MILITARY
CONFLICT

Also by Morris Janowitz:

Political Conflict: Essays in Political Sociology

MILITARY

CONFLICT

Essays in the Institutional
Analysis of War and Peace

MORRIS JANOWITZ

 SAGE Publications *Beverly Hills* · *London*

Copyright © 1975 by Sage Publications, Inc.

For information address:

SAGE PUBLICATIONS, INC.
275 South Beverly Drive
Beverly Hills, California 90212

SAGE PUBLICATIONS LTD
St George's House / 44 Hatton Garden
London E C 1

Printed in the United States of America

International Standard Book Number 0-8039-0560-2 (C)
0-8039-0561-0 (P)

Library of Congress Catalog Card No. 75-23610

FIRST PRINTING

CONTENTS

Acknowledgments   7

Introduction   10

**Part   I.   ARMED FORCES, NATIONALISM, AND
INTERNATIONAL RELATIONS**

Toward a Redefinition of Military Strategy in
International Relations   19

Military Elites and the Study of War   56

Military Institutions and Citizenship in Western Societies   70

Part II.   COMPARATIVE ANALYSIS OF MILITARY INSTITUTIONS

Armed Forces and Society: A World Perspective   89

Military Organization in Industrial Society   110

Civil-Military Relations in the New Nations   136

Comparative Analysis of Middle Eastern
Military Institutions   146

Part III.   THE IMPACT OF MILITARY AUTHORITY

Cohesion and Disintegration in the Wehrmacht in
World War II   177

Changing Patterns of Organizational Authority:
The Military Establishment   221

Part IV. CIVILIAN CONTROL AND THE MANAGEMENT OF CONFLICT

U.S. Forces and the Zero Draft   239

Racial Composition in the All-Volunteer Force:
    Policy Alternatives   284

Sociological Research on Arms Control   298

Index   315

ACKNOWLEDGMENTS

The contents of this volume obviously reflect the pervasive intellectual debt I owe to Harold D. Lasswell, whose writings and personality stimulated my interest both in political sociology and in the sociology of military institutions, war, revolutions, and peace-keeping, if such distinctions may be made. In the fall of 1938, it was through Bruce Lannes Smith, while he served as a member of the faculty of Washington Square College, New York University, that I was introduced to the work of Harold D. Lasswell and soon thereafter to Lasswell himself. At the same time, I was deeply moved by the lectures of Sidney Hook on the "philosophy of history" which supplied a context for my interests in both political and military institutions.

But it is, of course, impossible to separate intellectual biography from personal experience. Undoubtedly, a series of personal and historical events—worldwide and local—fashioned my predisposition to study military conflict and the management of military conflict. In retrospect, I would assert that the traumatic events of World War II rendered my research concerns with armed forces and collective coercion permanent and inescapable. But each event of sociopolitical importance implies a previous event which impinges on one's consciousness. When I was an undergraduate, it was the devastating impact of the "lost cause" of the Spanish Civil War which initially politicized the campuses and heightened my consciousness of the changing forms of collective violence. Antecedent was my boyhood involvement in the immigrant community of Paterson, New Jersey, which has a history of periodic outbursts of industrial violence and a transplanted group memory of European wars, militarism, and revolution that had driven generation after generation of textile workers from various parts of that continent and even the Middle East to this particular community. It can hardly be said that I left the tranquility of the hinterland to discover the realities of the "real world."

7

When I entered graduate school at the University of Chicago in 1946, the intellectual traditions of men such as Quincy Wright and William F. Ogburn and the colleagueship of my teachers, Bruno Bettelheim and Edward A. Shils, served to encourage my making an academic assessment of the events which I had recently experienced. It was a time when university sociology was generally indifferent to the study of military affairs and war-making.

The fact that I persisted in my writings and concerns I must attribute to a small group of intimate associates scattered throughout the United States and abroad with whom I shared common interests. These included Albert Biderman, Maury Feld, Oscar Grusky, Kurt Lang, Roger Little, Charles Moskos, David Segal, Allan Silver, and Mayer Zald. Their active assistance made it possible to create the Inter-University Seminar on Armed Forces and Society, which served as a focal point for social research on these topics. I am particularly indebted to Sam Sarkesian, James Linger, David Crider, and Nancy Goldman for their work in connection with the Inter-University Seminar.

On the international scene, I had read the writings of Raymond Aron and deeply respected his comprehensive outlook. I soon came into invaluable personal and intellectual contact with Jacques van Doorn of the Netherlands. Through collaborative efforts with him, it was possible to inject a comparative and international perspective on the study of militarism by means of the International Sociological Association. I owe acknowledgments to an ever-growing list of international scholars who have sought to correct my localistic tendencies. I can mention only some: Bengt Abrahamsson, Sweden; Anton Bebler, Yugoslavia; A. Bopegamage, India; Julian Busquets, Spain; Gwyn Harries-Jenkins, Great Britain; Fuad Khuri, Lebanon; Jae Souk Sohn, Korea. There are many others to whom I am obligated. More recently, I have had the assistance of Raymond Aron, Samuel Finer, and Jacques van Doorn in founding a new international and interdisciplinary journal, *Armed Forces and Society,* ‾concerned with military organization, civil-military relations, war, and the management of conflict.

In the development of contemporary research on armed forces and society, there has been a group of "old-fashioned" foundation executives who believed in the importance of scholarship. Their courage and support have made my work possible and their efforts support the growth of the Inter-University Seminar on Armed Forces and Society. They are Donald Young, Leonard Cottrell, Jr., and Orville Brim, all of whom have served as officers of the unique Russell Sage Foundation.

One cannot look back on the years during which these essays were written without acknowledging the important role Jeremiah Kaplan, head of the Free Press, played in contemporary social science and especially in the study of military institutions and collective violence. It is with great admiration that I recall that Jeremiah Kaplan risked publishing my earliest writings, without having recourse to the "professional" review process.

These papers constitute the second volume dealing with conflict and conflict management. The first volume, which appeared in 1970, is entitled *Political Conflict: Essays in Political Sociology*. I wish to acknowledge the efforts of Sara and George McCune in continuing the tradition of innovative publishing that their enterprise represents. I wish in particular to express my gratitude for the assistance that they have rendered and continue to render in connection with the publication program of the Inter-University Seminar on Armed Forces and Society.

M. J.

University of Chicago
Near South Side
Chicago, Illinois
January 1975

INTRODUCTION

In this collection of studies on armed forces and society, written over three decades, I have sought to make use of an "institutional" perspective. The "institutional" perspective implies that the study of war and peace requires an analysis of the organization of military forces and the manner in which they are used in the pursuit or the avoidance of conflict.

The institutional analysis of military organization and military elites has undergone a profound transformation, if only because of the marked increase in literature on the subject. In the 1930s, Harold D. Lasswell's formulation that the military could be considered as the managers of the "instruments of violence" was a unifying assertion for academic research. Lasswell was explicating Max Weber's "theory of history," which emphasized the growth and consequences of bureaucratic organization. His approach helped to focus on underlying realities and avoid formal institutional distinctions. It led to an emphasis on the political role of the military, domestic and international, and served its purpose in stimulating scholarly analysis and in raising fundamental policy questions about the objectives and legitimacy of the use of force, internally in the modern nation-state and externally in international relations.

Lasswell's analysis was, in effect, addressed to a very small group of academic scholars. Before 1940, scholarship on armed forces operated in very limited confines. The informed public, and certainly the mass public, were indifferent to its activities and results. But the effects of World War II, the development of nuclear weapons, and the worldwide trends toward decolonization have injected the work of the academic scholars on war and peace into the mass media and made military institutions and a "world without war" topics of widespread debate. The description of the military as managers of the "instruments of violence" has become a touchstone for counterformulations. The discussion has centered on its inherent clarity, precision, relevance, and moral and political implications.

10

Lasswell's formulation has come under criticism from two sets of intellectual specialists. Among professional officers, some "military" intellectuals have reacted negatively. They do not believe that military organization and the military profession are based exclusively on managerial personnel. They point to the body of social research that identifies an element of the heroic in military formations—be they regular professional forces or activist guerrilla units. Moreover, military intellectuals rebel at a conceptualization which they believe is stereotypic in their terms. Under the military logic of deterrence, they want to see themselves as managers of the instruments for the avoidance of violence. Lasswell's designation is, in their view, an unfortunate and erroneous label.

On the other hand, academic "peace" intellectuals who resist the Lasswell formulation do so because of presumed issues of values and ethics. There is a parallel in the basis of their argument with that of the "military" intellectual. Some academic intellectuals argue that Lasswell's conceptualization inadvertently, but certainly excessively, justifies the use of violence. In this view, the categories one uses influence one's orientation. Reliance on this naturalistic formulation serves to legitimate the use of force and inhibits the political struggle against militarism.

Of course, it is essential that academic research on armed forces and society and on the institutional perspective on war and peace be subject to continuous scrutiny in terms of value analysis. However, despite the "value" debate of recent years, the social science analysis of military institutions and military conflict persists in having a core focus on the "management of violence" and the institutions for conflict resolution. In fact, it can be argued that the social science analysis of military institutions has its current intellectual vitality—and it *is having* considerable intellectual vitality—precisely because of the persistence of a set of concepts and problems which have endured since the 1930s and which provide an arena of common inquiry among investigators with differing outlooks.

Of course, students of military organization and military conflict must face the changing historical context. It is all too often the case in social research and analysis that intellectual accomplishments—even the most modest accomplishments—become barriers to further inquiry. In particular, there is a tendency to use each new set of findings as a fixed basis for projecting and extrapolating trends, with profoundly distorting consequences. Social science research is supposed to have built-in self-criticism—ruthless self-criticism, at that—which implies in time even self-destruction of its own findings. Achieving balance between stability in an intellectual conceptual framework and modification of perspective to account for sociopolitical change is a delicate, difficult, and as yet unresolved task.

The institutional analysis of war and peace has to reassess the fundamental similarities and differences between the management of violence in a variety of industrialized nations and developing nations. Global and undifferentiated concepts, like modernization, have failed to help clarify the issues at stake. The routes to "modernity" are diverse, and students of sociopolitical change must keep in mind the divergent dimensions of urbanization and industrialization and modernization. The Western experience—Westernization—is but one. model of sociopolitical change.[1] At a minimum, for the issues at hand involving military organization and military conflict—domestic and international—among the industrialized nations, there is a fundamental and basic difference between the Western parliamentary state and those of Eastern Europe and the Soviet Union, with one mass party, where the central military forces have a critical internal security function. In so-called developing nations, there is a fundamental generic difference between those of Latin America, which achieved their independence in the nineteenth century, and those of Africa and Asia, which were decolonized after World War II. For both the industrialized nations and the developing nations, it is essential to avoid mechanical extrapolation from trends in military organization and civil-military relations in the recent past into the future.

The formulation inherent in the "management of violence" frees the institutional analysis perspective from a formal definition of the military. It becomes more and more necessary in analyzing the military from a worldwide perspective to be concerned with reserve forces, special security forces, national militarized police, new types of militia, and the variations in paramilitary forces—full-time and part-time. In fact, for markedly divergent reasons, in both the industrialized nations and the developing nations, the growth of the personnel in paramilitary institutions represents one of the most striking developments in the contemporary transformation of armed forces and society.

For the industrialized nations, the major emphasis of the research literature in the institutional perspective has been on the impact of total war—World War I and World War II—on military organization (namely, the long-term process of "civilianization" of the military—that is, of the interpenetration of the military and the society). But the emerging problem involves the outcome and the limits of this long-term trend, which had its origins in the American and French Revolutions and in the rise of the mass armed force. In nation-states with parliamentary regimes in Western Europe and in the United States, the new trend is toward the constriction and elimination of conscription, and thereby an alteration in the domestic sociopolitical balance. The impact of nuclear weapons and the changed internal value system are prime factors. The result is a decline in the size of the military establishment and a range of new tensions between the military and elements of the civilian society.

Moreover, this trend comes in a period of increased internal social conflict in the parliamentary political systems. Paradoxically, and despite the impacts of Vietnam on the United States and of Northern Ireland on Great Britain, popular confidence in the military establishment has increased, if only because it is judged—in comparison to other institutions such as industrial enterprises or trade unions—to have more concern with the national interest. It is striking that, in most Western parliamentary systems, there has been little effective increase in the size of paramilitary formations under the control of the central government during the last decade of political tension. For these advanced industrial societies, a central political issue is not the threat of a coup d'etat, but rather the necessity of insuring that the military are strictly limited in their internal police role. The hallmark of a political democracy is the sharp differentiation of the domestic police units from the military formations of national defense. With the trend toward an all-volunteer force, the military during a period of domestic tension run the risk of becoming a pressure group with a distinct right-wing ideological overtone that could serve as a source of political tension and political dissensus.

This pattern of changing military structure is in contrast to that in the advanced industrial nations of the Soviet Union and Eastern Europe. These nations have experienced the impact of nuclear weapons, and the size of their standing forces has been gradually reduced to a limited extent. But conscription remains unshaken, since the military are seen as an educational tool. The armed forces function as security elements both internally and for intervention to maintain the regimes of the Warsaw Pact nations. But most striking is the growth of paramilitary units—especially part-time forces—which have internal security functions. Thus, for nations with one-party political systems, the tensions of advanced industrialism are to be contained by the expansion of the armed forces available to the party regime.

In the new nations of Africa and Asia, the basic trends have been described in the research literature in terms of the breakdown of parliamentary institutions, the expansion of the role of the military into the political arena, and the resulting institutional instability. The military of the new nations—those which achieved their independence after 1945—have generally tended to be change-oriented. In Latin America, achieving independence in the nineteenth century produced a military which was linked to the landed interests and oriented toward the maintenance of the status quo or the limited incorporation of middle-class elements in the political arena. In recent years, these military formations of Latin America have become more and more change-oriented, paralleling the outlook of the military in the new nations of Africa and Asia.

There was never any doubt among serious scholars that the military of the developing nations had no special advantages in approaching the tasks of economic development, social change, and political institution-building. Their effectiveness would depend on the emergence of charismatic leadership supplemented by new forms of political organization with strong civilian overtones and involvements. But the findings of the research literature of the period to 1975, which stressed the barriers to economic development and the frequency of politico-military instability and fragmentation, need not be directly extrapolated into the years ahead.

While economic development in these nations has been slow, there are cases in which military regimes have produced pronounced economic progress. There are also cases in which civilian regimes have effective records of economic development. For the post-1975 period, the central question is whether there is an increased potential for political stability—military or civilian regime stability—in the developing nations. A variety of factors is at work, raising the likelihood of some increase in stability. In some cases, there has been a measure of economic progress; in others, a charismatic leader has held the regime intact. At times a military regime has demonstrated a measure of political skill and willingness to collaborate and move in the direction of civilian participation.

But one of the most striking developments in the period of 1965-75 has been the increase in paramilitary forces in the developing nations. These paramilitary forces, both symbolically and as organizations of coercion, have contributed to containing political instability, if only over the short run. There is a growing body of evidence that the expansion of military and paramilitary forces in the developing nations is less the result of U.S. and Soviet intervention and more the result of internal political decisions and regional rivalries.[2] In the recent past, the developing nations have seen considerable political instability, but with some major exceptions they have been ruled with limited internal coercion. In the years ahead, a period of greater political or regime stability, in the absence of a self-regulating electoral system, may well be purchased by increasingly resorting to internal coercion. The underlying issue is that there is no justification for the projection of the recent past into the emerging future for the new nations as well as the industrialized ones.

There has been an effort to designate the institutional analysis of armed forces and society as "military sociology." It is a matter of minor and at best passing concern, but the phrase "military sociology" has for a long time seemed to me both arbitrary and inappropriate. My reservations are varied and numerous. First, the term implies an excessively delimited scope of investigation. As mentioned above, the study of coercion and collective violence involves a wide range of military formations. At least in this respect, the term "armed forces" is much more relevant. Second, "military sociology" places excessive emphasis on the boundaries—the formal boundaries—of the military. In effect, it tends to remove the military as an object of research from the societal environment. Research into organizational behavior generally, and specifically in areas such as medical and educational sociology, has suffered in this regard. At a minimum, the notion of armed forces and society is a more adequate delimitation. Third, the intellectual issue runs even deeper; there is a powerful difference between a military organization in its routines in peacetime and one engaged in conflict. Moreover, under conditions of deterrence, the structure of the military undergoes basic changes as it moves from a mobilization cadre to more and more of a force "in being." Finally, military sociology as a term fails to emphasize the articulation of the sociological perspective with an interdisciplinary approach, and in particular the necessity for a historical perspective and a concern with long-term trends. All these points are well known and stress that the subject of the institutional analysis of war and peace encompasses military organization, civil-military relations, war, disarmament, peace-keeping, and the management and reduction of conflict.

In addition, the institutional perspective on war and peace requires interdisciplinary stimulation. The study of armed forces and society as pursued in these papers has been the result mainly of political science and sociological perspectives. One emerging intellectual frontier has been the application of institutional analysis and categories to earlier historical periods. In recent years, the number of analytical historical studies of military institutions has grown. Although analytical and comparative history is a worthy intellectual task in and of itself, its development also implies a broader historical approach to contemporary analysis of military institutions. In other words, in a day when policy studies are directed toward war and peace, analytic history becomes indispensable for developing a worldwide perspective.

There is no device for anticipating future intellectual progress, especially in empirical inquiry. But there is good reason to believe that the application of sociological and political science perspectives has run its course, or at least has become routinized. These perspectives do not necessarily serve as intellectual catalysts to the same degree as they did previously. Instead, it may well be that psychology—including depth psychology—will supply an important stimulus to new intellectual advances.

Psychological and social-psychological perspectives have been applied, with a measure of success, to the study of military organizations under stress. Through their focus on the interplay of primary groups with larger military structures, the realities of responses to combat have been laid bare. The transformation of combat, from World War II to Korea to Vietnam, is more than a matter of strategy and technology. It has been reflected in a series of field studies of the changing dynamics of primary groups. Primary-group structures served to strengthen military effectiveness in World War II. In Vietnam, while similar mechanisms were encountered, the special conditions of combat attenuated primary-group patterns in an important segment of the military, and under particular conditions developed into a source of resistance to combat goals.

Included in this tradition of research are the brilliant group interviews of S.L.A. Marshall, which demonstrated the importance of primary-group cohesion and highlighted the powerful resistance civilian soldiers have to using their weapons—even for self-preservation.[3] Likewise, interviews with psychiatric casualties—for example, those of Roy Grinker and J. P. Spiegel[4]—have contributed to research on the psychology of the military formation in combat, as have the more recent, psychiatrically oriented writings of Robert Lifton.[5]

But the psychology of military service under deterrence remains relatively unconceptualized and underdeveloped. Formulating a military psychology for a free society is both an intellectual and a policy-oriented task. A deterrent force under a "constabulary" organization requires men who will perform their military roles on the basis of training and organizational logic—and not in response to internal psychological pressures and distorted psychological imagery. The avant-garde of the military profession, those who are truly adaptive to change, already accept this notion. They cautiously point to research findings which attest to the existence of sectors in the military where effective performance is unrelated to aggressive personal motives or postures. The future trend in civilianization of the military under deterrence could be psychological, in which the personality of the professional military conforms more and more to the "modal personality" of civilian society.

The psychological dimension of the study of war and peace involves the study of the socialization of the military man and of the differing patterns of threat perception in the military. The term "psychological disarmament" seems confusing, but the patterns of personal and social control in military institutions rest at the heart of the matters at hand—even if our intellectual tools are hardly adequate.

At this moment, there is little point in seeking to justify the publication of a single volume of a series of studies which were prepared over a period of years. The arguments against such an effort are persistent, and there are many book reviewers who have made their critical reputations by pointing to the absence of a "central unifying theme" in volumes of collected papers. I do hope that the argument in favor—or at least in justification—rests on more than convenience and accessibility, although in the contemporary period of disciplinary journals with variegated content, a volume on a specific subject has its purpose and its audience. At critical points, I have updated the illustrative and statistical data, but, as indicated above, the main effort has been to select essays that have emphasized conceptual formulations as a basis for studying and assessing the continuities and changes in military organizations in a world perspective.

NOTES

1. Lloyd A. Fallers, *Inequality: Social Stratification Reconsidered* (Chicago, 1974).

2. Philippe C. Schmitter, editor, *Military Rule in Latin America* (Beverly Hills, 1973).

3. S.L.A. Marshall, *Men Against Fire* (Washington, D.C., 1945).

4. Roy Grinker and J. P. Spiegel, *Men Under Stress* (Philadelphia, 1945).

5. Robert Lifton, *Home from the War* (New York, 1973).

TOWARD A REDEFINITION OF MILITARY STRATEGY IN INTERNATIONAL RELATIONS

In a period of search for politico-military détente between the major nuclear powers, one cannot avoid the question of whether the theories and categories for the analysis of international relations, especially those involving the role of military force, are appropriate and clarifying. Although they strive to make use of timeless categories, social scientists, especially when analyzing international relations, must take into consideration the changing historical context.[1] In this paper I will attempt to reassess the well-known issue of the limits of military intervention in international relations by advanced industrial societies. I will seek to extend and formulate the ideas which, in *The Professional Soldier: A Social and Political Portrait,* were vaguely expressed in the notion of a constabulary.[2]

The intellectual approach rests on some standard notions of sociological analysis derived from the writings of Max Weber and Karl Mannheim on social structure and the growth of bureaucracy and large-scale organization under industrialism.[3] This type of "institutional" analysis focuses on the impact of goals and changes in goals on bureaucratic organization and the problem of implementing national policies. In particular, Mannheim's concept of "fundamental democratization," originally formulated to analyze the internal social structure of an advanced industrialized nation, can also be applied to characterize the transformation in the international arena which has produced the paradox of vastly increased concentrations of military power simultaneously with trends toward the diffusion of political power.[4] Most sociological writings about international relations have focused on attitudes and perceptions, when actually the categories of institutional analysis—currently relabeled "organization analysis"—are

From *World Politics,* XXVI (July 1974), pp. 473-508.

more appropriate.[5] Although the focus of this paper is on the military
organizations of the advanced industrial nations, the issues are applicable
to the political-diplomatic agencies of international relations as well.

The central argument of this essay is that the classical categories for
analyzing military organization and strategy must be reconceptualized in
the era of nuclear weapons and the decline of colonial rule.[6] The idea of
"stabilizing" and "destabilizing" military systems is offered as an
alternative to the classical language—balance of power, offensive-defensive,
and strategic-tactical military structures.

It is no simple matter to define and give concrete content to the terms
"stabilizing" and "destabilizing" military structures, but their essential
elements can be identified. These concepts supply a basis for reassessing
international relations during the years since 1945, and for examining
alternative approaches to the search for military détente. They also help to
give meaning to the oft-repeated observation that, from the point of view
of Western nations with multiparty political systems, the role of violence
in international relations has undergone fundamental changes.[7]

First, the concepts are based on the recognition that total war, as
prepared for and practiced by the nations of Europe and the United States
and Japan during World Wars I and II, is no longer viewed as an instrument
for achieving national goals.[8] To the extent that rationality operates, the
outbreak of "major" war between industrialized nations is no longer
defined as inevitable. A military force based on conventional mobilization
for total war gives way to a force in being, which is designed to achieve
deterrence.

Second, the overseas colonial empires of advanced industrial nations
have in the main come to an end through voluntary withdrawal or political
agitation, or, in a limited number of cases, as the result of military
engagements.[9] Colonial rule has given way to varieties of assistance for the
building of military institutions in the so-called developing nations, and to
support for armed conflict either between or within these nations.[10]

As a result, the legitimacy and utility of every specific military
preparation and operation must be judged in terms of new criteria which,
in a kind of shorthand, have come to be called deterrence. Deterrence in
turn is equated with a reduction of the chances and avoidance of the
outbreak of major war between the advanced industrial powers, and with
the inhibition of peripheral and limited war. But the term has
limitations—and not only because it has been overused and misused. It
deals mainly with military affairs and military goals and does not
adequately encompass the range of processes and objectives required for

an international order that seeks to avoid war.[11] To speak of stabilized military systems and the search for stabilization is, first, to indicate the multiple goals of military institutions of avoiding general war and reducing or inhibiting limited war.

But, second, an emphasis on stabilized military systems encompasses the goals of a declining level of military expenditures and expanding arms control, as well as a reduction in mass personal insecurity generated by the nuclear arms race. Given the dangers of accidental nuclear war, miscalculations leading to escalation of international tensions, and the sheer organizational complexity of managing nuclear military systems, new forms of communication and negotiation are required between "adversaries" if one is to speak of stabilized military systems.[12] In these terms, the management of military institutions involves the creation of an international arena which would improve economic intercourse and enhance the opportunity for political solutions to international tensions and imbalances. In short, deterrence as a concept has been mainly negative—and therefore of limited import for analyzing the organizational goals of military institutions.

Since, for industrialized nations, military intervention operates under marked limitations—and limitations which tend to increase—the notion of stabilizing versus destabilizing military systems is designed to explore these limitations and to assess the full range of impact that the military function has in the international arena. It is designed to avoid utopian thinking during a period of redefinition of national interests, since it assumes that stabilized military systems can have positive effects on the political, economic, and moral aspects of the international arena.

Obviously, in exploring the impact of the military function, we must distinguish between the nation-states with multiparty political systems and those with a single mass party, such as the Soviet Union and its associated nations, and Communist China. The political decision-making process of the single-party states enables them to allocate a larger share of the gross national product to military affairs, to mobilize—under conscription—a more extensive proportion of the available manpower, and to operate with less concern for currents of public opinion. In particular, any analysis of the consequences of military institutions on the international arena must assume this profound disparity in manpower resources when seeking to probe beyond the concept of deterrence.

But the disparity runs much deeper. In a parliamentary democracy, competing political elites strive to separate the police from the military and to remove the military from internal police functions except during gravest emergency. Competition between organized political parties depends on enforcing the nonpartisan role of the military. In a one-party state, the military is both an instrument of national defense and an active element in the internal police system. The military is also assigned a positive role in ideological indoctrination. It is an element in the "school of the nation," while remaining subject to extensive control by the party and the secret police.[13] In the Soviet Union, the military has to confront the realities of Sino-Soviet tension and the possibility of having to intervene to maintain allied governments in Eastern Europe.

Therefore, during a period when the military function is being transformed, the broader role of the military in one-party states implies that traditional assumptions about the military are less frequently and extensively called into question. Thus, the disparity in resources and manpower, plus the broader domestic role of the military, produces powerful elements of asymmetric response to issues of changed military functions. However, these crucial differences should not divert us from examining the extent to which complex technology and the social structure of advanced industrial society have produced important parallel consequences in military institutions in all advanced industrial nation-states.

Systemic Analysis of International Relations

The academic analysis of international relations is not based on a powerful or paradigmatic theory comparable to marginal utility analysis in economics or even to learning theory in behavioral psychology.[14] It would no doubt be asking too much to demand a "theory" of international relations, just as it is to search for a "theory" of the welfare state. Theories are formed by particular disciplines and not by areas of subject matter. The field of international relations invokes the application of a disciplinary orientation or a multidisciplinary orientation to a common set of problems of subject matter.

The classic formulations have been those related to the international balance of power; that is, they have been a form of political analysis. The balance-of-power model has had limited relevance, because it is so highly general that its plausibility hardly explains any particular set of circumstances or specifies the elements to be examined. The balance-of-power formula seems mainly to have served as a rationalization of power politics, if such rationalization were required. In the contemporary setting, the formula has even less explanatory relevance and is out of accord with the necessity of including "voluntaristic" factors, such as the initiative of political leaders and their "advisors" as independent dimensions in the analysis of international relations. Game theory, cybernetic models, and simulation modes of analysis which have come to the fore reflect effective rigor but have a tendency to mislead, since they cannot deal with change and transformation.[15] Their mechanistic assumptions bear limited relation to the realities of the world community. Because of their failure to deal with institutional and normative elements, they have not made a sufficient contribution to the clarification of the impact of particular means—especially military means—on political ends in the dynamics of international relations.

There is also a growing body of so-called revisionist literature about the origins of World War II and the immediate postwar period. The bulk of this literature is countermoralizing.[16] Paradoxically, despite the vast flow of literature, systematic and realistic analysis of the management of international relations is still hard to obtain; it is as if the analytical task were swamped by the magnitude of available documentation. Thus, despite the enormous efforts in international propaganda during World War II and the cold war, by all the participants, there is no book that comes to the heart of the matter so well as Harold D. Lasswell's classic study of World War I, *Propaganda Technique in the World War*.[17] It remains astounding, therefore, that the role of mass persuasion is for all practical purposes an issue of peripheral concern to the contemporary theorist of international relations. Likewise, the consequences of guerrilla warfare are a study area in which the assertions of ideologists and advocates serve as substitutes for effective analysis of realities and limitations.[18]

The best scholarship has succeeded in demolishing the single-variable theories of international relations which dominated the field before World War II, whether such theories be based on economic determinism, the psychological basis of organized aggression, or vague and almost metaphysical notions of geopolitical potentials. The present status of scholarship in international relations in part reflects the basic and persistent problem of the intellectual analysis of violence. Intellectuals are fascinated by violence and, despite condemning it morally, they are often bemused by it or romanticize its character and consequences.[19] There is a real danger of generating moral indifference if "objectivity" is pressed ruthlessly and without social and political responsibility. In the name of objectivity and detachment, a personal fascination and/or obsession may be encountered—a characteristic that is common to writings as different as

Herman Kahn's *On Thermonuclear War* and Frantz Fanon's *The Wretched of the Earth.*[20] But it is possible to delve into the study of violence with scholarly criteria in mind and with a sense of social and political responsibility.[21]

Because of the absence of a paradigmatic theory of international relations and the availability of a mass of information that must be confronted, the study of international relations is in actuality a process of forecasting—that is, extrapolating from existing trends, with an *ad hoc* focus on the search for limiting or even reversing conditions in concurrent trends.[22] Such extrapolation involves both internal national trends and trends in relations between nation-states. Since that is the present state of the field, the intellectual issue is to enrich this mode of analysis. The most effective approach is to identify the elements and dimensions that actually or potentially limit or reverse ongoing trends. Obviously, this involves an eclectic assembling of variables and dimensions from a number of different academic disciplines and some arbitrary ordering of their importance and consequences.

Morton Kaplan has pioneered in the systems analysis of international relations, but his aspiration appears to be too overreaching.[23] In a way, international relations can be considered as a system, but a system which is imperfect and unstable. In fact, it makes sense to speak of the systematic analysis of international relations if the model, rather than being a mechanistic and closed system, is a set of loose institutional arrangements based on the master trends of economic and military potentials, and reflects the voluntaristic and purposeful designs and accommodations of political leadership.

The term "systemic analysis" is designed to underline the assertion that there is no global, self-contained, and paradigmatic theory of international relations. Therefore, systemic analysis is not the same as systems analysis. Instead, the intellectual analysis of international relations can be pressed, not to predict the future, but to assist men in avoiding self-fulfilling prophecies. The purpose is to clarify present and emerging trends in order to assess the consequences of alternative policies and efforts at international institution building. Current exercises in "futurology" distort the real potentials of alternative models of international relations—highlighting the dilemmas which the leaders of advanced industrial societies face in adapting their institutions to economic and sociopolitical change.[24]

In building systemic models of international relations, one conventionally starts with economic and military elements and uses political elements as coordinating mechanisms. In recent years, there have also been efforts to incorporate psychological elements.[25] With the declining legitimacy of military force—because of the utter destructiveness of military technology and because of the internal sociopolitical tensions of an advanced industrial society—the social dimensions of international relations come into prominence. The notion of legitimacy and the crisis of legitimacy in military force is one formulation of the sociological dimension of international relations. It is dangerous to develop a sociological model of international relations, since it can quickly reduce itself to issues of manpower and morale or questions of ethics divorced from political reality. But basically, the changing function of the military is in part a reflection of these issues of norms and legitimacy.[26] Systemic analysis of international relations can therefore be enriched by the appropriate infusion of the sociological analysis of institutions, social structures, and institution building.

Two interrelated assumptions about the nature of advanced industrial societies and the impact of the industrial order offer a point of departure. They are relevant for linking the transformation of the internal social structure of an advanced industrial nation with trends in the international arena.

First, under conditions of advanced industrialism, there is a profound diffusion of dispersion of power and of authority within the nation-state and in the linkages between advanced industrialized states and the rest of the world community. There is, of course, a striking paradox: elements of diffusion and dispersion are compatible with elements of persistent and increased concentration of power and authority. We cannot assume that we are dealing with a closed system; however, the contemporary process of transformation of authority is difficult to comprehend.

Sociologists have spoken of functional interdependence to describe the process by which the division of labor in institutions becomes more complex and specialized. Mannheim has offered the notion of "fundamental democratization" to point to the normative and political implications of this development in the social order.[27] There is some merit in this formulation, although there is also a possibility of confusion, since he does not use "democracy" in the parliamentary sense. He is oriented to the residual power that emerges as formerly excluded groups increasingly enter the mainstream of society. In the United States, the trend toward fundamental democratization first became noticeable during the mobilization efforts of World War I, but its full implication developed and became more manifest during the Second Indochina War.

Since 1945, the most striking development in the internal social structure of Western parliamentary democracies has been the residual power that accrues to formerly excluded or low-status groups—minorities, unskilled workers, youth, old people, or women. The complexity of the division of labor and of functional interdependency plus new normative trends are key elements. Often the power of these groups is more negative than positive, but that is the implication of residual power. The new trends do not negate the persistence of extensive disparity and inequality in resources and privileges. This observation merely seeks to place the residual power in the context of the social structure of an advanced industrial society; its result is an increase in political tension and an undermining of political legitimacy. The difficulties of making effective political decisions become central. There is persistent tension between elite groups and pervasive veto groups. Political systems can operate on the basis of a gap between aspiration and actual practice, but the strains from the pressure of fundamental democratization are profound on the domestic scene. They result in chronic social conflict or national political stagnation, rather than in new revolutionary circumstances.[28]

At the international level, the same diffusion of power and authority can be noted. It reflects internal domestic changes and changes in the structure of international relations.[29] The phrase, "the shift from a bipolar to a multipolar world community," fails to capture adequately the complexity and content of this transformation. The diffusion of power involves the linkages between major nation-states; and simultaneously, within each region, a related process occurs among the smaller nation-states. The dispersion of residual power is striking, despite the enormous concentration of resources among the advanced industrial nations. As in the case of patterns of internal domestic authority, the increase in functional interdependence is operative; normative and ideological values have enlarged impact. Some writers believe that this fundamental democratization between nations, especially in the context of nuclear weapons systems, should result in invigorated competition between nations with attendant international stability, in an analog to the competitive process of the marketplace. However, the actual process of dispersion of power and authority produces no inherent increase in stability. As in the case of the impact of fundamental democratization on domestic social structure, the effect on international relations is persistent tension and great difficulty in achieving accommodation and effective political decisions.

Second, under advanced industrialism, both internally and

internationally, the interplay of force and persuasion undergoes a transformation. An admixture of persuasion and force has traditionally been the central element in diplomacy. The calculus of force and persuasion has been modified so that there is good reason to speak of an increase and intensification in the fusion or articulation of persuasion and force, including the threat of force. In the period of mass armies and traditional warfare among industrialized nations up through World War II, there seems to have been a phasing or periodicity in the use of persuasion and coercion.[30] There was more of a separation between normal international relations and the application of force. The breakdown of the balance of power led to the use of force, and "victory" was pursued by the means at hand. Although there were intermittent periods of high tension, war followed peace and peace followed hostilities.

Under the technology and politics of deterrence and involvement in peripheral warfare, the threat of force and force itself are more continually invoked with concurrent efforts at persuasion. The process is one of gradually escalating and de-escalating force, of "fighting" and simultaneously "negotiating," of pursuing divergent means in different specific sectors of the international arena. In part, this process reflects the effort to avoid the use of great amounts of force; in part, it reflects the consequences of greater functional interdependence, in which the opposing powers must take into consideration the enlarged arenas of common interest. There is, at each step, a potent inhibition against using more powerful weapons. The symbolic aspects of force become more and more central. The fusion of force and persuasion partially reflects changes in the normative structure of international relations.

In Western political democracies, the same transformation in the balance of force and persuasion manifests itself internally—for example, in the efforts to control race relations, student protests, and labor relations, and even in the handling of bank robbers. The police are prepared to use personnel who specialize in negotiations with bank robbers holding hostages rather than to apply the force at their disposal. The application of force is not a periodic, all-or-nothing event: it is a continuous aspect of the social process, which must be moderated in terms of self-interest and recognition of the unanticipated consequences of the use of force.

The consequence of both (a) increased functional interdependence and "fundamental democratization" of residual power and (b) the fusion and moderation in the use of force and persuasion is a new level of complexity and fragility in international relations. It is not enough to assert that, because of nuclear weapons, there has been no major or total war between advanced industrial nations for more than a quarter of a century although levels of tension and the scope of armed conflict have been persistent and unacceptably high. It is necessary to offer hypotheses about the increased limits of military intervention since the end of World War II.

Force and the International Order

Inequality is an outstanding aspect of the international order and the same can be said of the internal social structure of any society, including the advanced industrial societies. Over the last quarter-century, inequality between nations has probably declined less than inequality within nations, especially within advanced industrialized states. There is reason to believe that inequality between the industrialized and the less developed nations has in fact increased. Within advanced industrialized states, those persons who are not members of the middle majority—the sick, the aged, elements of the unskilled, and welfare recipients—may well find themselves with enduring disabilities that exclude them from the material benefits of affluence.

In some fundamental sense, the role of military force is designed to support the inequalities between nations or at least does so in fact (as domestic police power contributes to internal social stratification). This assertion does not deny that military force contributes to the maintenance of a world "order"—no matter how unstable—in which economic, educational, and administrative processes can and do operate to reduce existing degrees of inequality.

However, the hypothesis appears relevant that, at the international level, the capacity of advanced industrialized nations to maintain their economic advantages by reliance on military force has markedly declined. The cost of a military establishment is so huge that there is much greater advantage to be gained by reducing or even limiting military expenditures than by using the threat of force to achieve economic advantage.[31] Critics of a variety of political persuasions now generally concede that military expenditures are not needed to maintain the economic vitality of a "capitalist" society in the West, and that military expenditures are a tremendous burden to the Soviet Union during its continuing press for industrial growth.[32] Nuclear weapons rule out the possibility of drastically restructuring the "zones of influence," as was done after World War II. Moreover, on the contemporary international scene, the less developed nations will not as readily succumb to a show of the flag or a military presence. Of course, this does not rule out specific intervention to deny important resources to an opponent. To use the language of economics, the marginal utility of the military function has declined.

In addition, the psychological returns of a military force with nuclear weapons have grave limitations. "National security" and "defense of the motherland" are in part a matter of psychic security and of honor, prestige, and the positive attraction of membership in a collectivity. The phrase "world politics and personal insecurity," offered by Harold D. Lasswell, is a focal but neglected aspect of the transformation of international relations. The sheer accumulation of weapons—especially nuclear weapons—does not necessarily reduce anxiety.

The mass of the citizenry continues to support policies which are represented as essential for nuclear deterrence, although there may be extensive political debate about alternative strategies and levels of budgetary allocation. Popular support for national security is in part an expression of personal anxiety. However, the threat of mass destruction produces privatization as well as moral revulsion. There has been a long-term decline in enthusiasm for national war making. Popular support at the outbreak of World War I gave way to realistic participation during World War II, and the prospect of a third world war produces psychological numbness.[33] Since 1945, sharp outbursts of neutralism have demonstrated these pressures. During a period of military détente such feelings will become more prominent, and, although likely to be limited to a minority of the population, "psychological" neutralism can have extensive political consequences.

The mass media, especially television in its day-to-day reporting of violence from Indochina to Northern Ireland, serve to increase the negative psychological consequences of military intervention. Military institutions have a diminished ability to contribute to psychological security: the reality and the imagery of violence produce higher levels of personal insecurity, leading to apathy and withdrawal.[34]

At the same time, there is a countertrend that is difficult to explain but understandable. For some persons, prolonged exposure to the international threat of mass destruction contributes to a weakening of their commitment to the internal order. The consequences are increased personal expression of diffuse violence. Personal insecurity and generalized dissatisfactions, especially among young groups, produce a noteworthy incidence of diffuse violence—at times with political overtones, but more often simply sheer outbursts of aggressive behavior. Therefore, it is necessary to face the hypothesis that not only has the ability of the military to contribute to a sense of personal security declined; but massive military preparations and expenditures (including those on nuclear weapons) contribute to diffuse and aggressive internal disorder.

Any examination of weapons control thus involves an inquiry into fundamental psychological insecurities. For example, the atmospheric testing of nuclear weapons heightened personal insecurity and became the focal point for mass agitation. In turn, the ending of atmospheric testing of nuclear weapons was more a psychological advance than a strategic one, but it was a significant step because it reduced personal insecurity. The prospect of joint Russian-American exploration in space, given its dramatic content, offers an interesting and promising potential step for containing and reducing the massive insecurity that nuclear weapons have been generating since 1945.

At the political level, the utility and legitimacy of military forces and military intervention—particularly for the Western political democracies—in maintaining and strengthening political alliances have tended to develop built-in limitations. The United States and the Soviet Union and, increasingly, Communist China, have built their foreign policy on a tangled web of politico-military alliances of varying degrees of involvement. While the structures of NATO and of the Warsaw Pact operate as keystones in the existing definitions of national security, the effective utility of military forces for building political alliances requires reassessment on the basis of a worldwide perspective.

The NATO experience until the middle of the 1960s represents, for the United States, a case where a military alliance successfully served to strengthen political arrangements. The NATO system was built on existing elements of political agreement, plus the expectation that American military forces were designed to deal with the threats posed by the Soviet Union while being in fact excluded from the internal political affairs of the Western European states which were in the alliance. The Warsaw Pact, by contrast, was built on the basis of a military occupation. The Soviet Union has used its forces for intervention in the internal politics of Warsaw Pact states and continues to reserve the option for direct military intervention in their domestic affairs.

In the industrialized context of Europe, the patterns and consequences of military alliances are very different from those of the developing countries. Throughout most of the developing states, military alliances and support involve some measure of direct or indirect involvement in the domestic internal security of the assisted state. With few notable exceptions, attempts to build an immediate political base by military assistance to the developing countries have been of limited and problematic consequence. The effectiveness of military alliances rests on the important element of political stability. It seems military alliances can operate only if there already exists a strong political base for the alliance. But military assistance often weakens the required political support, especially if it becomes an object of domestic political attack.

These observations do not deny the significance of particular military alliances that exist. They also do not deny that particular developing countries seek to develop programs of multiple assistance in order to maintain an element of independence and flexibility. The essential issue in the case of the economic, psychological, and political utility of military forces and military assistance in the context of deterrence is not to be assessed in terms of immediate power positions alone, but also in the broader perspective of the stabilizing and destabilizing effects of military forces on the international order.

Strategy Versus Stabilization in International Relations

In the effort to reconceptualize the consequences—actual and desired —that the military systems of the advanced industrial states can have on international relations, it will be useful to assess the impact of some of the major intellectual formulations that have been developed since 1945.[35] The purpose is less to explore their actual influence—important though that may be—and more to evaluate in retrospect their analytic adequacy.

In the years immediately after 1945, basic political decisions about military policy were made in the United States amid a vast outpouring of military and governmental studies and writings from academic circles.[36] It will remain for future intellectual historians to evaluate this effort fully. But the interim assessment can be made that most of these sources failed to clarify the effective limits within which military intervention, actual and symbolic, could operate. In retrospect, the bulk of these intellectual efforts seems not as productive of detached analytical explorations of alternatives as it is representative of an obsessive drive to insure that technological and organizational resources have their "maximum" military utility. One only has to reread Henry A. Kissinger's *Nuclear Weapons and Foreign Policy,* published as late as 1957, to be reminded that the limitations of military intervention were not central to the mainstream of strategic analysis by academics.[37] The possibilities and conditions for a trend toward military détente were not even postulated in Kissinger's effort. Of course, there were writers who, after 1945, saw the fundamental transformation in the military function, but they were clearly in the minority.[38]

However, the issue is much more complex when one examines the link between the formulation of military strategy and the actualities of foreign relations. The central issue for the intellectual historian is not merely one of tracing the emergence of a transformation of strategic analysis. The essential historical problem is to explain why the traditional notions of the military function were immediately abandoned in the development of politico-military policy and practices in Western Europe, while in the Far East, and even more specifically in Southeast Asia, the process of adjustment to new realities came with agonizing slowness.[39] In fact, the outbreak of the Korean War and the first Indochina conflict acted as a stochastic process which inhibited adaptation to the requirements of a nuclear foreign policy.[40]

The dominant strategic "advice" offered from 1945 to 1960 was, on the whole, irrelevant to the central issues of the stabilization of nuclear weapons. During this period, the central strategic conception was the distinction between tactical and strategic nuclear weapons. No doubt this notion had a variety of origins, including internal military staff work, but the writings of civilian scholars contributed to its currency.[41] Even the most superficial examination of the literature reveals no conceptual or operational basis for the distinction, which was without rational purpose and lacked precision. At the time it was offered, it encountered determined and persistent critiques. It was one of those intellectual inventions which have little effective consequence, and it perished because of its political defects. It was essentially a notion generated by the intellectuals' fascination with violence, and designed to avoid the analysis of the limitations of military intervention in a nuclear context. Billions of dollars were spent on the development and deployment of tactical nuclear weapons. It is striking that the notion of tactical nuclear weapons was incorporated into the language of NATO defense exercises without significant destabilizing results. In effect, these weapons operated partially as elements in the strategic deployment of nuclear weapons—or were so considered by the Soviet Union.[42]

If, during the period after 1945, the main analytic contribution to military strategy was the distinction between strategic and tactical nuclear weapons, in the 1960s a new generation of nuclear weapons and a search for military détente were accompanied by an equally dubious strategic distinction, that between defensive and offensive nuclear weapons.

Technological developments and changes in the sociopolitical environment, both domestic and international, had signaled to the political leadership of both the Soviet Union and the United States that some form of strategic limitation on nuclear weapons would be required. To allow existing trends to continue would have created greater economic burdens and increasing international tension, because of the complexity and destructiveness of the new weapons. In more basic terms, some element of détente was needed to enhance the legitimacy of the political leadership and to allow them to govern with greater effectiveness. The pressure for détente did not mean that the new cycle of military preparation was abandoned, since existing internal political pressures and limitations on institutional arrangements for negotiations required its continuation. Nor did it imply that the Soviet Union, with its particular internal decision-making process, would not in specific arenas of international relations seek to press to the limits.

The core technological element in the transformation of the nuclear deterrent, which came into being in the 1960s, rested only in part on the increased destructive weight of the new weapons. It was rooted more in the imputed accuracy of delivery and, at the same time, in the greater capacity for directing nuclear weapons to alternative targets. In essence, these developments came to be defined as destabilizing; they caused a qualitative and quantitative intensification of the arms race. The response was to make launching sites more invulnerable, either by hardening them or by increasing their dispersion, and increasing reliance on submarines and the development of antiballistic missiles.

No doubt these technological developments were the precondition for a new threshold in the management of nuclear deterrence and, without political accommodation, they would have contributed markedly to an intensification of a "doomsday" sentiment. However, the emergence of the distinction between defensive and offensive weapons complicated and slowed the search for some form of strategic arms limitation, no matter how restricted. Although a variety of writers have contributed to the distinction, Fred C. Iklé's article, "Can Nuclear Deterrence Last Out the Century?" is a useful statement of the implication of this distinction, although he proceeds implicitly rather than explicitly.[43] According to Iklé, defensive weapons are those aimed at or threatening the enemy's offensive nuclear weapons, while offensive weapons are those aimed at or threatening civilian populations. When one superpower is faced with "numerical" parity in nuclear weapons, or even inferiority, as well as uncertainty about the vulnerability of its own nuclear deterrent, it will of necessity aim its weapons at the enemy's civilian population. It may, in this view, be forced to launch its weapons upon warning of attack rather than to respond in graduated measure. To hold civil populations hostage is considered immoral and unworthy of a nation such as the United States. Instead, the United States must emphasize the development of defensive nuclear weapons—that is, weapons invulnerable to enemy attack, which can be launched on a graduated basis and which, in particular, are aimed at the enemy's offensive weapons.

The fierce pressure, both in the United States and in the Soviet Union, to implement this strategic distinction can, at best, only slow the search for some form of strategic arms limitation. It is basically an imprecise distinction, which has the unanticipated consequence of continuing the image of an inevitable arms race. It will strengthen and perpetuate the prospect of the "doomsday machine," couched in the language of higher morality. First, the argument that it relies on defensive nuclear weapons has not produced and could not produce a positive ethical response. Advocates of the defensive nuclear strategy cannot in fact hold that such a strategy would make the use of nuclear weapons more acceptable, and their ethical argument is thus much too formalistic to have any transcendental value.

Second, there is no effective basis for making such a distinction. Of course an antiballistic missile is different from an intercontinental missile. However, the implementation of this concept would at best produce limited changes in the weapons systems being developed and deployed, would require greater expenditure of efforts, and, in reality, would increase the overall nuclear weapons apparatus. The advocates of the defensive-offensive distinction serve the useful purpose of alerting the political leadership and informed citizens to the complex and uncertain elements in the new nuclear deterrence. In particular, they emphasize the danger of accidents and of imprecise and ineffective control over nuclear weapons. These complexities and uncertainties would be applicable to defensive weapons in any enlarged system.

Third, politically the distinction between defensive and offensive strategy leads mainly to a continuation of nuclear weapons development, since the advocates are hardly concerned with assessing the mechanisms —technological and political—for containing the arms race. In essence, a massive system of nuclear weapons—if organized in terms of defensive-offensive weapons—presents the prospect of a never-ending and ever-accelerating arms race with profoundly destabilizing consequences. In contrast, recognition among political leaders of the Soviet Union and the United States that strategic arms agreements, no matter how limited, are a desirable goal appears powerful enough to overcome the argument of technical experts committed to the distinction between defensive and offensive nuclear systems, and to stimulate a search–political and technical–for alternatives.

Stabilizing Versus Destabilizing Military Systems

Instead of the classic concepts of strategic versus tactical, or offensive versus defensive, the alternative formulation, stabilizing versus destabilizing, is more useful for assessing the contemporary function of the military in international relations. The classic terms can be used to describe the technological dimensions of the military. But the notion of stabilizing and destabilizing is designed to reflect the politico-military processes at work in international relations. As shown above, the terms "stabilizing" and "destabilizing" compel one to consider the sociopolitical context of military systems in the search for a viable international system: the avoidance of nuclear war and the containment of peripheral military confrontations.

The central issue is to assess the stabilizing versus destabilizing consequences of alternative approaches to military détente, recognizing the asymmetrical constriction of conscripted manpower for the NATO forces in contrast to the Warsaw Pact states. A review of the years 1945 to 1968–from the first use of nuclear weapons to the active negotiations between the United States and the Soviet Union about strategic arms limitations–is a precondition for assessing the trends that emerged after 1968, when the second phase in post-World War II international relations began.

To speak of stabilized systems of nuclear weapons implies the expectation that future weapons development will be economically manageable and also will not present the political specter of a perpetual, overpowering, and uncontrollable "doomsday" arms race, although some continuous change would be built in. In other words, nuclear weapons can be managed without consuming excessively large amounts of resources and producing such high levels of personal insecurity as to transform advanced industrial society into a type of garrison state in which the search for more and "better" nuclear systems becomes an omnipotent goal.

The hypothesis can be offered that between 1945 and 1968, although there was no explicit system of arms control, the development of nuclear weapons remained within tolerable limits of stabilization. The deployment of conventional forces, especially ground forces in Western Europe, supported this stabilized development. In contrast, the use of conventional forces in Southeast Asia had a destabilizing effect on that area and, in turn, on worldwide international relations.

It was a period when deterrence operated to avoid the outbreak of nuclear war without any fundamental politico-military realignments that could be viewed by any of the three central powers as basically threatening to the structure of the world community. However, the period 1945-1968 was only partly stabilizing at the level of nuclear weapons. Insufficient steps were taken to develop explicit systems of arms control and to anticipate a future in which more complex nuclear weapons would be deployed, and economic and political factors would require a more active search for a military détente. The destabilizing consequences of military intervention in the Second Indochina War reduced and delayed the United States' ability to take the initiative in negotiating with the Soviet Union about strategic arms limitation and a restructuring of conventional forces in Western Europe, and contributed to increased destabilization throughout the world community, especially in the Middle East.

In 1945 it was clear that, while the United Stated had "numerical" superiority in nuclear weapons, the possibility of an outbreak of nuclear war was very remote, although effective steps had to be taken to prevent accidental warfare or miscalculation. The bulk of the strategic literature of that period, predicting or accounting for developments, can be readily dismissed. It would have been much too much to expect the United States' political elite to begin realistic negotiations with the Soviet Union in 1950 on the basis of nuclear parity, which was to develop only at the end of the 1960s as a prerequisite of the SALT talks. However, there was no possibility of preventing the Soviet Union from achieving such parity if the United States was to remain a humane and democratic society.

In essence, the political leadership of the Soviet Union and the United States recognized the utter destructive capacity and unpredictability of nuclear weapons in any military confrontation between NATO and Warsaw Pact nations. The achievement of nuclear deterrence and relative stability between 1945 and 1968 is a reflection, not merely of weapons systems, but of political arrangements and normative patterns at the international level. The social structure and political posture of the United States initially ruled out a preventive attack on the Soviet Union. The NATO military system had at its disposal an adequate number of ground forces to achieve its deterrent role in the nuclear context. The ground-force structure of NATO, especially the very sizable American contingent, indicated a relatively stable political context, uninfluenced by the fears of a nuclear holocaust that could have produced excessive neutralism. Nor, on the other hand, was there a move toward an independent European deterrent under Franco-German hegemony, which would have been highly destabilizing from the point of view of Soviet-American relations. Moreover, the military presence of the United States insured the continued division of Germany, which was essential for the postwar reconstruction of both Western and Eastern Europe and for the long-term stability of the West.

During the Eisenhower Administration, while the Soviet Union was engaged in the first steps toward nuclear parity, there was in the United States an extensive effort to develop civilian defense. These measures collapsed, initially because of public indifference and later because of congressional reluctance to allocate the required funds. After a very brief period of limited hysteria, the penetration of a "doomsday" outlook into their day-to-day life proved not to be acceptable to the citizens of the United States, who thereby served to contain the level of international tension. A massive civilian defense program would have been destabilizing at that time because it would have weakened the credibility of the United States' strategic intentions of avoiding nuclear war. It would also have weakened the social fabric of the United States by further distorting the values of everyday life.

The effectiveness of nuclear deterrence in the NATO-Warsaw Pact balance was enhanced by the limited but symbolically significant efforts at international arms control. These steps produced no more than marginal technical adjustments, but underlined the intention to keep military developments within credible and acceptable limits. (The accords started with the denuclearization of Antarctica, partial test bans, prohibition of nuclear weapons in outer space and in the sea bed, and the construction of the hot line.)

In contrast to the relatively stabilized military balance—conventional and nuclear—in Western Europe, which lasted until the middle of the 1960s, the progressive deployment and utilization of military force in the Far East had a very different impact, which was essentially destabilizing. In essence, the basic source of the destabilization was the failure to develop those political arrangements with Communist China which were blocked from 1947 on by domestic American political agitation. All available evidence indicates that, at the close of World War II and subsequently, Communist China would have been amenable to political initiatives comparable to those which were launched after 1968, and which would have taken into consideration the relations of China both with the Soviet Union and with other nation-states of the Far East and Southeast Asia. Instead, American foreign policy mechanically sought to apply the format of Western Europe without appropriate adaptation to the realities of the social structure of the Far East.

For a brief moment, the possibility of the use of "tactical" nuclear weapons to support the declining fortunes of the French in Indochina, particularly in the context of "white" military forces against Asiatic formations, proved highly destabilizing. This prospect created the specter of disaster for the world community. It was effectively avoided, but only after extensive destabilizing consequences.

Deployment of conventional forces, especially ground forces, failed to take into account the process of decolonization and emergent nationalism in the Far East and in Southeast Asia. After the defeat of Japan, the reimposition of colonial systems was not militarily feasible and was sure to be politically destabilizing. Initially, United States policy was oriented toward the goal of decolonization and the emergence of independent nation-states with their own indigenous military forces. The conventional United States military presence had to conform to these politico-military requirements. In the British and Dutch colonies, this objective was basically achieved, but lack of political decisiveness in Indochina presented the crucial and fatal exception. (The political error was rooted not only in tacit and then open support of French military intervention, but also in allocating a role to China in the initial occupation of Indochina.)

In retrospect—although there is no point in rewriting history—if the Nixon policies toward Nationalist China on Formosa which were implemented after 1968 had been initiated in 1946-47, alternative political and military arrangements for Korea and particularly Indochina might have been possible. However, the prolongation of the Second Indochina War was a major destabilizing process in the international arena after 1945. One of the causes was the limited effectiveness of U.S. military intervention, especially in its conventional strategic air attacks and the absence of adequate international political legitimacy of the effort. Later, limitations in the North Vietnamese military effort emerged. The failure of their tank offensive in spring 1972 (which was blunted by tactical airpower and the increased accuracy of United States bombing of the North in the fall of 1972) created the military conditions for the acceptance of a "cease-fire." It was clear, however, from the early 1960s on, that a contraction of American military involvement in the Second Indochina War depended on a direct initiative by the United States to satisfy the political objectives of Communist China.

The vast amount of documentation about the outbreak of the Second Indochina War has obscured the central issue: the demise of the determined United States military opposition to deploying ground forces on the mainland of Asia, which had become especially strong after Korea.

The leaders of this opposition were called members of the "never-again club." Before 1960, key U.S. military leaders had been opposed to large-scale ground involvement in Southeast Asia. Likewise, the limits of military intervention had been recognized in the military plans that were developed, calling for one million to one million two hundred thousand men as the requirement for a ground force in Vietnam.[44]

It is arbitrary to take 1968 as the starting date of the second era in post-World War II politico-military development; no doubt it will be subject to reformulation in later retrospection. In that year, however, the internal political scene in the United States—changed because of the election of President Richard M. Nixon—shifted to permit de-escalation of the war in Vietnam, and to make possible new political initiatives with the Soviet Union and, later, with Communist China. President Nixon's election also permitted the political decision to start unilateral disarmament in the United States by ending the draft. In effect, 1968 was a political benchmark for response to developments which had been in progress since the early 1960s—for example, the growing "numerical nuclear parity" of the Soviet Union, the increased complexity of nuclear weapons, the limitations on American intervention in the Second Indochina War, the increased recognition of the limitations of military assistance programs to developing nations, the emerging tension between the Soviet Union and China, and the internal problems of advanced industrial countries, including the Soviet Union.

The initiatives toward détente sought a new stabilization, but contained actual and potential elements of destabilization. Starting in 1968, the legitimate utility of military force required new arrangements to stabilize the nuclear deterrent under conditions of nominal nuclear parity. It is of course assumed that political elites in the United States would not accept "marked" Russian nuclear superiority. A stabilized nuclear deterrent cannot be defined only in technological terms, namely, as an inhibited commitment of economic resources. Politically, it would be necessary to prevent both reactive neutralism and aggressive nationalism in Western Europe. Reactive neutralism would lead to significant pressure to opt out of nuclear defense arrangements because of distrust of American intentions as being either too "forward" or too "unreliable," and could be assisted by high levels of privatization. On the other hand, aggressive nationalism might be attended by pressure for a more forward European defense posture. The political requirement of a stabilized nuclear deterrence would also involve the avoidance of an independent Western European deterrent, especially under Franco-German domination, which would be gravely destabilizing to United States-Soviet relations.

The complexities—technical, administrative, and political—encountered in the Strategic Arms Limitation Talks underline the enormous difficulties of institution building for military stabilization after 1968. However, the main lines of strategic arms limitations began to emerge. The stabilizing elements include: institutionalization of arms control; negotiations as permanent mechanisms; improved unilateral and bilateral photoelectronic surveillance; further limitations on weapons testing; limitations on new launching complexes, including antiballistic missile systems and submarines; and improved hot-line procedures, including the stationing of joint military commissions in neutral territories. Moreover, the emerging patterns of strategic arms limitations face the incredibly complex task of political accommodation with Communist China.[45] This last is especially crucial since the United States would produce gravely destabilizing potentials if it were to seek to enhance its world position by a balance-of-power strategy of "playing off" the Soviet Union against Communist China.[46] These rivalries are likely to maintain themselves on their own accord, with destabilizing consequences. Negotiations with Communist China on strategic arms limitations might well begin earlier rather than later.

However, the core problem is not technical. It remains political, and is related in particular to the changed military function. The major political thrust of the period after 1968 has been to link strategic arms limitation negotiation to the issues of conventional forces in Western Europe. The stability of deterrence depends on the relevant contribution of conventional forces to the mechanics of deterrence, to internal political balance in the NATO structure, and to the political stability of each constituent nation. Paradoxically, despite the vast expenditure of the United States military, the central stabilizing element rests on the supply of an adequate number of conventional ground forces in Western Europe. The unilateral introduction of the all-volunteer force complicated this task; but with a viable professional reorientation, an adequate force with legitimate military utility can be maintained even without conscription.[47]

In other words, under a stabilized foreign policy of "no more Vietnams," the United States would not station conventional ground forces outside Western Europe. (Correspondingly, the same would hold true for the Soviet Union and its external deployment in Eastern Europe.) The size of the remaining force has become subject to negotiation under a mutual balanced-reduction formula in the light of military and political requirements for nuclear deterrence and the worldwide search for military détente. Exceptions to the stationing of conventional forces by the United

States and the Soviet Union exist outside of Europe, in American commitments in Korea and parallel Russian involvement in Egypt and Syria. Although they constitute potential points of negotiation, the political context indicates the possibility of protracted commitment and destabilization, especially in the Middle East.

Under a policy of "no more Vietnams," the United States would also retain a limited and uncommitted multiple-purpose contingency force on active duty, supported by a contracted and effective ready reserve. This force would have a reinforcement potential for NATO and, at the same time, serve as a deterrent to Russian ground-force deployment outside the Warsaw Pact region.

These conditions alter the role of naval forces. A stabilized military balance would involve the deployment of naval forces by both sides as an element of the NATO-Warsaw Pact mutual deterrence on both the North Atlantic and the East Mediterranean flanks. It can be expected that a naval presence ranging widely over the globe, for diffuse objectives of national prestige and presumed political advantage, will continue with only marginal politico-military consequences. Greater expansion of naval power as, for example, in the Indian Ocean, presents potentials for delimited elements of destabilization, but local nationalist sentiment serves as a partial counterweight. There is also the ever-present issue of avoiding naval accidents, which is already being pursued by direct negotiation and treaty between the Soviet Union and the United States.[48]

Elements of destabilization also exist in the competition which the United States and the Soviet Union have generated with respect to the developing countries. However, since 1968 a more realistic perspective has been emerging as military assistance programs have been shown to have very limited military utility. Unilateral and bilateral restraint is the key device that can lead to relevant reductions and refinements without denying genuine national needs or a concern for regional security. One crucial exception, the military assistance race in the Middle East since 1968, has created a trend toward greater destabilization. The search for worldwide military détente between the major powers requires powerful initiatives to deal with these instabilities. The concern of the United States to reduce the instabilities that operated in Vietnam appear to have limited its intent and/or capacity to make the tensions of the Middle East a central element in its détente posture. Alternatively, the Soviet Union has defined the search for détente as compatible with a "forward" military assistance policy in the Middle East. However, the outbreak of military hostilities in 1973 can be taken to reflect the elements of initiative and dispersion of power to client states rather than merely the overriding calculus of the great powers.

The ability of major powers to alter the political structure of developing nations by political manipulation, subversion, support of guerrilla groups, and other types of covert operations has no doubt been exaggerated, although there have been particularly striking cases. These attempts may well continue, even though massive efforts in Latin America, for example, have failed. Moreover, in the Western political democracies, there is growing recognition that measures of defense against internal subversion depend on viable political leadership as much as on military or paramilitary institutions. The appeals to nationalistic sentiment and reliance on indigenous political resources have demonstrated their effectiveness, so that a belief in the inevitable success of Communist-dominated coups and revolts has come to an end. This is not to overlook the destabilizing elements of direct colonial rule where it still persists. However, under conditions of nuclear deterrence, there is real danger that military officers will seek to maintain a traditional definition of the military function by such means as a strong emphasis on various forms of "counterinsurgency." The specter of Western officers and intelligence operatives "going native" and leading indigenous forces dies hard, especially under the circumstances of continued military assistance from the Soviet Union and China to developing nations. However, for a stabilized world balance, the less direct the intervention the better, since such a policy allows nationalism to operate as a counterpressure.

In partial summary, it can be said that narrower limits of the military function have emerged for advanced industrialized nations, especially those with parliamentary institutions. But to speak of narrower limits hardly alters the centrality of force—especially force that is legitimate in international relations and oriented toward stabilizing international relations.

Institution Building for Military Stabilization

The fusion of new concepts with the day-to-day realities of military organization has presented, and continues to present, deep problems in institution building. The behavior and perspectives of the military are influenced by the immediate realities of manning particular weapons systems as much as they are by the formulation of doctrine. These day-to-day realities maintain traditional combat philosophies. It is true that, in the parliamentary nations of the West, the terminology of deterrence has been incorporated into the language of the professional officer. There is much discussion of the phrase, "peacekeeping through a military presence." The phraseology of the deterrent force in the format of a constabulary or various alternatives is extensively debated in military circles. The formulation presented in *The Professional Soldier* continues to require clarification and explication. "The military establishment becomes a constabulary force when it is continuously prepared to act, committed to the minimum use of force and seeks viable international relations rather than victory, because it has incorporated a protective military posture."[49] However, verbal pronouncements are not reliable indicators of institutional change.

It is difficult to assess the actual and potential capacity of a military organization to transform itself and to meet its changed function. To move beyond the strategy of deterrence and consider issues of stabilization versus destabilization will be even more difficult. In the Soviet Union, the existence of a capacity to fight a conventional war in Europe, the possibility of intervention in socialist countries of Eastern Europe, and the confrontation on the Sino-Soviet border help to maintain traditional perspectives. However, the specter of nuclear weapons and their relation to conventional military operations has produced an equivalent but highly muted debate in Soviet professional circles about the nature of the military profession under nuclear arms.[50]

Comparison with the medical profession may be appropriate. In order to develop preventive medicine, a separate structure and, in effect, a separate profession—the specialist in public health, with different training, career, and perspective—had to be brought into being. Clearly, it is not feasible to think in such terms in the case of the military. The transformation in professional capacities must take place within existing operational units. For the military profession, the overriding consideration is whether a force effectively committed to a deterrent philosophy and to peacekeeping and the concept of military presence can maintain its essential combat readiness.

To the detached outside observer, this problem hardly appears insoluble, but to the professional officer it is a central and overriding preoccupation. Does deterrence carry with it the seeds of its own destruction? Will such a strategy, especially under a parliamentary system, undermine the credibility of the military? Can a military force maintain combat readiness without any combat experience or an equivalent? Does not an inherent advantage accrue to nations under single-party political systems which accord the military a different social position and a broader range of functions—functions that presumably make it more viable?

Institution building in the military, creating and maintaining a stabilized military force for deterrence, must be seen as an aspect of the long-term decline of the mass armed force based on conscription. The expansion of the military organization to fight a total war had the paradoxical consequence of "civilizing" the military. The line between the military and the larger society weakened because of military dependence on civilian industry and science, and because of the impact of the mobilization of large numbers of civilians for wartime service. "Total war" made both soldier and civilian objects of attack and served further to attenuate the distinction between the military and civilian sectors of society. Notions such as Lasswell's "garrison state," Mills' "power elite," and Eisenhower's "industrial-military complex" served to highlight the political problems associated with the expansion of the military and the blurring of the distinction between the military and the civilian sectors.[51]

The emergence of an all-volunteer military slows the trend toward civilianization. While there is no return to a highly self-contained military establishment, the "new military" displays a strong preoccupation with maintaining its organizational boundaries and corporate identity. Top military leaders in particular struggle to maintain the distinctive features, qualities, and mystiques of military life as they see them. Although they are dependent on technical expertise, they press to select for the highest command posts those who have had combat experience; as the opportunities for combat decline, the emphasis is at least on operational experience. The military continues to recruit top leaders from those who have attended the prestigious military academies. It seeks to build housing on military bases and to maintain the separate structure of the community and its own style of life. The issues of civilian control are changed under the volunteer force structure, and focus more and more on maintaining the social integration of the military into the larger society.

In Great Britain and in the United States, conscription has been terminated. In France and in NATO nations, the trend is toward reduction in the length of service and toward exploration of new forms of military service (the Netherlands, Belgium, Denmark). Even in West Germany, questions of conscription and its form have come under continual administrative and political scrutiny. In the Western parliamentary democracies, the moral and political legitimacy of military service is thereby being transformed. The military profession and military occupations are seen as one set of "jobs" with special characteristics and qualifications, but the profession is weakened in its special mystique and special status.

Comparable trends are under way in the Soviet Union and the Warsaw Pact nations. The research of John Erickson has demonstrated that, although conscription remains intact and will continue to persist, forms of modern professionalism and an emphasis on "voluntarism" are increasing.[52] The military is becoming more and more concerned with recruiting and retaining volunteers who will man the highly complex weapons. In the navy and the air and rocket forces, manpower is volunteer—no doubt assisted by the volunteers' desire to avoid conscripted ground-force service. In the ground force, a double system—a fused organization of long-term professionals and conscripts—has been emerging. Military service for the conscript is less and less a positive experience, as the Russian equivalent of affluence creates its own youth culture. The military must reluctantly accept its role as an ideological indoctrinator while its main concern is with military effectiveness.

In any military organization, there is a gap between the "big ideas" of military function and the immediate tasks which military personnel must continually perform. Military leaders hope that day-to-day routine will create, or at least contribute to, a sense of military readiness and essential social solidarity. In essence, the more a unit during its normal routine is a military force in being, the more able it is to maintain the sense of military distinctiveness. There are, of course, limits to this observation—for example, when the task becomes excessively tedious or irksome.

Thus, the air force is the service most able to recruit personnel and maintain morale under voluntary manpower systems, because the routines of flying aircraft create military units in being. Even missile crews and radar units, because of the deadly character of the weapons which they handle, feel a sense of urgency which helps them to overcome boredom. Naval units have traditionally represented a force in being and maintained a group solidarity derived from the vitality of seamanship. However, the tedium and pressure of the new naval life—for example, of the submarine at sea for months and months—have transformed some of these conditions and increased the problems of recruitment and self-conception.

The crisis of the military style of life is sharpest in the ground forces. Here the gap between preparation and training and presumed combat is the greatest. Training is only periodic and often lacks the sense of urgency, reality, or risk that routine operations in the air force and navy entail. Airborne and parachute units are closest to units in being, because of the risk and danger in training. As a result, parachute training, ranger training, and wilderness activities are emphasized, not only because of their functional importance but to maintain the professional ideology of combat readiness and military distinctiveness.

The actual disposition of forces conditions military perspectives. The military man maintains his traditional conception of combat readiness more easily if he is stationed abroad or close to a strategic border. The Canadian military thinks of its NATO commitment as an essential ingredient in the military profession. Loss of its overseas assignment would reduce its self-esteem; it would become simply a super-gendarmerie. With the end of a commitment east of Suez, the British military establishment fears a loss of morale in the ground forces, which only operations in North Ireland have staved off temporarily.[53]

Such manifestations of organizational traditionalism raise grave questions about the capacity of the military to operate as a deterrent force in the context of changing military utility. Theoretically, the deterrent force must be prepared for combat regardless of previous combat experience or strategic disposition. Moreover, the more effective concepts of deterrence are, the fewer are the opportunities for traditional ways of maintaining combat readiness. There can be no doubt that the military seeks out opportunities to maintain and to perfect its combat readiness in training. Training exercises and the analysis of previous campaigns often leave the professional unsatisfied, although they are pursued relentlessly. Military observers are sent to wherever military confrontation occurs; peripheral warfare is still seen as a device for the experimental testing of new weapons and tactics. The military seeks to become involved in those operations which it defines as directly relevant for maintaining the combat mystique: intelligence operations, military assistance programs, and training foreign military personnel.

In parliamentary democracies, the preparation for and intervention in domestic disorders have become a highly divisive issue, one which has divided the military itself. Most officers see such involvements as weakening the legitimacy of the armed forces, and a task which must be assumed only under the gravest circumstances. A minority conceptualizes this domestic role of the military both as an essential aspect of the military operation and as a device for maintaining combat readiness. In the United States, the ground forces have, since their intervention in the race riots of 1968, pressed hard to have their role in domestic disorders curtailed. For example, in the events surrounding Wounded Knee, representatives of the ground forces counseled, and succeeded in implementing, a policy of restraint. Increased use of local and state police forces plus the expanded activities of federal marshals have been a resulting trend—but they have left many crucial legal and administrative issues unsolved.

The concern with combat readiness cannot be judged merely as irrational traditionalism, a desire to maintain special privilege, or a fetishistic involvement with the rituals of violence, although all these elements are involved. Combat readiness is a genuine problem, for there is insufficient experience to satisfy operational military officers.[54] The pressure of this uncertainty carries the danger that the military will develop an inflexible posture likely to stand in the way of pragmatic adjustment to emerging realities. One possible response is the acceptance of doctrines which distort the utility of military force in international relations and which are excessively ideological, absolutist, and assault-oriented.

The essential issue is to restructure the organizational milieu of the military so that combat readiness is not an expression of personal aggressiveness or rigid ideological perspectives, but rather a meaningful element of organizational effectiveness. To the outsider, a military organization appears to be a highly routinized institution—an agency governed by rules and regulations and concerned with the precision of its daily life.

However, such an image belies the essential character of military organization, whether a mass armed force based on conscription or an all-volunteer system. The routines of military organization obscure the sense of emergency and crisis to be found in the military. In the mass armed force, emergency and crisis were expected in time of mobilization and combat; for the volunteer force, they are an ever-present immediate potentiality. Emergencies and crises derive from both anticipated and unanticipated technological, economic, and political events; from accidents, miscalculations, or unforeseen contingencies. The military commander is the man who, in his own image, is able to respond to emergencies and crises. The expectation of risk and uncertainty, although narrowed under deterrence, pervades the military from lowest rifleman to operational leader to ranking commander. The capacity to restore balance effectively or to create a new balance is the contemporary dimension of the heroic.

As an element of continuity with the past, the capacity to respond to the unexpected is indeed a core military value, but one only dimly perceived and appreciated. That is the relevance of the "combat spirit" in the context of deterrence. Military men need to be able to act decisively to insure that accidents are avoided, resources mobilized, appropriate responses implemented, and information not distorted under pressure. Physical prowess is involved, but motor responses have always required mental precision; under deterrence, an element of rational steadfastness is paramount.

The notion of deterrence in a military organization is not merely a routine capacity; it requires ability to pursue existing, detailed operating procedures and to apply them with intelligence in new situations. When military men speak of problematic issues involved in maintaining combat readiness, they are in effect seeking to maintain this ability. Thus, for example, it is understandable that in 1973 the Royal Air Force seized the opportunity to mount a quick emergency food airlift to remote regions of Nepal. It thereby demonstrated its emergency capacity, since its pilots had to fly over unfamiliar and dangerous terrain. It was an acceptable exercise in the heroic impulse and a legitimate exposure to danger.

A military force is a complex organization, and the motives and interests of its professional perspective can certainly not be expected to be uniform. In the past, social background was believed to be an essential criterion for selecting military personnel. At present, professional socialization—that is, education and training—is considered essential to fashion and refashion the military man.

However, available data on education and socialization in the military supply no assurance that the process of transformation in the profession will be automatic or certain. In reality, the dominant impact of socialization is negative. Military socialization does not fundamentally alter the attitudes of recruits; it merely rejects those who do not conform to central norms and values. Moreover, the longer the time men spend in a military career, the more homogeneous their orientation becomes; and, all too often, the more pessimistic are their views about international relations.[55]

Tough training is necessary and may make for group loyalty, but it does not necessarily guarantee the professional perspectives required for a deterrent force. Moreover, as Marine Corps experience documents, there appears to be a modest supply of human beings, even in advanced industrial society, who are prepared to expose themselves to the extreme rigors of Marine Corps training. But the responsibilities given to such men are limited to initial military assaults.

To adapt to the new realities of international relations, the military profession must first have a conceptual clarity about its strategic purpose. The new element is that such understanding is not reserved to the top leadership. In appropriate degrees, all professional levels must be aware of the redefined aspects of the military function. In fact, professionalism is not to be delimited in terms of skill, but includes the dimension of awareness of the goals and purposes of deterrence. An educational system which assumes that an officer is trained for a tactical mission and subsequently educated for strategic goals as he advances through the military hierarchy has become irrelevant and outmoded.

Second, since men are not guided by strategic concepts alone, group cohesion and collective motives are essential. In the United States, particularly in the aftermath of the war in Vietnam, core elements in the military are deeply concerned with keeping alive their concept of the "fighter spirit." In Western Europe, the military forces acknowledge this problem but are less concerned, since they accept the validity of their training and operational format. One cannot separate self-conceptions from public reputations. In comparison with the military in Western Europe, and especially in Great Britain, it does appear that the lower prestige and social standing of the United States military contributes to its concern with "tough" military virtues.

In reality, most men in the military profession perform routine organizational tasks which need not attract any particular types of personality. However, military men think of themselves as specialists in violence. The deterrent force cannot have its organizational climate fashioned by men acting out aggressive impulses; rather, it must be the expression of effectively internalized professional norms and values.

The vast apparatus which the military has erected for personnel selection hardly solves the underlying issues.[56] Of course, it does serve to eliminate a tiny minority of unstable and undesirable personalities. The social personality of the military profession is the result of a complex series of training and operational assignments and an elaborate process of self-selection. In the past as well as the present, the military profession has placed great emphasis on rotation of assignment as a means of developing and testing for the kind of social personality desired. Although such a system is costly and disrupts family life, these procedures are stubbornly justified and maintained by the military. The content of military education and diversity of recruitment are key mechanisms of refashioning the military perspective. Another central step is the careful selection of innovative personnel for the role of chief of staff, a task which legitimately falls to civilian political leadership. It should also be possible to develop the military career so that it can be the first step in a lifetime of public service.

Predictably, sons of military personnel enter active duty already socialized to a considerable extent into the profession. It is doubtful whether the military could operate without a strong element of occupational inheritance from father to son. In addition, the military life appeals to men seeking an active athletic existence (although the image of engineer-technologist has been strong in recent years).[57] These men are initially prepared to learn to pilot a fighter aircraft, make repeated military parachute jumps, or navigate a fast destroyer escort. Although such experiences serve as rites of passage and create organizational solidarities, there is no reason to believe that they improve a person's capacities for the detachment and administration required for higher command. But in any career there are multiple requirements and contradictory pressures, and the military is no exception.

Standards of personal behavior are a central issue. If it is to be seen as legitimate and reliable, a force which handles nuclear weapons cannot engage in the deviant practices found in civilian life. The constant screening of "human factors" becomes part of military medicine, and the personal and social controls required to deal with the difficult and tedious tasks of the "new military" will have to be different and more constrained than those in the civilian society.

In a parliamentary democracy, it has been assumed that an officer corps which is not excessively self-recruited and which is reasonably represent- ative of the larger society would have a political orientation compatible with the larger society and would have internalized the advantages of civil control.[58] There can be no explicit political criteria of recruitment into the officer corps. The professional soldier—officer or enlisted man—has the right to personal privacy and to civic involvements, provided he does not engage in partisan behavior. Moreover, it is assumed that he will remain integrated into the larger society. (In the Soviet Union, political reliability is required and enforced by police controls, and the military is isolated from the larger society in order to insure continuing loyalty to the Party.)

However, in an all-volunteer force, especially in states with a long tradition of citizen-soldiers, all of these assumptions are being tested.[59] The strategic conceptions of deterrence and of stabilized military systems which do not produce tangible "victories" create high levels of profes- sional tension and frustration, especially in a period of strong antimilitary sentiment. Recruitment becomes more difficult and the recruits tend to be less representative of the larger society. The potential danger is not simply that the military will become ingrown and socially isolated, although there is clearly a trend in this direction. The real danger is that the military will become both ideologically rigid and more specialized in its contacts with civilian society, and that these contacts may move it toward a more explicitly conservative and rightist orientation.

The result is hardly to produce a potential cadre for counterrevolution. Rather, the military emerges as one additional element of political controversy in a society already racked with extensive political conflict and dissensus. Unless this alternative can be avoided, the military is likely to operate as a pressure group against the realistic military policies required in the search for a new pattern of stabilization in international relations.[60]

The formulations of social research are designed to clarify political and social alternatives; but they should be constructed so as to reduce the possibility of self-fulfilling prophecies. Thus it is necessary for this systemic analysis of international relations and military institutions to return to its point of departure. The assumptions of "fundamental democratization" and the interpenetration of coercion and persuasion reflect the continuity between the internal social structure of an advanced industrial society and the transformed processes of international relations. The emergence of nuclear weapons and the decline of colonial rule have combined to decrease the relevance of traditional conceptions of military intervention that are concerned with the "defeat" of national adversaries or the drastic restructuring of the balance of power. In a very crude way, the term "deterrence" represented a partial, incomplete, and ultimately unsatisfactory advance that sought to recognize realities and to reformulate international political analysis. The intellectual limitations of the notion of deterrence are varied; basically, the term denotes the military objectives without adequately encompassing the political, social, and moral ends.

In a period of search for military détente, the increased obsolescence of the notion of deterrence rests not merely on the changed character of the threat of national adversaries, although this is a relevant dimension. The concept of stabilizing versus destabilizing military systems is an attempt to move beyond the notion of deterrence. In particular, it is an attempt to explicate more specifically the political and moral objectives of military systems. It is an intellectual orientation concerned with the potentialities and limitations of military systems in creating new rules and new norms which are designed to reduce the threat of nuclear and limited war and at the same time to enhance the process of orderly change at the international level.

In each historical period, it is essential to avoid the extrapolation of trends that characterize much of international relations analysis. Therefore, my formulation of stabilizing versus destabilizing military systems should highlight the built-in limitations in the contemporary trend toward détente. It does not de-emphasize the centrality of force in international relations. I am hopeful, however, that it does offer a sharper set of categories for estimating changes in the utility and the legitimacy of the military function.

Notes

1. Quincy Wright, *A Study of War* (Chicago, 1942), Vols. I and II.
2. Morris Janowitz, *The Professional Soldier* (New York, 1971), pp. 418-430.
3. Max Weber, *General Economic History* (Glencoe, Ill., 1950); Karl Mannheim, *Man and Society in an Age of Reconstruction* (New York, 1940), pp. 44-49. See also Herbert Goldhamer and Edward A. Shils, "Types of Power and Status," *American Journal of Sociology*, XLV (September 8, 1939), pp. 171-182.
4. Mannheim, *Man and Society, passim.*
5. See for example, Louis Kriesberg, ed., *Social Process in International Relations: A Reader* (New York, 1968); Herbert Kelman, *International Behavior: A Social-Psychological Analysis* (New York, 1965).
6. Bernard Brodie, *Strategy in the Missile Age* (Princeton, 1959); D. Tarr, *American Strategy in the Nuclear Age* (New York, 1966).
7. Raymond Aron, *A Century of Total War* (New York, 1954); Albert Wohlstetter, "The Delicate Balance of Terror," *Foreign Affairs*, XXXVII (January 1959), pp. 211-234; Joseph Frankel, *International Politics: Conflict and Harmony* (London, 1969).
8. Thomas C. Schelling, *Arms and Influence* (New Haven, 1966). Despite this author's language and particular style, this volume contains valuable materials on the actual pattern of communication and interaction between the U.S. and the Soviet military force.
9. Rupert Emerson, *From Empire to Nation* (Cambridge, Mass., 1960); Clifford Geertz, ed., *Old Societies and New States: The Quest for Modernity in Asia and Africa* (Glencoe, Ill., 1963).
10. Morris Janowitz, *The Role of the Military in the Political Development of New Nations* (Chicago, 1964); S. F. Finer, *The Man on Horseback* (London, 1962); Philippe C. Schmitter, *Military Rule in Latin America* (Beverly Hills, 1973).
11. For an analysis of the changed meaning of nationalism in international relations, see John Herz, *International Politics in the Atomic Age* (New York, 1959); F. H. Hinsley, *Power and the Pursuit of Peace* (Cambridge, 1963).
12. The concept of "stabilizing" versus "destabilizing" military systems does not necessarily assume the idea of equilibrium in international relations, but is compatible with the analysis of historical change.
13. Raymond L. Garthoff, *Soviet Military Policy: A Historical Analysis* (New York, 1966); see esp. chap. 2.
14. Richard C. Snyder, "Some Recent Trends in International Relations Theory and Research," in Austin Ranney, ed., *Essays on the Behavioral Study of Politics* (Urbana, 1962), pp. 103-171.
15. Jessie Bernard, "The Theory of Games as a Modern Sociology of Conflict," *American Journal of Sociology*, LIX (March 1954), pp. 411-530; Anatol Rapoport, "Lewis F. Richardson's Mathematical Theory of War," *Journal of Conflict Resolution*, 1 (September 1957); Thomas C. Schelling, *The Strategy of Conflict* (Cambridge, Mass., 1963); Harold S. Guetzkow and others, *Simulation in Inter-*

national RElations: Developments for Research and Teaching (Englewood Cliffs, N.J., 1963); Bruce M. Russett, *Peace, War, and Numbers* (Beverly Hills, 1972), in particular R. J. Rummel, "U.S. Foreign Relations: Conflict, Cooperation, and Attribute Distances," pp. 71-115; J. W. Burton, *International Relations: A General Theory* (Cambridge, 1965).

16. Gabriel Kolko, *The Roots of American Foreign Policy* (Boston, 1969); Joyce and Gabriel Kolko, *The Limits of Power: The World and United States Foreign Policy: 1945-1954* (New York, 1972); see also Charles S. Maier, "Revisionism and the Interpretation of Cold War Origins," *Perspectives in American History,* IV (1970), pp. 313-347.

17. (New York, 1927, 1938).

18. For an exception, see Douglas Pike, *Viet Cong: The Organization and Techniques of the National Liberation Front of South Vietnam* (Cambridge, Mass., 1966).

19. See Edward Shils' introduction to Georges Sorel, *Reflections on Violence* (Glencoe, Ill., 1950).

20. (Princeton, 1960); (New York, 1965).

21. On the other hand, the United States Strategic Bombing Survey, which sought to assess the economic and sociopolitical consequences of strategic air warfare during World War II, constitutes an important large-scale *tour de force,* based on empirical efforts. In this case, the fact that it was sponsored by U.S. military authorities is irrelevant; the investigators' conclusions were at variance with the operational logic of the U.S. Air Force. Likewise, the fact that its findings had no impact on U.S. military policy is unfortunate, but its intellectual worth makes it a central contribution to the field of international relations. U.S. Strategic Bombing Survey, Morale Division, *The Effects of Strategic Bombing on German Morale, March-July, 1945,* I (Washington, D.C., 1947); U.S. Strategic Bombing Survey, Reports, *Pacific War, The Effects of Strategic Bombing on Japanese Morale* (Washington, D.C., 1945).

22. Otis Dudley Duncan, *Toward Social Reporting: Next Steps* (New York, 1969).

23. Morton Kaplan, *Systems and Process in International Politics* (New York, 1969).

24. Herman Kahn and Anthony J. Wiener, *The Year 2000: A Framework for Speculation on the Next Thirty-Three Years* (New York, 1967).

25. The pioneer effort was Harold D. Lasswell, *World Politics and Personal Insecurity* (New York, 1965); see also Alex Strachey, *The Unconscious Motives of War* (New York, 1957); Maurice L. Farber, "Psychoanalytic Hypotheses in the Study of War," *Journal of Social Issues,* XI, No. I (1955), pp. 29-35.

26. See, for example, Richard H. Tawney, *The Acquisitive Society* (New York, 1920).

27. Karl Mannheim, *Man and Society,* pp. 109-129.

28. Ralf Dahrendorf, *Class and Class Conflict in Industrial Society* (Stanford, 1959); Barrington Moore, Jr., *Reflections on the Causes of Human Misery and Upon Certain Proposals to Eliminate Them* (Boston, 1972).

29. F. H. Hinsley, *Sovereignty* (New York, 1966).

30. Hans Speier, *Social Order and the Risks of War* (Cambridge, Mass., 1969).

31. Stockholm International Peace Research Institute, *World Armaments and*

Disarmaments, SIPRI Yearbook 1973 (Stockholm, 1973); see also SIPRI Yearbooks for 1968-69, 1969-70, and 1972; United States Arms Control and Disarmament Agency, *World Military Expenditures,* 1971 (Washington, D.C., 1972).

32. Stanley Lieberson, "An Empirical Study of Military-Industrial Linkages," in Sam C. Sarkesian, ed., *The Military-Industrial Complex: A Reassessment,* Sage Research Series on War, Revolution, and Peacekeeping, Vol. II (Beverly Hills, 1972), pp. 53-94.

33. Ernst Kris and Nathan Leites, "Trends in Twentieth Century Propaganda," *Psychoanalysis and the Social Sciences,* I (1947), pp. 393-409.

34. For an evaluation of the impact on social personality of violence on television, see U.S. Public Health Service, The Surgeon-General's Scientific Advisory Committee on Television and Social Behavior *Television and Growing Up: The Impact of Televised Violence* (Washington, D.C., 1972).

35. The main outlines of "classical" military strategy in terms of which contemporary conceptions can be assessed are to be found in Gordon Craig, ed., *Makers of Modern Strategy* (Princeton, 1963).

36. See Cecil H. Uyehara, "Scientific Advice and the Nuclear Test Ban Treaty," in Sanford A. Lakoff, ed., *Knowledge and Power* (New York, 1966), pp. 112-161; Robert Gilpin, *American Scientists and Nuclear Weapons Policy* (Princeton, 1962); Gene M. Lyons and Louis Morton, *School for Strategy: Education and Research in National Security Affairs* (New York, 1965).

37. In assessing the marked difference in the success of U.S. foreign policy as between Western Europe and Southeast Asia, a reading of George Kennan, "The Sources of Soviet Conduct," *Foreign Affairs,* XXV (July 1947), pp. 566-582, is most helpful. First, there is no meaningful reference to nuclear weapons in his analysis. Second, he speaks of the need for "adroit and vigilant application of counter force at a series of constantly shifting geographical and political points." However, Kennan writes essentially about foreign policy in Europe, and does not draw the implication of his position for the Middle East or the Far East.

38. P.M.S. Blackett, *Atomic Weapons and East-West Relations* (New York 1956).

39. For an analysis of the "intelligence" dimension in U.S. decision making, see Roger Hilsman, *Strategic Intelligence and National Decisions* (Glencoe, Ill., 1956).

40. Townsend Hoopes, *The Limits of Intervention: An Inside Account of How the Johnson Policy of Escalation in Vietnam Was Reversed* (New York, 1969); Clark Clifford, "A Vietnam Reappraisal," *Foreign Affairs,* XLVII (July 1969), pp. 601-622. For an early assessment of the requirements for negotiating the end of the Indochina War, see Lloyd A. Fallers, Clifford Geertz, and Morris Janowitz, "The Policy Proposals: A Negotiated Stalemate," in *Bulletin of the Atomic Scientists: A Journal of Science and Public Affairs* (June 1965), pp. 42-45.

41. Bernard Brodie, "Nuclear Weapons: Strategic or Tactical," in *Foreign Affairs,* XXXII (January 1954), pp. 217-229, and *Escalation and the Nuclear Option* (Princeton, 1966); Henry A. Kissinger, *Nuclear Weapons and Foreign Policy* (New York, 1957).

42. Herbert S. Dinerstein, *War and the Soviet Union: Nuclear Weapons and the Revolution in Soviet Military and Political Thinking* (New York, 1959); Thomas W. Wolfe, *Soviet Strategy at the Crossroads* (Cambridge, Mass., 1964).

43. *Foreign Affairs,* LI (January 1973), pp. 267-285.

44. It remains to be explained why the U.S. military did not follow its own

professional judgment. The appropriate form of dissent would have been token resignation of the Chief of Staff, particularly the Chief of Staff of the ground forces, when he was assigned a task that he believed could obviously not be achieved with the resources placed at his disposal. The publication of the *Pentagon Papers* has probably postponed an analysis of this central issue, since the answer lies not in examination of specific documents but in the analysis of the workings of a military bureaucracy which in effect has become "overprofessionalized"—more prepared to follow orders than to exercise independent professional skill and judgment.

45. Morton Halperin, *China and Nuclear Proliferation* (Chicago, 1966).

46. Raymond L. Garthoff, *Sino-Soviet Military Relations* (New York, 1966).

47. Morris Janowitz, "Volunteer Armed Forces and Military Purpose," *Foreign Affairs*, L (April 1972), pp. 427-443; Erwin Hackel, "Military Manpower and Political Purpose," *Adelphi Papers*, No. 72 (London, 1970).

48. Union of Soviet Socialist Republics, *Prevention of Incidents on the High Seas* (Agreement signed at Moscow, 1972).

49. Morris Janowitz, *The Professional Soldier*, p. 418.

50. John Erickson, "Soviet Military Power," *Strategic Review* (Spring 1973).

51. Harold D. Lasswell, "The Garrison State," *American Journal of Sociology*, XLVI (January 1941); C. Wright Mills, *The Power Elite* (New York, 1956).

52. John Erickson, *Soviet Military Power* (London, 1972).

53. John Erickson and J. N. Wolfe, eds., *The Armed Services and Society* (Edinburgh, 1970).

54. The concern to maintain combat readiness also pervades the Russian forces. Their leaders are deeply concerned that they have had no combat experience for a quarter of a century; in their own terms, the occupation of allied socialist nations is not considered war. Their response has been to conduct frequent large-scale maneuvers, with which they are obsessed. The threat of a Sino-Soviet confrontation supplies a realistic stimulant. Russian military leaders cannot engage in candid discussion of these issues, and very little is known of the scope and quality of their thinking on these points. They must accept the insistence of political leaders that ideological training is a device for maintaining combat readiness—although, of course, they are fundamentally aware of its limitations.

55. Bengt Abrahamsson, *Military Professionalization and Political Power* (Beverly Hills, 1972); John P. Lovell, "The Professional Socialization of the West Point Cadet," in Morris Janowitz, ed., *The New Military: Changing Patterns of Organization* (New York, 1964), pp. 119-159; David E. Lebby, "Professional Socialization of the Naval Officer: The Effect of the Plebe Year at the U.S. Naval Academy," unpub. Ph.D. diss. (University of Pennsylvania, 1970).

56. Paul D. Nelson, "Personnel Performance Prediction," in Roger W. Little, ed., *Handbook of Military Institutions* (Beverly Hills, 1971), pp. 91-122.

57. Morris Janowitz, *The Professional Soldier*, pp. 21-37.

58. Samuel P. Huntington, *Soldier and State* (Cambridge, Mass., 1957).

59. Morris Janowitz, "The U.S. Forces and the Zero Draft," *Adelphi Papers*, No. 94 (London, 1973).

60. For one of the earliest sociological explications of the norms required for an international order, see Charles Horton Cooley, *Social Process* (New York, 1918), p. 256: "A ripe nationality is favorable to international order for the same reason that a ripe individuality is favorable to order in a small group. It means that we have coherent, self-conscious, and more or less self-controlled elements out of which to build our system. To destroy nationality because it causes wars would be like killing people to get rid of their selfishness. . . ."

MILITARY ELITES AND THE
STUDY OF WAR

Can war and war-making be seen as a special case of a general theory of social conflict? General theories of social conflict offered by Kenneth Boulding and Lewis Coser attempt to encompass forms as diverse as family, community, ethnic, and class conflict.[1] Clearly, the understanding of war would be a crucial test of any general theory of social conflict.[2] Despite the desire for generalized explanations of social conflicts, social scientists cannot overlook the highly distinctive aspects of war as a process of political conflict.

First, as of the second half of the twentieth century, wars are "unique" forms of social conflict because they are waged only by nation-states. War implies social conflict between nation-states whose ideologies legitimize the use of violence in the national interest. The nation-state is a territorially based social system which monopolizes the use of the instruments of violence for both internal and external objectives. Of central importance is armed conflict between established "imperial" nation-states and revolutionary political groups seeking to establish new and independent nation-states. In the last two decades political movements of national independence have been able to arm themselves. In the process of expelling imperial powers, these revolutionary movements only create new nation-states which become potential and actual war-makers.

Second, war is differentiated from other forms of social conflict because war-making relies on a highly professionalized and specialized occupation, the professional soldier. By contrast, for example, conflicts in the family, in community affairs, and even in wide aspects of economic relations involve little or no specialization of personnel. In these arenas the personnel are the same in conflict and in nonconflict situations.

From *Conflict Resolution,* I (March 1957), pp. 9-18.

Nevertheless, in most nation-states—totalitarian or democratic—the decision to threaten war or to make war involves "politicians" and "civilian" leaders with broad manipulative skills, and not primarily military professionals. Regardless of the political power of the military elite, the classical forms of absolute military dictatorship are not applicable to modern mass-industrialized social structure.

The transition from peace to war and from war to peace involves a calculus of political conflict in which the military elites participate from their specialized points of view. Where conventional weapons are involved, the essential calculus is not necessarily that which is found in other types of social and political conflict. At times the essential calculus of war-making does not rest on the postulate that any prolongation of peace will increase the probabilities for further prolongation of peace. Under specific conditions of a traditional arms race, the prolongation of peace brings with it increased uncertainty about the enemy's war-making potential and therefore may increase the probability of war because of attempts to maintain existing advantages. In other forms of social conflict, social inertia and the postponement of decisions may contribute to the nonviolent resolution of conflict differences.

The introduction of nuclear weapons alters the calculus of war-making, for the major powers who have these weapons cannot assume that the outbreak of major war will be to their advantage. To the contrary, the outbreak of major war would be judged as a failure of national policy.

In the language of social science, simple equilibrium models are difficult to apply to the process of war-making.[3] Instead, a process or developmental analysis which highlights the voluntaristic efforts and calculations of the elites within each nation-state is more appropriate. These considerations lead to the analysis of the organization and perspectives of political and military elites as a crucial mechanism in the analysis of war and war-making.

Is it possible to identify different models of political-military elite organization—models that reflect different social structures? Can the consequences of vast technological developments in war-making for the organization of elites be traced out, in order to infer emerging trends? Can important uniformities in the motivational and ideological components of differing political and military elites be established?

Models of Political-Military Elites

Four models of political-military elites can be identified—aristocratic, democratic, totalitarian, and garrison state. For a base line, it seems appropriate to speak of the aristocratic model of political-military elite structure. The *aristocratic model* is a composite estimate of Western European powers before industrialism began to have its full impact.[4] In the aristocratic model, civilian and military elites are socially and functionally integrated. The narrow base of recruitment for both elites and a relatively monolithic power structure provide the civilian elite with a method of "subjective control" of the military.[5]

There is an explicit hierarchy in the aristocratic model which delineates both the source of authority and the prestige of any member of the military elite. The low specialization of the military profession makes it possible for the political elite to supply the bulk of the necessary leadership for the military establishment. The classical pattern is the aristocratic family that supplies one son to politics and one to the military. Birth, family connections, and common ideology insure that the military will embody the ideology of the dominant groups in society. Political control is civilian control only because there is an identity of interest between aristocratic and military groups. The military is responsible because it is a part of the government. The officer fights because he feels that he is issuing the orders.

In contrast to the aristocratic model stands the democratic one. Under the democratic model the civilian and military elites are sharply differentiated. The civilian political elites exercise control over the military through a formal set of rules. These rules specify the functions of the military and the conditions under which the military may exercise its power. The military are professionals in the employ of the state. They are a small group, and their careers are distinct from civilian careers. In fact, being a professional soldier is incompatible with any other significant social or political role. The military leaders obey the government not because they believe in the goals of the war but because it is their duty and their profession to fight. Professional ethics as well as democratic parliamentary institutions guarantee civilian political supremacy. The officer fights because of his career commitment.

The *democratic model* is not a historical reality but rather an objective of political policy. Elements of the democratic model have been achieved only in certain Western industrialized countries, for it requires extremely viable parliamentary institutions and broad social consensus about the ends of government. The democratic model assumes that military leaders can be effectively motivated by professional ethics alone, and this is most difficult. Paradoxically, certain types of officers with aristocratic background have made important contributions to the development of the democratic model.

In the absence of development toward the democratic model, the *totalitarian model* tends to replace the aristocratic one.[6] The totalitarian model, as it developed in Germany, in Russia, and to a lesser degree in Italy, rests on a form of subjective control, as did the older aristocratic model. But the subjective control of the totalitarian model arises not from any natural or social unity of the political and military elites. On the contrary, a revolutionary political elite of relatively low social status and based on a mass authoritarian political party fashions a new type of control of the military elite. The revolutionary elite, bedecked with paramilitary symbols and yet forced into temporary alliance with older military professionals, is dedicated to reconstituting the military elites. Subjective control of the totalitarian variety is enforced by the secret police, by infiltrating party members into the military hierarchy, by arming its own military units, and by controlling the system of officer selection. Under subjective control of the totalitarian variety, the organizational independence of the professional military is destroyed. The officer fights because he has no alternative.[7]

The *garrison-state model,* as offered by Professor Harold D. Lasswell, is the weakening of civil supremacy which can arise even out of an effective democratic structure.[8] While the end result of the garrison state approximates aspects of the totalitarian model, the garrison state has a different natural history. It is, however, not the direct domination of politics by the military. As modern industrial nations cannot be ruled merely by the political domination of a single small leadership bloc, the garrison state is not a throwback to a military dictatorship. It is the end result of the ascent to power of the military elite under conditions of prolonged international tension. Internal freedom is hampered, and preparation for war becomes overriding. The garrison state is a new pattern of coalition in which military groups directly and indirectly wield unprecedented political and administrative power. The military retain their organizational independence, provided they make appropriate alliances with civil political factions. The officer fights for national survival and glory.

It cannot be assumed that all forms of militarism involve "designed militarism." Designed militarism—the type identified with Prussian militarism—involves the modification and destruction of civilian institutions by military leaders acting directly and premeditatedly through the state and other institutions. Equally significant and more likely to account for crucial aspects of the garrison state, as well as for contemporary American problems, is "unanticipated militarism." Unanticipated militarism develops from a lack of effective traditions and practices for controlling the military establishment, as well as from a failure of civilian political leaders to act relevantly and consistently. Under such circumstances a vacuum is created which not only encourages an extension of the tasks and power of military leaderships but actually forces such trends.

The threats to the democratic model cannot be meaningfully analyzed merely from the point of view of designed militarism. Designed militarism emphasizes the impact of military leadership on the civil social structure. Unanticipated militarism requires an analysis of the manner in which the military profession responds and reacts to developments in civilian society. The technology of war, which is the advanced technology of civilian society, lies at the root of and sets the preconditions in trends toward unanticipated militarism.

Consequences of Technological Trends

The long-term technological development of war and war-making has required the professionalization of the military elite. Such technological developments have been compatible with the democratic model of political-military elites, for this model rests on the differentiation of the functions of politicians and soldiers. But the current continuous advance in the technology of war begins to weaken the possibility of the democratic elite model.

The vast proliferation of the military establishments of the major industrialized nations is a direct consequence of the continuous development of the technology of warfare. The "permanent" character of these vast military establishments is linked to the "permanent" threat of war. It is well recognized that under these conditions the tasks that military leaders perform tend to widen. Their technological knowledge, their direct and indirect power, and their heightened prestige result in their entrance, of necessity, into arenas which have in the recent past been preserved for civilian and professional politicians. The result is a tremendous stress on traditional assumptions about the effectiveness of the democratic model for regulating political-military relations. Political leaders' need for active advice from professional soldiers about the strategic implications of technological change serves only to complicate the task of redefining spheres of competence and responsibility. Totalitarian as well as democratic nations are faced with these problems.

The impact of the technological development of warfare over the last half-century leads to a series of propositions about social change:

A large percentage of the national income of modern states is spent for the preparation, execution, and repair of the consequences of war.

There is more nearly total popular involvement in the consequences of war and war policy, for the military establishment is responsible for the distribution of a larger share of civilian values and the destructiveness of war has increased asymptotically.

The military's monopolization of legal armed violence has increased so greatly that the task of suppressing internal violence has declined, as compared with the external tasks of national security.[9]

The rate of technological change has accelerated, and a wider diversity of skill is required to maintain the military establishment.

The previous periodic character of the military establishment (rapid expansion, rapid dismantlement) has given way to a more permanent maintenance or expansion.

The permanent character of the military establishment has removed one important source of political-military conflict, i.e., the civilian tendency to abandon the military establishment after a war. Instead, because of the high rate of technological change, internal conflicts between segments of the military elite have been multiplied.

The diversification and specialization of military technology have lengthened the time of formal training required for mastery of military technology, with the result that the temporary citizen army will become less important and a completely professional army more vital.

The complexity of the machinery of warfare and the requirements for research, development, and technical maintenance tend to weaken the organization line between the military and the nonmilitary.

Because of these technological and large-scale administrative developments, civilian society as well as the military establishment is undergoing basic transformation. The contemporary tension in political-military organization within the major industrialized powers has a common basis to the degree that the technological requirements of war are highly universal. Yet differences in the amount or character of political power exercised by military leaders and the methods for resolving conflicts between political and military leaders as between the major nation-states cannot be explained primarily, or even to any great extent, by differences in the technological organization of their armed forces. This is not to deny that each weapons system—land, sea, or naval—tends to develop among its military managers characteristic orientations toward politics based on the technical potentialities of their weapons. The political outlook of any military establishment will be influenced by whether it is an organization dominated by army, navy, or air force. Nevertheless, technological developments merely set the limits within which the civilian and military elites will share power. National differences in the influence patterns of military elites must be linked to national differences in social structure and elite organization.

These technological trends in war-making have necessitated extensive common modification in the military profession in both democratic and totalitarian systems, and regardless of national and cultural differences. The changes in the military reflect organizational requirements which force the permanent military establishment to parallel other large-scale civilian organizations. As a result, the military takes on more and more the common characteristics of a government or business organization. Thus the differentiation between the military and the civilian—an assumed prerequisite for the democratic elite model—is seriously weakened. In all these trends the model of the professional soldier is being changed by "civilianizing" the military elite to a greater extent than the "militarizing" of the civilian elite.

What are some of these modifications in the military profession? They include (a) "democratization" of the officer recruitment base, (b) a shift in the basis of organization authority, and (c) a narrowing of the skill differential between military and civilian elites. Propositions concerning these trends for the United States military during the last fifty years are applicable in varying forms to the military establishments of the other major industrialized nations.[10]

"Democratization" of the Officer Recruitment Base: Since the turn of the century the highest military elites of the major industrialized nations have been undergoing a basic social transformation. They have been shifting their recruitment from a narrow, relatively high-status social base to a broader, lower-status, and more representative social base.

The broadening of the recruitment base reflects the demand for large numbers of trained specialists. As skill becomes the basis of recruitment and advancement, democratization of selection and mobility increases. This is a specific case of the general trend in modern social structure of the shift from criteria of ascription to those of achievement. In Western Europe the democratization of the military elites displaced the aristocratic monopoly of the officer corps; in the United States an equivalent process can be observed, although social lines are generally less stratified and more fluid. The sheer increase in size of the military establishment contributes to this democratization. For a period, the United States Air Force, with its large demand for technical skill, offered the greatest opportunity for rapid advancement.

From the point of view of the democratic model, democratization of social recruitment of military leaders is not necessarily accompanied by democratization of outlook and behavior. By democratization of outlook and behavior is meant an increase in accountability or an increase in the willingness to be accountable. In fact, the democratization of the military profession carries with it certain opposite tendencies. The newer strata are less aware of the traditions of the democratic model. Their opportunities for mobility make them impatient and demanding of even greater mobility. Their loyalty to the military establishment begins to depend more and more on the conditions of employment rather than on the commitment to the organization and its traditions.

The increased representativeness of social background of the military profession also results in an increased heterogeneity of the top leaders within the various military services. Under these conditions it is more difficult to maintain organization effectiveness and at the same time enforce the norms of civilian political control. (In a totalitarian society, it likewise becomes more difficult to maintain organization effectiveness and enforce party loyalty.) Of course, any large-scale organization develops devices for overcoming these forms of disruption. The military profession emphasizes honor as a unifying ideology, and intra-service marriage patterns have been a power device for assimilating newcomers into the military establishment. But requirements of bureaucratic efficiency corrode honor, and the military marriage, like civilian marriage, is currently more limited in its ability to transmit traditions.

Even more fundamental, the new democratization changes the prestige position of the military profession. The older traditional soldier has his social prestige regulated by his family of origin and by the civilian stratum from which he came. What society thought was of little importance as long as his immediate circle recognized his calling. This was true even in the democratic model. The British officer corps, with its aristocratic and landed-gentry background and its respectable middle-class service families, is the classic case in point. In varying degrees before World War II it was true for the United States Navy, with its socialite affiliations, and even the United States Army, with its Southern military family traditions. But with democratization of the profession, pressure develops for prestige recognitions by the public at large. A public-relations approach must supplant a set of personal relations. Public relations becomes not merely a task for those specialists assigned to developing public support for military establishment policies; every professional soldier, like every businessman or government official, must represent his establishment and work to enhance the prestige of the professional military. In turn, a military figure becomes a device of enhancing a civilian enterprise. Under these circumstances, objective control gives way to subjective identity.

Shift in the Basis of Organization Authority: It is common to point out that military organization is rigidly stratified and authoritarian in character because of the necessities of command. Moreover, since military routines are highly standardized, it is generally asserted that promotion is in good measure linked to compliance with existing procedures and existing goals of the organization. (These characteristics are found in "civilian" bureaucracies but supposedly not with the same high concentration and rigidity.) Once an individual has entered into the military establishment, he has embarked on a career within a single pervasive institution. Short of withdrawal, he thereby loses the "freedom of action" associated with occupational change in civilian life.

From such a point of view, the professional soldier is thought to be authoritarian in outlook. Status and the achievement of status are thought to be fundamental motivations. The organizing principle of authority is domination—the issuing of direct commands. The professional soldier is seen as limited in his ability and skill to participate in "civilian" political affairs which require flexibility, negotiation, and the "art of persuasion."

It is not generally recognized, however, that a great deal of the military establishment resembles a civilian bureaucracy as it deals with problems of research, development, supply, and logistics. Even in those areas of the military establishment that are dedicated primarily to combat or to the maintenance of combat readiness, a central concern of top commanders is not the enforcement of rigid discipline but rather the maintenance of high levels of initiative and morale. This is a crucial respect in which the military establishment has undergone a slow and continuing change since the origin of mass armies and rigid military discipline.[11]

Initiative rather than the enforcement of discipline is a consequence of the technical character of modern warfare, which requires highly skilled and highly motivated groups of individuals. Often these formations must operate as scattered and detached units, as opposed to the solid line of older formations. It is also a consequence of the recruitment policies of modern armies, which depend on representative cross-sections of the civilian population rather than on volunteers. Modern armies increasingly draw their recruits from urbanized and industrialized populations and less from illiterate agricultural groups, for whom response to discipline is a crucial and effective form of control. Tolerance for the discomforts of military life decreases. The "rationality" and skepticism of urban life carry over into military institutions to a greater degree than in previous generations. The rationalization of military life makes necessary the supplying of more explicit motives. Social relations, personal leadership, material benefits, ideological indoctrination, and the justice and meaningfulness of war aims are now all component parts of morale.

Short of complete automation, specialized units manning the crucial technical instruments of war must display fanatically high morale in order to achieve successful military offensive action. Although military formations are still organized on the basis of discipline, military command involves an extensive shift from domination to manipulation as a basis of authority. Manipulation implies persuasion, negotiation, and explanation of the ends of the organization. Direct orders give way to the command conference. Since manipulation involves high social interaction, differences in status are tempered by morale objectives. Shifts from domination to manipulation, from status to morale, are present in many aspects of civilian society. But the peculiar conditions of combat have obscured the extent to which morale leadership is especially required for military formations. This is not to imply that the military establishment has found a formula for approximately balancing domination and manipulation.

Narrowing the Skill Differential Between Military and Civilian Elites: The consequences of the new tasks of military management imply that the professional soldier must more and more acquire skills and orientations common to civilian administrators and even political leaders. He is more interested in the interpersonal techniques of organization, morale, negotiation, and symbolic interaction. He is forced to develop political orientations in order to explain the goals of military activities to his staff and subordinates. Not only must the professional soldier develop new skills necessary for internal management; he must develop a "public-relations" aptitude in order to relate his formation to other military formations and to civilian organizations. This is not to imply that these skills are found among all the top military professionals, but the concentration is indeed great and seems to be growing. The transferability of skills from the military establishment to civilian organizations is thereby increased. Within the military establishment, conflicts occur and deepen with greater acceleration between the old, traditionally oriented officers and the new, who are more sensitized to the emerging problems of morale and initiative.

Each of these three trends—(a) democratization of the officer recruitment base, (b) shift in the basis of organizational authority, and (c) narrowing the skill differential between military and civilian elites—has its limitations. These limitations derive from the need of the military establishment to maintain its organizational boundaries, and from the problems of organizing military technology. In other words, the trend toward civilianization modifies but does not eliminate civil-military differences, and especially raises crucial questions about the ideological perspective of the military profession.

Trends in Indoctrination

In the past, institutional indoctrination of the military professional in the United States avoided discussion of human factors in the military establishment and the political consequences of military operations. (It is, of course, difficult, if not impossible, to intellectualize at any length about the enforcement of discipline.) Before World War II, the United States professional military had a schooling which supplied little realistic orientation except to emphasize a simple mechanical version of ultimate civilian supremacy. Even before the outbreak of World War II, however, important sectors of the military elite had to reorient themselves slowly and painfully on these matters. Reorientation came about as a result of the realities of the war. Of course, much of the crucial work merely devolved upon lower-rank staff officers and technical specialists, with the "top military cadre" not fully in sympathy.

In the absence of institutional indoctrination for these tasks, the extent to which self-indoctrination succeeded in producing the number of officers capable of functioning in these areas is impressive. Nevertheless, the military establishment continues to be characterized by deep inner tensions because of its new responsibilities and because of the absence of a sufficiently large cadre of top officers sensitized to deal effectively with its broad administrative and political tasks.

Before World War II, whatever training and indoctrination existed for handling the complexities of civil-military relations and political tasks were primarily a self-generated mission. Some deviant career officers were not only sensitive to emerging problems within the military establishment, but many of these officers sought to indoctrinate themselves about emerging problems of civil-military relations and of the political aspects of military operations. They often accepted specialized assignments of a quasi-political nature or those involving communications skills which supplied relevant opportunities for indoctrination and training. (These assignments included military attaché, foreign-language officer, intelligence officer, and public relations.) Voluntary acceptance or pursuit of these assignments represented genuine efforts at self-indoctrination and thereby selected out for training those who felt inclined and had potentials for growth. In the United States especially, before 1939, these assignments had relatively low prestige. In fact, they were seen as interfering with one's career, and therefore they were avoided by all except those who had sufficient foresight to see their high relevance. For many, these assignments did involve risk and short-term disadvantages. But the results of such assignments in crucial cases were just the contrary. They helped officers to enter the very top of the military elite, since they did, in fact, represent realistic indoctrination for emerging tasks.

Since the end of World War II, institutional indoctrination at all levels of the military establishment encompasses much wider perspectives—social and political. Although much of the new indoctrination appears to be oriented to the broader problems of the military establishment—internal and external—it is very much an open question as to what the consequences are likely to be for civil-military relations in a democratic society.

Ideological indoctrination is now designed to eliminate the civilian contempt for the "military mind." The military mind has been charged with traditionalism and a lack of inventiveness. The new indoctrination stresses initiative and continuous innovation. This is appropriate for the career motives of the new recruits and is important in creating conditions for overcoming bureaucratic inertia. The military mind has been charged with an inclination toward ultra-nationalism and ethnocentrism. Professional soldiers are being taught to de-emphasize ethnocentric thinking, since ethnocentrism is detrimental to national and military policy. The military mind has been charged with being disciplinarian. The new indoctrination seeks to deal with human factors in combat and in large-scale organization in a manner similar to contemporary thought on human relations in industry. In short, the new indoctrination is designed to supply the professional soldier with an opinion on all political, social, and economic subjects which he feels obliged to have as a result of his new role.

The new "intellectualism" is a critical capacity and a critical orientation. The military officer must be realistic, and he must review the shortcomings of the past and contemporary record of political-military relations. Will the growth of critical capacities be destructive, or will it be productive of new solutions? The consequence could be a growth in hostility toward past arrangements, in particular toward past political leadership of the military establishment and toward the dogmas of civilian supremacy. The military profession runs the risk of confusing its technical competency with intellectual background. As a result, it could become critical and negative toward the military bureaucracy and toward civilian political leadership in the same way that Joseph Schumpeter speaks of the university-trained specialist becoming critical of the economic system. In the United States at least, such hostility is hardly likely to lead to open disaffection but more to passive resentment and bitterness.

In the long run, under either the democratic or the totalitarian model, the military establishment cannot be controlled and still remain effective by civilianizing it. Despite the growth of the logistical dimensions of warfare, the professional soldier is, in the last analysis, a military commander and not a business or organizational administrator. The democratic elite model of civilian supremacy must proceed on the assumption that the function of the professional military is to command soldiers into battle. There is no reason to believe that the characteristics of the ideal professional soldier as a military commander are compatible with the ideal professional soldier as an object of civilian control, although the differences seem to be growing less and less as the automation of war continues. The quality of political control of the professional soldier is not to be judged by examining those aspects of the military establishment that are most civilian but rather those that are least civilian. Here the willingness to submit to civilian control, rather than the actuality of civilian control, is crucial.

There is no reason to believe, in a democratic society, that the military can be controlled by offering them the conditions of employment found in civilian society. In the long run, civilian establishments would draw off all the best talent, especially in a business-dominated society. To achieve the objectives of the democratic elite model, it is necessary to maintain and build on the differentiation between civilian and military roles. A democratic society must accord the professional soldier a position based on his skill and on his special code of honor. He must be integrated because his fundamental differentiation is recognized. Under these circumstances, standards of behavior can be established and political directives enforced. The current drift toward the destruction of the differentiation of the military from the civilian cannot produce genuine similarity but runs the risk of creating new forms of hostility and unanticipated militarism.

Notes

1. Kenneth Boulding, *Conflict Resolution,* I, No. 2 (1957); Lewis Coser, *The Functions of Social Conflict* (Glencoe, Ill., 1956); Georg Simmel, *Conflict,* trans. Kurt H. Wolff (Glencoe, Ill., 1955).

2. See Quincy Wright, *A Study of War* (Chicago, 1942), esp. chap. XVI, "Scientific Method and the Study of War."

3. For a discussion of equilibrium models and social change, see Barrington Moore, Jr., "Sociological Theory and Contemporary Politics," *American Journal of Sociology,* LXI (September 1955), pp. 107-115.

4. Alfred Vagts, *The History of Militarism* (New York, 1937).

5. Samuel P. Huntington, "Civilian Control of the Military: A Theoretical Statement," in Heinz Eulau, Samuel Eldersveld, and Morris Janowits, eds., *Political Behavior: A Reader in Theory and Research* (Glencoe, Ill., 1956), pp. 380-385.

6. Hans Speier, *War and the Social Order: Papers in Political Sociology* (New York, 1952).

7. Coser, *Functions of Social Conflict.* The totalitarian model that developed in Western Europe is not the same as the traditional feudal-like military dictatorship found in parts of South America, in which a military junta directly dominates civilian military life. The Perón model was a strange combination of the old-style military dictatorship and the newer devices of the totalitarian model.

8. Harold D. Lasswell, "The Garrison State," *American Journal of Sociology,* XLVI (January 1941), pp. 455-468.

9. Katherine Chorley, *Armies and the Art of Revolution* (London, 1943).

10. Morris Janowitz, *The Professional Soldier and Political Power: A Theoretical Orientation and Selected Hypotheses* (University of Michigan, Bureau of Government, Institute of Public Administration, 1953).

11. S.L.A. Marshall, *Men Against Fire: The Problem of Battle Command in Future War* (Washington, D.C., 1947).

MILITARY INSTITUTIONS AND CITIZENSHIP
IN WESTERN SOCIETIES

Research literature on the "new" nations of Africa, the Middle East, and Asia, as well as on Latin America, reveals a persistent concern with the positive and negative contributions of military institutions to "nation building."[1] In particular, the perspective of macrosociology as it has been applied to the "developing" nations takes into consideration the impact of armies and armed political movements on the capacity of political parties to govern. By contrast, comparative macrosociology has shown very little interest in assessing the role of military institutions in the emergence of Western nation-states—that is, in Western Europe and the United States. This is particularly difficult to explain in the light of the central historical significance of armies and armed conflict in fashioning both the boundaries and the structure of the modern secular nation-state.[2]

Of course, historians have been aware and have written extensively of the military dimensions of Western European and American history. But they have not been concerned with the processes by which parliamentary multiparty systems have been able to emerge in this geographic and cultural region where modern professional military institutions, including "citizen" conscription, first emerged and were institutionalized.

Macrosociological Perspective

Therefore, this paper focuses on those socio-political changes in Western Europe and the United States that can be linked to the rise and subsequent decline of mass popular armies from the end of the eighteenth century to the present. The armies of Western Europe and the United States during this era can be called mass "citizen" armies, in varying degrees. They have embodied professional cadres of officers and enlisted personnel, augmented by conscripts and,in wartime, by mobilized citizen reservists. We are dealing with military institutions in which these conscripts and civilian reservists are defined as citizens rather than "mere" subjects. Citizenship focuses on the balance of individual rights versus the prerogatives of the state and its leaders. T. H. Marshall asserts the sequential development of three dimensions in citizenship in the Western nation-states: civil, in the eighteenth century; political, in the nineteenth century; and social (including economic welfare), in the twentieth.[3] Enlargement of the scope of citizenship in these terms has been accompanied by an expansion in the proportion of the population defined as citizens until formal citizenship becomes universal in a "mass society."[4] But at each point in the definition and redefinition of citizenship, the impact of military institutions must be taken into account. Citizenship in Western nation-states is not only a result of industrialism and urbanism and the associated socio-political movements. In fact, the thrust of my analysis is embodied in the formulation of Friedrich Engels: "Contrary to appearance compulsory military service surpasses general franchise as a democratic agency." In the 1960s, mass military institutions based on citizen conscription began to be transformed into smaller more "volunteer" forces—with profound implications for social structure, political power, and nationalism.[5]

How can one account for the simultaneous emergence of massive modern military institutions and of multi-party parliamentary institutions in the Western industrialized nations? The experiences of the Western nation-states are relatively distinct from those of other nation-states which underwent industrialization (e.g., Russia and Japan), and much more distinct from those of contemporary developing nations. The analysis offered here seeks to encompass three sets of factors in order to generate hypotheses which may help clarify the complex role of the military in the historical development of Western nation-states: (a) technology and organizational format; (b) social stratification and professionalization of the military institutions; and (c) the normative and symbolic content of the social and political movements supplying the ideological foundation of the Western nation and the rationale for its military institutions.

The modern professional mass armies of Western Europe emerged from the postfeudal institutions created in the eighteenth century by the absolute monarchies. The military institutions of the United States were deeply influenced by these developments. Only in the West was military service in mass conscript armies of the nineteenth century seen as compatible with the duties and rights of citizenship. In fact, military service was defined as an integral aspect of citizenship, and two general hypotheses emerge. First, the institutionalization of citizen conscription has been an essential component in the emergence of Western parliamentary institutions. The continuing task for research is to account for this variant of conscription as it appeared in the West, since conscription in the nineteenth century was also compatible with, for example, serflike socio-political relations in Czarist Russia. The second hypothesis also relates to the transformation from the feudal type of military to the bureaucratic and professional armies of the nineteenth century. It will be argued that the "heroic" model of the Western officer corps, rooted in European feudalism, has been significant in facilitating the acceptance of parliamentary and civilian control. The military elite, or at least a significant portion who were traditionally conservative because of their conception of personal fealty, could readily transfer their allegiance from the reigning monarchy to the leaders of the new political regimes. The failure or the reluctance of the professional military to intervene directly more extensively than they did in the political process in the nineteenth-century West requires explanation. Throughout the nineteenth century, their behavior was markedly contained, compared with the military groups of the developing nations since 1945. The military leaders at various points in the development of Western political institutions monopolized coercive power to at least as great a degree as the military in contemporary developing societies. Moreover, they often operated in a setting in which political parties were as weak as, or even weaker than, those in the new nations.

For the issue at hand, the term "military institution" is probably too circumscribed, and, in fact, misleading for a comprehensive and effective comparative macrosociology of nation building—in Western societies—or more generally. It refers to a concrete and specific institution rather than to the taxonomic elements involved in the "management of the instruments of violence."[6] Although this paper focuses on armies as military institutions, the term "armed forces" is more appropriate if it is conceived as describing the variety of organizations and groups which (a) use coercion and force in order to maintain or to alter the societal structure and power relations, and (b) seek to monopolize force in terms of a formula of political legitimacy. Therefore, "armed forces" encompasses the full range, from formally organized standing armies to armed revolutionary movements.[7]

The classical tradition of sociological analysis has investigated the problematic relations between industrialism and nationalism to explain the development of "modern" political institutions. The present state of investigation into the emergence of the nation-state in the West is different from that which existed when sociological thought was being formulated in the middle and end of the nineteenth century. In the intellectual origins of sociology as a distinct discipline, and especially in its initial interest in the comparative analysis of total societies and the rise of the nation-state, the classical writers demonstrated a central interest in military institutions and armed revolutionary conflict.

In Great Britain, Herbert Spencer, with his typology of the "militant" society, focused on the negative effects military institutions had on industrial society and its evolution.[8] In Germany, Max Weber interspersed his political sociology with a concern for the legitimate institutionalization of coercion as the essential element in the emergence of the nation-state. There can be no doubt that Weber was fully aware of the centrality of the armed forces in fashioning nationalism. He understood that military organization was the prototype of modern organizations: "The discipline of the army gives birth to all discipline."[9] He recognized the linkages between military service and citizenship. But, in the thousands of pages in his collected works, at most twenty are devoted to military themes.[10] As a result, it is understandable that the multitude of Weber disciples did not continue his approach and avoided such matters.[11] Karl Marx's theory of armed conflict and revolutionary change required him to describe military institutions, although this topic was actually of greater concern to his colleague, Friedrich Engels.[12] Perhaps the most comprehensive analysis of the connections between conscription and political forms presented during that period was by Gaetano Mosca in his *The Ruling Class.*[13]

However, since 1945, most sociologists involved in the comparative analysis of Western industrialized nations have carried out their research without regard to the impact the armed forces have had on social structure and political institutions. For example, in *Social Mobility in Industrial Society,* Reinhard Bendix and Seymour M. Lipset do not pose as a central theoretical issue the manner in which military institutions reflect and, in turn, fashion social structure.[14] Peter Blau's guide to sociology in *Reader's Guide to the Social Sciences* contains a single reference to the analysis of military institutions and that is to Herbert Spencer.[15] Ralf Dahrendorf's penetrating analysis of the transformation of Western industrial society, *Class and Class Conflict in Industrial Society,* in effect completely avoids the military's role in the emergence of Western nationalism.[16] Only Raymond Aron stands as a historical sociologist who has been centrally concerned with the interplay of military institutions, industrialism, and political democracy.[17] Two other sociologists have approached these issues from a very specialized point. Stanislaw Andreski, in *Military Organization and Society,* has sought to trace the connection between participation in military institutions and the degree of equalitarianism in the social stratification.[18] He proposes that greater participation leads to more equality—a suggestive notion, but one which requires extensive explication. Alternatively, Marion Levy offers a set of categories, derived from Talcott Parsons' scheme for investigating the role of the military, that he believes are applicable both to industrialized societies and to the developing nations.[19] It has become obvious that macrosociological analysis of Western nation-states must take into consideration the impact of military institutions and armed forces on political institutions.

Military Institutions and Citizenship

This paper maintains that military institutions have been of central importance in fashioning the type of nation-states that emerged in Western Europe and the United States. The role of the military is linked to nationalism; in fact, the armed forces of the nineteenth and twentieth centuries epitomize modern nationalism. But modern nationalism hardly insures the emergence of elements of political democracy.[20] For the purposes at hand political democracy is linked to the normative notion of "citizenship." The essential problematic issue is that of establishing the connections between military service in selected Western nation-states and the political concept of "citizenship." The analytic terrain that requires investigation is complex and the theoretical formulations involved are easily misunderstood. The first hypothesis offered above requires careful examination. To the extent that mass armies defined their recruits in terms of political and normative ideas of citizenship, military service functioned as an essential and necessary contribution to political institutions. Of course, the political meaning of military service is generated and imposed by political elites external to the military. There is another element in the mass conscript army which contributes to the democratic political institution. Revolutionary nationalism, in the United States, and also in France, broke the monopoly of the higher social groups over recruitment into the officer corps. In theory, and to some extent, all social groups were eligible to become officers.

However, it must be emphasized that military conflict and war created social and political tensions which weakened democratic political institutions. Moreover, throughout the nineteenth and early twentieth centuries, civil-military relations were influenced by the pattern of the "military-industrial complex" of that time. Industrial groups aligned themselves with the military (e.g., Krupp under Kaiser Wilhelm, and Schneider during the Third Republic) in such a manner as to strain parliamentary control over it.

Reinhard Bendix, in *Nation-Building and Citizenship,* argues that the extension of the franchise is the key indicator of nation building in Western Europe in the nineteenth century.[21] Stein Rokkan also has developed this theme in considerable detail.[22] Such analyses are too circumscribed. Alternatively or in amplification, I would argue that, starting with the French and American revolutions, participation in armed conflict has been an integral aspect of the normative definition of citizenship.

Historically, the American Revolution and the French Revolution were crucial points in the origin of the modern mass military formation. In those conflicts, political leaders armed extensive segments of the civil population, and thus broke decisively with traditional patterns. That the rank and file could and should be armed and that the armed citizenry would be loyal was a "revolutionary" formulation. In a similar vein, the establishment of the principle that the officer corps was open to recruits from all social groups was also revolutionary. Under feudal and postfeudal arrangements from the Renaissance to the neo-Classical age, 1417-1789, military formations were officered by groups dominated by the nobility and were manned by mercenaries, men impressed into service, and small delimited groups of volunteers.[23]

The citizen-soldier concept, of course, had its origins in the Greek city-state and in the early Roman military system. The interconnections among military service, control of the armed forces, and political democracy were explicitly formulated and institutionalized to varying degrees. It is significant that some of the central leaders of the French Revolution were explicit in their references to these ideas and practices. Moreover, the citizen-soldier format had its institutional antecedents, before the American and French revolutions, in the militia and national guard units. Variations of these types of units were widespread both in Western Europe and in the North American British and French colonies. The part-time character of their officers and the more representative character of their members anticipated the social format of the mass citizen-conscript armies. Particularly in France, the national guard units played an important role in armed conflicts of the Revolution.

The legitimacy of the revolutionary movements and the political democracies they sought to establish rested on the assertion that citizens had been armed and had demonstrated their loyalty through military service.[24] Military service emerged as a hallmark of citizenship and citizenship as the hallmark of a political democracy. The citizen army which made use of civilian reservists was not only an instrument of nationalism but a device for political control of the military professionals. To stress the political and normative consequences of mass military service is not to overlook the essential requirement that the military leadership of the mass armed forces which emerged during the nineteenth century had to be depoliticalized or politically contained if any variant of political democracy were to be achieved and institutionalized.

For purposes of comparative macrosociology, the worldwide view which assumes a general process of "modernization" of feudal, traditional, or peasant societies is much too global. In Western Europe, industrialism was well developed by the end of the nineteenth century, the emergence of modern large-scale military institutions was closely intertwined with the growth of industrial institutions, and, furthermore, both were relatively indigenous processes. While it is possible to speak of the emergence of modern armed forces in Western Europe in the nineteenth century, such a general observation cannot obscure the profound differences in the organizational and normative basis of mass participation in the military in different nations.

The linkage between citizen-soldier and the effective extension of the franchise, with its resulting impact on political institutions, reflects different historical patterns in Germany, France, Great Britain, and the United States. France can be taken as the nation where the conception of the citizen-conscript was most clearly enunciated as a principle designed to assist civilian political control of the military. Conscription was institutionalized early and widely accepted; it has been gradually reformed and expanded, with the result that it has served as an accepted institution in French social structure. In contemporary France, the political commitment to conscription remains the strongest among Western nations, although, with the development of nuclear weapons and the end of the French empire, it has come under increasing attack. The United States is the nation in which the ideological and political basis for the citizen-soldier has been strong and extensive from the period of the American Revolution. However, national and military requirements made it possible to avoid introducing conscription except in wartime, until the end of World War II. From World War I onward, citizen military service had been seen as a device by which excluded segments of society could achieve political legitimacy and rights. Until Vietnam, for example, blacks pressed to be armed and integrated into the fighting military as a sign that they had effectively attained citizenship and the concomitant privileges. While professional military officers have informally been excluded from elected office, with the exception of a few wartime heroes who became president, service as a citizen-soldier has been a powerful asset for candidates seeking election to the U.S. Senate and House of Representatives.

Germany and Great Britain can be considered as the limiting and alternative examples of the impact of mass military participation on citizenship. Germany's parliamentary institutions until after World War II were weak in comparison to those in France, Great Britain, and the United States. Nevertheless, the linkage between military service and the extension of the franchise was explicit in "nation building" in Germany. For example, in 1871 Bismarck institutionalized male suffrage immediately after the unification of Germany in response to the political realities created by new forms of military service. In contrast, throughout most of the nineteenth century, British military institutions were an admixture of feudal forms intertwined with slowly emerging professional officers. The extension of the franchise was likewise very gradual—indeed, limited. World War I transformed the structure of the British military and witnessed the dramatic extension of the franchise. It is striking that conscription was not instituted in Great Britain until after World War I had caused enormous manpower losses. The political consequences of extensive military mobilization produced legislation in 1918 which extended the franchise and was explicitly linked to the necessity of giving political rights to those who had been conscripted.

Moreover, it is obviously necessary to distinguish between the process of "modernization" in the West—Westernization, if you will—and the equivalent processes of socio-political change leading to the emergence of the nation-state in other regions and cultural areas that occurred later. For our purpose, it is well to recall that the traditional Ottoman Empire before the nineteenth century had large-scale military formations which rivaled those of the West. But the "modernization" of the Ottoman military depended on importing Western science and technology. The associated industrial development did not produce its own internal momentum until well into the middle of the twentieth century. Alternatively, Japan in the second half of the nineteenth century introduced both Western technology and military forms and experienced a simultaneous and continuous development of its industrial and military institutions. But it must be pointed out that during this period neither Japan nor the Ottomans

developed or assimilated the notion of citizenship—as a political definition
or as an aspect of military service.

Intellectual Traditions

Besides the classical writings, the comparative analysis of armed forces
and society draws its vigor and associated variables as well as its limitations
from three theoretical-empirical intellectual traditions. These focus on (a)
the technological and organizational dimensions; (b) the social stratification and professionalization of the armed forces; and (c) the normative
aspect of social and political movements, in particular of political
nationalism. The transformation of each of these variables is related
historically to the rise of the mass military and then to its contemporary
decline. While the variables illuminate the emergence of the mass armed
force in the Western nation-states and, to varying degrees, the incorporation of the notion of citizenship, they also are sources of the
contemporary dissolution of the mass army and the attenuation and, in
fact, separation of the notion of citizenship from military service.

a. *Technology and Organizational Format:* Technological explanations,
if one must select a single or unidimensional explanation, appear to have
great expository power but at the same time often seem to have
tautological elements. The bulk of historical writing on the emergence of
the mass armed force emphasizes the technological dimension. The
sociological approach, of course, is to regard technology as a set of factors
impinging on organizational format. The technological base of the mass
armed force has rested on two elements. One is the increase in firepower
effected by the introduction of the rifle and modern artillery. The other is
the development of transportation and communication systems, permitting the concentration of large numbers of men and machines.
Obviously, these technological innovations could utilize the manpower
generated by conscription and thereby contribute to the development of
large-scale bureaucratic military organization and the elimination of feudal
conceptions of military life. In short, a citizen's army is compatible with
such a military format.

However, citizen participation in the military antedated the full impact
of the new technology. Modern technology was only at the incipient stage
during the French and American revolutions. Likewise, modern technology has been incorporated into military systems where the notion of
citizenship and the attendant political implications have been completely
absent. At best, technology can be considered a facilitating variable in
determining the military's role in the emergence of the modern state.

Modern technology contributed to the development of the strategic conception of total war.[25] Progressively larger and larger proportions of the civilian population have been mobilized into the military or into war-related production. The slaughter of human beings has increased, especially with the introduction of airpower, with less and less regard to the distinction between the military and the civilian. The deployment of nuclear weapons represents the "perfection" of the modern military by vastly increasing its destructiveness. At the same time, the advanced technology carries the "seeds of its own destruction," since the outbreak of total nuclear war can no longer be perceived as in the national interest. After 1946, the military function shifted from making war to deterrence, to the extent that rational considerations could be applied.[26] Peripheral wars prolonged conscription in the United States, but the trend toward eliminating or reducing conscription has been a general development in Western industrialized nations, with a stronger emphasis on all-volunteer professional forces augmented by various types of part-time soldiers, or short-term militias. It is difficult, under these circumstances, to define military service as an integral aspect of citizenship or vice versa.

b. *Social Stratification and Professionalization:* The second continuing research tradition focuses on the changing social stratification of the military and the military's development into a bureaucratic institution with its particular format of professionalism. Despite important structural differences from nation-state to nation-state, a generalized pattern of stratification of the military in Western nations—including the United States—has been identified. It stands in marked contrast to the institutional history of other regions of the world. The officer corps of Western Europe before the French Revolution was an elite group whose social recruitment was rooted in the feudal-based landed aristocracy, especially the minor gentry. Its social recruitment not only gave it its conservative political outlook but was also an integral aspect of its code of honor, as the armed forces became more and more technical. The system of land tenure enabled a social enclave to persist in which these traditional values could be maintained and from which "reliable" officers were recruited.

A body of careful scholarship traces the broadening of the social origins of members of the military profession as new technology and mass armies developed. In all the militaries of Western Europe for which studies of historical trends are available, the professionalization of the military in the nineteenth century meant the introduction of middle-class elements into a structure dominated by the upper class with its close connections to the landed elements. Karl Demeter in his study on *The German Officer Corps* presents the prototype of this. Comparable trends have been documented in Great Britain, France, Italy, the Netherlands, Belgium, Sweden, and Norway.[27]

Even before the French Revolution, technological necessity and the growth in size of the military establishments in Western Europe required that middle-class officers be introduced to fill the cadres of artillery, engineering, and logistical specialists. The French Revolution, of course, speeded up the social transformation of the French military establishment (the absence of a comparative process in England permitted the feudal type of domination to persist through much of the nineteenth century).[28] In France, the transformation represents a balance between the infusion of new non-noble elements and the persistence of important elements of noble personnel. S. F. Scott, in "The French Revolution and the Professionalization of the French Officer Corps, 1789-1793," has traced the extent to which traditional elements persisted in the "revolutionary" armies.[29] At the lower ranks of the officer corps the influx of new personnel was most extensive, including men promoted from noncommissioned status; at the higher ranks, a carry-over in personnel predominated. As of 1793, nobles still constituted 70 percent of the generals.

By the end of the nineteenth century, throughout Western Europe, middle-class social elements were extensive in the military and frequently dominated it in number—except in selected elite infantry and cavalry units with high personal attachments to surviving monarchies. But the concentration of numbers was less important than the fact that political conservative traditions and the heroic model persisted until the outbreak of World War II. In the United States, although there was no feudal tradition, a comparable social selectivity in recruitment served to develop a similar set of values. Recruitment was concentrated among native-born white Protestant families from rural and hinterland backgrounds, especially in the South.

Social recruitment does not determine political behavior. In particular, with the growth of professionalization, there are more and more links between political behavior and professional socialization. Jacques van Doorn has traced the historical development of professionalism in the Western military and has focused on the type of professionalism, with its heroic element, which developed within a bureaucratic structure.[30] In the nineteenth century, the social role and professional format of the officer corps of Western industrialized nations were compatible with the variety of political forms, but such compatibility included acceptance and alliance with struggling democratic institutions. In England, France, and the

United States, revolutionary movements left their impact on the officer corps, although there were strong continuity and only gradual transformation from feudal types of forms. The heroic model inhibited the officers' direct intervention in politics.

Thus, the residues of the heroic model, with its emphasis on traditional values plus personal allegiance to the ruler, permitted acceptance of emerging parliamentary forms. This is not to assert that, in the nineteenth century, the military profession was without political influence, or that its political power was only the result of struggles between competing civilian elite groups. Rather, social origins, and the social mold of the military with its upper-class sense of guardianship of the state, worked in the United States and Great Britain, on balance, to serve the processes of internal parliamentary government. In France, the balance was more unstable and disruptive, but the military did not fundamentally undermine the parliamentary system—although they challenged its existence. One outcome of the Napoleonic period was a constitutional monarchy and a legislative arena. On the other hand, the officer corps that emerged in Germany was compatible with and served to support the monarchial-civil service regime.

In sharp contrast, for example, the Ottoman military did not rest on a feudal social structure as the term had meaning in Western Europe. The system of land tenure and the sultan's position ruled out an independent nobility either as a source of officer recruitment or as a political base for a check on the sultan's power. Instead, for centuries, the armed forces were recruited by the Ottoman Empire on a broad and diverse base, including a slave type of component, in order to strengthen the sultan's power. The military was a form of government service under the authority of the sultan.[31] It had no specific conservative orientation reflecting attachment to a landed upper class.

The significance of the Western military officer corps as a social type during the nineteenth century is highlighted in comparison with the posture of the Ottoman military—and the military of many new nations. In the absence of a feudal and heroic tradition, the new nations' military leaders, as they have developed modern armed forces, have been more committed to their own notions of revolutionary political change and more accessible to and involved in direct domestic political action.

During the first half of the twentieth century in Western industrialized nations, the growth of the military establishment, more than the social origins or professionalization of its officers, contributed to its markedly increased political weight. With the decline of the mass armed force and the movement to an all-volunteer system, social recruitment reemerges as a more relevant variable, since recruitment becomes less representative. In the post-World War II period, the trend in many Western industrialized nations has been toward a heavier concentration in the officer corps of self-recruitment, especially among sons of noncommissioned officers. There is evidence of disproportionate reliance on particularistic sources, such as special preparatory schools catering to old established families with regional affiliations. The existence of highly unrepresentative officer corps during the emergence of the all-volunteer force does not necessarily present a "putschist" threat to parliamentary institutions, but it does weaken the legitimacy of military institutions. Moreover, selective factors in recruitment are already tending to increase the conservative political bias of the officer corps and to produce more rigid attitudes toward international affairs.

c. *Natural History of Revolutionary Nationalism:* The third set of variables focuses on the normative and symbolic content of the social and political movements which have supplied the ideology of the nation-state. A wide range of economic and social structural variables have been offered to explain the transformation of European feudalism. Each of these theories must also be judged in terms of its ability to account for the variation in degree of political democracy that emerged in a particular nation-state. The tradition of such intellectual endeavors is rich and unending: for example, de Tocqueville's *The French Revolution and the Ancient Regime,* Thorstein Veblen's *Imperial Germany* and Barrington Moore, Jr.'s *Social Origins of Dictatorship and Democracy.*[32] However, the common concern of these analyses is with underlying economic and social structures. The explanations or at least prerequisites for the process of "modernization" and the emergence of political democracy versus totalitarianism are recognizably incomplete or partial.

The alternative or supplementary perspective in comparative macro-sociology seeks to conceptualize the process in terms of social and political movements—purposive and collective agitation, if you will. Such theorizing is hardly so systematic and comprehensive, but it does highlight the voluntaristic elements in historical processes. Of course, the writers who use social and economic structural explanations are fully aware of the limitations of their perspectives and the need to assign a degree of "independence" or causality of organized collective political agitations and institution building. One has only to examine the prerequisites for the development and growth of political democracy offered by Barrington Moore, Jr. In effect, they reduce to two elements: (a) an elaboration of de

Tocqueville's stress on an effective balance between central monarchial authority and local centers of power and initiative; and (b) Moore's social anthropology of peasant life and the importance of the commercialization of agriculture. He then adds a third: (c) the necessity of a "revolutionary break with the past"—which, in effect, is an undifferentiated awareness of the social and political movement perspective.

In short, it is necessary to join to the social structural analysis of nation building a systematic concern with "nation building" as a social and political movement, that is with the organizational and leadership aspects of mass agitation as elements of socio-political change.

One can point to the origins of contemporary theoretical-empirical research in this vein in the seminal and incisive monograph, *The Natural History of Revolution,* by Lyford P. Edwards, published in 1927. It served as the prototype for the much more widely recognized but derivative volume by Crane Brinton, *The Anatomy of Revolution.*[33] Edwards was strongly influenced by Robert E. Park of the University of Chicago, whose doctoral thesis on "Massen und Publikum" was an early effort to study, systematically, social and political movements in their own right.[34] Edwards's analysis included the sociology of the intellectual, and mass agitation as a central element in fashioning nationalistic movements. It anticipated contemporary studies of liberation movements in developing nations.

The American and French revolutions were social and political movements whose ideological and normative content and leadership styles had independent effects on the sequence of "nation" building. These were revolutionary movements whose ideological content fashioned the social cohesion of the central leadership and contributed to the mobilization of activist cadres, both military and civilian. These movements led to extensive armed conflict against existing standing armies, in which the revolutionary forces were victorious because they could mobilize new rank-and-file cadres and could use professional officer elements. Moreover, the effective consequences of these revolutionary movements were not military dictatorships or oligarchies, but parliamentary institutions with varying degrees of stability and effectiveness. The Cromwellian Revolution, which contributed to making England the first modern nation-state, had these elements as well. In England and in the United States, and to a lesser extent in France, military leaders did not succeed in establishing their legitimacy for political leadership.

For the purposes at hand, three elements in the ideological content of the American and French revolutions (and again, on an equivalent basis, of the Cromwellian Revolution) were significant in influencing their character and consequences. First, their ideology and political propaganda were explicitly nationalist. That is, they created a nationalist symbolism of identification within which to press for socio-political change and demand social and political justice. National symbols were offered in contrast to existing localistic and traditional boundaries of the polity. The idea and appeal of nationalism, as a basis for collective action, were extremely powerful and enduring. Nationalist symbolism supplied a basis for the political legitimacy of revolutionary leadership and a particularly effective basis for organizing the armed forces. The interpenetration of ideological nationalism and military organization persisted until the middle of the twentieth century. Nationalist ideology operated as a convenient vehicle by which feudal elements could find their social, professional, and political positions in the emerging polity and in the postrevolutionary mass armed forces.

Second, the ideological and normative definition of citizenship and the notion of civic participation in the revolutionary armed forces were equally pervasive and powerful. The legitimacy of these armed forces was based on an appeal to defend individual freedom and achieve social and political justice. To arm the ordinary person and to declare his right to bear arms constituted a revolutionary appeal, serving the immediate requirements of raising military cadres and drawing elements from a wide variety of social strata. But this ideological and propaganda call was not only a military formula. It was a political definition which served to enlarge the concept of those who were effective members of the polity. Like nationalism, it supplied a key ingredient in the expansion of the electorate. The duties and obligations of the armed citizen set the framework for the concept of the electorate in civil society, although actual enfranchisement came in subsequent steps.

From the Cromwellian Revolution onward, the actual competence of military leaders to rule as a leadership group in Western nation-states has, indeed, been limited. Philip Abrams's study of the Cromwell military government by generals and colonels has shown it had dilemmas and fatal shortcomings comparable to the difficulties of the contemporary military oligarchies of new nations.[35] The generals and colonels could not convert their ability to seize power into a legitimate base for a stable government. In the case of the United States, historians emphasize George Washington's political commitment to civilian rule, but this in turn represented the pervasive ideological and normative definitions of the American Revolution.

The intertwined notions of nationalism and citizenship participation had continuing impact until World War I, when the immense slaughter of alliance warfare weakened their viability. World War II only undermined their organizing effectiveness further. Nevertheless, for 150 years, they supplied a basis for transforming the military from a distinct status group into more and more of a civil service organ of the state. In Germany, where the concept of citizenship was indeed weak, the military continued to operate as a detached status group, as a state within a state, even after World War I. It remained for the National Socialist regime, with its ruthless and distorted forms of "democratization," to end the Prussian military assumptions. But the reconstructed armed forces, after the Allied victory, have assumed a conventional modern Western format. In most Western European nations where modern industrial systems have emerged, the standing armies could exist alongside parliamentary systems—a special historical development of limited frequency. This has been so, not only because of the patterns of civilian social structure, but because of the basis of legitimacy which the military has come to accept.

The weakening of the power and attraction of nationalism and the contraction of mass armed forces do not automatically strengthen parliamentary institutions. The attenuation of nationalist sentiments and ideology is not caused only by the increased destructiveness—actual and potential—of war. It is also a popular expression of an advanced industrial society with a high level of income and education that produces strong and powerful hedonistic concerns. Resistance to military service becomes widespread as the logic of nationalism is questioned and the rationale for the military is obscured by the reality of nuclear weapons. Social and political movements become intensified. A tiny minority of college-educated youth are prepared to engage in confrontation politics designed to "undermine" contemporary military institutions. However, their conspicuousness should not obscure the fact that there is a broader suspicion of existing authority, which has especially strong anti-military overtones.

There is a convergence of consequences which derives from the new dimensions of technology, social stratification, and the normative content of social and political movements in Western advanced industrial nations. All these dimensions threaten to separate the military from the larger society and render it an internal but more isolated body with selective linkages to that society. The consequence is a greater ideological differentiation between those who offer themselves for a military career and the wide segments of the population who accept the necessity of a military but accord it little moral legitimacy. S. M. Lipset and others have asserted that an advanced industrial society would not be racked by social and occupational cleavages.[36] This assertion has come to be rejected. Age, sex, ethnic-religious, and racial differences and new forms of occupational stratification do not supply the basis for "revolutionary" social conflict but do create social divisions which are persistent and deeply disruptive.[37] Issues of civil-military relations, such as the internal position of the military and the military's role in foreign affairs, also become another basis for profound cleavage which burdens the parliamentary system of an advanced industrial society.

Notes

1. Morris Janowitz, *The Military in the Political Development of New Nations* (Chicago, 1964).

2. Ernest Gellner, *Thought and Change* (London, 1964). See Chapter 7 for an analysis of the transformation of nationalism.

3. T. H. Marshall, *Citizenship and Social Class* (Cambridge, 1950).

4. Edward A. Shils, "The Theory of the Mass Society," *Diogenes*, No. 39 (1962).

5. Morris Janowitz, "The Decline of the Mass Army," *Military Review* (February 1972), pp. 10-17.

6. Harold Dwight Lasswell, *Politics: Who Gets What, When, How* (New York, 1936).

7. Morris Janowitz and Jacques van Doorn, eds., *On Military Intervention*, Vol. 2 (Rotterdam, 1971).

8. Herbert Spencer in "Heritage of Sociology" Series, *Herbert Spencer on Social Evolution,* selected writings edited by J.D.Y. Peel (Chicago, 1972).

9. Max Weber, *Economy and Society,* "The Discipline of Large-Scale Economic Organizations," edited by Gunther Roth and Claus Wittich (New York, 1968),Vol. 3, p. 1155.

10. Weber's essay entitled "The Origins of Discipline in War," constituted one of the most profound and penetrating portions of his writings. He probes the emergence of modern forms of military discipline, and is concerned with the impact of technology on modern military organization. His analysis rejects a technological determinism. Modern technology is an essential prerequisite for bureaucratic military discipline which was absent in the feudal armies. However, it was charismatic leadership and ideological content which established the basis of effective organized military discipline associated with the professional armies of the Western nation-state. See Max Weber "The Origins of Discipline in War," op. cit., pp. 1150-1155.

11. It is striking, by contrast, that Emile Durkheim revealed a complete absence of interest in the analysis of armed forces as part of the "social division of labor" and the processes of societal change.

12. Karl Marx, *The 18th Brumaire of Louis Bonaparte* (New York, 1969); Friedrich Engels, *Anti-Duhring: Herr Eugen Duhring's Revolution in Science* (Moscow, 1954), pp. 219-256.

13. Gaetano Mosca, *The Ruling Class* (New York, 1939).

14. Seymour M. Lipset and Reinhard Bendix, *Social Mobility in Industrial Society* (Berkeley, 1960).

15. Peter Blau, "Sociology," in *A Reader's Guide to the Social Sciences,* edited by Bert F. Hoselitz (Glencoe, 1959), p. 164.

16. Ralf Dahrendorf, *Class and Class Conflict in Industrial Society* (Stanford, 1959).

17. Raymond Aron, *The Century of Total War* (Boston, 1955).

18. Stanislav Andreski, *Military Organization and Society* (London, 1968).

19. Marion Levy, *Modernization and the Structure of Societies: A Setting for International Affairs* (Princeton, 1966), see Chapter 4, "Armed Force Organization."

20. Alfred Vagts, *A History of Militarism: Civilian and Military* (New York, 1937).

21. Reinhard Bendix, *Nation-Building and Citizenship: Studies of Our Changing Social Order* (New York, 1964). Bendix has a single sentence in this study on military institutions as part of his analysis of opposition to elementary education and the franchise. "Similar questions were raised with regard to universal conscription, since arms in the hands of the common people were considered a revolutionary threat."

22. Stein Rokkan, "Mass Suffrage, Secret Voting and Political Participation," *European Journal of Sociology,* II (1961), pp. 132-152. See also, "The Comparative Study of Political Participation" in A. Ranney, editor, *Recent Developments in the Behavioral Study of Politics* (Urbana).

23. T. Ropp, *War in the Modern World* (New York, 1962).

24. It is interesting to note that social anthropologists concerned with political institutions have turned their attention to the analogies of the presence or absence of the idea of "citizenship" as a central approach to the politico-jural structure of tribal and peasant societies. See for example, Meyer Fortes, *Kinship and the Social Order: The Legacy of Lewis Henry Morgan* (Chicago, 1969).

25. Hans Speier, *Social Order and the Risks of War* (New York, 1952).

26. Morris Janowitz, "Toward a Redefinition of Military Strategy in International Relations," *World Politics* (Summer 1974).

27. Karl Demeter, *The German Officer-Corps in Society and State 1650-1945* (New York, 1965); Morris Janowitz, *The Professional Soldier: A Social and Political Portrait* (Glencoe, Ill., 1960, 1971), pp. 79-103; Bengt Abrahamsson, *Military Professionalization and Political Power* (Beverly Hills, 1972), pp. 20-58.

28. Katharine Chorley has sought to investigate the conditions under which "armed forces" either support or do not oppose revolutionary movements, using the historical materials of Western Europe, Russia, and the United States. Katharine Chorley, *Armies and the Art of Revolution* (London, 1943).

29. S. F. Scott, "The French Revolution and the Professionalization of the French Officer Corps, 1789-1793," in Morris Janowitz and Jacques van Doorn, editors, *On Military Ideology* (Rotterdam, 1971), pp. 5-56.

30. Jacques van Doorn, "Political Change and the Control of the Military: Some General Remarks," in Jacques van Doorn, editor, *Military Profession and Military Regimes: Commitments and Conflicts* (The Hague, 1969), pp. 11-35.

31. Morris Janowitz, "The Comparative Analysis of Middle Eastern Military Institutions," in Morris Janowitz and Jacques van Doorn, eds., *On Military Intervention,* op. cit.

32. Alexis de Tocqueville, *The Ancient Regime and the French Revolution* (Paris, 1856); T. B. Veblen, *Imperial Germany and the Industrial Revolution* (New York, 1939); Barrington Moore, Jr., *Social Origins of Dictatorship and Democracy: Lord and Peasant in the Making of the Modern World* (Boston, 1966).

33. Lyford P. Edwards, *The Natural History of Revolution* (Chicago, 1970); Crane Brinton, *The Anatomy of Revolution.*

34. Robert E. Park, *Massen und Publikum (The Crowd and the Public and Other Essays)*, Henry Elsner, ed., Charlotte Elsner, trans. (Chicago, 1972) in "Heritage of Sociology" Series. Park was strongly influenced by W. I. Thomas, who presented a penetrating sociological analysis of the nationalist movements in subjugated Poland at the end of the nineteenth century. William I. Thomas and Florian Znaniecki, *The Polish Peasant in Europe and America*, 5 vols. (Boston, 1918-1920; Vols. I and II originally published by the University of Chicago Press, 1918).

35. Philip Abrams, "Resotring Order: Some Early European Cases," in Morris Janowitz and Jacques van Doorn, eds., *On Military Intervention*, Vol. 2, op. cit., pp. 37-61.

36. S. M. Lipset, "The Changing Class Structure and Contemporary European Politics," *Daedalus*, XCIII (Winter 1964), pp. 271-303; Robert E. Lane, "The Politics of Consensus in an Age of Affluence," *American Political Science Review*, LIX (December 1965), pp. 874-895.

37. Morris Janowitz, *Political Conflict* (Chicago, 1970), pp. 5-35.

ARMED FORCES AND SOCIETY:
A WORLD PERSPECTIVE

The Professional Military as an
Object of Sociological Investigation

In the last decade, there has been an increase in scholarly work on the sociology of military institutions and militarism. Despite the intrinsic intellectual interest of the field and its overriding substantive and policy importance, this aspect of sociology has lagged far behind other subjects in the discipline. However, one of the interesting intellectual trends in the emergence of research on these topics has been the conscious efforts at comparative analysis and the search for a world perspective. Comparative scholarship has developed not only as the work of single scholars using their own frames of reference but as the result of the interaction of numerous social scientists with different theoretical and national backgrounds.

The International Sociological Association, its various World Congresses, and in particular its Research Committee on Armed Forces and Society, have supplied a relevant focal point.[1] During the first four World Congresses of Sociology, in 1950, 1953, 1956, and 1959, the topic of military institutions was not directly discussed.[2] At the Fifth World Congress of Sociology, held in Washington, D.C., in 1962, a single paper was presented, in the session on political sociology, on "The Role of the Military in the Political Development of New Nations."

A preliminary effort at international exploration of the comparative sociology of military institutions was made at a Conference on Armed Forces and Society in London, July 1964, sponsored by the Committee on

This chapter is a revised version of a paper presented to the Working Group on Armed Forces and Society, Sixth World Congress, Evian, September 1966.

Political Sociology of the International Sociological Association. It brought together, for the first time, scholars from the United States and Western Europe and resulted in the publication of a special issue on the subject by *The European Journal of Sociology* (Archives Europénnes de Sociologie 6, no. 2, 1965). However, the Sixth World Congress of Sociology in Evian in 1966 marked an important departure, in that a series of sessions was devoted to the topic, "The Professional Military and Militarism." At these meetings, some seventy scholars from Western Europe, Eastern Europe (including the USSR), the Middle East, the Far East, and South America convened to evaluate the current state of sociology of military institutions, war, revolution, and international peace-keeping and arms control. One result of this conference was the publication of a volume edited by Jacques van Doorn, *Armed Forces and Society: Sociological Essays* (The Hague: Mouton, 1968). At Evian, a separate working group on Armed Forces and Society of the International Sociological Association was organized. It has continued to sponsor international sessions at the regular World Congresses of Sociology and at special interim meetings. The proceedings of these sessions have emerged as sources of documentation, research, and analysis on the comparative analysis of military institutions, war, and peace-keeping.

In September 1967, a special meeting was held in London. Although the actual number of participants was smaller than in Evian, the world coverage by twenty-four papers was much broader. The resulting volume, edited by Jacques van Doorn, was entitled, *Military Profession and Military Regimes* (The Hague: Mouton, 1969). Subsequently, very broad-scale sessions were held at the Seventh World Congress of Sociology in Varna in 1970. Two volumes of proceedings encompassed its work: Morris Janowitz and Jacques van Doorn, editors, *On Military Intervention* (vol. 1); and *On Military Ideology* (vol. 2) (Rotterdam: University of Rotterdam Press, 1971).

A special regional conference held in 1972 in Amsterdam was devoted to the topic of "The Decline of the Mass Army." Selected papers from this conference have appeared in *Armed Forces and Society: An Interdisciplinary Journal* (Winter 1975) and elsewhere. The theme of "The Crisis in Legitimacy" was considered at the Eighth World Congress in Toronto, August 1974, and the deliberation led to the publication of *The Military and the Problem of Legitimacy,* edited by Gwyn Harries-Jenkins and Jacques van Doorn (London: Sage Publications, 1975).

Barriers to Social Research on the Military

Despite the gradual development of international sociological interest in the changing nature of military institutions, we must note the resistances to such research so that these topics may be approached with the greatest amount of objectivity and thereby transcend national and personal prejudices. It would be a mistake to assume that the current literature has achieved the necessary levels of objectivity. However, there is a growing body of literature which, although based on existing national systems of sociological inquiry, seeks to apply the canons of sociological scholarship.

First, sociologists have avoided the study of war—internal and external—because of political pressures and personal values. The management of violence involves the most fundamental values and most significant considerations in a society. Only under the conditions of the widest intellectual freedom is it possible to pursue sociological research on such topics. The field is still not investigated in a great many countries. Even where adequate political conditions exist, personal and academic considerations continue to define the study of the military as outside the central core of sociological endeavor.

Second, the secrecy of military institutions, both official and professional, has been offered as a barrier to sociological analysis. There can be no doubt that this is important, with significant implications for the research sociologist. But it can hardly be offered as a fundamental explanation, if only because of the sheer amount of available material which is yet to be analyzed. This is particularly the case for historical materials and for the use of ex- and retired military professionals as sources of more contemporary materials. It has also been the experience of numerous research workers that direct contact with military professionals has produced more favorable conditions for research than they had anticipated. However, the central issue is that the recent growth, interest, and fruitful work have not been the result of a fundamental change in military practices concerning secrecy but, rather, of the orientation, diligence, and persistence of sociological investigators.

Third, and more important as a barrier than the practices resulting in secrecy, has been the intellectual posture of sociology. The discipline has failed to develop a realistic understanding of social structure that would include the military establishment and the role of force. Classical writers of sociology—Herbert Spencer, for example—could not be accused of such a failing. The growth of sociology as a specialized and technical discipline and as a diffuse form of social criticism seems to have been connected with this decline in realism.

ı, resistance to the growth of a sociology of the military can be
ı ideological terms. While there are many ideological sources at
ʋ.　　　　　ı sociological thought, it appears that sociology has flourished in
societies where there is a strong liberal tradition. But the liberal tradition
has served as a barrier to a sociology of the military, for those following
the liberal tradition have in general sought to handle the problem of
military institutions by denial. In fact, in the liberal tradition, some
sociologists have even believed that to study and analyze military
institutions would have the consequences of strengthening the role of
military leaders and militaristic forces.

Ideological opposition to the sociological study of military institutions
has receded, but the field is still confronted by complex questions of
"values"—in particular, the values of the sociologist. To the extent that
progress has been made, it is because the study of military institutions has
become a legitimate object of scientific analysis. The scholar worthy of
any contribution must be judged by the same standards of intellectual
progress as any other sociologist. This assertion does not imply that
sociologists in this field are not concerned with the responsible application
of knowledge to social problems. The very importance of the issues of war
and peace guarantees that the findings of sociologists will be subject to the
closest scrutiny by political leaders, policy makers, and the mass media.

As the barriers to research into the sociology of the military profession
and militarism are yielding, pressures on scholarship have changed and the
problems of maintaining objectivity have altered. During the period of
intellectual indifference to the study of military institutions, a strong bias
was operative. When social scientists approached the study of armed
forces, they did so with a civilian ideology which tended to overlook what
is common to large-scale organizations; in short they tended to over-
emphasize the differences between military and civilian organizations. In
the more recent period, the reverse has become the case; the social
scientist runs the risk of underemphasizing the special characteristics of
the military establishment.

The field of the sociology of war and peace has been, and is likely to
remain, strikingly different from other areas in sociology. First, in spite of
the increase in interest and work, only a handful of specialists are involved.
Even if the number were to double or triple, we would still be dealing with
a very small group. Second, it is a field in which there are more theoretical
ideal type analyses and suggestive propositions than empirical substance.
Nevertheless, even the limited available results have transformed the study
of comparative sociology and societal change. It is no longer possible to

deal with these problems—in either industrialized societies or developing nations—without due emphasis on the sociology of military institutions from a world perspective.

Military Establishments: A World Profile

The study of military institutions from a world perspective requires more adequate data and statistics on the forms, sizes, and structures of military establishments. International perspectives on armed forces and society that have been rooted in analytic and ideal-type models have been augmented by a continuing increase in the body of fundamental data organized on a world basis. These include comprehensive trend data and indicators of costs and manpower allocations.

The reliability of the available data requires careful assessment. Nevertheless, it is possible to point to increasingly relevant statistics. Three research groups, in Western political democracies, concentrate on collecting and assessing such information. The United States Arms Control and Disarmament Agency publishes *World Military Expenditures;* the International Institute of Strategic Studies, *The Military Balance;* and the Stockholm International Peace Research Institute, *World Armaments and Disarmament: SIPRI Yearbook.* Pertinent data are also presented in *The Statesman's Year-Book.* With these and other sources, we can organize a combined and assessed array of basic statistics.

Two different sets of indicators are of central importance, and each warrants different presentation and analysis. One set of data focus on budgetary expenditures and long-term trends therein. These data are best presented in terms of political power blocs (see Table 1). The other set focus on the number of personnel in various types of military units and the trends in manpower allocations. These data are presented by regional distributions, according to the system of classification of the United Nations statistical reports (see Table 2).[3]

Worldwide, expenditures on military budget grew in the 1960s: from $119 billion in 1961 to $216 billion in 1971.[4] More than half of the $97 billion increase could be accounted for by inflation. Thus, there was a real increase, of one-third over the 1961 level, in military expenditures. It has been estimated that one-third of the increase was for manpower and personnel, and the remaining two-thirds, research and development, equipment, and general support.

There has been a marked difference in the increased expenditures between the developed and the developing countries. While the bulk of the expenditures are concentrated in the developed nations, the rate of increase in the developing nations has been greater than in the developed nations. In 1971, military expenditures in constant prices exceeded 1961 expenditures by 24 percent on average in developed countries, by 114 percent in the developing countries. During the first years of the 1970s, the expansion of arms expenditures slowed to some degree in the developed nations; this can hardly be reported of the developing nations.

However, in order to examine in depth the world profile of military expenditures, we must consider the budgetary pattern in terms of political groupings, since there is a distinct difference between the developed and

TABLE 1
Long- and Short-Term Trends in the Volume of World Military Expenditure
1951-1971 (based on constant price figures)

| | Average per cent change per year | | | | | *Size of military expenditure in 1971, US $ bn, current prices and exchange rates* |
| | Long-term trend 1951-71 | Year-to-year changes | | | | |
		1967-68	1968-69	1969-70	1970-71	Budgeted change in 1972	
USA	+ 1.9	+ 2.7	− 4.2	− 9.8	− 7.8	+ 3.0	*74.9*
Other NATO	+ 2.6	− 2.9	− 0.2	+ 1.3	+ 4.9	+ 3.0	*31.7*
Total NATO	**+ 2.1**	**+ 1.4**	**− 3.3**	**− 7.1**	**− 4.5**	**+ 3.0**	*106.6*
USSR[a]	+ 3.1	+15.5	+ 5.9	+ 1.1	± 0	± 0	*42.6*
Other Warsaw Pact[a]	+ 5.9	+18.4	+12.3	+ 7.4	+ 5.6	(+ 5.4)	*7.9*
Total Warsaw Pact[a]	**+ 3.5**	**+15.9**	**+ 6.8**	**+ 2.0**	**+ 0.8**	**(+ 0.8)**	*50.5*
Other Europe	+ 4.7	+ 3.1	+ 3.6	+ 3.0	− 1.1	+ 6.6	*3.6*
Middle East	+13.2	+24.2	+18.5	+15.5	+11.3	···	*4.7*
South Asia	+ 5.5	+ 3.8	+ 6.7	+ 4.1	+11.1	···	*2.6*
Far East (excl. China)	+ 6.2	+12.4	+12.4	+11.0	+ 7.2	···	*6.3*
Oceania	+ 3.6	+ 6.1	+ 0.5	+ 0.8	− 3.0	+ 5.3	*1.5*
Africa[b]	+14.2	+ 7.4	+22.3	− 2.5	− 5.2	···	*1.6*
Central America	+ 3.9	+10.7	− 5.4	+10.2	+ 1.8	···	*0.6*
South America	+ 3.6	− 4.7	+ 7.2	+ 3.5	+10.0	···	*2.4*
World[c]	**+ 2.9**	**+ 5.5**	**+ 1.1**	**− 2.7**	**− 1.4**	···	*189.3*

a At current prices and Benoit-Lubell exchange rates.
b 1960-1971.
c Including an estimate for China of US $9.0 billion in 1971.

SOURCE: SIPRI Yearbook 1973, p. 207.

the developing nations. The data presented by the Stockholm Inter-national Peace Research Institute for long-term trends from 1951 to 1971 are appropriate in this regard (see Table 1). For the world as a whole, the average change per year was 2.9 percent. Among the developed nations, the NATO countries had an average increase of 2.1 percent, while the Warsaw Pact countries had an average annual increase of 3.5 percent. The rank order was: the United States, the lowest increase, 1.9 percent; other NATO nations, 2.6 percent; and the USSR, 3.1 percent; and other Warsaw Pact nations, 5.9 percent.

Among the developing nations, African countries showed the most rapid annual rate of increase. For 1960-1971, their average annual increase reached 14.2 percent. In part, this high rate was the result of the fact that, having achieved independence relatively late, some nations, particularly those in sub-Saharan Africa, sought to build up rapidly their military establishments which, at the time of independence, were relatively meager. But the rate of increase in the Middle East nations was not noticeably lower. In fact, in the Middle East (excluding those Arab nations which are classified as African and which also have high rates of expenditures), the average annual increase was 13.2 percent. In contrast, in South America the rate of annual increase was only 3.6 percent; and the rate of increase continues the traditionally low budgetary expenditures in that part of the world community.

For the comparative analysis of armed forces and society, the data on the size of the military forces and the pattern of increase in military manpower are essential. These data supply indicators of the changing structure and morphology of military establishments. They reveal not only the transformation of international relations under the impact of nuclear weapons but also the widened involvement of many military establish-ments in the internal policy-making processes of their own nations.

Table 2 presents, for the nations of the world with populations of over one million, the size of the armed forces for 1966, and, for 1973-1974, the size of the armed forces plus the regular reserves and the ratio of military manpower to the total population. Nations of fewer than one million were excluded, since they present special cases and are often so small as not to have articulated military institutions. (Nevertheless, even the 320-man army of Togo was capable of political intervention through the use of force.)

Aside from the basic question of the reliability of data, the definition of the term "armed forces" needs to be standardized. First, the available data on active duty military forces are defined as including the full-time

TABLE 2

World Profile of Armed Forces: 1966 to 1974

Country	Population 1973 est. (millions)	Active Duty Military Forces 1966	Active Duty Military Forces 1973-1974	Para-military 1973-1974	Reserves 1973-1974	Military Manpower Ratio* 1966	Military Manpower Ratio* 1973-1974
Africa							
1. Nigeria	59.4	8,000	157,000		102,000	.014	.264
2. Egypt	35.7	80,000-130,000	298,000	100,000	534,000	.464	.834
3. Ethiopia	26.5	30,000	44,500	20,400		.137	.168
4. Zaire	24.4		50,000	14,000			.205
5. South Africa	23.0	26,500	110,000	75,000	92,000	.155	.115
6. Sudan	17.0	12,000	38,600	5,000		.093	.270
7. Morocco	16.3	35,000	56,000	23,000		.270	.344
8. Algeria	15.7	65,000	63,000	10,000	12,000	.560	.401
9. Tanzania	14.4	1,500	11,600			.014	.081
10. Kenya	12.4	3,000	6,700	1,800		.033	.054
11. Uganda	10.8	2,000	12,600	15,000		.027	.117
12. Ghana	9.1	9,000	18,900	3,000		.122	.908
13. Malagasy	7.4	2,700-9,000	4,250	4,000		.151	.057
14. Cameroon	6.2	2,800	4,500	5,000		.055	.073
15. Upper Volta	5.6	1,000	2,000			.021	.036
16. Tunisia	5.5	20,000	24,000	15,000		.445	.436
17. Mali	5.4	3,000	3,650	1,500		.068	.068
18. Rhodesia	5.9	10,000	4,700	8,000	45,000	.249	.080
19. Malawi	5.2	1,500	1,000			.039	.019
20. Ivory Coast	4.6	1,500-4,000	3,500	3,000		.109	.076
21. Zambia	4.5	2,500	6,000	2,000		.071	.133

*Ratio of active duty military manpower to total population.

22. Guinea	4.2	2,500-5,000	6,000	7,700		.163	.143
23. Senegal	4.2	2,700-7,000	5,900			.210	.141
24. Niger	4.3	1,200-2,000	2,100	1,400		.064	.049
25. Rwanda	4.1	1,000	2,750	400		.035	.067
26. Chad	4.0	400	3,700	4,000		.014	.100
27. Burundi	3.5	1,000	2,000	900		.037	.057
28. Somalia	3.0	6,000	17,300	3,500		.260	.577
29. Dahomey	2.9	1,000	2,250	1,200		.044	.078
30. Sierra Leone	2.0	1,300	2,000			.059	.100
31. Togo	2.1	1,000	1,000			.063	.048
32. Libya	2.2	5,500	25,000			.365	1.114
33. Central African Republic	1.5	1,200	1,300			.092	.087
34. Liberia	1.7	3,800	5,150	1,300		.368	.303
35. Mauritania	1.3						
36. Congo (Brazeville)	1.0		2,300	4,800			.230
Subtotal		345,600-412,000	999,250	330,900	7,850,000		
Asia							
1. China	800.0	2,614,000	2,900,000	300,000	5,000,000	.348	.362
2. India	578.0	550,000	948,000	100,000	100,000	.119	.164
3. Indonesia	132.4	350,000	322,000	120,000		.349	.243
4. Bangladesh	76.0		17,900	13,000			.023
5. Pakistan	64.8	103,000-260,000	402,000		513,000	.263	.620
6. Japan	107.0	221,000	266,000		39,000	.230	.249
7. Turkey	37.9	428,000	455,000	75,000	800,000	1.414	1.200
8. Philippines	40.2	28,500	42,700	84,000	218,500	.094	.106
9. Thailand	36.7	81,000-134,000	180,000	18,000	300,000	.464	.490
10. South Korea	32.0	575,000	633,500	2,000,000	1,125,000	2.140	1.980

Country	Population 1973 est. (millions)	Active Duty Military Forces 1966	Active Duty Military Forces 1973-1974	Para-military 1973-1974	Reserves 1973-1974	Military Manpower Ratio 1966	Military Manpower Ratio 1973-1974
Asia (continued)							
11. Burma	29.1	149,000	149,000	25,000		.627	.512
12. Iran	30.8	150,000	211,500	70,000	315,000	.676	.686
13. North Vietnam	22.0	250,000	578,000	440,000		1.404	2.673
14. South Vietnam	20.0	225,000	572,000	570,000		1.468	2.910
15. Afghanistan	18.3	90,000	84,000	221,000	212,000	.604	.459
16. Taiwan	15.1	542,000	503,000	175,000	940,000	4.634	3.331
17. North Korea	15.0	309,000	470,000	1,500,000	765,000	.532	3.133
18. Ceylon	13.3	8,800	12,500	16,000	12,000	.082	.096
19. Nepal	11.5	20,800	20,000			.206	.174
20. Malaysia	11.5	7,600	56,000	54,000	50,600		.487
21. Iraq	10.1	60,000-70,000	101,800	18,800	260,000	.949	1.008
22. Saudi Arabia	8.4	30,000	42,500	11,000		.454	.506
23. Cambodia	7.5	32,000	187,200	150,000		.542	2.496
24. North Yemen	7.0		20,900				.299
South Yemen	1.6	Total: 10,000	9,500				.593
25. Syria	6.8	45,000	132,000	9,500	203,500	.856	1.941
26. Israel	3.2	75,000	115,000	9,000	185,000	3.156	3.594
27. Lebanon	3.0	10,800	15,250	5,000		.490	.508
28. Laos	3.1	94,000	74,200	40,000			2.314
29. Jordan	2.5	35,000	72,850	22,000	20,000	1.915	3.285
30. Singapore	2.2		20,600	9,000	30,000		.936
Subtotal		7,094,500	9,614,900	6,055,300	11,088,600		

Europe

1. West Germany	60.1	430,000	475,000	20,000	625,000	.775	.790
2. United Kingdom	56.3	435,000	361,500		435,000	.808	.642
3. Italy	54.4	390,000	427,500	80,700	545,000	.775	.786
4. France	52.0	880,400	503,600	85,000	540,000	1.839	.969
5. Spain	34.7	400,000	293,000	65,000		1.287	.844
6. Poland	33.7	285,000	280,000	73,000	600,000	.928	.831
7. Yugoslavia	21.0	347,000	240,000	1,019,000		1.820	1.142
8. Rumania	20.9	218,000	170,000	40,000, 500,000 militia	285,000	1.158	.813
9. East Germany	17.0	154,000	132,000	80,000, 400,000 armed workers' organization	250,000	.956	.777
10. Czechoslovakia	14.6	185,000	190,000	35,000, 250,000 people's militia	350,000	1.326	1.301
11. Netherlands	13.5	130,000	112,200	3,200	340,000	1.086	.831
12. Hungary	10.4	90,000	103,000	27,000, 250,000 workers' militia	163,000	.892	.990
13. Belgium	9.8	110,000	89,600	15,000	15,600	1.184	.914
14. Portugal	9.2	190,000	204,000	9,700	318,000	1.327	2.217
15. Greece	8.9	161,000	160,000	99,000	205,000	1.898	1.800

Country	Population 1973 est. (millions)	Active Duty Military Forces 1966	Active Duty Military Forces 1973-1974	Para-military 1973-1974	Reserves 1973-1974	Military Manpower Ratio 1966	Military Manpower Ratio 1973-1974
Europe (continued)							
16. Bulgaria	8.7	149,500	152,000	17,000, 150,000 people's militia	280,000	1.850	1.750
17. Sweden	8.2	23,000	74,800		675,000	.302	.912
18. Austria	7.5	14,000	52,000	11,250	100,000	.195	.693
19. Switzerland	6.5	12,000	33,500		567,000	.207	.515
20. Denmark	5.0	42,500	39,800		91,000	.907	.796
21. Finland	4.7	41,900	39,500	4,000	685,000	.922	.840
22. Norway	4.0	35,000	35,400		158,000	.954	.885
23. Ireland	3.0	13,000	10,570		20,000	.457	.352
24. Albania	2.4	28,000	38,000	15,000		1.589	1.500
Subtotal		4,764,300	4,216,970	3,248,850	7,247,600		
North and Central America							
1. U.S.A.	210.9	2,702,000	2,252,000		883,000	1.426	1.068
2. Mexico	53.4	62,200	71,000	250,000 part-time conscripts		.161	.133
3. Canada	22.3	119,700	83,000		23,000	.632	.372
4. Cuba	8.8	43,000	108,500	10,000 people's militia	200,000	.596	1.233
5. Haiti	5.2	5,000	6,500	14,900		.112	.125
6. Guatemala	5.7	8,000	11,200	13,000		.193	.197
7. Dominican Republic	4.4	19,000	15,800	10,000		.569	.359

North and Central America (continued)

8. El Salvador	3.9	4,000	5,600	3,000		.147	.144
9. Honduras	2.9	2,500	5,700	2,500		.123	.197
10. Nicaragua	2.2	5,000	7,100	4,000		.324	.323
11. Costa Rica	1.8			1,200			
12. Panama	1.5			6,000			
Subtotal		2,970,400	2,566,400	514,600	906,000		
Oceania							
1. Australia	13.0	52,000	73,300			.476	.481
2. New Zealand	3.0	12,500	12,800			.492	.427
Subtotal		64,500	86,100				
U.S.S.R.	205.5	3,850,000	3,425,000	125,000	3,000,000	1.713	1.667
South America							
1. Brazil	100.8	272,700	208,000	150,000		.356	.206
2. Argentina	24.3	116,000	135,000	19,000	250,000	.534	.556
3. Columbia	23.2	19,000-22,000	63,000	35,000	250,000	.145	.272
4. Peru	14.9	37,000	54,000	20,000		.334	.362
5. Chile	9.2	42,300	60,000	30,000	200,000	.514	.652
6. Venezuela	11.5	19,700	37,500	10,000		.241	.326
7. Ecuador	6.6	15,800	22,200	5,800		.334	.336
8. Bolivia	5.3	8,000-15,000	21,800	5,000		.417	.441
9. Uruguay	3.0	17,000	21,000	22,000	100,000	.618	.700
10. Paraguay	2.5	9,600	14,900	8,500		.504	.596
Subtotal		557,100-567,100	637,400	305,300	800,000		
Grand TOTAL		19,646,400-19,722,800	21,546,020	10,579,950	30,892,200		

101

military establishment and are limited to each nation's central government's army, navy, and air force. The forces can be volunteer or conscript or both; but they must be full-time, whatever the length of service required. This definition includes only those personnel who are designated as being on full-time active duty. Second, the data on the reserve forces are limited to those trained personnel designated to be called to duty to the central full-time active duty forces. Third, these data seek to present information about paramilitary forces of the nations of the world community. Paramilitary forces can be full-time or part-time and include a wide range of formations, such as frontier guards, national militarized police units, workers' militia, and village defense corps. The analysis of these data is designed, not to obscure these different types of formations, but to explore them.

The data about paramilitary forces are crucial for the analysis of the changes in the world profile of armed forces and society. During the last two decades, the armed forces everywhere appear to be differentiating themselves into three different patterns which highlight actual changes in their functions. In the developed and industrialized Western parliamentary nations, the personnel size of the military has been steadily declining, as their military forces rely more and more on capital, intensive arms, and advanced technology. In these states, there has been no marked increase in the size of the paramilitary forces. Second, in the developed nations of Eastern Europe and the Soviet Union with one-party mass regimes, a similar decline in the size of military manpower and increased reliance on advanced technology can be observed, but the rate of decline has been much less noticeable. Among these one-party nations, the growth in size of paramilitary units with a clear internal security function has been most pronounced.

In contrast, in the developing nations, there has been a significant increase in the manpower involved in the central active duty military forces. In addition, there has been pronounced growth in a variety of paramilitary formations. In fact, this growth in paramilitary units, in the one-party states and especially in developing nations, is one of the central and dramatic trends in the contemporary organization of armed forces.

On a worldwide basis, for those nations with populations of more than one million, the total active duty military forces in 1966 numbered 19.6 million persons. By 1973-1974, the number had risen to 21.6 million—a growth of 9.1 percent. The size of the regular reserve units of the world community in 1973-1974 reached 30.9 million persons, while 10.6 million were involved in various types of paramilitary forces. (This figure of 10.6

million does not include members of local police forces or political or secret police units.)

However, it must be stressed that the pattern of change from 1966 to 1973-1974 varied greatly, according to region and type of political regime. To make worldwide comparisons, we must compute a military manpower ratio—that is, the ratio of active duty military manpower to the total population. This supplies a crude standardized measure of changes in military manpower in terms of population growth. Of the 110 nations in this array of data on a worldwide basis, 57 experienced an increase in military manpower ratio from 1966 to 1974-1975, while 36 decreased, and 6 remained stable; for 11, there were no comparable data for this period. Thus, when nations did have military growth, it was often significant.

The difference in structure and morphology can be seen through examining the three groups of nations categorized above. First, it is appropriate to examine the Western parliamentary democracies—West Germany, United Kingdom, Italy, France, Netherlands, Belgium, Sweden, Austria, Switzerland, Denmark, Finland, Norway, Ireland, and the United States, Canada, Australia, and New Zealand. The overall trend in military manpower in this group is downward, despite the fact that, during this period, West Germany continued to build up its forces in order to complete its treaty obligations. The overall total of military manpower for these 17 nations in 1966 was 5,443,000, and it declined to 4,676,070 in 1973-1974. The rate of decline was therefore 14.1 percent. Except for France and Italy, these nations have minor paramilitary forces, limited to border guards. Even in France and Italy, with their national militarized police forces, there has been no notable increase in size of the paramilitary units (gendarmerie) during this time.

In the Eastern Europe one-party states (USSR, Poland, Yugoslavia, Rumania, East Germany, Czechoslovakia, Hungary, Bulgaria), the total active duty regular military forces declined from 5,278,500 in 1966 to 4,692,000 in 1973-1974. The rate of decline was 10.9 percent, compared to 14.1 for the Western nations. By contrast, there has been a marked increase in the size of paramilitary units among these Eastern European nations. This increase is not mainly the result of an expansion of the full-time border guards and security police forces but rather of the variously designated part-time armed workers' units. The pattern is similar in four of the members of the Warsaw Pact nations for 1966 to 1973-1974. East Germany increased its paramilitary units from 70,000 to 80,000 while it developed an armed workers' organization of 400,000.

Czechoslovakia's full-time paramilitary units remained at 35,000, while its "People's Millitia" reached a total of 250,000. In Hungary, the standing paramilitary units declined from 35,000 to 27,000, while its workers' militia in 1973-1974 stood at 250,000. In Bulgaria, the full-time paramilitary units increased from 15,000 to 17,000 while the People's Militia rose to 150,000.

In each of the other Eastern European nations there has been a related pattern which in part reflected particular internal political arrangements. In Poland from 1966 to 1973-1974, there was an increase in the full-time security troops, from 45,000 to 73,000. However, Poland has not emphasized the development of armed workers' militia. Rumania reduced the size of its standing paramilitary formations from 60,000 to 40,000; however, it maintained, in 1973-1974, a paramilitary militia of 500,000. Yugoslavia's standing paramilitary force, the Frontier Guard, has remained stable at 19,000 persons; however, the government has developed a part-time militia of 1,000,000 which, because of its national defense function, is more accurately considered a form of reserve force rather than a paramilitary force.

In the developing nations, the paramilitary forces are generally of two types. One is the militarized national police force—variants of the European gendarmerie; the other comprises part-time local defense or militia-type forces organized in connection with civil war and insurrection movements.

Among the developing nations, those in Africa have experienced a growth in full-time active duty military manpower from an estimated 345,000 to 409,500 in 1966 to 994,000 in 1973-1974. This is a growth of 185 percent. In 1973-1974, the size of the paramilitary forces in Africa, based on less reliable data, stood at 330,000. For Asia, military manpower rose during this period from 7,094,500 to 9,594,900—an increase of 35 percent. Paramilitary forces were particularly large in Asia—in 1973-1974, 6,055,300. (This figure does not include the 1.5 million village defense forces of South Vietnam.)

The data for China are, of course, particularly subject to question. However, from 1966 to 1973-1974, the size of the regular military forces did increase, at least as reflected by the reported growth from 2,614,000 to 2,900,000. The figure of 300,000 paramilitary encompasses the full-time security and border troops. It does not include the local militia, whose status was undermined by the cultural revolution.

Among the Latin-American countries, the rate of expansion of the active duty military has been much less than in the developing nations of

Africa and Asia. In the Central American countries—Mexico, Cuba, Haiti, Guatemala, the Dominican Republic, El Salvador, Honduras, Nicaragua —the size of the active duty military increased from 148,700 to 231,400. In Cuba, the pattern is an admixture of that of a developing nation and that of a one-party mass regime. There has been a marked increase in the size of the military, from 43,000 to 108,000; and, in addition to a 10,000 man full-time security force, the regime has developed a People's Militia of 200,000. In South America, the total military manpower has increased from the 1966 level of 557,100 to 637,400, or by 14 percent. The level of paramilitary forces stood at 305,300, and no country had developed an extensive part-time militia formation.

Aggregate Analysis

The availability of an increasing body of worldwide data on military expenditures and military institutions has resulted in a variety of gross analyses based on aggregate statistics. An analysis based on a worldwide array of data must be crude, because of the difficulties of developing a set of concepts adequate for handling the wide heterogeneity of the nations and military establishments. For example, in the developing nations, the 200-man force of Upper Volta, composed almost exclusively of infantry, is hardly the same type of organization as the Indian defense forces of over 948,000, with first-line jet planes and naval units. Again, in Western Europe, despite the similarities in societal setting and technology, there are, for example, important differences between the military profession in Switzerland and Sweden, which were able to be neutral during the last wars, and the military formations of Holland and Belgium, which have been deeply influenced by their wartime experiences.

The initial attempts at cross-national aggregate analysis sought to determine whether there were any relationship between economic development or its absence and the political role of the military, especially its political role in the developing nations. Students of cross-national research have offered the proposition that there is a positive association between economic development and democratic political competitiveness. By inference, the more economically developed a nation is—again, especially a new nation—the less likely it is that the military can hinder the competitive process in politics and government.

This type of analysis was pioneered by S. M. Lipset, who made use of selected indexes of economic development to compare Western European and Latin American democracies as a basis for testing this hypothesis about the positive association between economic development and political competitiveness.[5] He concluded that there were grounds for accepting this hypothesis. James Coleman, the political scientist, employed the same type of analysis for the new nations of Asia, the Middle East, and Africa and concluded that "the major hypothesis that economic development and competitiveness are positively correlated is validated when countries are grouped into major differentiating categories of competitiveness and when mean scores are employed."[6]

Conceptually, the weakness of such analysis rests in the arbitrary categories used to classify the political role of the military and the value of political competitiveness. To group together as "authoritarian" at a given time the political system of Afghanistan, at the time the exercise of power was based on personal rule, and that of Sudan, where it was the result of a coup d'etat by a professional military group, is to obscure comparative analysis. Moreover, statistical support for this proposition is hardly impressive; and this type of analysis appears to have limited relevance for understanding, on a comparative basis, the dynamic relationship between economic development and political forms. Since there are only a limited number of cases in the analysis, even a minor redefinition of the universe significantly alters the statistical conclusions. More important, in order to avoid a mechanical test of the proposition, one would expect over a period of time changes in political competitiveness in these nations, since the original analysis would be congruent with the basic proposition. This means that those nations high on the economic development index should have moved toward more competitiveness. In Latin America, the trend has been toward less political competitiveness; and this trend cannot directly be related to the increased level of economic development—in some cases, it is inversely related. The same lack of support of the hypothesis is presented by the countries of Africa and Asia. Lipset's and Coleman's efforts have produced a series of subsequent studies in the same format but with more refined techniques.[7]

An alternative approach is developed when a narrower and more homogeneous group of military establishments are examined in terms of a specific issue. Janowitz explored whether there is any relationship between economic development and limitations on the political role of the military in a sample of fifty-one developing nations.[8] The empirical results are mainly negative. Some of the difficulties of this type of analysis rest within the crude nature of the political categories even when more refined categories of military involvement in politics are employed among the new nations studied. However, there is no basis for asserting that, with higher levels of economic development, there is a movement toward restriction of the military's involvement with the domestic political system. In fact, among those new nations with the highest levels of economic development, the absence of democratic competitive systems is more noteworthy than their presence, since competitive systems are concentrated in the middle level of economic development. On the other hand, there is an apparent but not profoundly explanatory relation between the length of time that a new nation has been independent and the increased political role of the military. The chance of political involvement has increased year by year after independence, while contraction of the military's political role remains highly problematic.

With the expansion of military manpower and of the political role of the military in the developing nations, it was to be anticipated that aggregate analysis would shift to an examination of the capacity of the military regimes to effect economic development. Statistical studies have been completed by Irma Adelman and Cynthia Morris and by Eric Nordlinger.[9]

Conceptually, these suffer because all nations are treated as if they had equal potential for economic development and the researchers fail to confront the basic issues of available resources. Again, statistical problems compounded the research results. However, these findings argue against any special ability that military regimes may have to perform in a superior fashion in producing economic development. It would be more appropriate to conclude that aggregate analysis of military regimes and economic development indicates, for the time being, that some military regimes perform better than others and better than some civilian regimes.

It is also the case that aggregate analyses of military regimes, military expenditures, and their consequences are better accomplished on relatively homogeneous groups of nation-states. The analysis should also be extended over a longer period. Thus, for example, the research findings of Philippe C. Schmitter meet these two essential criteria.[10] He concludes, predictably, that "the military in power definitely tend to spend more on themselves of defense spending . . . civilian regimes definitely spend less on defense (here they are not plagued by frequent military interruptions and threats) and more on welfare." However, in summary, he adds that "no regime-type seems to be exclusively responsible for 'developmental success'." In subsequent related studies on Latin America, Schmitter and his associates are concerned with the effects of military assistance programs by the major powers on the arms races in the developing nations.[11] The results of these researches on the Latin American environment clearly undermine the notion that arms races in Latin America are a reaction to the international rivalries of the great powers. The notion of dependence gives way to a fuller understanding of the role that national rivalries play in developing the conditions for regional patterns of increases in military expenditures.

In summary, it is possible to point to a body of emerging data which describe the trends and indicators of the changing profile of military institutions from a world perspective. None of these trends should be mechanically extrapolated, although they all help to present the parameters of emerging models. Given the increase of internal tensions in the developed nations with parliamentary institutions, it is striking that there has been no marked increase in paramilitary formations sponsored by central governments. The prospect of private paramilitary units, of course, cannot be ruled out. In the developing nations, the central question is whether the growth of paramilitary institutions is likely to lead to regional stability. There is good reason to expect such a trend.

But the purpose of the world perspective and profile of military institutions is not to predict but to assess the contemporary scene. In this regard, it is already clear that statistical analysis of aggregate data makes for relevant cross-national comparison and interpretations when there is an emphasis on trend data and when relatively homogeneous groups of nations are examined in order that the underlying realities be kept clearly in mind. Thus, in a period of continued growth of military institutions and expenditures, worldwide research perspective has grown, but at a more limited rate than the institutions themselves.

Notes

1. Morris Janowitz, "International Perspectives on Militarism," *The American Sociologist* (February 1968), pp. 12-16.

2. Morris Janowitz and Reuben Hill, "Internationalizing American Sociology," *The American Sociologist* 8, 2 (May 1973).

3. For an alternative array of data on military manpower, see Bruce M. Russett et al., *World Handbook of Political and Social Indicators* (New Haven, 1964), pp. 72-80. See also Charles L. Taylor and Michael C. Hudson, eds., *World Handbook of Political and Social Indicators* (New Haven, 1972).

4. United States Arms Control and Disarmament Agency, *World Military Expenditures, 1971* (Washington, D.C., 1971), pp. 1 f.

5. S. M. Lipset, "Some Social Requisites of Democracy: Economic Development and Political Legitimacy," *American Political Science Review* 53 (March 1959), pp. 69-105.

6. James S. Coleman, "Conclusion: The Political Systems of the Developing

Areas," in Gabriel A. Almond and James S. Coleman, eds., *The Politics of the Developing Areas* (Princeton, 1960).

7. Phillips Cutright, "National Political Development: Measurement and Analysis," *American Sociological Review* 28 (April 1963), pp. 253-264; Dick Simpson, "The Congruence of Political, Social, and Economic Aspects of Development," *International Development Review* 6 (June 1964), pp. 21-25; Deane E. Neubauer, "Some Conditions of Democracy," *American Political Science Review* 61, no. 4 (December 1967), pp. 1002-1009; Marvin E. Olsen, "Multivariate Analysis of National Political Development," *American Sociological Review* 33, no. 5 (October 1968), pp. 699-712; Phillips Cutright and James A. Wiley, "Modernization and Political Representation: 1927-1966," *Studies in Comparative International Development* 5, no. 2 (1969-1970).

8. Morris Janowitz, *The Military in the Political Development of New Nations* (Chicago, 1964).

9. Irma Adelman and Cynthia Morris, *Society, Politics and Economic Development* (Baltimore, 1967); and Eric A. Nordlinger, "Soldiers in Mufti: The Impact of Military Rule Upon Economics and Social Change in the Non-Western States," *American Political Science Review* 64 (December 1970), pp. 1112-1130.

10. Philippe C. Schmitter, "Military Intervention, Political Competitiveness, and Public Policy in Latin America: 1950-1967," in *On Military Intervention,* Morris Janowitz and Jacques van Doorn, eds. (Rotterdam: University of Rotterdam Press, 1971).

11. Philippe C. Schmitter, ed., *Military Rule in Latin America: Function, Consequences and Perspectives* (Beverly Hills, 1973).

MILITARY ORGANIZATION IN
INDUSTRIAL SOCIETY

Military organization is a reflection of the technology of war. Therefore, the history of military organization and the military professional is generally written from the point of view of changes in weapons systems. But from the perspective of the social scientist, and especially the sociologist, military organization is thought of in different terms and at a different level of abstraction. Although social scientists make similar assumptions about the central significance of technology and technological change, military organization is defined as a comprehensive social system and is analyzed by means of institutional and social-psychological categories.

Technology and Military Organization

In light of the overriding reality that military formations are organized on a national basis, social research into military organization is faced with two sets of problems. First is the effort to highlight common patterns and uniformities in military institutions regardless of national or cultural settings. In this regard, the concept "organizational analysis" or "organization behavior" has gained widespread currency. Second, social scientists are aware that military organization reflects the social structure and political and cultural values of each particular environment. Because military formations are organized as national units, they reveal the consequences of historical and traditional values. These national differences influence not only organizational effectiveness, but also are basic elements in accounting for various patterns of civil-military relations.

This chapter is adapted from "Military Organization," in Roger W. Little, ed., *Handbook of Military Institutions* (Beverly Hills, 1971), pp. 13-51.

The purpose of this essay is to review some of the central concepts and available hypotheses about contemporary military institutions from the sociological perspectives both of institutional and organizational analysis, for these terms can be used interchangeably. The focus is on the United States military establishment as a particular manifestation of the more general experience of the Western European armed forces. This task also requires the additional perspective of the analysis of a profession. The essential elements of a professional group are (a) a system of training, (b) a body of expert knowledge and skill practices, (c) group cohesion and solidarity, (d) a body of ethics and a sense of responsibility, and (e) mechanisms of self-regulation. It is essential to apply the idea of responsibility to the military profession although it is a complex task. In fact, the military is a highly specialized profession because it is a profession that can only be practiced in modern times in governmental employment. Therefore, the notion of responsibility must always be evaluated in collective terms as well as individual terms.

In the contemporary period of rapid social and political change, that is, since the end of World War II, two basic assumptions about the nature of warfare seem essential.

First, the impact of technology and new mass destructive weapons has changed the pattern of international relations and altered the threat of general war. The major nuclear powers, while pursuing a policy of mutual deterrence, have had to face the severe limitation which mass destruction instruments place on the conduct of traditional diplomacy and international relations. For the military profession, the implication has been not merely that new weapons have had to be incorporated but that there has been a fundamental crisis in the profession itself. The military profession as it emerged in the nineteenth century had the overriding orientation that the outbreak of general war was inevitable. This inevitability, the profession assumed, was rooted in the nature of man, in the conduct of international relations, and in the consequences of each new arms race.

In the contemporary scene, the military profession must face the political imperative that the outbreak of general war is no longer defined as inevitable or in the national interest. General war continues to be a contingency, and an undesirable one at that, and it is recognized as such by a significant proportion of the military profession. Therefore, the study of the military profession involves its reaction to the actual and proposed international schemes of arms control and disarmament. The sociology of the military must also encompass the consequences of multilateral arrangements and United Nations peace-keeping activities which are designed to contain or reduce limited wars, especially those limited wars which might increase the possibility of general war.

Second, limited war is no longer "traditional." Since 1945, limited war has less often been a struggle between two legitimate governments, and more often a violent contest within a nation by some group against the existing regime. These wars are conflicts into which external national powers are drawn. These struggles involve use of nonprofessional forces and, therefore, the study of military organization shades off into the analysis of various forms of armed revolts, police systems, paramilitary formations, and other agencies of internal warfare.

"Morale" Versus Organization

The contemporary study of the sociology of military organization in an institutional framework had its intellectual origins in the classical writings of Max Weber on bureaucratic organization. The core works of Max Weber have been assembled and translated into a three-volume work entitled *Economy and Society.*[1] The most relevant sections are contained in Volume Three, Chapter XI, "Bureaucracy," and especially in the analysis of "The Origins of Discipline in War." Weber emphasizes the central importance of managerial forms and the emergence of discipline as the basic features of modern armies.

The early writings of political sociologists Harold D. Lasswell and Hans Speier elaborated the outlook of Max Weber.[2] These two men displayed a continuing and systematic concern with the implication of military organizations for social and political change.

Closely related is the pioneer social and institutional history of the German officer corps, by Karl Demeter, entitled *The German Officer Corps in Society and State.*[3] This seminal volume supplied the prototype for the study of the social recruitment and career lines of professional military officers.

The development of the sociology of military organization derives from a long tradition of empirical research much of which has been carried out by civilians called to military duty during war time. The history of these efforts reveals a shift in interest from a concern with "morale" to that of "organization."

During World War I, empirical research on American military institutions was first launched from a concern with the characteristics and motivations of recruits. A good deal of effort has been expended by social psychologists on this selected and specific aspect of military life. During World War I, a new approach to the use of military personnel was stimulated by social research, namely, the importance of considering a person's intelligence, skills, and aptitudes in assigning him to a military occupation. The experiences of military psychologists of this period provided a basis for the subsequent rapid development of personnel selection in civilian industry and business.

During World War II, an elaborate machinery was erected for matching men's skills to the jobs required. No large-scale organization as vast as the military establishment can operate without a standardized personnel selection system. But any personnel testing procedure runs the risk of developing overspecialization in both training procedures and personnel. It has even been argued that military personnel selection as administered during World War II resulted in draining off superior talent from essential but "unglamorous" assignments, such as the infantry. Moreover, no responsible personnel selector will claim that the dimensions of aggressive leadership in combat or strategic command have been satisfactorily conceptualized to the point where reliable personnel testing is possible.

Thus it was understandable that during World War II, social scientists broadened their interests beyond personnel selection and stressed the importance of research into motives and attitudes in military units. Research on "morale" was by no means a new approach to the analysis of complex and large-scale organizations. But the armed forces, that is, the ground and air forces, undertook morale studies on a most extensive scale. In the summary study of these efforts, *The American Soldier,* prepared under the guidance of Samuel A. Stouffer et al., the potentialities and limitations of attitude and morale research were assessed.[4] And again, as with the development of personnel selection during World War I, industry and business have continued morale and attitude studies which have been extended to a wide variety of civilian agencies and organizations, including welfare and educational settings.

Social research on attitudes and morale in the armed forces provides useful information for specific problems where it is assumed that the executive of a policy requires cooperation. The limitation of attitude research is not that the strategy and tactics of war cannot be based on the preferences of soldiers. This is obvious to all, including the social scientist. But, in fact, attitude research fails to describe the underlying social system—the realities of bureaucratic organization—of the armed forces. "Morale" is much too limited a concept to understand the coercive force of bureaucratic organization, especially of military formations as they operate in combat. The findings of *The American Soldier* studies serve to underline and reaffirm this sociological observation:

Thus we are forced to the conclusion that personal motives and relationships are not uniquely determinate for organization in combat ... officers and men must be motivated to make the organization work, but not *all* of them have to be so motivated, nor must they all agree on details of social philosophy or be bound by ties of personal friendship in order for a functioning organization to exist. To put it another way, the best single predictor of combat behavior is the simple fact of institutionalized role: knowing that a man is a soldier rather than a civilian. The soldier role is a vehicle for getting a man into the position in which he has to fight or take the institutionally sanctioned consequences.[5]

Therefore, in turn, the single concept of morale has been displaced by a theory of organizational and professional behavior in which an array of concepts are integrated: authority, communications, hierarchy, sanction, status, social role, and socialization.[6] Intellectual influences from historical writings, economic analysis, and social anthropology and sociological theory have emphasized the need for a comprehensive focus on the totality of the military, not merely on part of it. The line of analysis that has been developed has paralleled the institutional and organizational study of the factory, the mental hospital, the prison, and the school as a social system.[7]

Interestingly, the operational requirements of political warfare against the German and Japanese armed forces led to research efforts in which these forces were regarded as total social systems. During World War II, two social science units working independently recast operational and strategic intelligence into sociological models for explaining the strength and vulnerability of the Axis armed forces as they came under Allied attack. One group, the Foreign Morale Analysis Division, Military Intelligence Service, was concerned with Japan, while the other worked on Germany and, in particular, on the Wehrmacht. This latter group, Intelligence Branch, Psychological Warfare Divison, SHAEF, produced the research data on which the analysis by Edward A. Shils and Morris Janowitz, "Cohesion and Disintegration in the Wehrmacht in World War II," was based.[8]

Their findings, as well as those reported in *The American Soldier,* showed high convergence in underscoring the central importance of primary group solidarity, seen in totalitarian armies, as a crucial source of military effectiveness. Specifically, a social system perspective helped to focus attention on the important conclusion that it was not Nazi ideology which was at the root of German fanatical resistance, but rather the military and organizational practices which the Nazis permitted, encouraged, and required.[9] In the Korean conflict, the focus of attention shifted to a research concern with the social organization and behavior of U.S. prisoners of war. Albert Biderman undertook careful evaluation of the impact of prison experience on American military personnel and refuted popular stereotypes.[10] An important body of research was completed on the military and battle behavior of the Communist military formation.[11]

Since the end of World War II, the U.S. military establishment has conducted a series of ongoing periodic attitude studies for administrative purposes. In particular, to the outside observer, it would appear that the effort of military agencies has been at times sporadic. To be sure, the growth of social science in the military has been beset by organizational rivalries and difficulties. Such research has had to confront shortages of trained and committed personnel. But these efforts have produced a body of data relevant to the work of university-based specialists who are responsible for the major thrust.

The development of sociological research in the military is described by Raymond V. Bowers in the volume entitled *The Uses of Sociology*.[12] The diffuse structure which has emerged for social science and sociological research in the armed forces articulates with the structure of the military establishment. At the level of the Department of Defense, there has been since 1947 a series of groups charged with planning and coordinating social science research. In each of the three major services, there is a centralized research office which grants funds, including funds for social science research, to civilian groups. Military-sponsored research on social science aspects of military organization is undertaken by "in-house" agencies and laboratories and such efforts are stronger in data collection than in analysis.

With the advent of the all-volunteer military system and increased concern with race tensions and deviant behavior in the armed forces, the military has expanded its social research efforts. The bulk of these efforts focuses on sample surveys and is concerned with specific operational and administrative problems.

In the past, research in military organization was conducted mainly by individuals outside the military establishment. One of the major contributions to the analysis of military organization by an individual scholar since the end of World War II has been the volume by Samuel Huntington, *The Soldier and the State*.[13] Huntington is a political scientist who has sought to bridge political and organizational analysis. While his work has been subject to a variety of criticisms because of its implicit ideological overtones, his analysis highlights the effects of the political process on the historical development of American political institutions. A focal point for the work of university-based social scientists has been the efforts of the Inter-University Seminar on Armed Forces and Society. No single university has emerged as a center for research in this area, but through the efforts of this group independent research specialists are in communication. Through their efforts, including assembling existing sources of data, a limited body of research findings has developed. In *Sociology and the Military Establishment* by Morris Janowitz and Roger Little,[14] an overview of some of the essential materials is presented. The work of the Inter-University Seminar encompasses not only the internal organization of the American military, but is concerned both with comparative and cross-national analysis of armed forces and society.

Organization: Civilian Versus Military

If an institutional or organizational perspective is applied to the armed forces, it then becomes appropriate to contrast civilian and military organizations. Many features and characteristics of military organization, such as authoritarian and stratified hierarchical structures, are, in fact, to be found in varying degrees in civilian organizations. Moreover, transformations in technology and in military operations have brought about marked changes in the inner format of the military establishment. Speier points out that civilian social scientists tend to exaggerate and distort the differences between military and civilian organizations and overlook what is common to large-scale organization in general.[15]

The special characteristics of military organization derive from its goals, namely, the management of instruments of violence. However, the content of military goals has undergone tremendous changes under the impact of new technology. Furthermore, the range of political considerations which impinge on military operations has been altered. In general, the trend has been toward narrowing the differences between military organization and civilian organizations.

To analyze the contemporary military establishment in the United States as a social system, it is therefore necessary to assume that it has tended to display more and more of the characteristics typical of any large-scale, nonmilitary bureaucracy. The transformation of the military profession between World War I and World War II was based on existing trends in invention, organization, and firepower. The outcome was a convergence of military and civilian organization; the interpenetration of the civilian and the military is required as more and more of the resources of the nation-state are used in preparing for and making war. It became appropriate to speak of the "civilianization" of the military profession and of the parallel penetration of military forms into civilian social structure. The decreasing difference is a result of continuous technological change which vastly expands the size of the military establishment, increases its interdependence with civilian society, and alters its internal social structure. These technological developments in war-making require more and more professionalization of military personnel. At the same time, the impact of military technology during the past half-century can be described in a series of propositions about social change. Each of the conditions symbolized by these propositions has had the effect of "civilianizing" military institutions and of blurring the distinction between the civilian and the military. Each of these trends has, of course, actual and potential built-in limitations:

(1) A significant percentage of the national income of a modern nation is spent for the preparation, execution, and repair of the consequences of war. Thus there is a secular trend toward total popular involvement in the consequences of war and war policy, since the military establishment is responsible for the distribution of a progressively larger share of available economic resources.

(2) Military technology both vastly increases the destructiveness of warfare and widens the scope of automation in new weapons. It is commonplace that both of these trends tend to weaken the distinction between military roles and civilian roles as the destructiveness of war has increased. Weapons of mass destruction socialize danger to the point of equalizing the risks of warfare for both soldier and civilian.

(3) The revolution in military technology means that the military mission of deterring violence becomes more and more central as compared with preparing to apply violence. This shift in mission tends to civilianize military thought and organization as military leaders concern themselves with broad ranges of political, social, and economic policies.

(4) The complexity of the machinery of warfare and the requirements for research, development, and technical maintenance tend to weaken the organizational boundary between the military and the nonmilitary, since the maintenance and manning of new weapons require a greater reliance on civilian-oriented technicians. The countertrend, or at least limitation, is the greater effort by the military establishment to develop and train military officers with scientific and engineering backgrounds.

(5) Given the "permanent" threat of war, it is well recognized that the tasks which military leaders perform tend to widen. Their technological knowledge, their direct and indirect power, and their heightened prestige result in their entrance, of necessity, into arenas that in the recent past have been reserved for civilians and professional politicians. The need that political and civilian leaders have for expert advice from professional soldiers about the strategic implications of technological change serves to mix the roles of the military and the civilian.

These propositions do not deny the crucial differences that persist between military and nonmilitary bureaucracies. The goals of an organization supply a meaningful basis for understanding differences in organizational behavior. The military establishment as a social system has unique characteristics because the possibility of hostilities is a permanent reality to its leadership. The fact that thermonuclear weapons alter the role of force in international relations does not deny this proposition. The consequences of preparation for future combat and the results of previous combat pervade the entire organization. The unique character of the military establishment derives from the requirement that its members be specialists in making use of violence and mass destruction.

Thus, the narrowing distinction between military and nonmilitary bureaucracies can never result in the elimination of fundamental organizational differences. Two pervasive requirements for combat set limits to these civilizing tendencies.

First, while it is true that modern warfare exposes the civilian and the soldier more to equal risks, the distinction between military roles and civilian roles has not been eliminated. Traditional combat-ready military formations are maintained for limited warfare. The necessity for naval and air units to carry on the hazardous tasks of continuous and long-range reconnaissance and detection demands organizational forms that will bear the stamp of conventional formations. Even with fully automated missile systems, conventional units must be maintained as auxiliary forces for the delivery of new types of weapons.

More important, no military system can rely on expectation of victory based on the initial exchange of firepower, whatever the form that the initial exchange may be. Subsequent exchanges will involve military personnel—again regardless of their armament—who are prepared to carry on the struggle as soldiers, that is, subject themselves to military authority and to continue to fight. The automation of war civilized wide sectors of the military establishment; yet the need to maintain combat readiness and to develop centers of resistance after initial hostilities ensures the continued importance of military organization and authority.

Second, what about the consequences of the increased importance of deterrence as a military mission? Should one not expect that such a shift would also result in civilizing the military establishment? If the military is forced to think about deterring wars rather than fighting them, the traditions of the "military mind" based on the inevitability of hostilities must change, and military authority must undergo transformation as well. There can be no doubt that this shift in mission is having important effects on military thought and organization. In fact, military pragmatism which questions the inevitability of total war is an important trend in modern society as the destructiveness of war forces military leaders to concern themselves with the political consequences of violence.

Again, there are limits to the consequences of this civilizing trend. The role of deterrence is not a uniquely new mission for the military establishment. Historically, the contribution of the military to the balance of power has not been made because of the civilian character of the military establishment. On the contrary, the balance of power formula operates, when it does, because the military establishment is prepared to fight.

With the increase in the importance of deterrence, military elites become more and more involved in diplomatic and political warfare, regardless of their preparation for such tasks. Yet the specific and unique contribution of the military to deterrence is the threat of violence which has currency, that is, it can be taken seriously because of the real possibility of violence. Old or new types of weapons do not alter this basic formula. In short, deterrence still requires organization prepared for combat. Moreover, the actuality and possibility of limited war permit the military to persist in maintaining conceptions of combat. These conceptions come to include a wide variety of functions with civilian and political components, but which are defined at least in part as military: guerrilla and counterguerrilla warfare, psychological warfare, military assistance and training, or even "nation-building."

These trends in self-concepts and roles are described and analyzed in *The Professional Soldier: A Social and Political Portrait* as they have affected the officer corps during the past half-century in the United States.[16] The military profession which has centered on the self-conception of the warrior types or the "heroic leader" requires the incorporation of new roles, namely, the "military manager" and the "military technologist." For the military establishment to accomplish its multiple goals, it must develop and maintain a balance between these different military types.

These basic changes in the military over the past fifty years can be summarized by a series of basic propositions on the transformation of military organization in response both to the changing technology of war and to the transformation of the societal context in which the armed forces operate.[17]

Changing organizational authority. There has been a change in the basis of authority and discipline in the military establishment, a shift from authoritarian domination to greater reliance on manipulation, persuasion, and group consensus. The organizational revolution which pervades contemporary society, and which implies management by means of persuasion, explanation, and expertise, is also to be found in the military.

Narrowing skill differential between military and civilian elites. The new tasks of the military require that the professional officer develop more and more skills and orientations common to civilian administrators and civilian leaders. The narrowing difference in skill between military and civilian society is an outgrowth of the increasing concentration of technical specialists in the military.

Shift in officer recruitment. The military elite has been undergoing a basic social transformation since the turn of the century. These elites have been shifting their recruitment from a narrow, relatively high social status base, to a broader base more representative of the population as a whole.

Significance of career patterns. Prescribed careers performed with high competence lead to entrance into the professional elite, the highest point in the military hierarchy at which technical and routinized functions are performed. By contrast, entrance into the smaller group, the elite nucleus—where innovative perspectives, discretionary responsibility, and political skills are required—is assigned to persons with unconventional and adaptive careers.

Trends in political indoctrination. The growth of the military establishment into a vast managerial enterprise with increased political responsibilities has produced a strain on traditional military self-images and concepts of honor. The officer is less and less prepared to think of himself as merely a military technician. As a result, the profession, especially within its strategic leadership, has developed a more explicit political ethos.

Thus, in partial summary, since the turn of the century, the military establishment has been fusing with civilian enterprise. There has been a weakening of organizational boundaries. This organizational trend has been encountered in many other sectors of modern society, for example, the increased fusion of industrial and governmental agencies or of higher educational and business organizations. But this process of fusion of the military and civilian sectors had reached its systemic limits by the early 1960s.

This is not to postulate that there is a trend toward a return to a distinct, separate, and isolated military establishment. The fusion of military and political goals alone makes this impossible. However, there is a trend in the military which seeks to strengthen its distinctive boundaries, jurisdictions, and competence while at the same time the military is deeply intertwined with the larger society.

The Decline of Mass Armed Force

The transformation of the mass armed force in the Western multi-party parliamentary system, and in the United States, is obviously not linked to a single historical event although clearly the application of nuclear theory to military enterprise is crucial. It must be remembered these are not inevitable and predetermined trends but institutional developments which are subject to political intervention and voluntaristic initiative.

It is not possible to fix a terminal date for the historical period of the mass armed force, since the end of its dominance is a long term and gradual process. Therefore, the main outlines of the new directions in military organization were manifest after the end of World War II. In varying degrees, in most industrialized nations, especially those with nuclear weapons or in alliance with nuclear powers, the new long term trend was toward smaller, fully professional, and more fully alerted and self-contained military forces; the direction was away from a mobilization force to a military force "in being."

The development of nuclear weapons and their use against Japan in 1945 signaled both the end of World War II and the introduction of the technology out of which the new trend would develop. Korea was fought as a continuation of the World War II format. However, in the year 1952, with the assumption of power of President Eisenhower, the promulgation of the doctrine of "massive retaliation" may well be taken by historians as a crucial point in the movement away from the dominance of the mass armed force. However, the Eisenhower administration continued the draft system in order to maintain and extend the system of international alliances which required important elements of the mass armed force. After the end of military operations in Vietnam, the system of conscription was terminated and in 1973 an all-volunteer military came into being.

The emergence of the new format marked the halt, at least temporarily, in the trend toward civilianization. It is possible to offer a number of basic propositions related to those presented above, which highlight the possible outcome.

1. CHANGING ORGANIZATIONAL AUTHORITY

The shift from authoritative domination to greater reliance on explanation, expertise, and group consensus continued through the period of the Vietnam war. The realities and pressures of combat required the continuation of such a trend. However, with the actual implementation of the all-volunteer force and the elimination of "reluctant" draftees, there has been clear evidence that the limits of change have been reached for the time being. The debate within the military concerning those elements of discipline which are essential has produced powerful ideological and organizational pressures to resist additional change which military professionals believe weaken military authority.

The transition to an all-volunteer manpower system in the United States had to be instituted during a period of immense organizational strain and turbulence. The strategy of Congressional and Executive leadership to achieve the all-volunteer force rested mainly on increased pay to make the military competitive with civilian employment. However, the character and quality of military life, especially its forms of authority and visible purpose, were crucial elements in the recruitment and retention of personnel.

The response of the military leadership to the all-volunteer force has involved two elements. On the one hand, there has been a strong emphasis on reestablishing organizational control and "strengthening discipline." With the end of combat, and the elimination of "reluctant" draftees, a variety of organizational practices could be more directly implemented. There can be no doubt that, under the conditions of the all-volunteer force, military leadership has been concerned with the reestablishment of elements of traditional practices. However, there are powerful limits to these efforts. The other response of the military was to strive to make the volunteer system work. Thus, in reality, in the implementation of the all-volunteer force, the basic issue has to be faced as to what was the legitimate scope of military authority over the personal behavior of its members, since elaborate constraining practices had been justified as effective training necessary to prepare men to accept military discipline and to face combat. The control of personal behavior had involved hazing and harsh treatment in basic training, and trivial "mickey mouse" inspections and duties in garrison life.

The military elite justified such control of personal behavior by the absence of an effective military tradition among civilians and because of the lack of an immediate and direct threat. Under the all-volunteer system the trend has been toward a very gradual elimination of brutal induction procedures and excessive inspections. In training, the objective is to expose men to realistic problems and to avoid degrading experiences. Military leadership therefore undertook programs to promote a private life in military barracks, to eliminate "make work" assignments, needless inspections, and personal harassment, but the implementation of such changes encounters pervasive organizational rigidities. The impact of official policies of change have been indeed limited. As was to be expected, these reforms were viewed as overreaching by some professionals, especially in matters dealing with personal appearance, and after a period a reversal of policy could be noticed.

On balance, the end of hostilities in Vietnam and the advent of the all-volunteer force has resulted in stronger internal organization control, although the scope of discipline over private behavior within operational units has been limited. No doubt, much of the excessive ritualism and "mickey mouse" will never be reinstated, but some degree of ceremony and protocol will continue to be important in professional military life.

2. NARROWING SKILL DIFFERENTIAL BETWEEN MILITARY AND CIVILIAN ELITES

One of the more precise indicators of the interpenetration of military institutions and civilian society has been the long-term increase in the transferability of skills from the military to the civilian sector. During the period 1960-1970, the limits of this trend were reached.

For enlisted personnel, Harold Wool's comprehensive study, *The Military Specialist,* documents post-World War II changes in skill structure.[18] During the first part of this period, 1945-1957, the trend in the Army toward a greater proportion of technical specialists with direct counterparts in the civilian economy increased, but then leveled out in succeeding years. Thus, the proportion of Army enlisted personnel whose primary specialty was ground combat fell from 39.3 percent in 1945 to 28.1 percent in 1960, but by 1963 the figure remained at 28.8 percent. A similar pattern was seen in the Marine Corps.

Wool also points to another aspect which limited the trend of convergence of civilian and military skills. Enlisted personnel engage in a variety of generalized assignments, such as guard duty and housekeeping, regardless of occupational specialty and rank. The practice of having civilians employed, directly or by contract, to perform logistical and supply assignments means a greater tendency to assign uniformed personnel to purely military or combat functions.

3. SHIFT IN OFFICER RECRUITMENT

From 1910 to 1960, the data support the hypothesis that the military elites were shifting their recruitment from a narrow base, with regard to social status, to a broader base, more representative of the population as a whole. Since 1945, and especially since 1960, new trends in social recruitment have developed, particularly for academy cadets. First, the military profession has continued to be an avenue of social mobility for the working class. Thus, 17.6 percent of the class of 1971 at the U.S. Military Academy were from the working class, mainly the sons of skilled workers. This figure was a continuation of post-World War II patterns, and is markedly higher than figures at civilian universities of comparable quality. Even at the U.S. Naval Academy, 20.1 percent of cadets in the same class described their background as blue collar.

Second, the armed forces lost their last direct linkage with sons of the upper class. Such recruits, especially those who rose to the highest ranks, had been steadily declining, faster in the Army and Air Force than in the Navy. There has even been a decline in sons from upper-middle-class business and professional backgrounds and a strong emphasis on lower-middle-class business and professional backgrounds and a strong emphasis on lower-middle-class sources of recruitment. The number of recruits from families in high-status professions—such as medicine, law, and even teaching—is limited (about 3 percent, which is less than in comparable civilian institutions). The modest background of cadets can be inferred from the modest incomes of their families. Men from such backgrounds must rely more heavily on their education to develop broad cosmopolitan perspectives.

Third, self-recruitment has increased sharply in all three services since 1945. In the 1960s, more than one-quarter of entering cadets at the service academies came from career military families. They had fathers who either were on full-time career duty or had completed twenty years of service. If one were to include uncles and close relatives who were career military men, the percentage would, of course, greatly increase. Although precise data are not available, there has been a marked increase in the number of sons of noncommissioned officers at service academies. For these young men entrance into the officer corps, especially as academy graduates, is a sign of social mobility and personal achievement. Among military offsprings, linkages with civilian society tend to be attenuated, and a sense of social isolation is an often present potential. Likewise, recruitment from the ROTC into the officer cadres has become more and more unrepresentative as the ROTC have been abandoned in the Northeast and Midwest and transferred to the South and Southwest. A military of overemphasized lower-middle class origins with strong ties to the hinterland of "middle America," plus a strong element of self-recruitment, supplies potentials for increased social isolation and differentiation from the full structure of United States society, and as would be expected, would prove to have the strongest elements of nationalistic sentiments.

4. SIGNIFICANCE OF CAREER PATTERNS

The advent of nuclear weapons and the burdens of prolonged conflict in South Vietnam have not altered the notion or the content of the prescribed career—the accepted career ladder into the military elite. With the introduction of the all-volunteer force in 1973, in each service, there remained a discernible series of steps which alternate between staff and command assignments plus successful course completion at service schools, and these have changed only very slightly. On the contrary, faced with the prospect of a declining military force in the 1970s, officers strove as before to pass through the prescribed stages of career training as they searched for essential command assignments. Career management has been described by the professionals themselves as "having your ticket punched." The higher schools emphasize conventional staff and command procedures and offer considerable content on public affairs and current international events. However, they are not centers for fundamental self-criticism or reformulation of doctrine, but forums for transmitting existing policy. Laurence I. Radway, long-time student of higher military education, emphasizes "the frequent testimony of many graduates that 'what you learn there is less important than the friends you make there'."

The prescribed career has been broadened to include some involvement in politico-military assignments and "stability operations." But most of these operations are carried out by specialists who frequently do not rise into the military elite. Command of troops, vessels, aircraft, or missiles remains central, and a politico-military assignment. Excessive involvement in politico-military tasks is thought to thwart career advancement. A military establishment dominated by men who have had uniform and traditional careers is likely to face strain in the process of adaptation to change.

But what of the hypothesis, offered in *The Professional Soldier,* that in contrast to a prescribed career, entrance into the small elite nucleus —where innovating perspectives, discretionary responsibility, and political skills are required—is given to persons with unconventional and adaptive careers? The number of officers who enter the elite nucleus via an unconventional career varies. It was high during and immediately after World War II. However, in the decade 1960-1970, the route to the very top became narrower and these posts were more often filled by men pursuing conventional careers.

There were reasons for this. First, many assignments and skills that formerly marked an adaptive career have become routinized and hence have developed into career specialties. This has occurred, for example, with language skills and staff service in joint and international commands. Likewise, in the past, especially between World War I and World War II, the adaptive and unconventional career was reflected in a personal decision to become associated with new and experimental weapons such as the submarine, the tank, and the airplane. However, that type of innovative career has been closed, as weapons development has become an institutionalized process. In fact, the innovators now are the men who resist needless and marginal differentiation in weapons systems. But negative contributions like these are seldom recognized as innovative or generously rewarded. If an adaptive career is indeed a reflection of self-motivation, initiative, and risk taking, then the scope has narrowed and the signs are more difficult to determine.

Second, while men make careers for themselves and contribute importantly to the changing military by pursuing innovative assignments, the military circumstances must be appropriate. The war in Vietnam has meant that the men who sought to innovate—mainly in the field of counterguerrilla warfare—failed. Brig. General William P. Yarborough, a strong advocate of "unconventional warfare," was a conspicuous example of a group of aspirants. They failed both because of the inherent impossibility of their task and because command decisions after 1964 meant that conventional forces and leaders with prescribed careers had come into dominance. With the advent of the all-volunteer force, the trend appears to continue and to be reinforced.

5. BOUNDARIES OF MILITARY ORGANIZATION

With the end of World War II, the military establishment, like any other institution, struggled to defend its boundaries against external intrusion and to maintain its distinctive character. Above all else, all three services have sought to increase the number and proportion of officers trained at the service academies and to maintain a strong emphasis on academy training as a criterion for elite positions. Before the Air Force Academy was established in 1955, enrollment at the two service academies numbered less than 6,200. By 1970, there were approximately 13,000 military cadets in the academies, because of the establishment of the Air Force Academy and the expansion of West Point and Annapolis.

The Academy system is based on the notion that an early decision to become a career officer plus four years of military academy education will produce strong commitments to the military establishment. Since the end of World War II youngsters graduating from high school who are college bound find it more and more difficult to make an early career decision. As many as one-third change their academic specialization or professional goals. With the end of conscription, resignation of cadets while studying at the academies, especially at the Air Force Academy, rose to the point where they attracted attention; in 1972, more than one-third of the entering class terminated their work. This reflects the general trend of shifting undergraduate choices plus special concerns about a military career.

Moreover, although between 20 and 25 percent of academy graduates leave the service after their obligated tour of duty, those who remain have the strongest commitments to the autonomy of the profession and to the values of military honor. They have, in fact, risen to dominate the general and flag-officer ranks. The concentration of academy graduates among general and flag officers decreased somewhat during the early 1960s as high-caliber personnel who had entered the officer corps directly from civilian life during World War II, and who had stayed in the service after the war, were promoted into those ranks. But at no time was the overall dominance of academy officers threatened. Even in the Air Force, with the most open system of promotion, all thirteen generals in 1968 and 41 percent of lieutenant generals were graduates of a service academy. For that same year in the Army, all fourteen generals and 79 percent of the forty-three lt. generals were academy graduates; while in the Navy all of the forty-three admirals and vice-admirals were graduates. Even 40 percent of the 186 rear admirals were of this category. As the total size of the armed force is reduced, the increasingly large numbers of new academy graduates will have an even more decisive effect.

Second, the realities of military strategy, the admixture of weapons systems and the politico-military rules for employing them, have served gradually since 1945 (and more decisively since 1960) to limit the trend toward civilianization and to reinforce the boundaries of military organization. A national defense strategy which relies on nuclear weapons produces a military force with increasingly distinct boundaries and one which is more sharply differentiated from civilian society. At the upper end of the destructive continuum, nuclear weapons of mass destruction must be manned by a "force in being." The Air Force and even the Army have become more and more a force in being, similar in this aspect to the Navy. The key training periods are extended. A man is either in the nuclear deterrent or not. In this respect, the dividing line is more distinct than during the period of conventional weapons and mass civilian mobilization. Those who manage mass destruction weapons are exposed to grave risks. The need to deal with the unexpected is not a matter of actual battle but an ongoing concern: a military atmosphere becomes pervasive. In short, nuclear weapons are fundamentally different from nonnuclear weapons in that their military character derives from their mere existence, even without their being used. The incorporation of nuclear weapons creates an organizational climate which is military and distinct from civilian institutions.

At the lower end of the continuum of destructive capacity, under a nuclear strategy, conventional war units tend to be converted, although very slowly, more and more to forces in being, that is, into smaller segments, more self-contained and readily alerted. The withdrawal of the ground forces from Vietnam accelerated this trend. Mobilization plans are deemphasized and the role of the reserves, except for those units actually in the effective ready reserves, becomes more circumscribed. Every deployment of conventional forces becomes part of the logic of strategic deterrence and the need to avoid nuclear confrontation. These forces do not have a strategy of their own, since their operations derive from the larger goal of preventing the outbreak of nuclear war. The scope of conventional military action becomes highly delimited, and, to be effective, such forces must be fully trained and prepared for immediate action—again, a force in being.

Redefinition of Military Organization

The sociological and institutional analysis of military organization implies an observational standpoint. In other words, it requires a standard of evaluation or a set of judgments for interpreting the performance of military institutions. The student of military affairs, of course, strives to apply the scientific method and especially to be concerned with objectivity. He must face a series of complex research issues such as access to documentary sources, overcoming secrecy, and the avoidance of nationalistic biases. But only by placing his effort in some broad and evaluative framework, does he serve the purpose of intellectual enlightenment. The development of social science is a collective enterprise which transcends national barriers. Therefore, research on the military is a positive force for peace.[19]

The distinction offered by Alfred Vagts, the historian, between "militarism" and "the military way" represents a powerful frame of reference and a useful approach for the study of military organization undergoing change:

The military way is marked by a primary concentration of men and materials on winning specific objectives of power with the utmost efficiency, that is, with the least expenditure of blood and treasure. Militarism, on the other hand, presents a vast array of customs, interests, prestige, actions, and thought associated with armies and wars and yet transcending true military purposes. Indeed militarism is so constituted that it may hamper and defeat the purposes of the military way.[20]

This distinction is a specific application to military organization of the classic problem of rationality in large-scale organization, that is, the conditions promoting or hampering the effective adjustment of means to ends. Internally, militarism implies the development and persistence of practices which block scientific and administrative procedures designed to produce greater professionalism. Externally, militarism encompasses the social, economic, and political power that the military generates and its consequences on domestic social structure and international politics.

To the extent that the military officer is a professional, to that extent he must relate himself to the profound uncertainties in planning for and conducting military hostilities. Therefore, the ideal model of the military professional is not that of the scientist or the engineer or the business administrator. There is an irreducible component of a heroic posture in his professional self-image, for he must be prepared to face danger.

The development of the military profession has been a continuous struggle to be rational and scientific in the context of military requirements. Thus, it is possible to describe the history of the modern military establishment as a struggle between the previously identified military types—heroic leaders who embody traditionalism and glory—and military managers who are concerned with the scientific and rational conduct of war. Internal militarism in the sense that the military blocks technical progress has waned in most military establishments. As the military establishment becomes progressively dependent on more complex technology, the importance of the military manager increases. He does not displace the heroic leader, but he undermines the long-standing traditionalism of the military. As a result, there is a crisis in the strain between military managers and heroic leaders. However, this is a professional crisis that can be controlled by organizational resources, by compromise, and because the military manager acknowledges the worth and instrumental value of the heroic leaders in the military profession.

The proposition can be offered that the crisis in the professional self-image of the military man derives not primarily from internal organizational problems but from the crisis in military goals. At the upper end of the violence continuum, the development of nuclear weapons and strategic conceptions of deterrence means that the military officer—both the military manager and the heroic leader—is transformed into a teacher, that is, an instructor of men who will man and maintain a machine designed not to be employed. The past supplies little basis for organizing and maintaining a professional self-image under such conditions. At the lower end of the violence continuum, the scope of conventional warfare narrows. The tactics and techniques of limited war and internal warfare limit the authority of the military professional at the expense of civilian experts and civilian political leadership. It is almost possible to speak of civilian militarism as each aspect of military operations comes under the elaborate control of civilian leaders—democratic and authoritarian—and as the mechanics of warfare must be integrated with political strategy in the absence of an opportunity for traditional-type military victory.[21]

The constabulary force. The notion of the constabulary force is one conception designed to contribute to the issues of restructuring military institutions to emerging technological, political, and moral considerations. In *The Professional Soldier: A Social and Political Portrait,* the constabulary concept is defined in the following way: the military establishment becomes a constabulary force when it is continuously prepared to act, committed to the minimum use of force, and seeks viable international relations rather than victory because it has incorporated a protective military posture.[22] For industrialized nations, the constabulary force concept encompasses the entire range of military power and organization, including the military contribution to arms control and disarmament. For developing nations, the constabulary concept involves reasoned and careful use of the military for social and national development, including civic action. The military is viewed moving in the direction of becoming a police-type operation in the sense that "victory" against a specific enemy is no longer its major goal, but creating stable conditions for social and political change is its major goal instead.

The constabulary concept is not tied to a specific strategic outlook; it is a concept designed to relate institutional analysis to enlightened self-interest.[23] It is designed to facilitate creative innovation in military organization and doctrine to permit modification in national policy in order to reduce the risk of war.

The peace-keeping operations of the United Nations can be viewed as an application of the constabulary concept at the level of the world community. In the early evolution of the United Nations, there was considerable discussion of the possibility of a world military force to enforce the political and legal decisions of the United Nations. This would be a force recruited and staffed directly under United Nations jurisdiction, as a step toward "world government." The pressure of international relations plus the organizational defects of this approach rendered the concept inoperative from the very beginning.

The actual pattern of military operations of the United Nations has in effect conformed to a constabulary pattern. Peace-keeping operations have been undertaken by conventional national forces which have been welded into ad hoc organizations, and given political and administrative direction by United Nations organs. It is striking to note that, while there have been factual and operational reports of the United Nations peace-keeping operations, they have not been studied in depth from a sociological perspective.

Equally significant is the analysis of the impact of United Nations military experiences on member nations and their constituent forces. A large number of nations have sent forces to participate in United Nations operations with discernible impact on the participants and, in turn, on the internal processes of the particular member nation involved. One such study is available on the Irish Army, where the impact of United Nations peace-keeping activity has been of considerable importance for political integration of the home country. Victory in the traditional military sense is not relevant, but success in the constabulary sense of making a contribution to the world community is relevant. This was precisely the case for the Irish troops, which were hardly "victorious" in the field operations but succeeded in their operational mission. Charles Moskos has undertaken a more comprehensive study of the impact of participation in the U.N. peace-keeping operation in Cyprus on the individual soldiers who were involved.[24] He found that traditional training as soldiers supplied the basis for peace-keeping operations. The constabulary ethic developed under the impact of operational realities and was not incompatible with national pride and sentiments.

In recent years planning for United Nations military operations has, as a result of experience, undergone a radical change, and the notion of a permanent United Nations force has receded. Obviously, this is a result of international politics and the burden of existing United Nations military operations. It is also the result of creative thinking which is seeking to develop professional military forms appropriate to the political and administrative tasks of the United Nations. As a result, thinking and planning have progressed in the constabulary direction, namely, to create that kind of force which would satisfy the needs of the United Nations and which, in its organization format, would contribute to the reduction of tensions per se rather than create new imbalances. The evolving format is that of national standby forces which are designated in advance as potential United Nations units. These units are housed in member nations and are part of their national defense forces but are available on a constabulary basis for United Nations emergencies. It is noteworthy that some small nations, namely, Norway, Sweden, and Denmark, have designated specific units for such activities. It is, of course, such small nations that will be called on for United Nations constabulary duty. Canada has taken the lead and organized an international conference on these problems. As a result, the United Nations has the rudiments of a military force at its disposal without the political instabilities and administrative difficulties that would be generated if it had a force in being.

Arms control and disarmament. Beyond peace-keeping operations is the arena of arms control and disarmament. It is possible to develop sociological models of the world community under conditions of radical disarmament. Walter Millis and James Real in *The Abolition of War* are concerned with eliminating war as an instrument of national policy.[25] Yet they conclude with an organizational concept which they label "national police forces." National police forces—not a world police—are seen as elements to enforce the domestic conditions required for a world community. The idea of the national police force converges with the concept of a constabulary force. Not only are specialists in violence seen to operate in a protective military posture, but by whatever name, they are seen to have a positive role in arms control and disarmament.

In the long run, successful systems of accommodation and arms control would reduce the size of the military, but in the very short run, such schemes are likely to require a shift in the pattern of military activity. From this point of view, each step and each type of international accommodation require new involvements and adaptations by the military if the accommodations of arms control are to be stable, relatively enduring, and expanding in scope.

On the level more specifically related to the mechanics of arms control is the formulation of Thomas C. Schelling of a special surveillance force.[26] The special surveillance force is seen as an instrument for implementing an arms control arrangement. It is an organizational device for making treaties and formal arrangements enforceable, effective, and expanding. The special surveillance force is an example of institution-building which would function "to observe the enemy's behavior, at the enemy's invitation, and to report home instantly through authentic channels. The purpose is to help tranquilize crises that threaten to erupt into general war, particularly crises aggravated by the instability of strategic deterrence." Thus, it is striking to note that Schelling sees arms control in part as a crash program in which new arrangements—formal and informal, unilateral and bilateral—can emerge in response to a sudden crisis. It is even more striking to note that the organizational characteristics he describes for his special surveillance force are military characteristics in part, and more specifically converge with the constabulary concept, namely, "the attributes of the forces should be readiness, speed and reliability, self-sufficiency, versatility and ability to improvise."

It is necessary to examine the full range of the nonmilitary activities of constabulary forces. At a minimum, national disasters are likely to persist whose consequences can be coped with in part by military forces. In addition to these national disasters, there are the continuous rescue missions and responses to the failure and breakdown of man-made systems of transportation, power, navigation, and the like. All of these adjunct roles can enhance military effectiveness to cope with its central function in a rational and adaptive fashion.

Notes

1. Max Weber, *Economy and Society*, Guenther Roth and Claus Wittich, eds. (New York, 1968).

2. Harold D. Lasswell, *Politics: Who Gets What, When, How* (New York, 1951); Hans Speier, *Social Order and the Risks of War* (New York, 1952).

3. Karl Demeter, *The German Officer Corps in Society and State* (New York, 1965).

4. Samuel A. Stouffer et al., *The American Soldier* (Princeton, 1949).

5. Ibid., vol. 2, p. 101.

6. See S. Andreski, *Military Organization and Society* (London, 1954); R. H. Williams, *Human Factors in Military Operations: Some Applications of the Social Sciences to Operations Research,* Technical Memorandum ORO-T-259 (Chevy Chase, Md., 1954); U.S. Department of Defense, Office of the Secretary of Defense, *Report of the Working Group on Human Behavior Under Conditions of Military Service,* A Joint Project of the Research and Development Board and the Personnel Policy Board (Washington, D.C., 1951); J.A.A. van Doorn, *Sociologie van de organisatie: beschouwingen over ograniseren in het bijzonder gebaseerd op eeen onderzoek van het militaire sustem* (Leiden, 1956).

7. J. G. March, ed., *Handbook of Organizations* (Chicago, 1965).

8. Edward A. Shils and Morris Janowitz, "Cohesion and Disintegration in the Wehrmacht in World War II," *Public Opinion Quarterly,* XII (1948), pp. 280-315; see also A. Leighton, *Human Relations in a Changing World* (New York, 1949), for the research findings on Japanese institutions.

9. For example, see S.L.A. Marshall, *Men Against Fire* (New York, 1947).

10. Albert Biderman, *The March to Calumny* (New York, 1963).

11. Alexander L. George, *The Chinese Communist Army in Action: The Korean War and its Aftermath* (New York and London, 1967); William C. Bradbury, *Mass Behavior in Battle and Captivity: The Communist Soldier in the Korean War,* Samuel M. Meyers and Albert D. Biderman, eds. (Chicago, 1968).

12. Raymond V. Bowers, "The Military Establishment," in P. F. Lazarsfeld et al., eds., *The Uses of Sociology* (New York, 1967), pp. 234-274. See also G. W. Crocker, "Some Principles Regarding the Utilization of Social Science Research within the Military," in E. T. Crawford and A. Biderman, eds., *Social Scientists and International Affairs* (New York, 1969), pp. 185-194.

13. Samuel Huntington, *The Soldier and the State* (Cambridge, Mass., 1957).

14. Morris Janowitz and Roger Little, *Sociology and the Military Establishment* (New York, 1965); also see Kurt Lang, *The Sociology of War: A Selected and Annotated Bibliography,* Inter-University Seminar on Armed Forces and Society (Chicago, 1969).

15. Speier, *Social Order and the Risks of War.*

16. Morris Janowitz, *The Professional Soldier: A Social and Political Portrait* (New York, 1960, 1971).

17. Ibid., pp. 7-16, 21-36.

18. Harold Wool, *The Military Specialist: Skilled Manpower for the Armed Forces* (Baltimore, 1968).

19. See Morris Janowitz, "International Perspectives on Militarism," *The American Sociologist,* III, No. 1 (February 1968), pp. 12-16.

20. Alfred Vagts, *A History of Militarism* (New York, 1937), p. 13.

21. Morris Janowitz, "Toward a Redefinition of Military Strategy in International Relations," *World Politics,* XXVI, No. 4 (July 1974), pp. 473-508.

22. Janowitz, *The Professional Soldier,* p. 418.

23. J. A. Jackson, "The Irish Army and the Development of the Constabulary Concept," in Jacques van Doorn, ed., *Armed Forces and Society: Sociological Essays* (The Hague, 1968).

24. Charles C. Moskos, Jr., forthcoming.

25. Walter Millis and James Real, *The Abolition of War* (New York, 1963).

26. Thomas C. Schelling, "A Special Surveillance Force," in I. Wright, W. M. Evan, and D. Morton, eds., *Preventing World War III* (New York, 1962), pp. 87-105.

CIVIL-MILITARY RELATIONS IN THE
NEW NATIONS

In the comparative study of new nations, two different questions can be asked about the role of the military in political change. First, what characteristics of the military establishment of a new nation facilitate its involvement in domestic politics? Second, what are the capacities of the military to supply effective political leadership for a new nation striving for rapid economic development and social modernization?

These two questions seem to generate very similar answers. Those organizational and professional qualities that make it possible for the military of a new nation to accumulate political power, and even to take over political power, are the same as those which limit its ability to rule effectively. Thus, once political power has been achieved, the military must develop mass political organizations of a civilian type, or it must work out viable relations with civilian political groups. In short, while it is relatively easy for the military to seize power in a new nation, it is much more difficult for it to govern.

Social science literature is rich in its analysis of the social, economic, and political conditions of new nations that weaken parliamentary institutions and civilian political organizations and thereby increase the possibility of military intervention. It is the· purpose of this essay, however, to explore civil-military relations from the point of view of the internal social organization of the military, which conditions its political capacities. This includes the dimensions of organizational format, skill structure and career lines, social recruitment and education, and professional and political ideology, as well as cohesion and cleavage.

Adapted from *The Role of the Military in the Political Development of New Nations* (Chicago, 1964), pp. 1-29.

The focus of this essay can be stated alternatively in comparative terms. First, there is the comparative analysis of the military profession in old nations and new ones. Why are military officers of new nations, as compared with those in Western industrialized societies, more involved and more influential in domestic politics? Clearly, the social structure of their countries predisposes them to political activism. But to what extent can this greater involvement be accounted for by particular sociological characteristics of the military profession? Second, comparative analysis deals with variations in the extent and form of military involvement in domestic politics from country to country. The capacity to act in politics is hardly a constant. What characteristics of the military profession help account for differences in civil-military relations in different new nations?

Civil-Military Relations: Old Nations and New

Experience in civil-military relations in different Western nation-states has hardly been uniform. But where mass democracy has emerged, the intervention of the military establishment in domestic politics has become limited, and its influence is felt mainly in the conduct of foreign affairs and defense policies. Similarly, in one-party Communist regimes, the military has been neutralized in its internal political power, although, as in mass democratic states, it remains an important agent in influencing foreign affairs.

As a basis for comparing industrialized states with new nations, it is possible to identify two models of political-military or civilian-military relations—democratic and totalitarian.[1] Neither the democratic nor the totalitarian model, however, adequately describes civil-military relations in the "typical" new nation. These models are not applicable because the military has wider involvement in domestic economic, social, and political change.[2] Fundamentally, this derives from the weakness of civilian political institutions, as described by Edward Shils[3] and others. It is the result of the sheer quantity of resources that the military establishment, in comparison with other bureaucratic institutions and professional groups, has been able to accumulate.

In the second half of the twentieth century, the processes of government are so complex, even in the new nations, and the pressures of mass political movements are so intense, that personal military dictators are outmoded, or at best transitional devices. Therefore, models for describing the political activities of the military in new nations during the last fifteen years range from performing the minimal governmental functions essential for any nation-state to constituting themselves as the exclusive governing political group. For the purposes of analyzing the military in the political development of new nations, five types of civil-military relations can be identified: (1) authoritarian-personal control, (2) authoritarian-mass party, (3) democratic competitive and semi-competitive systems, (4) civil-military coalition, and (5) military oligarchy.

Although the first three differ markedly in the form of internal political control, they have the common feature that the military's involvement in domestic politics is at the minimal level; it is therefore possible to describe its activities as limited to the mark of sovereignty. As such, the officer corps is not involved in domestic partisan politics but functions as an institution symbolizing the independent and legitimate sovereignty of the new nation, both at home and abroad. The mark of sovereignty includes the military's contribution to internal law and order and to the policing of the nation's borders. Since new nations are immediately involved in international relations, the military is required as a token force for United Nations operations and regional security affairs.

Alternative political formats may limit the military to the role of a mark of sovereignty. The first is an authoritarian regime, which may be based on personal and traditional power, as formerly in Ethiopia, or it may be a newly developed personal autocracy, as formerly in South Vietnam. This is the (1) *authoritarian-personal* type of civil-military control and is likely to be found in nations just beginning the process of modernization. In a few countries the military is no more than a mark of sovereignty and is excluded from domestic politics by the power of civilian authoritarian political power; for example, in Ghana under Nkrumah, Mali, and Guinea. Such authoritarian power may be rooted in a one-party state, under strong personal leadership, without parliamentary institutions. This type of civil-military relations can be labeled (2) *authoritarian-mass party* control. In these states both the civilian police and paramilitary insti-tutions operate as counterweights to the military, which is small and not yet fully expanded. On the other hand, in a few nations, e.g., in Malaya and India, the military is limited to these functions because of the strength of competitive democratic institutions, and the pattern of civil-military relations which is based on civilian control can be called (3) *democratic-competitive.* In the democratic-competitive system, which must be defined to include semi-competitive systems, as in Tunisia and Morocco, civilian supremacy operates to limit the role of the military in part because colonial traditions have implanted a strong sense of self-restraint on the military. In these countries there are competing civilian institutions and power groups, as well as a mass political party which dominates domestic politics but permits a measure of political competition.

When the military expands its political activity and becomes a political bloc, the civilian leadership remains in power only because of the military's passive assent or active assistance. The extent of political competition decreases; and it is appropriate to describe such a pattern as a (4) *civil-military coalition* because of the crucial role of the armed forces. Here the military serves as an active political bloc in its support of civilian parties and other bureaucratic power groups. The civilian group is in power because of the assistance of the military. Indonesia provides an example of such political intervention. The military may act as an informal, or even explicit, umpire between competing political parties and political groups as it does in, for example, Turkey. The military may, at this level, be forced to establish a caretaker government, with a view to returning power to civilian political groups. Such were the intention and practice of the first Burmese military government and the intention of Pakistani military leaders. These alliances and caretaker governments are unstable; they frequently lead to a third and wider level of involvement, where the military sets itself up as the political ruling group as in, for example, Thailand, Egypt, and Sudan. The result is a (5) *military oligarchy,* because for a limited time, at least, the political initiative passes to the military. When an actual takeover occurs and the military becomes the ruling group, civilian political activity is transformed, constricted, and repressed.

But it is our basic assumption that the military operates at each level of political intervention, including the takeover of political power, as incomplete agents of political change. Thus an additional type of civil-military relations, in part hypothetical, and to some degree actually emerging, must be postulated. After "takeover," the military regime can begin to recognize the task of supplying national political leaders. At this level the military recognizes the need for a mass political base. It seeks to develop a broader political apparatus, either with its own personnel, under its direct supervision, or through a system of alliances with civilians. Trends in this direction already can be noted in Egypt, South Korea, and to a lesser extent in Pakistan.

There is no evolutionary process by which a new nation passes from one level of intervention to another, although a pattern of broadening commitments is discernible. It may well be possible for the military in some nations to limit its intervention to that of an active political bloc, along with other groups, and avoid becoming the political ruling group. But the task remains of clarifying the contributions of professional military to these different patterns of domestic politics, since these types give more concrete meaning to the forms of militarism in the new nations.

Historical and Economic Dimensions

The initial step in the comparative analysis of the military in the political development of new nations is to examine, even briefly, the historical and economic factors that fashioned these military establishments. That the objects of our analysis are highly diverse is an obvious fact, but one which complicates our task. The population range of new nations in 1960 varied from India with over 400 million to Gabon with less than .05 million. *The United Nations Demographic Yearbook* for 1960 lists, for Africa and Asia, sixty-four political reporting units with a population of over one million inhabitants, if China, Taiwan, Japan, and the Union of South Africa are excluded as special cases. From a population basis, is there a minimum level required to support, even with outside assistance, a military establishment which has internal political consequences? The level of one million population seems to include all the smaller nations with politically relevant military establishments, even though some of these establishments may be dependent on foreign assistance.

Among those nations with the highest level of economic development, the absence of democratic competitive systems is more noteworthy than their presence, for competitive systems are concentrated in the middle level of economic development. But the analysis is not without meaning if the general hypothesis is abandoned and the underlying process examined. Authoritarian-personal regimes are heavily concentrated among the nations with low economic development, for these nations are just embarking on economic development. These nations have a pattern of civil-military relations which reflects the past, for this is essentially the character of their authoritarian regimes. Moreover, it is true that there are no democratic-competitive regimes at the very bottom of the economic ladder. But the economic threshold is rather low for a democratic-competitive system. The basic conclusion is that, with higher economic levels, the outcome is as likely as not to be in the direction of military oligarchy, and perhaps somewhat more likely. Thus factors such as natural history of origin, time since independence, or level of economic development supply, at best, a limited point of entrance for understanding differences in the political role of the military in the new nations.

Social Structure and Military Organization

By what intellectual strategy can comparative analysis of the military be pursued if there is such marked variation between cultural-geographic area, natural history of origin, and sheer size? There are two strategies for extending the analysis beyond the case-study level. One approach is to focus on paired comparisons of two countries which have important similarities and yet have emerged with marked differences in civil-military relations: India and Pakistan, Nigeria and Ghana, Morocco and Indonesia. Despite the complexities, the alternative approach pursued in this essay is to make some simplifying assumptions and to extend the range of analysis to a very wide, if not the full, range of new nations.

Basically, the analysis rests on two pervasive assumptions about social structure and military organization. One focuses on the common societal context of the military in new nations, namely, new nations have chosen without exception the goal of modernization. They have embarked in varying degree on programs of managed rapid modernization and social change designed to transform their traditional social structure. Thus, despite differences in national culture and history, from this point of view it is assumed that the military is operating in societies which are confronted with rather similar political, economic, and social require-ments. Second, as compared with other institutions and bureaucracies, it is assumed that the military establishment has a variety of common organizational features. These common features condition and limit the capacity of the military profession to exercise political power.

The first assumption raises the question of what is meant when new nations are described as traditional societies in the process of social change. One conception of a traditional society focuses on stability and integration. A traditional society is one with long-standing and relatively unchanged social structure. In this view, the persistence of social and cultural forms is highlighted. Social changes start and become accelerated with the recent introduction of modern technology, modern adminis-tration, and Western values. The process produces increased economic potential, literacy, and urbanism, which corrode traditional forms. Social change is a new process in which there is a passage from traditional society through a transitional phase to modernity. It is a continuation of the "idea of progress" in a non-Western context.[4]

Such a view of social change in the new nations seems inadequate on various grounds. It fails to acknowledge the vast changes in economic and demographic growth that were transforming peasant economies even under colonial rule. It seems to assume that these peasant economies, before the advent of colonialism and Western contact, did not have societal-wide political institutions with strong influence on traditional social structure. It seems to imply that traditional societies were merely a collection of villages and communities with no superstructure; but, most important, this view fails to recognize the manner in which traditional values and traditional forms persist during modernization, even though these traditions become modified. Neo-traditional political movements arise which leave their mark on the meaning of "modernity" in non-Western nation-states.

Thus an alternative view of traditional society seems more appropriate for the task of analyzing the role of the military as an agent of social and political change. In this view, traditional society is a peasant society. Because it is a peasant society, the rate of social change may generally be slow; but peasant societies undergo change, including rapid and drastic change, on occasion, as peasant technology changes. In particular, as peasant societies, new nations were touched by colonialism in the past, and some were completely transformed by colonial agricultural and plantation systems. As most of the population is engaged in agriculture, the organization of a peasant society rests in the linkage between vast masses of rural population and tiny urban elites who manage the societal institutions. The peasant society is a society in which religious values are paramount. Therefore, an understanding of the sociological implications of traditional religion is essential for understanding the structure of these societies.[5]

The peasant society, like any form of social organization, has its sources of consensus and dissensus. One of the main characteristics of a peasant society is that it can tolerate or accommodate more social dissensus than can a modernized society. The simpler level of technology and division of labor requires less consensus and permits more disarticulation. Even more important in this regard, peasant societies have more limited collective aims and goals. As governments, the colonial regimes were political caretakers, concerned with avoiding the development of native political demands. Under colonialism, and under the impact of Western indirect rule, forms of accommodation had to emerge. But the processes of accommodation generally did not increase internal consensus. On the contrary, internal differentiation increased. In all emerging nations, new groups and new contenders for elite power arose who were oriented toward modernization in terms derived from the West. Dissensus increased with the advent of independence, as the governments strove to develop a base of popular support. But these same nations produced social movements which embodied traditional values. In some areas, traditional religious and political values had weakened under colonialism but became strengthened as independence became a reality. The success of these neo-traditional movements varies from country to country, and in the long run they may atrophy under the impact of modernization. But these neo-traditional movements have had significant impact in heightening nationalism. It is popular to think of the military in new nations as technocratic in orientation and as concerned with modernization, but the military is also concerned with legitimate authority and with historical and national traditions. In analyzing its political ideology and political behavior, one cannot overlook the impact of neo-traditionalism on the military.

The second assumption concerning the special organizational character of the military flows from the notion that the goals of an organization supply a meaningful basis for analyzing its bureaucratic structure. In some respects, the contemporary military establishment has the characteristics of any large-scale bureaucracy. But the military establishment—regardless of its societal context—has a unique character because the threat of violence is a permanent reality to its leaders. The results of previous combat and the pressure to prepare for future combat pervade the entire organization. The unique character of the military derives from the requirement that its key members be specialists in the use of violence.

Changing technology creates new patterns of combat and thereby modifies organizational behavior in the military. The more complex the technology of warfare, the narrower are the differences between military and nonmilitary establishments, because more officers have managerial and technical skills applicable to civilian enterprise. Yet even the most automated military establishment retains an organizational format that reflects the necessities of combat. Since the military establishments of new nations do not have nuclear capabilities, they still bear many essential characteristics of World War II military organization. Because their technology is relatively similar, they have relatively similar organizational features, particularly in their systems of hierarchy, status, and authority. They tend to develop similar procedures of recruitment and training, as well as of internal control, that in turn control the capacity of the military to intervene in domestic politics. On the other hand, it is more difficult to isolate internal factors which vary from one military establishment to another and which account for differences in political behavior.

The following illustrative propositions about internal organization are offered to help explain the patterns of political behavior of the military in new nations as compared with industrialized nations, on the basis of available data. They are also designed to throw light on differences among the new nations and on the difficulties that confront the military when it becomes the ruling group and must seek to develop mass political support.

1. *Organizational format.* The capacity of the military establishment in new nations to intervene in domestic politics derives from its distinctive military format, namely, its control of the instruments of violence; its ethos of public service and national identification; and its skill structure, which combines managerial ability with a heroic posture. (In part, this proposition is designed to help explain the greater initial political capacity of the military in comparison with other, civilian groups.)

2. *Skill structure and career lines.* While there has been a trend toward "civilianizing" the military profession, the officer corps in the new nations have important limitations in producing those leadership skills in bargaining and political communication that are required for sustained political leadership. These limitations include the absence of a tradition for dealing with clients and publics outside of the military. (While this proposition applies to both industrialized and new nations, it has particular relevance to new nations because of the relative absence of parliamentary and legal institutions for controlling the military.)

3. *Social recruitment and education.* In the new nations, the military establishment is recruited from the middle and lower-middle classes, drawn mainly from rural areas or hinterlands. In comparison with Western European professional armies, there is a marked absence of a history of feudal domination. As a result, the military profession does not have strong allegiance to an integrated upper class which it accepts as its political leader, nor does it have a pervasive conservative outlook. Military education contributed to an innovating outlook toward modernization. (This proposition helps to account for the differences between "army and society" in the new nations and the industrialized ones.)

4. *Professional and political ideology.* While it is impossible to identify a military ideology in the new nations, common ideological themes are found which help to explain the professional officers' political behavior. These include a strong sense of nationalism, a puritanical outlook, acceptance of extensive government control of social and economic change, and a deep distrust of organized civilian politics. As a result of social background, education, and career experiences, military personnel of the new nations become interested in politics, but they maintain a strong distrust of organized politics and civilian political leaders. (As in the case of social recruitment and education, the analysis of political ideology

presents a proposition which contrasts the military of industrialized nations with that of the new nations.)

5. *Social cohesion.* The ability of officers to intervene in domestic politics and produce stable leadership is related to internal social cohesion. The military establishments of new nations differ markedly in their internal social cohesion because of differences in training, indoctrination, operational experience, and intergenerational cleavages. (This proposition relates to differences among the armed forces of the various new nations.)

6. *Political intervention.* The "takeover" of power by the military in new nations has generally followed the collapse of efforts to create democratic-type institutions; the military has tended not to displace the single mass-party authoritarian political regimes. After "takeover," the military regime faces the task of supplying national political leadership and of developing mass support for its programs. While this phase is only emerging, the evidence seems to indicate that, if the military is to succeed in this political goal, it must develop a political apparatus outside of the military establishment but under its direct domination. (Comparative analysis in the case of this proposition is designed to help clarify the conditions under which the military comes to recognize the need for mass political support and is able to develop it.)

Notes

1. For exposition of these models, see "Military Elites and the Study of War," above.

2. Harold Lasswell's concept of the "garrison state" is more applicable (see "The Garrison State and Specialist on Violence," *American Journal of Sociology,* XLVI [January 1941], pp. 455-468). The garrison state is a model for describing the weakening of civil supremacy, especially in democratic states, because of the "permanent" threat of mass warfare. While the end result of the garrison state approximates aspects of the totalitarian state, the garrison state has a different natural history. It is, however, not the direct domination of politics by the military. Since modern industrial nations cannot be ruled merely by the political domination of a single small leadership bloc, the garrison state is not a throwback to a military dictatorship. It is the end result of the growth of power by the military elite under conditions of prolonged international tension. The garrison state is a new pattern of coalition in which military groups, directly and indirectly, wield unprecedented political and administrative power. The military retains its organizational independence provided it makes appropriate alliances with civil political factions. As the garrison state requires a highly developed industrial base, the concept is not directly applicable to the new nations.

3. Edward A. Shils, *Political Development in the New States* (The Hague, 1962).

4. For an exposition of this point of view, see Daniel Lerner, *The Passing of Traditional Society: Modernizing the Middle East* (Glencoe, Ill., 1958).

5. See Clifford Geertz, *The Religion of Java* (Glencoe, Ill., 1960), for an example of this type of approach to the analysis of peasant society.

COMPARATIVE ANALYSIS OF
MIDDLE EASTERN MILITARY INSTITUTIONS

Introduction

Despite the extensive participation of the military in Middle Eastern politics, past and present, research on these armed forces has not been a central ingredient in the contemporary emergence of the comparative analysis of social and political change. Scholarship on Muslim military institutions has been mainly descriptive; and even the amount of such literature has been limited as compared with work in other regions. The publication of the expanded version of *Army Officers in Arab Politics and Society* by Eliezer Be'eri is an ambitious effort at comparative analysis.[1]

To the outsider like myself, the field of Middle Eastern studies generally is characterized by particular outstanding monographic contributions and a growing body of highly competent writings. Analytic and comparative studies have not been pursued with vigor or intensity since the intellectual ferment of comparative history and comparative sociology has been slow to manifest itself for this area, at least slower than for other areas of the world.

No doubt specialists on the Middle East will explain to the outsider the special problems of their scholarship. It has been argued that the lack of primary data and research is an issue at hand; but this appears to be more of a description of the state of affairs than an explanation. The same can be said of the claim about the difficulty of undertaking research in the Middle East although work on the military faces formidable obstacles. One can be intrigued by the repeated observation of Middle Eastern scholars that the internal diversity of the region presents a subject matter which defies or at least complicates systematic comparative analysis. Every specialist sees his topic as more difficult than any other comparable problem. Some Middle Eastern specialists continually seem to emphasize the ideographic and complex aspects of their subject matter. For example, J. C. Hurewitz has proclaimed 'the study of military politics in nonindustrial states is a good deal more complicated than scholars, policy-makers and journalists, to say nothing of laymen, seem ready to admit.'[2] Fortunately, in his volume he is concerned with an emerging comparative approach. Within limits diversity and complexity offer the basis of comparative analysis. The real issue is the adequacy of alternative explanations and their limitations.

The provocative idea has been offered that the Middle East, until the early 1960s, with such exceptions as Turkey, Lebanon and Israel, had been a center of resistance to social and political change. Such resistance apparently does not stimulate the same intellectual interest—both internal and external to the area—as does the actual process of change. Therefore, it is not an accident that for the Middle East, scholarship on Turkey has been the locus of some of the best systematic research on societal processes. With the quickening of the pace of change, a broader focus of scholarship is likewise anticipated.

The explanation of the present state of Middle Eastern comparative studies is in good measure an expression of the training, perspectives and organization of scholars who work on these matters. The study of the classical periods has been developed and it has served as the center of interest; scholars have had to devote extensive energy to the study of difficult languages. The field has not been successful in incorporating 'outsiders' concerned with analytic issues nor has it had sufficient 'insiders' who have been profoundly sympathetic if not leaders in the development of more explicit analytic and comparative approaches. The contributions of Gustav E. von Grunebaum are representative of a social science approach to the traditional subject matter of Islamic studies.[3]

The state of research on a given geographic area can be judged on the basis of the extent to which its results become part of the general literature of social science.[4] In other words, to what extent are the available writings incorporated in the thinking and scholarship of those whose interests are not mainly on that particular area? The last three decades have seen the completion of a growing series of studies which contribute to a deeper understanding of the emergence and contemporary transformation of the nation state in its variant forms. From a growing range of efforts in depth the following are but illustrative of the range of writings on particular societies which bear with them explicit analytical frameworks: Franz Neumann's *Behemoth*[5] on the rise and decline of Nazi

Germany; Barrington Moore's *Terror and Progress in the U.S.S.R.;* Chalmers Johnson in *Peasant Nationalism and Communist Power;* and Ronald Dore, *Land Reform in Japan.* Of course, Bernard Lewis' *The Emergence of Modern Turkey* needs to be included; but this does not deny the observation on the relative state of Middle Eastern studies.[6] In the execution of explicit and 'grand' comparative macro-sociological analyses, the Middle East tends to be deemphasized precisely because of the state of the available literature. Thus, again by way of example, Barrington Moore's *Social Origins of Dictatorship and Democracy* does not include comparative materials from the Middle East; and this cannot be the case because of the lack of analytical relevance for his basic thesis.[7]

In preparing my *The Military in the Political Development of New Nations,* I found the greatest difficulty in assembling materials on the Middle East.[8] I would also claim that this part of the analysis is the weakest. In the years since the completion of this essay new monographic literature bearing on armed forces and society has appeared but, again, compared with other areas, such as Africa and Latin America, even the descriptive study materials still lag very much behind.

This paper is based on a review of available literature and seeks to offer some illustrative hypotheses.[9] The underlying assumption is that the comparative analysis of armed forces and society suffers precisely because of the inability to incorporate the experiences and transformations of the Middle East. One of the core intellectual problems is the role of Islamic religious values in influencing the development of military institutions and conditioning the forms of political behavior of the military.[10] The outsider and the student of comparative institutions look forward to an adequate exploration of this issue which of necessity remains mainly outside the scope of the paper. Western military institutions, correspondingly, have been rooted in the religious values and cultural patterns of Christianity. For Europe the work of Max Weber on economic organization requires renewal in terms of the emergence of military institutions and of 'rationality' in the military context.

Instead, the focus of this paper is on two key issues dealing with the political behavior of the armed forces in the Middle East. First is the need to offer some hypotheses to explain the socio-political perspectives and ideology of the profession, including its elite members, starting with the period after World War I and continuing into the contemporary period. Long standing historical traditions cannot be overlooked. While there are variations in particular nation states, fundamentally in contrast to the persistence of a conservative or status quo outlook of the military profession of the industrialized nations of Western Europe which arose from a feudal background (and correspondingly of the United States), the officer corps of the Middle East have shown a markedly different and positive commitment toward societal change, with progressively greater emphasis on 'socialist' and radical symbolism. The strategy of this type of analysis involves a broad 'idea type' analysis of the socio-political history of the military profession in Western European feudalism in contrast to its emergence in the societies of the Middle East. Social origins and social recruitment are the obvious points of entrance for this comparative problem. Ozbudun's formulation directed to Turkey has relevance for the Middle East more generally, 'It may be hypothesized that armies recruited essentially from lower and middle classes are more likely to produce reformist military regimes than armies of feudal or upper class origin.[11] Such a proposition is at best a starting point for a more detailed analysis since it is essential to make use of more refined categories which reflect the details of occupational structure, geographic affiliation and cultural elements.

It is hazardous to compare the social recruitment of military groups in the developing nations with their counterparts in the Western world if the analysis proceeds solely in terms of Western concepts and categories. American sociologists have been prepared to engage in comparative analysis of social stratification by applying those categories which they have found appropriate to the social structure of the United States and Western Europeans to other countries. It is not adequate to make use of a single and uniform set of categories for the comparison of a group of industrialized countries, let alone for a broader range of new nations and old. Nevertheless, even broad comparative analysis highlights differences in social recruitment. Moreover, the conceptual approach of this paper will seek to focus on the interplay of social background with professional socialization (military education and career experiences).

The second objective of this paper is the more specific task to explain the relative success and failure of military leaders and military regimes after the assumption of power, particularly in political affairs. There exists a rich body of comparative political sociology on the developing nations which focuses attention on the social structural and cultural dimensions of the developing nations and which accounts for the weakness of political movements which have sought to implant constitutional democracies.[12] The intervention of the military in domestic politics is the norm; persistent patterns of civil supremacy are the deviant cases that require special exploration. It needs to be kept in mind that, as both Halpern and Hurewitz point out, in the majority of military Middle East nation states, military intervention in internal political regimes follow the crisis or breakdown in efforts to create parliamentary systems.[13] There is also a body of literature on the characteristics of military forces which, in one form or another, enable them to intervene so rapidly and dramatically in internal politics.[14]

The central issue is to account for the relative performance, or at least realism, of leaders of military regimes once an intervention has taken place. In this regard, the strategy of comparative analysis focuses on a point by point comparison of one specific country with another; in such an approach Turkey emerges as a nodal point for comparative analysis.

The question of the criteria for assessing realism or political effectiveness is by no means clear cut, but an effort as assessment is worthwhile. Has enough time elapsed in order to make a judgment? The question of leadership succession can be viewed as one crucial aspect. On the other hand, ability to hand power back to civilian leaders including even the recognition of the importance of such a goal is an equally relevant dimension. Economic progress is essential, e.g., Pakistan and Algeria; but in the case of Pakistan, it was not accompanied by sufficient political innovation.

It is assumed that military establishments are at best only partially equipped to serve as the political regimes, regardless of the form of government they are able to impose. The successful military regime —whether it holds power for a short or long period of time, whether it operates as a coalition partner on the basis of a personal authoritarian leader or an oligarchic ruling group—must recognize this fact and respond accordingly. The options available to it may vary—supplying energetic leaders to civilian parties, serving as an umpire between competing groups, or creating its own mass political organization. But the essential question is to probe the factors that lead military groups which become involved in politics to take steps to separate (in the language of the sociologist to differentiate) themselves from political organizations, or at least to contribute to institution building in the political arena.

The Emergence of Modern Military Institutions:
Europe Versus Middle East

Exploration of the first hypothesis concerning difference in the orientation—conservative versus innovative or radical as between Western

Europe versus the Middle East—rests on an examination of the long term emergence of the military profession. Despite the prior existence of large scale military formations in the Middle East and the Far East, the modern military establishment is a contribution of Western industrial civilization. In essence, modern military institutions have had their origin in Northwest Europe and have slowly diffused throughout the world community. Armies can be thought of as being modern when they (a) incorporate the result of intensive scientific and technological progress and (b) make use of bureaucratic and managerial forms; that is, they are 'rational' in the sense of the term as used by Max Weber. Modern military institutions—and the various political militarism and civil supremacy that have resulted—have meant the gradual emergence of a military profession with a system of selection, education and training, career promotion, honor (code of ethics) and a measure of self-regulation.[15]

The conception of the military profession in the literature of social science, and especially as used by the students of comparative civil-military relations, takes the case of the European profession as the 'ideal type,' as the mode, so to speak.[16] The widely divergent experiences in military organization of the Ottoman Empire or the case of Communist China have yet to be incorporated effectively into comparative analysis.

But the historical model of the European military (and derivatively of the United States), supplies a basis for understanding its conservative socio-political bias and the range and forms of its political behavior as the West became industrialized.

In this conception, the military professional is rooted in the historical experiences of European feudalism—and the emphasis is on the term European. Military defeats, political and social revolutions, and the profound transformations that major advances in technology have produced have not eliminated this historical continuity and the relevance of organizational traditions. Up to the end of World War II, there was a reality and imagery of professional continuity which has been equalled in few professional groups.

The following elements are part of the composite model of the feudal or aristocratic model of the military before industrialism had its full impact and out of which the contemporary professional forms developed. Basically, the military were not a distinct social or functional group. To the contrary, the size of the skilled officer group was small and the civilian and military elites were socially and functionally integrated. There was a rigorous hierarchy in both the civilian and military sectors which delineated both the source of authority and the prestige of any member of the military. The low specialization of the military made it possible for the political elites and their kin to supply the bulk of the necessary leadership for the military establishment. Birth, family connections, and common ideology insured that the military would embody the ideology of the dominant groups in society.

The feudal military was in effect based on landed position. Land remained in the hands of family groups through various patterns of primogeniture. Military victories (and correspondingly military defeats) influenced the distribution and redistribution of land; but the essential values of the military were an expression of a conservative maintenance of the privileged position of a landed elite group. The classic pattern has been viewed as one in which the aristocratic family which supplied one son to politics (or governmental administration) and one to the military. In effect and especially in the later historical phases the main source of officers was the families of the lower aristocracy or rural gentry. This was in part necessitated by the sheer manpower requirements.

Progressively the tasks of military life became more and more irksome, time consuming and interfered with the way of the life of a nobleman. The history of the emergence of the military profession was one of an ever broadening base of recruitment during the nineteenth century.[17] Mass armies, because of the sheer numbers, required ever greater reliance on middle class sons to man the officer corps. Middle class personnel first entered the profession of arms in the artillery and engineers where scientific and technical training were required, and where the style of life not only required more diligent preparation but was more and more at variance with the self-conceptions of upper class gentry of heroism and gallantry. In turn middle class elements spread steadily through the essential infantry units. In France, the French Revolution brought some of these changes earlier and with drastic abruptness, but the long term trends were not at marked variance with those of the other nations of Western Europe.[18] Only in the selected infantry units with special attachment to the royal household and in the cavalry did the predominance of the nobility and gentry persist until the outbreak of World War I.

What was crucial in this process was that the middle class cadres were recruited at a rate which permitted them to be assimilated into the norms and values of the existing feudal officer corps. Moreover, the impact of the professional education served to maintain the existing standards of behavior and the conservative socio-political outlook. Officer cadets were recruited early and sent to special preparatory schools. The German Kadettenschule represented the most intensive example of this type of education and indoctrination in support of the ethos of the military profession. Officer education was mainly technical, plus a continued informal exposure to the dominant political outlook. There was no development of a significant or politically important modernizing outlook even among the most technically oriented officer cadres. In short, the interplay of social recruitment and professionalization produced a politics of being above politics—with an inherently conservative orientation for the bulk of the officer corps. (These orientations persisted up through the outbreak of World War I when the actual contributions of the landed upper social classes had become most limited in numbers.)

For Western Europe, it is impossible to make categorical statements about differences toward politics in armies whose officers came from aristocratic background as opposed to middle class based institutions. The aristocratic oulook, which operated to inhibit direct intervention by the military in domestic partisan politics, was compatible with different internal socio-political arrangements. In England, the military profession found itself integrated into a parliamentary system with effective civilian supremacy and a military policy which supported an active overseas imperialism. In Germany, the aristocratic outlook led to Prussian type militarism which actively supported the content of conservative politics and, subsequently, to the acceptance of National Socialism. The Prussian military outlook did seek to infuse civilian society with its notion of service to the state; but it was basically conservative, and hardly reformist, in any fundamental social or political sense.

By contrast, in the Middle East the traditions of the military—as a social group and, subsequently, as an emerging professional cadre in the nineteenth century—were very different. With specific exceptions, described below, the military operated or were created as a civil service type establishment of the central government without the social and personal connections to landed upper strata. There were examples of a 'gentry' type cavalry but of limited scope and importance. Mostly in the Ottoman Empire, it was a long standing practice for the Sultanate to recruit and develop a distinct bureaucratic stratum from various social groups including the very lowest to staff the military.[19] There was a strong emphasis on wide geographic dispersion of recruitment. As a result these officers had primary attachments to the 'government.' Feudalism as it was known in Western Europe was not to be found in the Ottoman Empire. Bernard Lewis describes the elements of feudalism[20] that existed; and he uses the term 'bureaucratic feudalism' which helps highlight the essential differences.

There was no process by which land was accumulated by a nobility and passed on to the eldest son and which supplied an independent powerbase. Moreover, land was not the basis of a culture and value system which penetrated into the life of the military. Land was used as a reward for outstanding military service to specific figures, but the scope of such distribution seems to have been limited and the results subject to redistribution by the monarch.

The Janissaries were, of course, the epitome of this type of military. As the need for technological innovation became more and more pressing at the end of the eighteenth century, they became a source of resistance to improved organization. When in 1826 they were abolished, this act represented at most a shift in the source of recruitment in a long established civil service type military establishment. Thus, within the Ottoman Empire which became the base of modern Turkey, there was no feudal tradition nor did the colonial power encounter an aristocratic based military when the dismembered portions of the Ottoman Empire came under Western rule.

What were the exceptions to this pattern? There were some instances where for long or shorter periods of time a social equivalent to the Western model developed, but these were of limited political consequence. In fact, in a sample of fifty-two nations of Africa, South East and Far East Asia, residues of 'feudal' or upper social strata in the military were more present in the Middle East than for the other culture areas of the new nations.[21] Colonial domination of this area came comparatively late, and was more indirect and more limited in scope. Therefore, the standard practice of the colonial powers of disbanding the existing traditional armies was not universal.

One interesting case was British rule in Pakistan where sons of leading families from the northern hill country were recruited in regiments of the Indian Army, which later became the core of the Pakistan army at the time of the partition. This process was more a reflection of the recruitment of distant ethnic groups who were assumed to be loyal to the British government if only because of their opposition to Hindu political movements. In nineteenth century Egypt, the upper ranks of the officer corps were heavily weighted with alien elements—Turks, Kurds and Albanians—who were a kind of foreign elite rather than an indigenous landed aristocracy. Under British mandate, Egyptians of upper class and landed background were concentrated in a number of elite cavalry units patterned after the image of British high status regiments.[22] They were part of the system of indirect rule that supported the pashas, and, in fact, these cavalry units were the locus of momentary opposition to the Nasser movement. In the early years of the independent Syrian Army, 'leadership came largely from the upper echelons of Syrian society' and in many ways was connected with the country and 'fifty families.'[23] But even in these cases, these upper status groups did not exercise effective dominance or they were rapidly submerged in the transitional period after independence. Other exceptions could be found in those nations where colonial rule was essentially absent, such as Saudi Arabia and Persia. In these cases the military was built on tribal loyalties and one cannot speak of the emergence of a modern military force until after World War II. The military force created in Jordan is the exceptional case of a modern type army force which emphasized a network of tribal loyalties and which, as of 1970, remained loyal to the existing monarch.[24] In the early 1920s the Arab officers in the Jordanian Legion had seen service in the Ottoman Empire. The new recruitment was mainly Bedouin with many coming from non-Jordanian tribes—mostly from Saudi Arabia and Iraq. Gradually there was a weakening of the heavy reliance on such Bedouin personnel.[25]

In assessing the consequences of the social origins of the military in the Middle East, the argument being offered is not the one presented by Manfred Halpern in *The Politics of Social Change in the Middle East and North Africa.*[26] He argues that 'as the army officer corps came to represent the interests and views of the new middle class, it became the most powerful instrument of that class.' In this view, the the process of social and political change and the political behavior of the military are expressions of social class interest. The source of military strength depends on its ability to reflect and to implement the requirements of the middle class, especially those portions which have come to be called the new middle class. He is aware and enters a note of caution by raising the direct alternative proposition supplied by Morroe Berger, namely, that the 'military regime, it might be more accurate to say, has really been seeking to create a class to represent.'[27]

Both of these formulations are much too oversimplified to encompass societal change in the Middle East. As mentioned above, the broad idea of class structure as derived from Western Europe must be applied to Middle Eastern societies, especially to the Ottoman Empire, with reservation and discretion. Second, the term new middle classes is hardly appropriate to describe in a refined fashion the social recruitment of the military, as shall be elaborated below. Third, the notion—broad or narrow—of socio-economic strata does not encompass the other essential aspects of social structure of the Middle East, namely, bureaucratic institutions, ethnic-communal solidarities and urban aggregations.

The issue for sociological investigation needs to be stated in different
and more sequential terms, for we are not seeking to account for military
takeovers but rather to explicate the political orientations and ideology of
the military officer corps. In 1964, I wrote that 'there are many steps
between the impact of social origins and the political perspectives of a
professional group. Especially in the military, the values of early
socialization are refashioned by education and career experience.'[28] This
was a general formulation, for I was quick to add that 'in shaping the
political perspectives of the military, however, social origins seem to be of
greater importance in the new nations than in contemporary Western
industrialized nations. Differences in background, such as rural versus
urban, are sharper in their social meaning.' It is with this perspective that I
approach the data on both the nineteenth century and the more
contemporary period.

Social Origins and Professional Socialization

In assessing the available data on the more contemporary social
recruitment of the Middle East, it would be highly appropriate if
independent and primary sources could be presented confirming the
arguments presented above. Much of what has been said about historical
origins and entered into the literature is based on impressionistic
observations and especially on inferences drawn from the institutional
practices of the military in the Ottoman Empire and elsewhere in the
Middle East.[29] For the period since World War I, there are some more
adequate data on Turkey collected by Frederick W. Frey, on Egypt by
Eliezer Be'eri and by Ayad al-Qazzas on Iraq.[30]

The limited available amount of data, plus the historical arguments
about institutional practices present a plausible case. The available data
make it possible for us to move beyond the notion of 'lower middle-
class'—which probably did not fit the structure of the Middle East in the
nineteenth century—to an investigation of the specific occupation groups
which contributed their sons to the military. We are dealing with a
professional bureaucratic group whose social composition derived from an
amalgam of three major sources of recruitments. In each case, it is possible
to make inferences about the motivation which led them into the military
and the kinds of values they brought into the military.

Using the Turkish case as the modal type and the case for which some
of the best data exist, there is reason to believe that there has been a great
deal of stability in the social recruitment from the end of the nineteenth

century to the middle of the twentieth century. The first source for the officer corps is the sons of the officer corps itself. In part, this is the normal process of occupational inheritance in any profession which is particularly strong in the military profession (but on the basis of detailed studies, no stronger than selected professions such as the medical profession). In addition, special emphasis on self-recruitment derives from the political reliability that such recruitment is presumed to generate. The same emphasis has been reported for the Egyptian army.[31] Second, are the sons of the minor civil servants, bureaucrats and closely related occupations with modest educational background but for whom service in the state apparatus is important. Third are the sons of small land holders and merchants located in provincial towns and capitals. The absence of the sons of doctors, lawyers, and journalists is striking. We are not dealing with the 'free professions' as representatives of the new middle class, particularly those based on scientific and intellectual pursuits.[32]

This pattern is documented indirectly by the data on the social background of samples of deputies in the Turkish assembly for the period 1920-1957. Of the sample of 32 from whom social background data could be collected, their fathers' occupations were distributed as follows: the largest group were sons of the military, 47 percent; next trade and agriculture with 25 percent, followed by government, 13 percent. From the professions only 3 percent were from law, in addition to 3 percent from religious backgrounds (16 percent were other).[33]

Ayad al-Qazzaz's analysis of the occupational origins of the Iraqi military officers converges with the findings of those from Turkey.[34] Eliezer Be'eri has reported a study of the social origins of a sample of 87 Egyptian officers who were killed in the Palestine War, 1948-1949; for 54 adequate biographical data are available.[35] The mixture of social origins was the familiar pattern of sons of middle level civil servants, a considerable number of army officers, merchants, village notables, including numerous sons of umda, and small landholders. (An additional measure of the extent of military sons, especially among the activists was the fact that half of the officers of the Revolutionary Command Council of 1953 had relatives who were officers.)

These findings parallel those for Turkey, although Be'eri gives the impression in his interpretation that there was a somewhat larger contribution from higher social status groups, including the upper middle class. This may have reflected differences in Egyptian social structure, differences in recruitment patterns under the mandate, but it may merely reflect differences in categorization since I found the data difficult to assess at points.

The comparability with the Turkish data and with the 'ideal typical' pattern of the Middle East can be seen from Be'eri's observation that there was not a single officer from the top hundred great landowning group, nor were any related to the 'few hundred families of great landowners, bankers, industrialists and big business.' To the contrary, even the proportion living off the rents from landed property—even small estates was limited; rather, two-thirds were of families whose relatives were salaried employees.[36]

The selective recruitment into the military profession in the Middle East (and for that matter in developing nations more generally) is conditioned by the relative prestige of the military as a professional opportunity for one's son. The historical traditions of the military in the Middle East, including Turkey as the heritage of the Ottoman Empire, have conditioned favorable military self-concepts and positive popular attitudes toward the importance of the military as a social institution. However, the military profession has not emerged as one of the highest ranks in prestige as a vocation. In a more precise formulation, the interest of a family in having sons enter the military is related to the social position of the fathers. This is even the case for Turkey in the 1950s. Ergun Ozbudun argues that 'the military . . . has always offered better avenues of advancement to the sons of lower and lower-middle classes. The appeal of the military profession to what is identified as the "growth elements" of the society—modern intellectuals, technicians, the innovators and entrepreneurs—has never been great during the history of the Republic and was even less so in the 1950s. In fact, if any trend could be established it would in all probability indicate a marked decline in the prestige of the military profession. Engineering, law, medicine, commerce and banking were the most sought after careers during this period: few sons of middle class families ever thought of the military as a career.'[37]

He offers as evidence the vocational prestige in a 1959 survey of Lycee-level students. For regular Lycee students, he reported their response to the question as to which occupation did they feel the greatest respect: 55.9 percent stated the free professions while only 13.1 percent mentioned the military.[38]

There is another element in the status factors and values at work in recruitment into the military profession; namely, the intellectual level and analytical powers of the military profession. Of course, men of great intellectual powers have entered the military and the impact of a major war can bring to the fore individuals of remarkable capacities. But the military as a bureaucratic group cannot be judged by its exceptional and conspicuous leaders. The military strives to recruit the most intelligent and able men it can. But there is a difference between intelligence and intellectuality (including both analytic and abstract skills). The military competes with free professions and with a range of other science based professions in recruiting its cadres. In developing and in industrialized nations, it does not get the most intellectual and science oriented personnel—both in terms of personal interests and family background. The military is more of a heroic profession—with strong administrative components—which are required to directly impose some order on an intractable environment.

Harold Lasswell's notion of the skill structure and the skill requirements of political activists is crucial. In general, the military does not attract men who have strong symbolic interests and skills which are part of the requirements of political leadership. This is less the case for the Middle East because of the traditions of the military; and in specific cases, men have even entered the military with political interests in mind because other avenues were blocked. Those military officers who develop political involvements are revealing skills and orientations which were originally secondary or which were accumulated in the course of their career. As one rises in the military, abilities in interpersonal and symbolic skill are necessary and are often developed. These skills carry over to the requirements of political leadership generally.[39]

In interpreting these data on occupational background of military officers, three points should be kept in mind. First, we are dealing not only with status and professional aspirations. The career choice of those who enter the military reflects also the values of their families. This is patently obvious in the case of a military family. In addition, for the sons of the minor civil servants and even the small landholder and merchant, there is a built-in commitment to the model of personal success in a bureaucratic setting, and the concomitant inclination toward statism or etatism as the legitimate basis for social and political change. The individual entrepreneur and the sense of individual responsibility which one would associate with the urban families of the free professions and of highly developed finance and trade are relatively absent.

Second, occupational origins and background cannot be separated from geographical affiliation. Because of the practice of recruitment the sources of personnel are highly dispersed and tend to represent the hinterland rather than the major urban centers. The low importance placed on prior higher education operates to facilitate recruitment from the hinterland; the military serves as an avenue for social mobility for those who do not have access to the superior educational institutions of the major urban areas. The result is to produce a professional group with wide geographical representation and a strong potential for developing a sense of national identity. Third, nevertheless, there are cases of imbalances in regional recruitment which have the result of emphasizing particular religious or political minorities. Hurewitz is justified in emphasizing the importance of 'such horizontal cleavages' (ethnic, linguistic, sectarian and even at times nomadic communities).[40]

He points out that such cleavages contributed to the difficulties which the military elites of Syria and Iraq had to face. These cleavages in effect have resulted from the fact that the officers were disproportionately recruited from particular primordial groups, often minority groups. In Syria, it was from the Alawis and the Druze; in Iraq, from the Sunni Muslims. While comparable measures are hard to develop, it does appear that for the Middle East, within existing national entities, these sources of cleavage are probably less marked than in other cultural areas of Africa and Asia. Moreover, in many countries after independence, there is a conscious effort to reduce such regional imbalances precisely because of the political instabilities they generate.

It is at this point that it is possible to note the interplay of social recruitment and professional socialization. Basically, while in Western Europe the social origin factors worked to support the professional education in producing political isolation and a conservative commitment to the status quo, the interaction of these two dimensions in the Ottoman Empire and, subsequently, in other parts of the Middle East, worked in the opposite direction. We are here dealing not only with the formal instruction but with the effective impact of the experiences of cadet officer training. The German officers who taught technical subjects in the military organization had very different consequences in Germany than in Turkey. In fact, it is striking to note that some of the strongest political commitments were developed in the men who were being trained in technical and medical subjects. Moreover, political interests developed very early while in officer training, not too many years later with higher rank as is the case in the U.S. military. In short, the absence of an aristocratic tradition has meant the absence of common restraint in military education which would limit the military in its political orientations.

In the Middle East, the military is a bureaucratic group, and like other such groups, it is more directly involved in administrative politics. When the Turkish army began to accept the notion that it was above politics, it was the result of the efforts of a charismatic leader; it was a norm which, during the period of modernization, had to be developed. Likewise the absence of an aristocratic social tradition implies that the military has less stake in the existing social structure. While the social origin hardly determined its professional ideology, it did contribute to a bureaucratic and managerial outlook which has been congenial to social change.

As a result of this interplay of social background and professional indoctrination, a number of 'ideological' orientations of the Middle Eastern military can be noted. First, it is common place that the military in general are fiercely nationalistic, and in the Middle East, the military are highly developed in this regard. However, in examining military nationalism there are more questions to be raised than answers in the existing literature, for we are dealing with the interplay of traditional Muslim values with modern conceptions of national statehood. In examining Middle Eastern nationalism, I would offer the hypothesis, contrary to much of the literature, that the military reflect the development of nationalist sentiment by civilian political and intellectual groups as much as they are active agents of nationalist sentiment. Moreover, as mentioned above, there are examples of powerful internal 'nationalistic' cleavages which the military as military cannot eliminate or even contain. In the case of Turkey, the role of the military in 'nation building' was grounded in the ability of Ataturk to define more meaningfully national boundaries. The army he constructed reflected a greater degree of homogeneity. The extent to which truncated Turkey had a more homogeneous and more nationalistic military force can be seen by Rustow's analysis of the social composition of the Ottoman Army Commanders, 1914-1918, as compared with the nationalist commanders in 1919-1922.[41] Not only were the Ankara government's military officers much younger, but their geographic background was now much more concentrated in Anatolia. In short, the ability of the military to perform a 'nation building role' depends on the existence of a pre-existing base of ethnic and cultural homogeneity.

Second, at the root of the military ideology of the Middle East is the theme of the acceptance, in varying degrees, of collective public enterprise as a basis for achieving social and economic change. In the Ottoman Empire the conception of statism was central and the military an integral part of this ideology. Social origins and professional indoctrination served to perpetuate and strengthen such thinking. While attraction for statism in a mild or undifferentiated form is present in most of the military of the developing nations of the Middle East, it has emerged more rapidly and more extensively into an active socialist language—without necessary regard to actual practices. Here the impact of the Western colonialism is at work. Western powers have come to be thought of antagonistically not only in terms of their colonial past, but in terms of a contemporary economic system which despite its material achievement is not worthy of emulation. The desire for governmental intervention and preoccupation with applying military planning to economic problems lead rapidly to a language of socialism.

Third, there is a pervasive paradox in the political ideology of the military which is relevant for understanding their actual political behavior. Social background, together with professional education, operate to make the military accessible to politics, but at the same time there are important factors which serve to create barriers between the military and civilian political elites. The rural, or more accurately, the hinterland social background coupled with lower middle class or bureaucratic occupational origins, contributed to a lack of social integration with other elites, especially political elites. In many Middle Eastern countries there is a split in values between the hinterland and the metropolitan social fabric. Since the officer corps has its roots in the countryside, its social orientation is critical of sophisticated upper status urban values, which it comes to consider corrupt and even decadent.[42]

This anti-urban outlook seems to be reenforced by the professional indoctrination and style of life of the military community. Elsewhere I have written that 'these aspects of the social background of the officer corps seem to have almost contradictory implications. The military is hostile to what it believes are self-indulgent urban values; it is oriented to modernization and to technological development.' This does not mean that the military are free of corruption when they enter politics; it does mean that the military—both before and after political involvement— display a strong skepticism and even hostility to professional political leaders. It is essential to recall that in most Middle Eastern countries the military have become involved in politics after the failure of civilian parliamentary efforts. These failures serve to strengthen military stereo-types that political leaders are talkers and not doers. But the split runs deeper reflecting differences in social groupings, professional styles of life and conceptions of social reality. The professional military do not readily display appreciation of the skills of political leadership which seeks to proceed on the basis of discussion, persuasion and negotiation. These ideological cleavages deeply influence the capacity of the military when they become directly involved in the exercise of domestic political power.

THE PERFORMANCE OF MILITARY REGIMES

The second focus of interest is on the comparative analysis of the performance of the military after the seizure of power. The actual policies and practices that are pursued or are not pursued represent considerable diversity. Yet to highlight the extent of uniformity, the basic argument or hypothesis that requires examination is that the capacity of the military to contribute to social and economic change depends on (a) the extent to which it is conscious of its limitations as a political instrument and (b) takes steps to separate itself from direct and tenuous political intervention.

This central hypothesis derives from the structural features of the military profession which limit its capacities to supply cadres of political leaders. In the Middle East the analysis of social origins and professional socialization, it was argued, tends to make these structural restraints less operative. Nevertheless, the individual officer of great political effectiveness is in a sense a deviant—or least at variance from the cadres of his professional colleagues; even the small groups of key officers who become the center of military politics or actual military oligarchies require specific explanation as compared with the bulk of their colleagues. They represent not merely the ethos of the military profession but they have extra opportunities for exposure to the political process in the society, specialized career experiences or civilian contacts which may not adequately prepare them for political tasks—but at least propel them in such a direction. Often they have served together in particular military academy classes, on particular command, or are part of particular friendship and clique networks.

There are a wide range of political tactics that military regimes have employed as they expand the scope of political involvement. However, there is no single predetermined pattern of steps or stages. In particular, the ability to control internal factional splits over a given period of time reveals considerable diversity. Clearly, the societal context presents the central dimension; namely, the real economic issues that have to be faced and the available resources; the patterns of internal social and ethnic stratification; and, of course, the nation's international position. The focus of this essay seeks to encompass additional dimensions, namely, of the internal structure and organization of the armed forces, since the internal military setting is a dimension which permits comparative analysis to be pressed with some rigor.

The case of Turkey under Ataturk is crucial for comparative analysis not only because of the relative success of his regime, but because of the clarity of his intentions to remove the army from corporate, direct and continuous involvement in partisan political life of the nation. The available literature documents his early commitment to such a strategy and unfolds his deliberate policies to achieve this goal. His famous pronouncement of 1908 is entered frequently in the research on civil-military relations in Turkey; 'Commanders, while thinking of carrying out the duties and requirements of the army, must beware of letting their minds be influenced by political consideration. They must not forget that there are other officials whose duty is to think of the requirements of the political side' (Nutuk, 1943, ii 43). While this statement is striking given its time and circumstance, it offers little insight to the complex and realistic thinking that Ataturk revealed on the role of the army in the process of political change. Moreover, to point out Ataturk's commitment to separate the military from direct intervention in politics, does not explain how and why he developed his commitment or what factors enabled him to pursue such a leadership strategy. Again, the available literature is rich in historical detail but offers few explanations.

Three interrelated elements seem at work in accounting for Ataturk's commitments and achievements; and these elements in turn highlight some of the conditions under which military intervention can contribute to political change—including effective self-restraint or separation from domestic politics. First, was the security role that the armed forces performed for the Turkish nation. Second, was the underlying structural features of the Ottoman government, particularly the civil service, which could be utilized in the early Ataturk period. Third, was the leadership element including the specific career experiences, personality and political conceptions of Ataturk himself.

First, the security role of the Turkish army reflects the imprint of Ataturk himself. The overriding and obvious consideration was that under Ataturk its national defense mission was a manageable one in contrast to the all consuming stance of other Middle East countries, such as the Nasser regime. Ataturk assumed power not as a defeated leader—but as a hero and national figure. The notion that military defeat propels military officers into political intervention does not encompass the Turkish situation. Ataturk was the victor of Gallipoli and the architect of the defeat of Allied and Greek intervention forces.[43] As a result, it was possible for Ataturk to impose his definition of the boundaries of Turkey and to avoid costly struggles over border irredenta which would have complicated the ethnic and cultural unity of Turkey. The international balance of power was such that an understanding with the Soviet Union could be arranged rapidly and without conspicuous diplomacy.

Robinson reports that it has been estimated that by 1932, the Turkish army was approximately the same size as it was in 1927—78,000. The portion of the general government budget consumed by national defense fell accordingly from 40 percent in 1926 to about 28 percent in the early 1930s,[44] as increases in the gross national product were allocated to the civilian sector. The army did not use its funds for heavy investment in new weapons or in motorized transports. This does not mean that it was stagnant and without internal vitality; such a point of view implies that only by mechanization could there be a basis of self-esteem.

The nation took pride in its military forces. Despite the international arrangements the military had a realistic strategic goal. Military service was thought of as being important regardless of the actual limitations of the Turkish army which remained extant until the build up of, before and during World War II. Moreover, while steps were taken to remove the military establishment from the day-to-day intervention in internal policy and security tasks, the army was still essential for the stability of the regime; it was used to repress the Kurdish uprisings in 1925 and 1930. Between the first and second World Wars the army served as the mark of sovereignty—it was the ultimate symbol of the authority and security of the Turkish government. It was not an institution in search of a mission. Turkey remained at peace with its neighbors, and in its own eyes the military succeeded in its essential mission.

The military also assumed specific and delimited tasks in the development sector which it was able to perform with relative effectiveness. But these were secondary. The contribution to national cohesion rested on the fact that Turkey had a draft system in contrast to most of the contemporary Middle Eastern nations. Men who served felt the pride of participation in the armed forces; and it was this collective experience which contributed to Turkish nationalism, rather than the specific educational and training programs. In fact, the proposition can be offered that precisely because it was a draft force with a turnover of personnel (rather than a long term standing service force) that it served as an institution for building national cohesion. The ability of an army to serve the nation building function varies inversely with its level of technology; small highly technical armies with complex weapons are not able to serve this function. Such armies in fact compete with rather than complement civilian education and nation building institutions.

It is within this context that one can approach the role of Ataturk in removing the military from active domestic political affairs. There is an immediate inclination to emphasize the powerful personality of Ataturk in explaining the political change in Turkey. For that matter, the study of new nations immediately before independence and in the first phases of post independence has led scholars to a deep concern with the role of charismatic leadership.[45] However, before examining the role of charismatic leadership, the second element, certain structural features of Turkey, particularly its civil service, and the relative absence of these in the bulk of the other Middle Eastern nations help clarify the context of the Ataturk experience and distinguish the Turkish case from the bulk of the rest of the Middle East. Turkey was a 'traditional' empire which was not occupied by the colonial powers, and which had a long standing governmental system, particularly a civil bureaucracy of considerable effectiveness.[46] The Ataturk regime could make use of its civil service tradition and bureaucratic resources regardless of the disruption it suffered. One should not underestimate the impact the civil bureaucracy had on the outlook and political behavior of the military. The military saw itself as part of a government structure, with its own special, and in its own eyes, superior status and virtues. However, it could look outward toward complementary relations with the civil service. It had the image and reality of these organizational resources to undertake important and central tasks if appropriate direction and leadership would be supplied.

The setting which the military of Turkey found itself, even during the greatest turmoil of the early 1920s, was one in which the military leaders could look back on as a long tradition of functioning government. The army was aware that civil government had put at its disposal extensive sources which produced a highly developed Turkish military force for World War I. Its failure was, in part, the result of military leadership. Such a history tended to place limitations on the conceptions of the military and introduce a strong note of realism. In fact, the opposite was the case; the role of key military leaders in the conduct of the Turkish national policies and domestic politics during World War I was extensive and hardly brilliant or successful. There is such a process as social learning. For some of the officers, including Ataturk himself, these immediate experiences underlined the difficulties of exercising power.

This is what is meant by the third element, the leadership which involves a focus on the education and ideology of Ataturk. The issue is not only that Ataturk was committed to a separation of the military from civilian political organization. Rather he was exposed to a series of career experiences and had the opportunities to be influenced in this direction, and was intelligent enough to learn the essential problems and develop an appropriate formula to handle them.

The Young Turk movement which engulfed Ataturk produced an insurrection in 1908 which, from its very origins, was an alliance between military personnel and civilian activists. Such a coalition was very different from the National Unity Committee and the 1960 coup which was a purely military activity and which conformed much more to the type of military conspiratorial takeover typical for the post-World War II Middle Eastern nations. The Young Turk movement in 1908 was primarily a civilian enterprise with only limited military overtones. In 1909 after the civilians had demonstrated their limitations the military intervened; and, interestingly enough, it was the junior officers who were most active. The civilian-military coalition of the Young Turks exemplified the exposure of the military to outside political ideas, especially those imported into Turkey at the end of the nineteenth century from France.

Ataturk was immediately off to a military and political career from the very start, since the 1908 events took place only three years after he had graduated from the General Staff Academy in 1905 at the age of 24. He was not a 'firebrand,' but rather was concerned with an appropriate role of the military. Four years later he served as Chief of Staff under Mahmud Sevket Pasa, commander of III Army which crushed the counterrevolution in 1909; and from this vantage point Ataturk got his first exposure in depth to the military in a balancing role. He continued to mix military assignments with politically oriented ones in his appointment as Military Attaché in Sofia, 1913. By the time he completed his military operations of World War I, he had an education in the realities of Turkish politics. On the one hand, he learned of the weakness of the parliamentary system that had been created by the events of 1908. On the other hand, the gradual involvement of ranking Ottoman generals in the Imperial government during the deterioration of World War I hardly encouraged Ataturk to rely on a military oligarchy. His own self-confidence grew instead.

Ataturk never lost sight of his fundamental belief that the military should remain out of the management of organized domestic politics while he made use of the military as the core of his underlying power base. Military personnel supplied important elements in the mass-type party which he created with the decision that those officers who wished to be active had to leave the army. His personal power dominated the military apparatus and prevented factional countercoups.[47]

From this point of view, the reentry of the Turkish military into party politics in 1961 represents a continuation of an emergent trend in Turkish society initiated by Ataturk. Frederick Frey has emphasized the decline in the access of the Turkish military to politics as an underlying element. He documents the decline from 1920 to 1954 in the military, that is, retired officers, from 'the most favored' group in the assembly to less than three percent. In his terms: 'This loss by the military first of its over-all strength in the assembly and then of its lingering strength at top leadership levels seems to be one important background factor in understanding the military coup d'état of May 27, 1960.' This observation appears to be much too narrow and is more of a description of the patterns of military politics than a central explanation. Likewise, Lerner's and Robinson's emphasis on changes in social mobility opportunities seems much too narrow to be relevant in explaining either the withdrawal from political involvement or the return in 1960.[48] They claim that during 1923-1948 there was a decline in career opportunities and vitality in the Turkish army which accompanied the declining military involvement. After 1948 under American military assistance, there followed a period of rapid rejuvenation which increased the attractiveness of the military and brought in a spirit which lies behind the subsequent intervention in domestic politics. Again this argument appears much too narrow in scope and distorts the fundamental and basic position of the Turkish military in its society. Moreover, as Ozbudun points out, it overstated the case during both periods. First, during the period of World War I to World War II, the internal vitality and career opportunities and ability basis for promotion did not suffer as much as presumed by this argument. For the subsequent period, Ozbudun refutes this social vitality argument by stating 'in short, the Turkish Army in 1960 was not appreciably more modern than Turkish civilian political institutions. It had neither a monopoly of technological skills nor a monopoly of social mobility. This does not mean, however, that the army did not have an image of modernization quite different from that of the D.P. leaders.'[49]

More essential for understanding the events of 1960 is that the Turkish army maintained its organizational solidarity since the assumption of the power of Ataturk. The social background of its officers and its professional socialization and the norms created by Ataturk meant that it retained its potentials for intervention in domestic politics. The barrier to intervention was the effectiveness of the domestic economic and civilian political arrangements. Once there was an internal crisis, a crisis in the legitimacy of the civilian leadership, the military responded in terms of its own logic.

The analysis of the social composition of the leadership of the National Unity Committee was a microcosm of the Turkish officer corps—as described above, with the persistence of a strong hinterland affiliation.

Again there were few representatives of the upper professional groups, and there were even fewer who had family or social connections with the 'top political or economic elite.'[50] It is most noteworthy that the National Unity Committee was able to resist internal factionalization even though this required drastic action and the expulsion of the more 'radical' members. The armed forces were able to continue their long standing posture as a balancing agent, with limited political objectives and return the government to civilians. After the election of October 15, 1961, on February 22, 1962, and on May 20, 21, 1963, there were unsuccessful attempts by more activists and 'radicals' to intervene in politics.

In each case, the efforts failed because of counter-interventions by the more moderates. The split ran along younger and less senior officers against older and more senior, reflecting differences in professional careers rather than sharp differences in social background. An implicit trend toward a more leftist or rather more comprehensive etatism is implied by the pronouncements of General Mashin Batu, Air Force general who warned in 1970 of the spread of leftist ideas among the officers during a period of increased social and economic unrest in Turkey. However, there is no documentation of the extent of such attitudes.

The military regimes of Egypt and Algeria can be taken as representative of two different models of military performance from that of Turkey. In the Turkish case, military intervention produced a 'personal' authoritarian regime which, while it rested on the military, had a leader whose goal was the creation of a viable civilian mass party and to keep the military intact by removing it from direct and continuous intervention. In Egypt, the 'personal' authoritarian regime rested on military authority but Nasser had no Ataturk-type goals. Instead, personal rule was enforced by secret police tactics and a balancing of personal cliques and interest groups. (Syria and Iraq have close parallels except that internal factionalization has prevented even the emergence of a Nasser-type regime.)[51] By contrast the model of Algeria is closest to what the political scientists have called a mobilization state. There are strong drawbacks to the term mobilization, but the essential element is that the regime, based on a military leader supported by a military oligarchy, is committed to a 'radical' collectivist program. The emergence of the regime from a national liberation movement means that its leaders were concerned with the issues of political organization. While they do not accept the Ataturk model, they are sensitive to the need for political organization. This model can be thought of as a military-mass party organization since the military are not separated from political activity but seek to dominate it directly and continuously. The spectrum of comparative analysis can be broadened. In the cases of Morocco and Iran, we are dealing with a traditional type of authority structure in which the military are an implicit coalition partner and the problems such as regime succession or rate of economic growth are likely to precipitate military intervention. On the other hand, the Sudan is the case where the circle has made a full turn and the army has been forced by civilian agitation to relinquish direct political responsibility.

To what extent do the above three elements or dimensions explain the different patterns of performance of particular military regimes; at least, for example, to help highlight the effectiveness of short term performance of the Algerian regime in contrast to that of the Egyptian regime. Our focus has shifted from the military as a social institution to broader relations between the military and the political process. First, as to the role of the military in national security, patently the overriding commitment of the Egyptian armed forces to the Israel war for twenty years and its inability to effect a political decision has been at the root of the limited effectiveness of the Nasser regime. While the Algerian regime as a 'forward' policy in the international arena was based on its revolutionary symbolism, the tasks of the military have been more limited and realistic; they have not distorted domestic politics. The one 'adventure' of military operations against the Morocco government ended quickly enough to prevent any internal disruption to the regime. The revolutionary government's contributions to wars of national liberation have been mainly political and symbolic and the training of foreign guerillas in Algeria with limited costs and even more limited results. Second, the Nasser government did not have a civil service comparable to either the Turkish government of the 1920s or for that matter other colonial dependencies of Great Britain such as India. Algeria on this dimension was much better off although during the first years after its national independence it faced very grave problems. There were some significant elements of a French trained civil service, and the removal of French personnel, particularly in education, proceeded gradually. Moreover, since so much of the economic development of Algeria was linked to the profits of oil extraction, foreign administrative and technical personnel for these specific tasks were permitted to operate and did so effectively. Thus, both of these factors have, over the short run, assisted the Algerian government to a greater extent than the Egyptian.

In assessing the performance of these military regimes, the third factor, the voluntaristic element of leadership and ideology, is of real importance.

The Nasser coup was engineered by a group of relatively unknown middle level Egyptian officers, many of whom became close personal friends because they attended military academy at the same time. They were a group who had few previous contacts with civilian political leaders, and little exposure to alternative political ideas. As mentioned above, Nasser was not attracted by the image of Ataturk and, although he did some political writing which did not reveal a deep understanding of the problems he would have to face, he had no effective prior experience. The Nasser regime repeatedly sought to develop various types of 'socialist unions' as political mechanisms but without noteworthy success and with little concern about the relation of army and party.

It would not be appropriate to call his regime totalitarian—or that of any Middle Eastern regime, because these societies are predominately peasant in their social structure. However, in the absence of a political formula, internal coercion remains a dominant ingredient on which the regime's authority rests. Neither the posture of the leader nor the ideology employed indicates an orientation toward greater reliance on consent and symbolic persuasion. In addition to most limited economic development, the regime faces neither the long term issues of succession and the development of political cadres, nor the immediate tasks of nation building except by a strategy of crisis management and a concern for its position in the Arab world.

By contrast, the regime of Algeria has a different political logic, which together with the fortunes of oil extraction has permitted some measure of economic development and political stability. This is not to prejudge the amount of consent and support that exists. It is to point out that the national liberation movement and the long struggle for independence have produced a sensitivity to the issues of political management. The process of liberation politicized both the top military and guerilla leaders. The FLN supplied a format in which the struggles between factional groupings and between civilian political leaders, guerilla commanders and the leader of the external army took place. It is striking to note the speed with which the external army when it returned to Algeria, with its limited numbers, organization and discipline overtook the internal guerilla forces. The temporary alliance between Ben Bella, representative of nationalist civilian political leadership and the commander of the external army, Boumedienne, in turn gave way to the emergence of Boumedienne leadership. But the heritage of the revolutionary movement left its deep mark. Leftist symbolism was an accepted aspect of the ideology of the armed forces—although pragmatic considerations placed restraints in dealing with social and economic development. The military leader, and the military oligarchy on which he rests, is fused with a series of political entities which are dedicated in principle to the development of some sort of political organization. As of 1970, there is no Ataturk goal, and in this sense Algeria has a military-single mass party structure. The ideology and operation of this amalgam is diffuse enough to permit or not permit the emergence of a civilian dominated organization which would require military support but might not fractionize the military.

Comparative analysis of the military regimes in the Middle East needs to proceed both by broad scale analysis of the military as a social institution and by detailed case studies of political performance in depth which permit point by point comparisons between particular nations. In partial summary, the Middle East by 1970 represents an area in which the performance of military regimes has proceeded far enough to reveal patterns of underlying uniformity and elements of diversity. It may well be the case that the thrust of the analysis presented here is not adequate because it is not sufficiently comprehensive. However, there is no reason that a more explicit comparative approach needs to be deferred.

Notes

1. Eliezer Be'eri, *Army Officers in Arab Politics and Society* (New York, 1970).

2. J. C. Hurewitz, *Middle East Politics: The Military Dimension* (New York, 1969), p. 6.

3. Gustave E. Grunebaum, *Medieval Islam: A Study in Cultural Orientation* (Chicago, 1953); and *Modern Islam: The Search for Cultural Identity* (New York, 1964).

4. See Lloyd Fallers, "Societal Analysis," *International Encyclopedia of Social Sciences,* XIV, David Sills, ed. (New York, 1968), pp. 562-572, for an overview of comparative societal research.

5. Franz L. Neumann, *Behemoth: The Structure and Practice of National Socialism* (New York, 1942); Barrington Moore, *Terror and Progress in the USSR: Some Source of Change and Stability in the Soviet Dictatorship* (Cambridge, Mass., 1954); Chalmers A. Johnson, *Peasant Nationalism and Communist Power* (Stanford, 1962); Ronald Dore, *Land Reform in Japan* (London, 1959).

6. Bernard Lewis, *The Emergence of Modern Turkey* (London, 1961).

7. Barrington Moore, *Social Origins of Dictatorship and Democracy* (Boston, 1966).

8. Morris Janowitz, *The Military in the Political Development of New Nations* (Chicago, 1964).

9. The works cited in these notes constitute a selected bibliography relevant to the hypotheses.

10. For an exploration of this topic see Hurewitz, *Middle East Politics,* Chap. 2, passim, and Be'eri, *Army Officers,* pp. 279-286.

11. Ergun Ozbudun, "The Role of the Military in Recent Turkish Politics," Harvard University, Center for International Affairs, *Occasional Papers in International Affairs,* No. 14 (November, 1966), p. 3.

12. Edward A. Shils, *The Political Development of New States* (The Hague, 1963).

13. Manfred Halpern, *The Politics of Social Change in the Middle East and North Africa* (Princeton, 1963); Hurewitz, *Middle East Politics.* D. Rustow has offered the observation that it takes four to five years after de facto independence before such efforts are sufficiently discredited to produce the conditions for military intervention. Dankwart A. Rustow, "The Military in Middle Eastern Society," in Sydney Nettleton Fisher, ed., *The Military in the Middle East* (Columbus, 1963).

14. Janowitz, *The Military in the Political Development of New Nations* (Chicago, 1964), p. 50.

15. Alfred Vagts, *The History of Militarism* (New York, 1937).

16. Karl Demeter, *Das deutsche Heer und seine Offiziere* (Berlin, 1935); *Das deutsche Offizierskorps in seinen historisch-soziologischen Grundlagen* (Berlin, 1930).

17. Ibid.; Morris Janowitz, *The Professional Soldier* (Glencoe, Ill., 1960), pp. 93-97, presents the statistical details.

18. Samuel R. Scott, "The French Revolution and the Professionalization of the French Officer Corps, 1789-1793," in Morris Janowitz and Jacques van Doorn, eds., *On Military Ideology* (Rotterdam, 1971), pp. 3-56.

19. The Ottoman focus was of course preceded by the Mamaluke formation in the Middle East. They existed from the middle of the ninth century up until the early 1900s and had many similar characteristics. See Be'eri, *Army Officers in Arab Politics,* pp. 296 ff.

20. Lewis, *Emergence of Modern Turkey,* p. 89, passim and p. 474.

21. Janowitz, *The Military in the Political Development of New Nations,* p. 50.

22. A. V. Sherman, "The Social Roots of Nasser's Egypt," *Commentary,* XXIV (1957), pp. 410-416.

23. Gordon H. Torrey, "The Role of the Military in Society and Government in Syria and the Formation of the UAR," in Fisher, ed., *Military in Middle East,* p. 53; see also Be'eri, *Army Officers,* p. 339..

24. P. J. Vatikiotis, *Politics and the Military in Jordan: A Study of the Arab Legion 1921-1957* (London, 1967).

25. Be'eri, *Army Officers,* p. 347.

26. Halpern, *Politics of Social Change,* p. 258.

27. Morroe Berger, *Bureaucracy and Society in Modern Egypt* (Princeton, 1957), p. 185.

28. Janowitz, *The Military in the Political Development of New Nations,* p. 56.

29. "The officer corps had always had a wide base of social and geographic recruitment as a result of the nineteenth century reforms, it also became one of the most conspicuous channels for advancement within the Empire's social structure." D. Rustow, *World Politics,* XI, No. 4 (July 1959), p. 515.

30. Frederick W. Frey, *The Turkish Political Elite* (Cambridge, Mass., 1965); Be'eri, *Army Officers;* Ayad al-Qazzaz, "The Changing Pattern of the Politics of the Iraqi Army," in Morris Janowitz and Jacques van Doorn, eds., *On Military Intervention* (Rotterdam, 1971), pp. 335-361.

31. P. J. Vatikiotis, *The Egyptian Army in Politics* (Bloomington, Ind., 1961), p. 232.

32. It is equally striking to note the widespread applicability of these observations to the developing nations. For example, William Gutteridge used the case of Ghana to summarize the question of social recruitment. "An army officer at present is much more likely to be the son of a peasant cocoa farmer or a post office employee, than of a professional man who probably has educated his son for the bar of the (higher) civil service or a similar occupation of established prestige." William Gutteridge, *Armed Forces in New States* (London, 1962), p. 44.

33. Frey, *Turkish Political Elite*, p. 141. Clearly this cannot be viewed as a representative sample, but if those officers who rose in rank and who also became politically active subsequently had such a lower-middle class, non-professional background, it would be doubtful whether the broader cadre, which would be presumed less cosmopolitan, would have a higher representation of the "new middle" classes.

34. Al-Qazzaz, "Changing Pattern of Politics of Iraqi Army," passim.

35. Be'eri, *Army Officers*, pp. 483-496.

36. Ibid., pp. 311-316.

37. Ozbudun, "The Role of the Military in Turkish Politics," p. 11. A similar argument is presented by Fisher, ed., *Military in Middle East*, p. 2.

38. For the total sample as reported by Ozbudun, the distribution of responses was as follows: free profession; 44.4 percent; education: 23.2 percent; government and politics: 10.6 percent; business and commerce: 9.5 percent; military: 9.1 percent; others: 3.2 percent. Ozbudun pointed out that the prestige attributed to the military profession tends to vary inversely with the economic well being of the respondents' families. Reported source: Frederick W. Frey, George W. Angell and Abdurrahman S. Sanay, *Ogrencilerin Meslek Gruplarina Bagladiklari Dergerler* (Ankara, 1962).

39. Morris Janowitz, *The Professional Soldier*, Chap. 18; these issues are raised by Daniel Lerner and Richard D. Robinson in the case of Turkey when they discuss the differences between the military profession and these occupational groups which they label the "secular intelligentsia." Unfortunately the term "secular intelligentsia" is too broad and diffuse since they include in it "the free professions—composed of teachers, students, journalists, engineers and doctors and the full array of quasi-intellectual roles of a predominately secular nature." Teachers are not members of a "free profession" and the intellectual component of engineers is indeed very "quasi." Daniel Lerner and Richard D. Robinson, "Swords and Ploughshares: The Turkish Army as a Modernizing Force," *World Politics*, XIII (October 1960), pp. 23-24.

40. Hurewitz, *Middle East Politics*, p. 428.

41. Dankwart Rustow, *World Politics*, II (July 1959), p. 526, passim.

42. See Ayad al-Qazzaz for an analysis of the social basis of the "provincial" outlook of the Iraq officer corps, "Changing Patterns," p. 11.

43. In a parallel but much more limited fashion Nasser achieved some personal reputation as a local commander in the 1948 Israeli war.

44. Richard D. Robinson, *The First Turkish Republic: A Case Study in National Development* (Cambridge, Mass., 1963), pp. 239-240.

45. Edward A. Shils, "Concentration and Dispersion of Charisma: Their Bearings on Economic Policy in Underdeveloped Countries," in *Selected Essays by Edward Shils* (Chicago, 1970).

46. The parallel of Turkey and Japan has been noted repeatedly since Japan and Turkey are the two cases of non-Western nations, especially Japan, which have been able to push rapidly toward their economic development and their general schemes of modernization. See Robert E. Ward and Dankwart A. Rustow, eds., *Political Modernization in Japan and Turkey* (Princeton, 1964).

47. One is struck with the similarity of David Ben-Gurion's personal authority in containing the Israeli military, after the war of independence, in their very limited political objective. He contributed decisively to the development of a non-political civil service military. For a revealing description of these details see David Kimche and Dan Bawly, *The Sandstorm: The Arab Israeli War of June 1967: Prelude and Aftermath* (London, 1968).

48. Lerner and Robinson, "Swords and Ploughshares," pp. 27-41.

49. Ozbudun, "Role of Military in Recent Turkish Politics," p. 12.

50. Ibid., p. 29. Similar conclusions are presented in Walter Weiker, *The Turkish Revolution 1960-1961, Aspects of Military Politics* (Washington, D.C., 1963), pp. 118-119.

51. See al-Qazzaz, "Changing Patterns of Politics of Iraqi Army," passim, for the political performance of the military while in power.

COHESION AND DISINTEGRATION IN THE WEHRMACHT IN WORLD WAR II

The Army as a Social Group

This study is an attempt to analyze the relative influence of primary and secondary group situations on the high degree of stability of the German Army in World War II. It also seeks to evaluate the impact of the Western Allies' propaganda on the German Army's fighting effectiveness.[1]

Although distinctly outnumbered and in a strategic sense quantitatively inferior in equipment, the German Army, on all fronts, maintained a high degree of organizational integrity and fighting effectiveness through a series of almost unbroken retreats over a period of several years. In the final phase, the German armies were broken into unconnected segments, and the remnants were overrun as the major lines of communication and command were broken. Nevertheless, resistance which was more than token resistance on the part of most divisions continued until they were overpowered or overrun in a way which, by breaking communication lines, prevented individual battalions and companies from operating in a coherent fashion. Disintegration through desertion was insignificant, while active surrender, individually or in groups, remained extremely limited throughout the entire Western campaign.

In one sense the German High Command effected as complete a defense of the "European Fortress" as its own leadership qualities and the technical means at its disposal permitted. Official military analyses, including General Eisenhower's report, have shown that lack of manpower, equipment, and transportation, as well as certain strategical errors, were the limiting factors.[2] There was neither complete collapse nor internally

This article, written with Edward A. Shils, is reprinted from *Public Opinion Quarterly*, XII (Summer, 1948), pp. 280-315.

organized effort to terminate hostilities, such as signalized the end of the first world war.

This extraordinary tenacity of the German Army has frequently been attributed to the strong National Socialist political convictions of the German soldiers. It is the main hypothesis of this paper, however, that the unity of the German Army was in fact sustained only to a very slight extent by the National Socialist political convictions of its members, and that more important in the motivation of the determined resistance of the German soldier was the steady satisfaction of certain *primary* personality demands afforded by the social organization of the army.

This basic hypothesis may be elaborated in the following terms.

1. It appears that a soldier's ability to resist is a function of the capacity of his immediate primary group (his squad or section) to avoid social disintegration. When the individual's immediate group, and its supporting formations, met his basic organic needs, offered him affection and esteem from both officers and comrades, supplied him with a sense of power and adequately regulated his relations with authority, the element of self-concern in battle, which would lead to disruption of the effective functioning of his primary group, was minimized.

2. The capacity of the primary group to resist disintegration was dependent on the acceptance of political, ideological, and cultural symbols (all secondary symbols) only to the extent that these secondary symbols became directly associated with primary gratifications.

3. Once disruption of primary group life resulted through separation, breaks in communications, loss of leadership, depletion of personnel, or major and prolonged breaks in the supply of food and medical care, such an ascendancy of preoccupation with physical survival developed that there was very little "last-ditch" resistance.

4. Finally, as long as the primary group structure of the component units of the Wehrmacht persisted, attempts by the Allies to cause disaffection by the invocation of secondary and political symbols (e.g., about the ethical wrongfulness of the National Socialist system) were mainly unsuccessful. By contrast, where Allied propaganda dealt with primary and personal values, particularly physical survival, it was more likely to be effective.

Long before D-Day in Western France, research was undertaken in the United Kingdom and North Africa on these social psychological aspects of the enemy's forces. These studies were continued after D-Day by the Intelligence Section of the Psychological Warfare Division of SHAEF. Although of course they are subject to many scientific strictures, they provide a groundwork for the evaluation of the experiences of the German soldier and for the analysis of the social organization of the German Army. Methods of collecting data included front line interrogation of prisoners of war (Ps/W) and intensive psychological interviews in rear areas. Captured enemy documents, statements of recaptured Allied military personnel, and the reports of combat observers were also studied. A monthly opinion poll of random samples of large numbers of Ps/W was also undertaken. This paper is based on a review of all these data.

Modes of disintegration. Preliminary to the analysis of the function of the primary group in the maintenance of cohesion in the German Army, it is necessary to classify the modes of social disintegration found in any modern army:

1. Desertion (deliberately going over to the enemy lines)
    a) by individual action
        (1) after discussion with comrades
        (2) without prior discussion with others
    b) by groups acting in concert
2. Active surrender (deliberate decision to give up to the enemy as he approaches and taking steps to facilitate capture, e.g., by sending emissaries, by calling out, by signalling, etc.)
    a) by single individuals
    b) by group as a unit
        (1) by mutual agreement
        (2) by order of or with approval of NCO or officer
    c) by plurality of uncoordinated individuals
3. Passive surrender
    a) by individuals acting alone
        (1) non-resistance (allowing oneself to be taken prisoner without taking effective steps to facilitate or obstruct capture; passivity may be a means of facilitating surrender)
        (2) token resistance (allowing oneself to be taken prisoner with nominal face-saving gestures of obstruction to capture)
    b) by plurality of uncoordinated individuals
4. Routine resistance: rote or mechanical, but effective execution of orders as given from above with discontinuance when the enemy becomes overwhelmingly powerful and aggressive.
5. "Last-ditch" resistance which ends only with the exhaustion of fighting equipment and subsequent surrender or death. (This type of soldier is greatly underrepresented in studies of samples of Ps/W. Therefore the study of Ps/W alone does not give an adequate picture of the resistive qualities of the German soldier.)

A more detailed description of each of the above classes will be useful in the following analysis:

Desertion involved positive and deliberate action by the German soldier to deliver himself to Allied soldiers for capture by crossing the lines, e.g., by planfully "losing himself" while on patrol and "blundering" into the enemy's area of control or by deliberately remaining behind during a withdrawal from a given position so that when the Allied troops came up they could take him.

In *active surrender* by the group as a unit, the positive act of moving across to enemy lines was absent but there was an element common with desertion in the deliberate attempt to withdraw from further combat. Like many cases of desertion, the decision to surrender as a group was arrived at as a result of group discussion and mutual agreement. The dividing line between active surrender and desertion brought about by lagging behind was shadowy. There were other forms of group surrender which were clearly different from desertion, e.g., the sending of an emissary to arrange terms with the enemy, the refusal to carry out aggressive orders, or to fight a way out of encirclement.

In *passive surrender,* the intention of a soldier to remove himself from the battle was often not clear even to himself. The soldier who was taken prisoner by passive surrender might have been immobilized or apathetic due to anxiety; he might have been in a state of bewildered isolation and not have thought of passive surrender until the perception of an opportunity brought it to his mind. Non-resistant passive surrender frequently occurred in the case of soldiers who lay in their foxholes or hid in the cellars or barns, sometimes self-narcotized by fear, or sometimes deliberately waiting to be overrun. In both cases, they made only the most limited external gestures of resistance when the enemy approached. In the second type of passive surrender—token resistance—the surrendering soldier desired to avoid all the stigma of desertion or surrender but nevertheless showed reluctance to undertake aggressive or defensive actions which might have interfered with his survival.

An examination of the basic social organization of the German Army, in terms of its primary group structure and the factors which strengthened and weakened its component primary groups, is first required in order to account for the stability and cohesion of resistance, and in order to evaluate the impact of Allied propaganda.

The Function of the Primary Group[3]

"The company is the only truly existent community. This community allows neither time nor rest for a personal life. It forces us into its circle, for life is at stake. Obviously compromises must be made and claims be surrendered. . . . Therefore the idea of fighting, living, and dying for the fatherland, for the cultural possessions of the fatherland, is but a relatively distant thought. At least it does not play a great role in the practical motivations of the individual."[4]

Thus wrote an idealistic German student in the first world war. A German sergeant, captured toward the end of the second world war, was asked by his interrogators about the political opinions of his men. In reply, he laughed and said, "When you ask such a question, I realize well that you have no idea of what makes a soldier fight. The soldiers lie in their holes and are happy if they live through the next day. If we think at all, it's about the end of the war and then home."

The fighting effectiveness of the vast majority of soldiers in combat depends only to a small extent on their preoccupation with the major political values which might be affected by the outcome of the war and which are the object of concern to statesmen and publicists. There are of course soldiers in whom such motivations are important. Volunteer armies recruited on the basis of ethical or political loyalties, such as the International Brigade in the Spanish Civil War, are affected by their degree of orientation toward major political goals. In the German Army, the "hard core" of National Socialists were similarly motivated.

But in a conscript army, the criterion of recruitment is much less specialized and the army is more representative of the total population liable to conscription. Therefore the values involved in political and social systems or ethical schemes do not have much impact on the determination of a soldier to fight to the best of his ability and to hold out as long as possible. For the ordinary German soldier the decisive fact was that he was a member of a squad or section which maintained its structural integrity and which coincided roughly with the *social* unit which satisfied some of his major primary needs.[5] He was likely to go on fighting, provided he had the necessary weapons, as long as the group possessed leadership with which he could identify himself, and as long as he gave affection to and received affection from the other members of his squad and platoon. In other words, as long as he felt himself to be a member of his primary group and therefore bound by the expectations and demands of its other members, his soldierly achievement was likely to be good.

Modern social research has shown that the primary group is not merely the chief source of affection and accordingly the major factor in personality formation in infancy and childhood. The primary group continues to be the major source of social and psychological sustenance through adulthood.[6] In the army, when isolated from civilian primary groups, the individual soldier comes to depend more and more on his military primary group. His spontaneous loyalties are to its immediate members whom he sees daily and with whom he develops a high degree of intimacy. For the German soldier in particular, the demands of his group, reinforced by officially prescribed rules, had the effect of an external authority. It held his aggressiveness in check; it provided discipline, protection, and freedom from autonomous decision.[7]

Army units with a high degree of primary group integrity suffered little from desertions or from individually contrived surrenders. In the Wehrmacht, desertions and surrenders were most frequent in groups of heterogeneous ethnic composition in which Austrians, Czechs, and Poles were randomly intermixed with each other. In such groups the difficulties of linguistic communication, the large amount of individual resentment and aggressiveness about coercion into German service, the weakened support of leadership due to their inability to identify with German officers—all these factors hampered the formation of cohesive groups.

Sample interviews with Wehrmacht deserters made in North Africa in 1943 and in France and Germany in 1944 and 1945 showed an overwhelmingly disproportionate representation of elements which could not be assimilated into primary groups. A total of 443 Wehrmacht Ps/W captured toward the end of the North African campaign, consisting of 180 Germans, 200 Austrians and 63 others (Czechs, Poles, Yugoslavs, etc.), had very markedly different tendencies toward desertion: 29 percent of the Germans were deserters or potential deserters; 55 percent of the Austrians fell into these two classes, as did 78 percent of the Czechs, Poles, and Yugoslavs. Of the 53 German deserters, only one declared that he had "political" motives for desertion. In the Western European campaign, the bulk of the deserters came from among the "Volksdeutsche,"[8] Austrians, Poles, and Russians who had been coerced into German military service. It was clear that in view of the apolitical character of most of the deserters, the grounds for their desertion were to be sought among those variables which prevented the formation of close primary group bonds, the chief of which were insuperable language differences, bitter resentment against their coerced condition, and the unfriendliness of the Germans in their units.

Among German deserters, who remained few until the close of the war, the failure to assimilate into the primary group life of the Wehrmacht was the most important factor, more important indeed than political dissidence. Deserters were on the whole men who had difficulty in personal adjustment, e.g., in the acceptance of affection or in the giving of affection. They were men who had shown these same difficulties in civilian life, having had difficulties with friends, work associates, and their own families, or having had criminal records. Political dissidents on the other hand, when captured, justified their failure to desert by invoking their sense of solidarity with their comrades and expressed the feeling that had they deserted when given a post of responsibility their comrades would have interpreted it as a breach of solidarity. For the political dissident, the verbal expression of political dissent was as much anti-authoritarianism as he could afford, and submission to his group was the price which he had to pay for it.

The persistent strength of primary group controls was manifested even in the last month of the war, when many deserters felt that they would not have been able to have taken the initial step in their desertion unless they had discussed the matter with their comrades and received some kind of legitimation for the action, such as a statement of approval.[9] And, on the other hand, the same ongoing efficacy of primary group sentiment was evident in the statements of would-be deserters who declared they had never been able to cross the threshold because they had been told by their officers that the comrades who remained behind (i.e., the comrades of the men who had deserted) would be shot. Hence, one of the chief forms of disintegration which occurred in the last stages of the war took the form of group surrender in which, after ample discussion within the unit, the authorization of the leading personalities and often of the NCO's had been granted for the offering of token resistance to facilitate capture, or even for outright group surrender.

Factors Strengthening Primary Group Solidarity

The Nazi nucleus of the primary group: the "hard core." The stability and military effectiveness of the military primary group were in large measure a function of the "hard core," who approximated about ten to fifteen percent of the total of enlisted men; the percentage was higher for non-commissioned officers and was very much higher among the junior officers.[10] These were, on the whole, young men between 24 and 28 years of age who had had a gratifying adolescence in the most rewarding period of National Socialism. They were imbued with the ideology of *Gemein-schaft* (community solidarity),[11] were enthusiasts for the military life, had definite homo-erotic tendencies and accordingly placed a very high value on "toughness," manly comradeliness, and group solidarity.[12] The presence of a few such men in the group, zealous, energetic, and unsparing of themselves, provided models for weaker men, and facilitated the process of identification. For those for whom their charisma did not suffice and who were accordingly difficult to incorporate fully into the intimate primary group, frowns, harsh words, and threats served as a check on divisive tendencies. The fact that the elite SS divisions and paratroop divisions had a larger "hard core" than other divisions of the army—so large as to embrace almost the entire group membership during most of the war—accounted for their greater fighting effectiveness. And the fact that such a "hard core" was almost entirely lacking from certain *Volksgrenadier* divisions helped to a considerable extent to account for the military inferiority of these units.

One of the functions of the "hard core" was to minimize the probability of divisive political discussions. There was, of course, little inclination to discuss political matters or even strategic aspects of the war among German soldiers. For this reason widespread defeatism concerning the outcome of the war had little consequence in affecting behavior (until the spring of 1945) because of the near impossibility—objective as well as subjective—of discussing or carrying out alternative plans of action.

In contrast with the "hard core," which was a disproportionately large strengthening factor in the integrity of the military primary group, the "soft core" was a source of infection which was by no means comparable in effectiveness. Unlike the first world war experience in which anti-war attitudes were often vigorously expressed and eagerly listened to by men who were "good comrades," in the second world war the political anti-militarist or anti-Nazi who expressed his views with frequency and vigor was also in the main not a "good comrade." There was a complete absence of soldiers' committees and organized opposition, even in March and April 1945 (except for the Bavarian Freiheitsaktion which was constituted by rear-echelon troops). On isolated occasions, the Western Allies were able to exploit a man who had been a "good comrade" and who, after having been captured, expressed his defeatism and willingness to help end the war; he was thereupon sent back into the German line to talk his comrades into going over with him to the Allied lines. Here the "soft core" man exploited his comradely solidarity and it was only on that basis that he was able to remove some of the members of his group from the influence of the "hard core."

Community of experience as a cohesive force. The factors which affect group solidarity in general were on the whole carefully manipulated by the German general staff. Although during the war Germany was more permeated by foreigners than it had ever been before in its history, the army was to a great extent carefully protected from disintegrating influences of heterogeneity of ethnic and national origin, at least in crucial military situations. German officers saw that solidarity is fostered by the recollection of jointly experienced gratifications and that accordingly the groups who had gone through a victory together should not be dissolved but should be maintained as units to the greatest degree possible.

The replacement system of the Wehrmacht operated to the same end.[13] The entire personnel of a division would be withdrawn from the front simultaneously and refitted as a unit with replacements. Since new members were added to the division while it was out of line they were thereby given the opportunity to assimilate themselves into the group; then the group as a whole was sent forward. This system continued until close to the end of the war and helped to explain the durability of the German Army in the face of the overwhelming numerical and material superiority of the Allied forces.

Deterioration of group solidarity in the Wehrmacht which began to appear toward the very end of the war was most frequently found in hastily fabricated units. These were made up of new recruits, dragooned stragglers, air force men who had been forced into the infantry (and who felt a loss of status in the change), men transferred from the navy into the infantry to meet the emergency of manpower shortage, older factory workers, concentration camp inmates, and older married men who had been kept in reserve throughout the war and who had remained with the familial primary group until the last moment. The latter, who were the "catch" of the last "total mobilization," carried with them the resentment and bitterness which the "total mobilization" produced and which prevented the flow of affection necessary for group formation. It was clear that groups so diverse in age composition and background, and especially so mixed in their reactions to becoming infantrymen, could not very quickly become effective fighting units. They had no time to become used to one another and to develop the type of friendliness which is possible only when loyalties to outside groups have been renounced—or at least put into the background. A preview of what was to occur when units became mixed was provided by the 275th Fusilier Battalion which broke up before the First U.S. Army drive in November. Thirty-five Ps/W interrogated from this unit turned out to have been recently scraped together from fifteen different army units.

The most ineffective of all the military formations employed by the Wehrmacht during the war were the Volkssturm units. They ranged in age from boys to old men, and were not even given basic training in the weapons which they were supposed to use. Their officers were Nazi local functionaries who were already objects of hostility and who were therefore unable to release a flow of affection among equals. They had moreover not broken their family ties to the slightest extent. They still remained members of a primary group which did not fuse into the military primary group. Finally, they had no uniforms. They had only brassards to identify them and through which to identify themselves with one another. The mutual identification function of the uniform which plays so great a role in military units was thereby lost. As soon as they were left to their own devices, they disintegrated from within, deserting in large numbers to their homes, hiding, permitting themselves to be captured, etc.

Factors Weakening Primary Group Solidarity

Isolation. The disintegration of a primary group depends in part on the physical and spatial variables which isolate it from the continuous pressure of face-to-face contact. The factor of spatial proximity in the maintenance of group solidarity in military situations must not be underestimated. In February and March of 1945, isolated remnants of platoons and companies were surrendering in groups with increasing frequency. The tactical situation of defensive fighting under heavy American artillery bombardment and the deployment of rear outposts forced soldiers to take refuge in cellars, trenches, and other underground shelters in small groups of three and four. This prolonged isolation from the nucleus of the primary group for several days worked to reinforce the fear of destruction of the self, and thus had a disintegrative influence on primary group relations.[14] A soldier who was isolated in a cellar or in a concrete bunker for several days and whose anxieties about physical survival were aggravated by the tactical hopelessness of his situation, was a much more easily separable member of his group than one who, though fearing physical destruction, was still bound by the continuous and vital ties of working, eating, sleeping, and being at leisure together with his fellow soldiers.

This proposition regarding the high significance of the spatial variable for primary group solidarity and the maintenance of the fighting effectiveness of an army is supported by the behavior of the retreating German Army in North Africa in 1943, and in France and Germany in September-October 1944 and March 1945. As long as a retreat is orderly and the structure of the component units of an army is maintained, strategic difficulties do not break up the army. An army in retreat breaks up only when the retreat is poorly organized, when command is lost over the men, so that they become separated from their units and become stragglers, or when enemy penetrations isolate larger or smaller formations from the main group.[15]

Stragglers first became a moderately serious problem in the German Army in October 1944. On October 22, 1944, General Keitel ordered that a maximum of one to three days be allowed for stragglers to reattach themselves to their units. The previous limit had been five days. The aggravation of the straggler problem was further documented by General Blaskowitz's order of March 5, 1945, according to which the category of stragglers was declared to have ceased to exist. Soldiers who lost contact with their own units were directed to attach themselves immediately to the "first troops in the line which he can contact. . . ."

Familial ties and primary group disintegration. Prisoners of war remarked with considerable frequency that discussions about alternative paths of action by groups of soldiers who were entirely defeatist arose not from discussions about the war in its political or strategic aspects, but rather from discussions about the soldiers' families.[16] The recollection of concrete family experiences reactivated sentiments of dependence on the family for psychological support and correspondingly weakened the hold of the military primary group. It was in such contexts that German soldiers toward the end of the war were willing to discuss group surrender.

To prevent preoccupation with family concerns, the families of German soldiers were given strict instructions to avoid references to family deprivations in letters to the front. In the winter and spring of 1945, when Allied air raids became so destructive of communal life, all telegrams to soldiers at the front had to be passed by party officials in order to insure that no distracting news reached the soldiers. On the other hand, care was taken by party and army authorities that soldiers should not be left in a state of anxiety about their families and to this end vigorous propaganda was carried on to stimulate correspondence with soldiers at the front. For those who had no families and who needed the supplementary affection which the army unit could not provide, provisions were made to obtain mail from individuals (including party officials) who would befriend unmarried or family-less soldiers, with the result that the psychic economy of the soldier was kept in equilibrium.

There was, however, a special type of situation in which the very strength of familial ties served to keep the army from further disintegration. This arose toward the end of the war, when soldiers were warned that desertion would result in severe sanctions being inflicted on the deserter's family.[17]

Toward the end of the war, soldiers tended to break away from the army more often while they were on leave and with their families, and therefore isolated from personal contact with their primary group fellows. When soldiers returned to visit their families, then the conflict between contradictory primary group loyalties became acute. The hold of the military primary group became debilitated in the absence of face-to-face contacts. The prospect of facing, on return to the front, physical destruction or a prolonged loss of affection from the civilian primary group, especially the family, prompted an increasing number of desertions while on furlough.

All of these factors contributed to loosen the solidarity of the German Army, especially when the prospect of physical destruction began to weigh more heavily. Severe threats to the safety of the civilian primary group created anxiety which often weakened the hold of the military primary group. When the area of the soldier's home was occupied by the enemy or when the soldier himself was fighting in the area, there was strong disposition to desert homeward. One such soldier said: "Now I have nothing more for which to fight, because my home is occupied."

The strong pull of the civilian primary group became stronger as the coherence of the army group weakened. But sometimes, the former worked to keep the men fighting in their units, i.e., when they reasoned that the shortest way home was to keep the group intact and to avoid capture or desertion. Otherwise there would ensue a long period in an enemy P/W camp. On the other hand, in event of the defeat of a still intact army, there would be only a short period of waiting before demobilization.

Demand for physical survival. The individual soldier's fear of destruction ultimately pressed to weaken primary group cohesion; nevertheless it is striking to note the degree to which demands for physical survival could be exploited by Wehrmacht authority to the end of prolonging resistance. Where the social conditions were otherwise favorable, the primary bonds of group solidarity were dissolved only under the most extreme circumstances of threat to the individual organism—in situations where the tactical prospects were utterly hopeless, under devastating artillery and air bombardment, or where the basic food and medical requirements were not being met. Although aware for a long time of the high probability of German defeat in the war and of the hopelessness of the numerous individual battles, very many German soldiers continued to resist without any serious deterioration in the quality of their fighting skill. But where the most basic physiological demands of the German soldier were threatened with complete frustration, the bonds of group solidarity were broken.

Concern about food and about health always reduces the solidarity of a group. Throughout the war, and until the period just before the end, German army medical services were maintained at a high level of efficiency; the decline in their efficiency coincides with the deterioration in the morale of the men. Special care was also observed in the management of the food supply and accordingly few German soldiers felt that the food supplies were inadequate. Indeed, as late as October 1944, only 15 percent of a sample of 92 Ps/W decalred that they were at all dissatisfied with army food. By January, however, the situation changed and Ps/W reported increased preoccupation with physical survival, with food, and the shortage of clothing. Soldiers in certain units were beginning to "scrounge." The extreme cold of the winter of '44-'45 also began to tell on the men whose military self-esteem was being reduced by the raggedness of their uniforms and the failure to obtain replacements for unsatisfactory equipment.

Thus, to keep groups integral, it was necessary not only to provide positive gratifications but also to reduce to a minimum the alternative possibilities of increasing the chances for survival by leaving the unit. For this reason the Nazis sought to counteract the fear of personal physical destruction in battle by telling the men that accurate records were kept on deserters and that not only would their families and property be made to suffer in the event of their desertion, but that after the war, upon their return to Germany, they, too, would be very severely punished. They were also told by their officers that German agents were operating in American and British P/W cages in order to report on violations of security and on deserters. A Wehrmacht leaflet to German soldiers mentioned the names of two deserters of the 980th Volksgrenadiere who were alleged to have divulged information and stated that not only would their families be sent to prison and suffer the loss of their property and ration cards, but that the men themselves would also be punished after the war. In actuality, they were often punished in the P/W camps by the extreme Nazis who exercised some control in certain camps.

For the same reason, as long as the front was relatively stable, the Wehrmacht officers increased the natural hazards of war by ordering mine fields to be laid, barbed wire to be set up, and special guards to be posted to limit the freedom of movement of isolated and psychologically unattached individuals who, in situations which offered the chance of safely withdrawing from the war, would have moved over to the enemy's lines. Although the number of avowedly would-be deserters remained very small until near the end of the war, even they were frequently immobilized for fear of being killed by the devices set up to prevent their separation from the group. The danger of destruction by the Allies in event of desertion also played a part in keeping men attached to their military units. As one P/W who had thought of desertion but who never took action said, "by day our own people shoot us, by night yours do."

Another physical narcissistic element which contributed somewhat to resistance on the Western front was fear of castration in event of the loss of the war. (This was effective only among a minority of the German soldiers.) The guilt feelings of the Nazi soldiers who had slaughtered and marauded on the Eastern front, and elsewhere in Europe, and their projection onto the enemy of their own sadistic impulses, heightened their narcissistic apprehensiveness about damage to their vital organs and to their physical organism as a whole. Rumors of castration at the hands of the Russians circulated in the German Army throughout the last three years of the war and it is likely that they were largely the result of ruthless methods on both sides.

The Nazis perceived the function of fear of personal destruction in the event of capture as a factor in keeping a group intact after the internal bonds had been loosened. There were accordingly situations in which SS detachments deliberately committed atrocities on enemy civilians and soldiers in order to increase the anxieties of German soldiers as to what would befall them in the event of their defeat and capture. This latter policy was particularly drastically applied by the Waffen-SS in the von Rundstedt counter-offensive. It appears to have been an effort to convince German soldiers that there were no alternatives but victory or resistance to the very end and that surrender or desertion would end with slaughter of the German soldiers, as it has in the cases of the Allied soldiers. This was not effective for the mass of the German soldiers, however, who were becoming convinced that the law-abiding British and Americans would not in most situations harm them upon capture.

The dread of destruction of the self, and the demand for physical survival, while breaking up the spontaneous solidarity of the military primary group in most cases, thus served under certain conditions to coerce the soldier into adherence to his group and to the execution of the orders of his superiors.

The Role of "Soldierly Honor"

American and British soldiers tend to consider their wartime service as a disagreeable necessity, as a task which had to be performed because there were no alternatives. For the German, being a soldier was a more than acceptable status. It was indeed honorable. The King's Regulations which govern the British Army (1940) begin with the statement that the army consists of officers and men serving for various lengths of time. The German equivalent in the Defense Laws of 1935 opens with a declaration that "military service is a service of honor for the German people, the Wehrmacht is the armed barrier and the soldierly school of the German people."

Emphasis on the element of honor in the military profession has led in Germany to the promulgation of elaborate rules of conduct regulating the behavior of both officers and men in a great variety of specific military and extra-military situations.[18] The explicit and implicit code of soldierly honor, regulating the responsibilities of officers for their men, determined behavior in battle and established conditions under which surrender was honorable. It also provided a very comprehensive body of etiquette. This elaborate ritualization of the military profession had a significantly positive influence on group solidarity and efficiency during periods of stress. "Honor" rooted in a rigid conscience (superego) served in the German Army to keep men at their tasks better than individual reflection and evaluation could have done. When the individual was left to make decisions for himself, the whole host of contradictory impulses toward authority of officers and of the group as an entity was stimulated.

Domination by higher authority was eagerly accepted by most ordinary soldiers, who feared that if they were allowed to exercise their initiative their *innere Schweinhunde*, i.e., their own narcissistic and rebellious impulses, would come to the fore. On the other hand, rigorous suppression of these impulses constituted an appeasement of the superego which allowed the group machinery to function in an orderly manner.

The belief in the efficacy and moral worth of discipline and in the inferiority of the spontaneous, primary reactions of the personality was expressed in the jettisoning of the German Army Psychiatric Selection Services in 1942. When the manpower shortage became stringent and superfluities had to be scrapped, the personnel selection system based on personality analyses was one of those activities which was thought to be dispensable. Apparently taking individual personality differences into account was thought to be too much of a concession to moral weakness which could and in any case *should* be overcome by hard, soldierly discipline.

Strength as an element in honor. For persons who have deep-lying uncertainties over their own weaknesses, who fear situations which will reveal their weakness in controlling themselves and their lack of manliness, membership in an army will tend to reduce anxieties. Subjugation to discipline gives such persons support; it means that they do not have to depend on themselves, that someone stronger than themselves is guiding and protecting them. Among young males in middle and late adolescence, the challenges of love and vocation aggravate anxieties about weakness. At this stage fears about potency are considerable. When men who have passed through this stage are placed in the entirely male society of a military unit, freed from the control of adult civilian society and missing its gratifications, they tend to regress to the adolescent condition. The show of "toughness" and hardness which is regarded as a virtue among soldiers is a response to these reactivated adolescent anxieties about weakness.

In the German Army, all these tendencies were intensified by the military code, and they accounted for a considerable share of the cohesion and resistance up to the very last stages of the war. Among those at the extreme end of the scale—the "hard core" of Nazi last-ditch resisters—in whom the preoccupation with strength and weakness is to be found in most pronounced forms—this attitude was manifested in unwillingness of some to acknowledge defeat even after capture.

The honor of the officer. To control the behavior of officers and to protect soldierly honor, the Court of Honor procedure of the Imperial Army was reestablished when the Nazis came into power. Its function was to adjudicate disagreements and quarrels between officers in an author-itative way, and it did succeed in minimizing disagreements and unpleasant tensions among officers in both professional and private affairs which might otherwise have endangered solidarity of the group by division among those in immediate authority. The settlement, which was arrived at in secret by officers of the same rank as those involved in the dispute, was almost always accepted without a murmur by both parties. Its minutely detailed procedural and substantive rules reduced to a minimum the possibility that an officer might feel that the collective authority which ruled over him was weak, negligible, or impotent in any sphere. The code went so far as to empower the court to recommend suspension from duty simply on the grounds of *unehrliche Gesinnung* (dishonorable attitude) derogatory to the status of the officer class. External discipline penetrated thus into even the most private sphere to give assurance that soldierly honor would be operative even in the recesses of the individual mind.[19]

The officers' court of honor not only served as an "external superego," but by its continuous emphasis on "honor" and "dishonor," it heightened the sensibilities of the officers to the demands of their own superego.

One of the most elaborated aspects of soldierly honor as related to combat behavior dealt with the conditions under which surrender could be honorably performed. In this respect, great stress was laid on the oath which bound soldiers not to desert or surrender, and much casuistical effort was expended to make surrender compatible with soldierly honor. In some cases soldiers arranged circumstances in such a way as would appear to others, as well as to themselves, that they had been captured against their will. In other cases, surrender was excused as legitimate according to accepted military standards. In a few cases, fortification commanders required that a token round of phosphorous shells be fired against their position in order to satisfy the requirements of their honor. Deserters often attempted to appease their conscience by ingenious arguments to the effect that the oaths which they took were signed with pencil, or that the sergeant who administered the oath turned his back on them, or that they had been forced into signing the oath which was incompatible with the "requirements of a free conscience."

The stout defense of the Channel ports, which denied vital communication centers to the Allies, was in large part the result of the determination of the commanding officers whose sense of military honor required them to carry out to the letter orders for resistance, regardless of the cost in men or of the apparent strategic futility of their operation.

Even after the extreme reverses in February and March of 1945, German colonels and generals sought to have their units captured and overrun in an approved manner. Captured German senior officers often declared that they had been aware of certain defeat in their sector but, despite this, they took little or no action to terminate hostilities. The most positive action some of them were able to take was to follow their instructions to hold fast in such a manner as to facilitate the capture of their own command posts when they were not able to retreat. But the various subterfuges to make their surrender or capture acceptable to their superego were apparently insufficient, and after capture their sense of guilt for having infringed on the moral requirements of officership usually produced regressive manifestations in the form of elaborate self-justifications for their inadequacy. In some cases it went to the extreme form of imagining how they would justify themselves in the event that Hitler were to confront them at the very moment and were to ask them why they had allowed themselves to be captured.

The reluctance of senior and general officers to enter into negotiations to surrender on their own initiative was of course not due exclusively to motivations of conscience; it was buttressed by the efficient functioning of the security system. The failure of the July 20 *Putsch* resulted in the carefully contrived isolation of senior commanding officers and their domination by Nazi secret police. The establishment of an independent chain of command for National Socialist *Führungs-offiziere* (Guidance Officers) was an additional technique established for spying on generals. Aside from their morale duties, which are described elsewhere, these fanatical Nazi Guidance Officers at higher headquarters busied themselves in reporting on German generals who appeared to be unlikely to carry out orders for final resistance.

Company grade and battalion officers on the whole behaved similarly to their superiors. The deterioration of their effectiveness which occurred was due in greater measure to the great reduction in their numbers rather than to any loss of skill or determination. At the end, the German Army suffered severely from being underofficered, rather than poorly officered. As early as January 1945, the ratio of officers to enlisted men fell to about 50 percent of what it had been under normal conditions.

Tension between officer's honor and solicitude of men. There was, however, a difference between the behavior of junior and senior officers, which can in part be explained by the latter's closer physical proximity and more extensive contact with their men. The sense of obligation which the junior officer felt for the welfare of his men often tempered his conception of the proper relations between soldierly honor and surrender, especially when he was in a position to recognize that there was no military value in further resistance. Nonetheless, desertion by German officers was extremely rare, and only occasionally did they bring about the group surrender of their men; more typically they protected their soldierly honor by allowing themselves to be overrun.

Senior non-commissioned officers displayed a sense of military honor very similar to that of junior officers, but even closer identification with their comrades precipitated a crisis in loyalties which weighed still more heavily on their consciences. Ordinarily, soldierly honor and primary group solidarity are not only congruous with one another but actually mutually supporting. In crisis situations, however, the divergence between them begins to appear and loyalty to the larger army group (the strategically relevant unit), which is an essential component of soldierly honor, enters into contradiction to loyalty to the primary group.

Until the failure of von Rundstedt's counter-offensive, soldierly honor on the part of senior NCO's tended to outweigh primary group solidarity wherever they came into conflict with each other. As the final Allied drive against the homeland developed, they became less disposed to carry out "last-ditch" resistance, but when captured they showed signs of having experienced guilt feelings for not having done so. The recognition of the overwhelming Allied strength in their particular sectors, together with physical absence from the immediate environment of their superior officers (which was a function of the decreasing ratio of officers to men) made it possible for them to offer only token resistance or to allow themselves to be overrun. They relieved their consciences by declaring that further bloodshed would have served no further *military purpose.*

The infantry soldier's honor. The code of soldierly honor and its ramifications took a deep root in the personality of the German soldiers of the line—even those who were totally apolitical. Identification with the stern authority associated with the symbols of state power gave the ordinary German soldier a feeling that he became strong and morally elevated by submitting to discipline. For these people a military career was a good and noble one, enjoying high intrinsic ethical value. Even apathetic and inarticulate soldiers sometimes grew eloquent on the values of the military life.

The most defeatist soldier, who insisted that he longed to be captured and that he offered little or no resistance, was careful to point out that he was not a deserter, and showed anxiety lest the conditions under which he was captured might be interpreted as desertion. This was of course to some extent the result of the fear that German police would retaliate against his family if his company commander reported that he had deserted and that the Nazis would seek revenge against him, either in the P/W camp, or after the war in Germany. But at least of equal significance was his desire to maintain his pride in having been a good soldier who had done his duty.[20] Anti-Nazi German soldiers who went to some length to inform the interrogators of their anti-Nazi political attitudes felt no inconsistency in insisting that despite everything they were "100 percent soldiers." Only a very small minority admitted freely that they deserted.

Relations with Authority: Officer-Man Relations

The basis of the officers' status. The primary group relations in modern armies, especially in the German Army, depend as much on the acceptance of the various authorities to which the soldier is subjected as on mutual respect and love between individuals of equal rank. The non-commissioned and the junior officers are the agents on whom the individual soldier depends in his relationships with the rest of the army outside his immediate group, and in his relations with the outer world (the home front and the enemy). They have charge of his safety, and they are the channels through which flow food, equipment, and other types of supplies as well as chance symbolic gratifications such as decorations, promotions, leave, etc. For the German soldier, with his authoritarian background, the officer-man relation is one of submission to an overriding authority.

An exceptionally talented regular German Army officer, bred in the German military tradition, once tried to summarize to his interrogator what made the German Army "work": political indoctrination and "pep talks" were "all rot"; whether the men would follow him depended upon the personality of the officer. The leader must be a man who possesses military skill: then his men will know that he is protecting them. He must be a model to his men; he must be an all-powerful, and still benevolent, authority.

He must look after his men's needs, and be able to do all the men's duties better than they themselves in training and under combat conditions. The men must also be sure that their officer is duly considerate of their lives: they must know that he does not squander his human resources, that the losses of life which occur under his command will be minimal and justified. In the training of NCO's for officers, the German Army acted on the basis of such maxims, despite the Nazi Party's propagandistic preoccupation with such secondary aspects of morale as political ideology.

The positions of the officer and of the NCO were dependent on discipline and on the sanctions by which discipline is maintained and enforced. During training the Wehrmacht laid down the most severe disciplinary rules. In combat, even before Germany's military fortunes began to contract, life and death powers over the troops were vested in lower commanders. At the same time elaborate precautions were taken to control and even to counteract their severity in certain spheres of behavior. Officers were warned against senseless and unnecessary insults directed against their men. Special orders were issued and particular attention was paid in the training of officers to fatherly and considerate behavior in relations with their men; the combination of sternness and benevolence was strongly counseled. Numerous small indications of affection such as congratulations on birthdays and on anniversaries, and fatherly modes of address, e.g., *"Kinder"* (children), were recommended as helping to build the proper relations between officers and men.

The results of this approach to status relationships appear to have been good. Differences in privileges between officers and enlisted men in combat units almost never emerged as an object of complaint on the part of enlisted Ps/W. On the contrary, complaints of "softness" were more frequently directed against officers and enlisted men in the rear. The infantry soldier seldom attempted to attribute deficiencies in military operations to his immediate superiors. Spontaneous praise, in fact, was frequent.

German soldiers—both officers and men—greatly appreciated the ceremonial acknowledgment of hierarchical differences as expressed, for example, in the military salute. Captured Germans who saw the American Army in Great Britain before D-Day were often contemptuous of an enemy who was obviously so lax in dress and salute. Many of them said that the American Army could not be expected to fight well since the relations between officers and enlisted men were so informal. "This is no army." Such views of the value of the ceremonial aspects of discipline persisted in defeat. Ps/W taken late in the war, when they commented on American officer-man relations, often remarked with incredulous wonderment: "I don't see how it works!"

Not only was the position of German officers strengthened by their mixture of severe dominion and benevolence, but additional support for their authority came from the provision for the blameless gratification of primitive impulses and from the sanctioning of all types of aggressive social behavior outside the army group. Private personal transgressions of "civil" ethics were regarded as of slight importance, since they were outside the limits of the "manly comradeship" of the military primary group. Drunkenness and having women in the barracks were crimes which the officers overlooked; in occupied and enemy countries the latitude in personal and private transgressions was even greater. Provision was made for official houses of prostitution in which soldiers could reassure themselves about their manliness without disrupting the disciplinary structure of the Wehrmacht. This combination of practices lowered the probability of tensions in officer-man relationships.

NCO's and junior officers. In battle, leadership responsibility devolved in actuality on the senior NCO's (the opposite numbers of American platoon sergeants) and on the company grade officers. Only seldom did a line soldier see his battalion commander and even less frequently was he spoken to by him. Thus battalion commanders and other higher officers played a less central role in the personality system of the German soldier. They were therefore less directly related to the solidarity of the military primary group.

Nearly all non-commissioned and commissioned officers of the company grade level were regarded by the German soldier throughout the Western campaign as brave, efficient, and considerate. It was only in the very final phases of the war that Ps/W occasionally complained that they had been abandoned by their officers, and there was reason to believe that such complaints were justified not by facts but by the resurgence of uninhibited hostility against officers who, having been defeated, could now be looked upon as having shown weakness.

In addition, the slight increase in anti-officer sentiment which occurred during the last two months of the war may be related, not to the decline in competence, courage, or devotion on the part of the officers, but rather to the fact that the heavy losses of the Wehrmacht's trained junior officers had led to a large reduction in the ratio of the junior officers to men. In consequence, in order to use the available officers most economically, it was necessary to "thin" them out.[21] This resulted in a reduction in the amount of face-to-face contact between officers and men and in reduced feeling of the officers' protective function. And this, in turn, sometimes tipped the balance of the submissiveness-rebelliousness scale, in the successful manipulation of which lay the secret of the effective control of the German Army.

The junior officers of the Wehrmacht were, in general, very well selected. They were better educated than the average German, and had received extensive preliminary training. Although Nazi Party politics played a role in the general selection of officers (despite the façade of a non-political Wehrmacht) the junior officer ranks never became a field of patronage. High technical and personality requirements were made of all candidates for officership, Nazi and non-Nazi.

These facts were appreciated by many of the more intelligent enlisted Ps/W who testified that the influence of highly placed friends or of Party connections had practically no effect on an officer candidate's chances for selection, if he lacked the necessary qualifications for making a good officer.

Equally important in the provision of firm, "hard," and protective leadership, were the senior non-commissioned officers, who were everywhere appreciated as the most solid asset of the Wehrmacht. Until 1943, more than half of the NCO's who became Ps/W had belonged to the pre-1935 German Army. These men were neither very interested in politics nor very aggressive, but were thoroughly trained, solid men who were doing their job out of a deeply-rooted sense of duty to the soldierly profession.

As the war progressed, their numbers declined and less well-trained men took their place. In the last stages of the war, when the speed in reforming units was increased, the top non-commissioned officers often did not have sufficient time to promote the growth of strong identifications between themselves and their men. In February 1945, for the first time, Ps/W began to complain that "they didn't even have time to learn our names." The disintegration which set in in the Wehrmacht at this time was in part due to the declining value of the NCO as a cohesive factor in the military primary group.

Senior officers. The High Command and the senior officers, although generally esteemed, were not directly relevant in the psychological structure of the military primary group. They were in the main less admired than the junior officers because their physical remoteness made it easier to express hostile sentiments against them; they stood between the Führer and the junior officers and NCO's. And while the latter three obtained a positive affect from the ambivalent attitude toward authority of so many of the soldiers, the general officers themselves were made to some extent into the recipients of the hostile component of the soldier's authority-attitude. The failure of the *Putsch* of July 20 served to lower the esteem in which the High Command was held, although in general there was not a very lively reaction to that incident. Stalwart Nazis viewed it as a case of treason, and for the time being the concentration of their hostility on generals whose names were announced in public increased their confidence in those generals whom the Führer left in charge. Other soldiers, less passionately political, were inclined to turn their backs on the unsuccessful plotters because of the weakness manifested in their failures. But the situation was only temporary, and in any case the officers on whom the men in the field felt they depended were but little affected. The loss of prestige of the immediate officers was too small to make any difference in battle behavior, while senior officers in whom confidence had declined to a greater extent were too remote in the soldier's mind to make much difference in his combat efficiency.

Secondary Symbols

From the preceding section it is apparent that the immediately present agents and symbols of political authority—junior officers, NCO's, and conceptions of soldierly honor—were effective because of their consistency with the personality system of the individual soldier. In this section, we shall examine the effectiveness of the remoter—or secondary—agents and symbols of state authority.

Strategic aspects of the war. For the mass of the German Army, the strategic phases of the war were viewed apathetically. The ignorance of the German troops about important military events, even on their own front, was partly a result of the poverty of information about the actual course of the war—itself a part of Nazi policy.[22] But the deliberate management of ignorance need not always result in such far-reaching indifference as the German soldiers showed. Deliberately maintained ignorance would have resulted in a flood of rumors, had the German soldiers been more eager to know about the strategic phases of the war. As it was, there were very few rumors on the subject—merely apathy. Three weeks after the fall of the city of Aachen, there were still many prisoners being taken in the adjoining area who did not know that the city had fallen. For at least a week after the beginning of von Rundstedt's counter-offensive, most of the troops on the northern hinge of the bulge did not know that the offensive was taking place and were not much interested when they were told after capture. Of 140 Ps/W taken between December 23-24, 1944, only 35 percent had heard of the counter-offensive and only 7 percent said that they thought it significant.[23]

Some exception to this extensive strategic indifference existed with respect to the Eastern front. Although the German soldiers were extremely ignorant of the state of affairs on that front and made little attempt to reduce their ignorance, still the question of Russians was so emotionally charged, so much the source of anxiety, that it is quite likely that fear of the Russians did play a role in strengthening resistance. National Socialist propaganda had long worked on the traditional repugnance and fear of the German toward the Russian. The experience of the German soldiers in Russia in 1941 and 1942 increased this repugnance by direct perception of the primitive life of the Russian villager. But probably more important was the projection onto the Russians of the guilt feelings generated by the ruthless brutality of the Germans in Russia during the occupation period. The shudder of horror which frequently accompanied a German soldier's remarks about Russia was a result of all of these factors. These attitudes influenced German resistance in the West through the shift of soldiers from East to West and the consequent diffusion of their attitudes among their comrades. They also took effect by making soldiers worry about what would happen to their families if the Russians entered Germany. Of course, it should also be mentioned that this fear of the Russians also made some German soldiers welcome a speedier collapse on the Western front in the hope that a larger part of Germany would fall under Anglo-American control.

Before the actual occupation, only a small minority expressed fear of the consequences of an Anglo-American occupation. The continuing monthly opinion poll conducted by the Psychological Warfare Branch, mentioned elsewhere, never showed more than 20 percent of the prisoners answering "yes" to the question, "Do you believe that revenge will be taken against the population after the war?" Those who feared retribution were confirmed Nazis. Yet the general absence of fear of revenge did not cause a diminution of German resistance.

Neither did expectations about the outcome of the war play a great role in the integration or disintegration of the German Army. The statistics regarding German soldier opinion cited below show that pessimism as to final triumph was quite compatible with excellence in fighting behavior. The far greater effectiveness of considerations of self-preservation, and their vast preponderance over interest in the outcome of the war and the strategic situation, is shown by German prisoner recall of the contents of Allied propaganda leaflets (see Table 1). In the last two months of 1944 and the first two months of 1945, not less than 59 percent of the sample of prisoners taken each month recalled references to the preservation of the individual, and the figure rose to 76 percent in February of 1945. On the other hand, the proportion of prisoners recalling references to the total strategic situation of the war and the prospect of the outcome of the war seldom amounted to more than 20 percent, while references to political subjects seldom amounted to more than 10 percent. The general tendency was not to think about the outcome of the war unless forced to do so by direct interrogation. Even pessimism was counter-balanced by the reassurances provided by identification with a strong and benevolent Führer, by identification with good officers, and by the psychological support of a closely integrated primary group.

The ethics of war and patriotism. Quite consistently, ethical aspects of the war did not trouble the German soldier much. When pressed by Allied interrogators, Ps/W said that Germany had been forced to fight for its life. There were very few German soldiers who said that Germany had been morally wrong to attack Poland, or Russia. Most of them thought that if anything had been wrong about the war, it was largely in the realm of technical decisions. The decision to extirpate the Jews had been too drastic not because of its immorality but because it united the world against Germany. The declaration of war against the Soviet Union was wrong only because it created a two-front war. But these were all arguments which had to be forced from the Ps/W. Left to themselves, they seldom mentioned them.

TABLE 1

Tabulation of Allied Leaflet Propaganda Themes Remembered by German Ps/W

	Dec. 15-31 1944	Jan. 1-15 1945	Jan. 15-31 1945	Feb. 1-15 1945
Number of Ps/W	60	83	99	135
Themes and appeals remembered:				
a. Promise of good treatment as Ps/W and self-preservation through surrender	63%	65%	59%	76%
b. Military news	15	17	19	30
c. Strategical hopelessness of Germany's position	13	12	25	26
d. Hopelessness of a local tactical situation	3	1	7	7
e. Political attacks on German leaders	7	5	4	8
f. Bombing of German cities	2	8	6	--
g. Allied Military Government	7	3	--	--
h. Appeals to civilians	5	4	2	--

NOTE: The percentages add up to more than 100% since some Ps/W remembered more than one topic. Only Ps/W remembering at least one theme were included in this tabulation.

The assumption underlying these arguments was that the strong national state is a good in itself. But it was not, in fact, the highest good for any but the "hard core." In September 1944, for example, only 5 percent of a sample of 634 Ps/W said that they were worried about anything other than personal or familial problems, while in the very same survey, more than half of the Ps/W said they believed that Germany was losing the war or that they were at best uncertain of the war's outcome. In brief, fear for Germany's future as a nation does not seem to have been very important in the ordinary soldier's outlook and in motivating his combat behavior. As a matter of fact, as the war became more and more patently a threat to the persistence of the German national state, the narcissism of the German soldier increased correspondingly, so that the idea of national survival did not become an object of widespread preoccupation even when it might have been expected to become so.[24]

Ethical-religious scruples seem to have played an equally small role. Although there were a few interesting cases of Roman Catholic deserters, Roman Catholics (except Austrians, Czechs, and Polish nationals) do not seem to have deserted disproportionately. Prisoners seldom expressed remorse for Nazi atrocities, and practically no case was, noted of a desertion because of moral repugnance against Nazi atrocities.

Political ideals. The significance of political ideals, of symbols of political systems, was rather pronounced in the case of the "hard core" minority of fervent Nazis in the German Army. Their desire for discipline under a strong leader made them enthusiasts for the totalitarian political system. Their passionate aggressiveness also promoted projective tendencies which facilitated their acceptance of the Nazi picture of an innocent and harmless Germany encircled by the dark, threatening cloud of Bolsheviks, Jews, Negroes, etc., and perpetually in danger from inner enemies as well. But for most of the German soldiers, the political system of National Socialism was of little interest.

The *system* was indeed of very slight concern to German civilians also, even though dissatisfaction increased to a high pitch toward the end of the war. Soldiers on the whole were out of touch with the operation of the Party on the home front. Hence the political system impinged little on their consciousness. Thus, for example, of 53 potential and actual deserters in the Mediterranean theater, only one alleged political grounds for his action. The irrelevance of party politics to effective soldiering has already been treated above: here we need only repeat the statement of a German soldier, "Nazism begins ten miles behind the front line."

Nor did the soldiers react in any noticeable way to the various attempts to Nazify the army. When the Nazi Party salute was introduced in 1944, it was accepted as just one more army order, about equal in significance to an order requiring the carrying of gas masks. The introduction of the *National Socialistische Führungsoffiziere* (Guidance, or Indoctrination Officer), usually known as the NSFO, was regarded apathetically or as a joke. The contempt for the NSFO was derived not from his Nazi connection but from his status as an "outsider" who was not a real soldier. The especially Nazified Waffen SS divisions were never the object of hostility on the part of the ordinary soldier, even when the responsibility for atrocities was attributed to them. On the contrary, the Waffen SS was highly esteemed, not as a Nazi formation, but for its excellent fighting capacity. Wehrmacht soldiers always felt safer when there was a Waffen SS unit on their flank.

Devotion to Hitler. In contrast to the utterly apolitical attitude of the German infantry soldier toward almost all secondary symbols, an intense and personal devotion to Adolph Hitler was maintained in the German Army throughout the war. There could be little doubt that a high degree of identification with the Führer was an important factor in prolonging

German resistance. Despite fluctuations in expectations as to the outcome of the war, the trust in Hitler remained at a very high level even after the beginning of the serious reverses in France and Germany. In monthly opinion polls of German Ps/W opinion from D-Day until January 1945, in all but two samples over 60 percent expressed confidence in Hitler,[25] and confidence in January was nearly as high as it was in the preceding June. During this same period considerably more than half of the German soldiers in seven out of eight polls said they believed that it was impossible for the German Army to defeat the Allies in France. Only when the German Army began to break up in the face of overwhelming Allied fire power and deep, communications-cutting penetrations, did confidence in Hitler fall to the unprecedentedly low level of 30 percent. Even when defeatism was rising to the point at which only one-tenth of the prisoners taken as of March 1945 believed that the Germans had any chance of success, still a third retained confidence in Hitler.[26]

Belief in the good intentions of the Führer, in his eminent moral qualities, in his devotion and contributions to the well-being of the German people, continued on an even higher level. This strong attachment grew in large part from the feeling of strength and protection which the German soldier got from his conception of the Führer personality.

For older men, who had lived through the unemployment of the closing years of the Weimar Republic and who experienced the joy of being reinstated in gainful employment by Nazi full-employment policies, Hitler was above all the man who had provided economic security. This attitude extended even to left wing soldiers of this generation, who denounced the National Socialist political system, but found occasion to say a good word for Hitler as a man who had restored order and work in Germany. For men of the generation between 22-35, who had first experienced Hitler's charisma in the struggles to establish their manliness during late adolescence, Hitler was the prototype of strength and masculinity. For the younger Nazi fanatics, he was a father substitute, providing the vigilant discipline and the repression of dangerous impulses both in the individual and in the social environment; for them he had the additional merit of legitimating revolt against the family and traditional restraints.

Prisoners spoke of Hitler with enthusiasm, and even those who expressed regret over the difficulties which his policies had brought on Germany by engendering a two-front war and by allowing the Jews to be persecuted so fiercely as to arouse world hatred—even these men retained their warm esteem for his good intentions. They found it necessary to exculpate him in some way by attributing his errors to dishonest advisors who kept the truth from him, or to certain technical difficulties in his strategic doctrines which did not in any way reflect on his fundamental moral greatness or nobility.

It was difficult for German soldiers, as long as they had this attitude toward Hitler, to rebel mentally against the war. Time after time, prisoners who were asked why Hitler continued the war when they themselves admitted it was so obviously lost, said he would not continue the war and waste lives if he did not have a good, even though undisclosed, strategic reason for doing so, of if he did not have the resources to realize his ends. Nazis as well as non-Nazis answered in this way. Or else they would say, "the Führer has never deceived us," or, "he must have a good reason for doing what he does."

There was obviously a fear of rendering an independent judgment of events among the German soldiers and a desire for some strong leader to assume the responsibility for determining their fate. American and British soldiers often complained that the complexity of the army organization and strategy was so great and their own particular part was so small that they could not see the role of their personal missions. Their failure to see the connection made them miserable because it reduced their sense of personal autonomy. In the German Army, on the other hand, there was no difficulty for soldiers who were used throughout their lives to having other persons determine their objectives for them.

It is also possible that the very high devotion to Hitler under conditions of great stress was in part a reaction formation growing from a hostility against lesser authorities, which emerged as the weakness of these authorities became more manifest. In the last year of the war, hostility and contempt on the part of the German soldiers toward Nazi Party functionaries and toward Nazi Party leaders below Hitler (particularly Goebbels and Goering) were increasing. After the *Putsch* of July 20, hostility toward senior Wehrmacht officers also increased somewhat, although it never reached the levels of hostiiity displayed by civilians against local civilian Party officials and leaders. It is possible, therefore, that guilt created in ambivalent personalities by giving expression, even though verbally, to hostility against subordinate agents of authority, had to be alleviated by reaffirmed belief in the central and highest authority.

Weakening of the Hitler symbol. As the integral pattern of defense was broken down, however, and as danger to physical survival increased, devotion to Hitler deteriorated. The tendency to attribute virtue to the strong and immorality to the weak took hold increasingly, and while it did not lead to a complete rejection of Hitler, it reached a higher point than at any other stage in the history of National Socialism. The announcement of Hitler's death met an incapacity to respond on the part of many soldiers. There seemed to be no willingness to question the truth of the report, but the great upsurge of preoccupation with physical survival as a result of disintegration of the military primary group, the loss of contact with junior officers and the greatly intensified threat of destruction, caused a deadening of the power to respond to this event. For the vast horde of dishevelled, dirty, bewildered prisoners, who were being taken in the last weeks of the war, Hitler was of slight importance alongside the problem of their own biological survival and the welfare of their families. For the small minority who still had sufficient energy to occupy themselves with "larger problems," the news of Hitler's death released a sort of amorphous resentment against the fallen leader whose weakness and immorality had been proven by the failure of his strategy. But even here, the resentment was not expressed in explicit denunciations of Hitler's character or personality. The emphasis was all on technical deficiencies and weaknesses.

The explanation of the deterioration and final—though probably only temporary—hostility toward Hitler may in part be sought in the average German soldier's ambivalence toward the symbols of authority. This psychological mechanism, which also helps to explain the lack of a significant resistance movement inside Germany, enables us to understand the curve of Hitler's fame among the German people. Hitler, the father symbol, was loved for his power and his great accomplishments and hated for his oppressiveness, but the latter sentiment was repressed. While he remained strong it was psychologically expedient—as well as politically expedient—to identify with Hitler and to displace hostility on to weaker minority groups and foreigners. But once Hitler's authority had been undermined, the German soldiers rejected it and tended to express their hostility by projecting their own weakness on to him.

Thus the only important secondary symbol in motivating the behavior of the German soldiers during the recent war also lost its efficacy when the primary group relations of comradeliness, solidarity, and subordination to junior officers broke down, and with it the superego of the individual, on which the effective functioning of the primary group depends.[27]

Nazi Machinery for Maintaining Army Solidarity and Fighting Effectiveness

Administrative machinery and personnel. Even before the outbreak of the war, the Nazi Party took an active hand in the internal high policy of the Wehrmacht and in the selection of the Chief of Staff and his entourage. From September 1939 to the signing of the capitulation in May 1945 this process of Nazification continued steadily until the Wehrmacht was finally rendered powerless to make its own decisions. Nazi Party control over the Wehrmacht was designed to insure (1) that Nazi strategic intentions would be carried out (2) that capitulation would be made impossible and (3) that internal solidarity down to the lowest private would be maintained.

Most ambitious and successful of the early efforts at Nazification were the recruitment and training of the special Waffen SS (Elite) Divisions. These units initially contained only fanatically devoted Nazi volunteers and had officer staffs which were thoroughly permeated with Nazi stalwarts. They became the Nazi Party army within the Wehrmacht, and their military prowess greatly enhanced the prestige of the Nazi Party and weakened the position of the General Staff.

At the outbreak of the war, the domestic security and police services inside the Reich were completely unified under the command of Himmler. Although the Wehrmacht had its own elaborate system of security, elements of the *Sicherheitsdienst* operated in occupied areas, in conjunction with the Wehrmacht. As the fortunes of war declined, the Nazi Party accelerated the extension of its security and indoctrination services over the Wehrmacht. The security net around the German High Command was drawn most tightly in response to the 20th of July *Putsch*. In addition to those officers who were executed, a large number of doubtful loyalty were removed or put into commands where they could be closely supervised.

As the German troops retreated into Germany, SS and state police units, instead of the Wehrmacht military police, were given the normal military function of maintaining the line of demarcation between the front lines and the rear areas. A captured order, issued by the CO of the SS forces in the West on September 21, 1944, indicated that these units would have the task of preventing contact between the civilian population and the troops, as well as the arrest and execution of deserters from the army.[28] In addition to these security procedures, the Nazis made effective use of exploiting the individual German soldier's fear of physical destruction as was described above in the section, *Demand for physical survival.*

But these measures were of a negative nature. In order to strengthen the traditional Wehrmacht indoctrination efforts, the Nazi Party appointed in the winter of 1943 political indoctrination officers, called *National*

Socialistische Führungsoffiziere (NSFO), to all military formations. Later, in September 1944, when the Nazis felt the need for intensifying their indoctrination efforts, the position of these officers was strengthened by the establishment of an independent chain of command which enabled them to communicate with higher headquarters without Wehrmacht interference.[29] The NSFO's were given the power, in cases of "particular political significance or where delay implies danger" to report immediately and directly to NSF officers of higher commands and upward to the highest command, irrespective of routine communication channels. To interfere with the NSFO chain of command was made a military crime. The NSFO "organization" came to publish or directly supervise most of the publications and radio stations for the troops, and to prepare the leaflets which were distributed to or dropped on the German troops. Their job also included periodic indoctrination meetings. The official publication for the indoctrination of the officers' corps, *Mitteilung für die Truppe,* which had been published throughout the war by the Wehrmacht, was also taken over by Nazi Party functionaries *(NS Führungsstab der Wehrmacht)* in November 1944.

The NSF officers, with their independent chain of command, also became security officers of the Nazi Party. They spent a great deal of time prying into the morale and political convictions of higher officers in order to warn headquarters of the need to replace men of faltering faith.[30] Captured German generals, perhaps motivated by a desire to exculpate themselves, told how during the closing months of the war, they came to feel completely subjugated by the indoctrination officers. They reported that these Nazi junior officers maintained an independent reporting system on senior officers and often said "You're done if he gives a bad account of you."

The final step in the Nazi Party encroachment on the administration of the Wehrmacht came when the *levee en masse,* the *Volkssturm,* was raised. Here, the Nazi Party assumed complete control of training and indoctrination and units were to be turned over to the Wehrmacht only for actual deployment. No doubt the Wehrmacht was glad to be relieved of this unpopular task, as well as the even more unpopular task of organizing the Werewolf resistance, which the Nazi Party assumed for itself completely.

Propaganda themes. The most striking aspect of Nazi indoctrination of their own men during combat was the employment of negative appeals and counter-propaganda, which attempted less to reply directly to the substance of our claims than to explain the reasons why the Allies were using propaganda.

The Nazis frankly believed that they could employ our propaganda efforts as a point of departure for strengthening the unpolitical resolve of their men. They had the legend of the effectiveness of Allied propaganda in World War I as a warning from which to "conclude" that if the Germans failed to be tricked by propaganda this time, success was assured. A typical instance of this attitude was contained in a captured order issued by the Officer in Command of the garrison of Boulogne on September 11, 1944, in which he appealed to his men not to be misled by Allied propaganda. The German order claimed that the propaganda attack in the form of leaflets was in itself an expression of the weakness of the Allied offensive, which was in desperate need of the port for communications. During the same period, an NSF officer issued an elaborate statement in which he reminded the garrison at Le Havre that the "enemy resorts to propaganda as a weapon which he used in the last stages of the first world war," in order to point out that German victory depended on the determination of the German soldier to resist Allied propaganda.

In the fall and winter of 1944, the campaign to counteract Allied propaganda by "exposing" it was intensified and elaborated. (This method had the obvious advantage that direct refutations of Allied claims could largely be avoided.) *Mitteilung für die Truppe* (October 1944), a newspaper for officer indoctrination, reviewed the major weapons in the "poison offensive." They included: attacks against the Party and its predominant leaders ("this is not surprising as the enemy will, of course, attack those institutions which give us our greatest strength"); appeals to the Austrians to separate themselves from the Germans ("the time when we were split up in small states was the time of our greatest weakness"); sympathy with the poor German women who work in hellish factories ("the institution must be a good one, otherwise the enemy would not attack it").

Other themes "exposed" in leaflets were: the enemy attempts to separate the leaders from the people ("Just as the Kaiser was blamed in 1918, it now is Hitler who is supposed to be responsible"); the enemy admits his own losses in an exaggerated way in order to obtain the reputation of veracity and to lie all the more at the opportune moment.

Even earlier in the Western campaign, the Germans followed the policy of stamping Allied leaflets with the imprint, "Hostile Propaganda," and then allowing them to circulate in limited numbers. This was being carried out at the same time that mutually contradictory orders for the complete destruction of all enemy propaganda were being issued. The explanation, in part, is that the Nazis realized that it would be impossible to suppress the flood of Allied leaflets, and therefore sought to clearly label them as such and to employ them as a point of departure for counter-propaganda.

The procedure of overstamping Allied leaflets was linked with follow-up indoctrination talks. Such indoctrination lectures, which were conducted by the Nazi NSFO's, became toward the end of the war one of the main vehicles of Nazi indoctrination of their own troops. Ps/W claimed, although it was probably not entirely correct, that they usually slept through such sessions, or at least paid little attention, until the closing *Sieg Heil* was sounded. At this late date in the war, emphasis on oral propaganda was made necessary by the marked disruption of communications. Radio listening at the front was almost non-existent due to the lack of equipment; when in reserve, troops listened more frequently. Newspapers were distributed only with great difficulty. More important were the leaflets which were either dropped by air on their own troops or distributed through command channels.

"Strength through fear." Major lines of the negative approach employed in these leaflets, in indoctrination talks, in the rumors circulated by NSF officers, stressed "strength through fear," particularly fear of Russia and the general consequences of complete destruction that would follow defeat.

Because of the German soldier's concern about the welfare of his family living inside Germany, Nazi agencies were constantly issuing statements about the successful evacuation of German civilians to the east bank of the Rhine.

Equally stressed in the strength through fear theme were retaliation threats against the families of deserters, mistreatment of prisoners of war in Anglo-American prison camps, and the ultimate fate of prisoners. The phrase *Sieg oder Sibirien* (Victory or Siberia) was emphasized and much material was released to prove that the Anglo-Americans planned to turn over their prisoners to the Russians. When the U.S. Army stopped shipping German Ps/W to the United States, Nazi propaganda officers spread the rumor among German soldiers "that the way to Siberia is shorter from France than from the United States."

Statements by Ps/W revealed that shortly before the Rundstedt counter-attack, speeches by NSFO's were increased. One of the main subjects seems to have been weapons. In retrospect, the intent of the directives under which they were working was obvious. Attempts were made to explain the absence of the Luftwaffe, while the arrival in the near future of new and better weapons was guaranteed.

Psychological preparation for the December counter-offensive was built around the Rundstedt order of the day that "everything is at stake." Exhortations were backed up with exaggerated statements by unit commanders that large amounts of men and material were to be employed. Immediately thereafter official statements were issued that significant penetrations had been achieved; special editions of troop papers were prepared announcing that 40,000 Americans had been killed.

Such announcements received little attention among the troops actually engaged in the counter-offensive because of the obvious difficulties in disseminating propaganda to fighting troops.

Nevertheless, after the failure of the counter-attack, the Nazis felt called upon to formulate a plausible line to explain the sum total result of that military effort, especially for those who felt that better military judgment would have resulted in a purely defensive strategy against Russia. On January 25, *Front und Heimat* announced that the December offensive had smashed the plan for a simultaneous onslaught: "The East can hold only if the West does too. . . . Every fighting man in the West knows that the Anglo-Americans are doing all they can, although belatedly, to start the assault on the Fortress Germany. Our task in the West now is to postpone that time as long as possible and to guard the back of our Armies in the East."

Despite the obvious limitations on the efficacy of propaganda during March and April 1945, the Nazis continued to the very end to keep up their propaganda efforts. Due to the confusion within the ranks of the Wehrmacht and the resulting difficulties of dissemination, the task devolved almost wholly on the NSFO's who spent much of their time reading to the troops the most recent orders governing desertion. Leaflets called largely on the Landser's military spirit to carry on. One even demanded that he remain silent *(zu schweigen)*. The Nazis taxed their fancy to create rumors as the last means of bolstering morale. Here a favorite technique for stimulating favorable rumors was for CO's to read to their men "classified" documents from official sources which contained promises of secret weapons or discussed the great losses being inflicted upon the Allies.

The Impact of Allied Propaganda on Wehrmacht Solidarity

The system of controls which the social structure of the Wehrmacht exercised over its individual members greatly reduced those areas in which symbolic appeals of the Allies could work. But the millions of leaflets which were dropped weekly and the "round-the-clock" broadcasts to the German troops certainly did not fail to produce some reactions.

The very first German Ps/W who were interrogated directly on their reactions to Allied propaganda soon revealed a stereotyped range of answers which could be predicted from their degree of Nazification. The fanatical Nazi claimed, "No German would believe anything the enemy has to say," while an extreme attitude of acceptance was typified by a confirmed anti-Nazi who pleaded with his captors: "Now is the moment to flood the troops with leaflets. You have no idea of the effect sober and effective leaflets have on retreating troops." But these extreme reactions of soldiers were of low frequency; Nazi soldiers might admit the truth of our leaflets but usually would not accept their conclusions and implications.

The fundamentally indifferent reaction to Allied propaganda was most interestingly shown in an intensive study of 150 Ps/W captured in October 1944 of whom 65 percent had seen our leaflets and for the most part professed that they believed their contents. This was a group which had fought very obstinately, and the number of active deserters, if any, was extremely small. Some forty of these Ps/W offered extended comments as to what they meant when they said they believed the contents of Allied leaflets.

Five stated outright that they believed the messages and that the leaflets assisted them and their comrades to surrender.

Seven declared they believed the leaflets, but were powerless to do anything about appeals to surrender.

Eight stated that they believed the contents, but nevertheless as soldiers and decent individuals would never think of deserting.

Twenty-two declared that events justified belief in the leaflets, but they clearly implied that this had been of little importance in their battle experiences.

In Normandy, where the relatively small front was blanketed with printed material, up to 90 percent of the Ps/W reported that they had read Allied leaflets, yet this period was characterized by very high German morale and stiff resistance.

Throughout the Western campaign, with the exception of periods of extremely bad weather or when the front was fluid, the cumulative percentage of exposure ranged between 60 and 80 percent. (This cumulative percentage of exposure was based on statements by Ps/W that they had seen leaflets sometime while fighting on the Western front after D-Day. A few samples indicated that penetration during any single month covered about 20 percent of the prisoners.) Radio listening among combat troops was confined to a minute fraction due to the lack of equipment; rear troops listened more frequently. In the case of both leaflets and radio it was found that there was widespread but desultory comment on the propaganda, much of which comment distorted the actual contents.

Not only was there wide penetration by Allied leaflets and newssheets, but German soldiers frequently circulated them extensively among their comrades. A readership study of *Nachrichten für die Truppe,* a daily newssheet published by the Allied Psychological Warfare Division, showed that each copy which was picked up had an average readership of between four and five soldiers—a figure which is extremely large in view of the conditions of combat life. Not only were leaflets widely circulated, but it became a widespread practice for soldiers to carry Allied leaflets on their person, especially the "safe conduct pass" leaflets which bore a statement by General Eisenhower guaranteeing the bearer swift and safe conduct through Allied lines and the protection of the Geneva Convention. There is evidence that in certain sectors of the front, German soldiers even organized black-market trading in Allied propaganda materials.

It is relevant to discuss here the differences in effectiveness between tactical and strategic propaganda. By tactical propaganda, we refer to propaganda which seeks to promise immediate results in the tactical situation. The clearest example of this type of propaganda is afforded by "across the lines" loudspeaker broadcasts, which sometimes facilitated immediate capture of the prisoners of war—not by propaganda in the ordinary sense, but by giving instructions on how to surrender safely, once the wish to surrender was present.

No sufficiently accurate estimate is available of the total number of prisoners captured by the use of such techniques, but signal successes involving hundreds of isolated troops in the Normandy campaign have been credited to psychological warfare combat teams. Even more successful were the loudspeaker-carrying tanks employed in the Rhine River offensive, when the first signs of weakening resistance were encountered. For example, the Fourth Armored Division reported that its psychological warfare unit captured over 500 prisoners in a four-day dash from the Kyll River to the Rhine. Firsthand investigation of these loudspeaker missions, and interrogation of prisoners captured under such circumstances, establish that Allied propaganda was effective in describing the tactical situation to totally isolated and helpless soldiers and in arranging an Allied cease fire and thereby presenting an assurance to the German soldier of a safe surrender. The successful targets for such broadcasts were groups where solidarity and ability to function as a unit were largely destroyed. Leaflets especially written for specific sectors and dropped on pinpoint targets by fighter-bombers were used instead of loudspeakers where larger units were cut off. This method proved less successful, since the units to which they were addressed were usually better integrated and the necessary cease fire conditions could not be arranged.

Less spectacular, but more extensive, was strategic propaganda. Allied directives called for emphasis on four themes in this type of propaganda: (1) Ideological attacks on the Nazi Party and Germany's war aims, (2) the strategical hopelessness of German's military and economic position, (3) the justness of the United Nations war aims and their unity and determination to carry them out (unconditional surrender, although made known to the troops, was never stressed), (4) promises of good treatment to prisoners of war, with appeals to self-preservation through surrender.

Although it is extremely difficult, especially in view of the lack of essential data, to assess the efficacy of these various themes, some tentative clues might be seen in the answers given to the key attitude questions in the monthly Psychological Warfare opinion poll of captured German soldiers.[31] Thus, there was no significant decline in attachment to Nazi ideology until February and March 1945. In other words, propaganda attacks on Nazi ideology seem to have been of little avail, and attachment to secondary symbols, e.g., Hitler, declined only when the smaller military units began to break up under very heavy pressure.

Since the German soldier was quite ignorant of military news on other fronts, it was believed that a great deal of printed material should contain factual reports of the military situation, stressing the strategical hopelessness of the German position. As a result, the third most frequently recalled items of our propaganda were the military news reports. It seems reasonable to believe that the emphasis on these subjects did contribute to the development of defeatist sentiment.

Despite the vast amount of space devoted to ideological attacks on German leaders, only about five percent of the Ps/W mentioned this topic—a fact which supported the contention as to the general failure of ideological or secondary appeals. Finally, the presentation of the justness of our war aims was carried out in such a way as to avoid stressing the unconditional surrender aspects of our intentions, while emphasizing postwar peace intentions and organizational efforts; much was made of United Nations unity. All this fell on deaf ears, for of this material only a small minority of Ps/W (about five percent) recalled specific statements about military government plans for the German occupation.

As has been pointed out previously, the themes which were most successful at least in attracting attention and remaining fixed in the memory, were those promising good treatment as prisoners of war. In other words, propaganda referring to immediate concrete situations and problems seems to have been most effective in some respects.

The single leaflet most effective in communicating the promise of good treatment was the "safe conduct pass." Significantly, it was usually printed on the back of leaflets which contained no elaborate propaganda appeals except those of self-preservation. The rank and file tended to be favorably disposed to its official language and legal, document-like character. In one sector where General Eisenhower's signature was left off the leaflet, doubt was cast on its authenticity.

Belief in the veracity of this appeal was no doubt based on the attitude that the British and the Americans were respectable law-abiding soldiers who would treat their captives according to international law. As a result of this predisposition and the wide use of the safe conduct leaflets, as well as our actual practices in treating prisoners well, the German soldier came to have no fear of capture by British or American troops. The most that can be claimed for this lack of fear was that it may have decreased or undercut any tendency to fight to the death; it produced no active opposition to continued hostilities.

As an extension of the safe-conduct approach, leaflets were prepared instructing non-commissioned officers in detailed procedures by which their men could safely be removed from battle so as to avoid our fire and at the same time avoid evacuation by the German field police. If the Germans could not be induced to withdraw from combat actively, Allied propaganda appealed to them to hide in cellars. This in fact became a favorite technique of surrender, since it avoided the need of facing the conscience-twinging desertion problem.

As a result of psychological warfare research, a series of leaflets was prepared whose attack was aimed at primary group organization in the German Army, without recourse to ideological symbols. Group organization depended on the acceptance of immediate leadership and mutual trust. Therefore this series of leaflets sought to stimulate group discussion among the men and to bring into their focus of attention concerns which would loosen solidarity. One leaflet declared, "Do not take our (the Allies) word for it; ask your comrade; find out how he feels." Thereupon followed a series of questions on personal concerns, family problems, tactical consideration and supply problems. Discussion of these problems was expected to increase anxiety. It was assumed that to the degree that the soldier found that he was not isolated in his opinion, to that degree he would be strengthened in his resolve to end hostilities, for himself at least.

Conclusion. At the beginning of the second world war, many publicists and specialists in propaganda attributed almost supreme importance to psychological warfare operations. The legendary successes of Allied propaganda against the German Army at the end of the first world war and the tremendous expansion of the advertising and mass communications industries in the ensuing two decades had convinced many people that human behavior could be extensively manipulated by mass communications. They tended furthermore to stress that military morale was to a great extent a function of the belief in the rightness of the "larger" cause which was at issue in the war; good soldiers were therefore those who clearly understood the political and moral implications of what was at stake. They explained the striking success of the German Army in the early phases of the war by the "ideological possession" of the German soldiers, and they accordingly thought that propaganda attacking doctrinal conceptions would be defeating this army.

Studies of the German Army's morale and fighting effectiveness made during the last three years of the war throw considerable doubt on these hypotheses. The solidarity of the German Army was discovered by these studies—which left much to be desired from the standpoint of scientific rigor—to be based only very indirectly and very partially on political convictions or broader ethical beliefs. Where conditions were such as to allow primary group life to function smoothly, and where the primary group developed a high degree of cohesion, morale was high and resistance effective or at least very determined, regardless in the main of the political attitudes of the soldiers. The conditions of primary group life were related to spatial proximity, the capacity for intimate communication, the provision of paternal protectiveness by NCO's and junior officers, and the gratification of certain personality needs, e.g., manliness, by the military organization and its activities. The larger structure of the army served to maintain morale through the provision of the framework in which potentially individuating physical threats were kept at a minimum—through the organization of supplies and through adequate strategic dispositions.

The behavior of the German Army demonstrated that the focus of attention and concern beyond one's immediate face-to-face social circles might be slight indeed and still not interfere with the achievement of a high degree of military effectiveness. It also showed that attempts to modify behavior by means of symbols referring to events or values outside the focus of attention and concern would be given an indifferent response by the vast majority of the German soldiers. This was almost equally true under conditions of primary group integrity and under conditions of extreme primary group disintegration. In the former, primary needs were met adequately through the gratifications provided by the other members of the group; in the latter, the individual had regressed to a narcissistic state in which symbols referring to the outer world were irrelevant to his first concern—"saving his own skin."

At moments of primary group disintegration, a particular kind of propaganda, less hortatory or analytical, but addressing the intensified desire to survive, and describing the precise procedures by which physical survival could be achieved, was likely to facilitate further disintegration. Furthermore, in some cases aspects of the environment toward which the soldier might hitherto have been emotionally indifferent were defined for him by prolonged exposure to propaganda under conditions of disintegration. Some of these wider aspects, e.g., particular strategic considerations, then tended to be taken into account in his motivation and he was more likely to implement his defeatist mood by surrender than he would have been without exposure to propaganda.

It seems necessary, therefore, to reconsider the potentialities of propaganda in the context of all the other variables which influence behavior. The erroneous views concerning the omnipotence of propaganda must be given up and their place must be taken by much more differentiated views as to the possibilities of certain kinds of propaganda under different sets of conditions.

It must be recognized that on the moral plane most men are members of the larger society by virtue of identifications which are mediated through the human beings with whom they are in personal relationships. Many are bound into the larger society only by primary group identifications. Only a small proportion possessing special training or rather particular kinds of personalities are capable of giving a preponderant share of their attention and concern to the symbols of the larger world. The conditions under which these different groups will respond to propaganda will differ, as will also the type of propaganda to which they will respond.

Notes

1. For a further treatment of these problems see Henry V. Dicks, "Personality Traits and National Socialist Ideology," *Human Relations*, III, No. 1 (June 1950), pp. 111-155.

2. Report by the Supreme Commander on operations in Europe by Allied Expeditionary Force, June 6, 1944 to May 8, 1945.

3. Charles Horton Cooley, in *Social Organization* (New York, 1909), defines primary groups: "By primary groups I mean those characterized by intimate face-to-face association and cooperation . . . it is 'we'; it involves the sort of sympathy and mutual identification for which 'we' is the natural expression. One lives in the feeling of the whole and finds the chief aims of his will in that feeling" (p. 23). "The most important spheres of this intimate association and cooperation —though by no means the only ones—are the family, the play group of children, and the neighborhood or community group of elders" (p. 24). "The only essential thing being a certain intimacy and fusion of personalities" (p. 26).

4. *Kriegsbriefe gefallener Studenten,* 1928, pp. 167-172. Quoted by William K. Pfeiler, *War and the German Mind* (New York, 1941), p. 77.

5. On the relations between the *technical* group and *social* group, cf. T. N. Whitehead, *Leadership in a Free Society* (Cambridge, Mass., 1936), Chap. IV.

6. Cooley, *Social Organization,* Part I, pp. 3-57; S. Freud, *Group Psychology and the Analysis of the Ego,* Chap. IV; Elton Mayo, *The Human Problems of an Industrial Civilization* (New York, 1933); A.T.M. Wilson, "The Service Man Comes Home," *Pilot Papers: Social Essays and Documents,* I, No. 2 (April 1946), pp. 9-28; R. R. Grinker and J. P. Spiegel, *Men Under Stress* (Philadelphia, 1945), Chap. 3; T. N. Whitehead, *Leadership in Free Society,* Chaps. 1, 7, 10; also A. D. Lindsay, *The Essentials of Democracy* (Oxford, 1935), pp. 78-81.

7. German combat soldiers almost always stressed the high level of camaraderie in their units. They frequently referred to their units as "one big family."

8. Individuals of German extraction residing outside the boundaries of Germany.

9. Approval of desertion by a married man with a large family or with heavy familial obligations was often noted near the war's end. For such men, the stronger ties to the family prevented the growth of insuperably strong ties to the army unit.

10. The "hard core" corresponds to opinion leaders, as the term is currently used in opinion research.

11. Herman Schmalenbach, "Die soziologische Kategorien des Bundes," *Die Dioskuren,* I (München, 1922), pp. 35-105; and Hellmuth Plessner, *Grenzen der Gemeinschaft* (Bonn, 1924).

12. Hans Bluher, *Die Rolle der Erotik in der männlichen Gesellschaft* (Jena, 1921), Vol. II, part II, especially pp. 91-109, 154-177.

13. This policy sometimes created a serious dilemma for the Wehrmacht. Increasingly, to preserve the sense of group identity and the benefits of solidarity which arose from it, regiments were allowed to become depleted in manpower by as much as 50 to 75 percent. This, however, generated such feelings of weakness that the solidarity gains were cancelled.

14. This proposition is in opposition to the frequently asserted view that social solidarity of an intense sort is positively and linearly related to fear of threat from the outside.

15. The Germans in the Channel ports were able to resist so long partly because the men remained together where they were constantly in each other's presence. Thus the authority of the group over the individual was constantly in play.

16. A 36-year-old soldier—a Berlin radio worker—who surrendered prematurely,

said: "During one month in a bunker without light and without much to do, the men often discussed capture. Conversation usually started about families: who was married and what was to become of his family? The subject became more acute as the Americans approached."

17. This threat was never actually carried out. Furthermore, the *Sicherheitsdienst* (Security Service) admitted the impossibility of taking sanctions against the deserter's family because of the difficulty of locating them in the disorder of German civilian life. As the German soldiers became aware of the impotence of the SD in this respect, this barrier against desertion weakened.

18. Karl Demeter, *Das deutsche Heer und seine Offiziere* (Berlin, n.d.), Chaps. 3 and 5; Hermann Broch, *The Sleepwalkers* (London, n.d.).

19. Indeed, a well-known German general during the period of captivity felt so strongly the pressure of soldierly honor that he always went to sleep wearing his monocle.

20. Frequently German soldiers who were reluctant to desert separated themselves from battle by hiding in cellars or dugouts, waiting to be overrun. Such soldiers often thought it morally necessary to volunteer the explanation for their capture that they had been found by the enemy because they had fallen asleep from exhaustion and had been taken against their will.

21. The absence of officers relaxed disciplinary controls. Thus soldiers who lay in bunkers and who "didn't see any officers for weeks" were more likely to desert or to allow themselves to be captured. The presence of the officer had the same function as other primary group members—he strengthened the superego by granting affection for duties performed and by threatening to withdraw it for duties disregarded.

22. Nazi propagandists, with their hyperpolitical orientation, tended to overestimate the German soldier's responsiveness to politics.

23. The fact that the High Command made no attempt to explain away the defeat of the counter-offensive may have been due, among other things, to its conviction of the irrelevance of strategic consideration in the morale of the ordinary soldier.

24. The proposition often asserted during the war that the Allies' refusal to promise a "soft peace" to the Germans was prolonging the war, i.e., that German military resistance was motivated by fear of what the Allies would do to Germany in the event of its defeat, scarcely finds support in the fact that in October 1944, when the German front was stiffening, 74 percent of a sample of 345 Ps/W said they did not expect revenge to be taken against the German population after the war.

25. See M. I. Gurfein and Morris Janowitz, "Trends in Wehrmacht Morale," *Public Opinion Quarterly* X, No. 1 (1946), p. 78.

26. Much of the reduction of trust in Hitler which occurred in this final period was simply a diminution in esteem for Hitler's technical skill as a strategist and as a diplomat.

27. The mixture of apathy and resentment against Hitler persisted through the first part of the demobilization period following the end of the war, but as life began to reorganize and to take on new meaning and the attitudes toward authority, which sustain and are sustained by the routines of daily life, revived, esteem for Hitler also began to revive. It is likely to revive still further and to assume a prominent place in German life once more, if the new elite which is being created under the Allied occupation shows weakness and lack of decisiveness and self-confidence.

28. Order of Commanding Officer of SS Forces in the West, September 21, 1944.

29. This step was regarded as sufficiently important to be promulgated in an Order appearing over Hitler's signature.

30. Numerous orders menaced officers who might become political dissidents. One such document circulated in Army Group B, dated January 21, 1945, stated that Himmler had drawn up a set of instructions concerning officer offenders which were to be reviewed at least once a month. Political divergences were to be harshly dealt with, regardless of the previous military or political service of the officer in question.

31. Cf. Gurfein and Janowitz, "Trends in Wehrmacht Morale."

CHANGING PATTERNS OF
ORGANIZATIONAL AUTHORITY:
THE MILITARY ESTABLISHMENT

Sociological perspectives toward organization have brought into focus the informal and interactive processes which modify legal and formal authority structures. Empirical research in this area emphasizes an equilibrium analysis—the striving to achieve adjustment, balance, and the like. What processes favor or hinder a large-scale bureaucracy in the maintenance of its organizational identity under pressure of internal and external demands? Equilibrium analysis focuses on limited time spans, and as a result organizational change is seen only as it takes place within definite and prescribed limits.[1]

Much less emphasized is the necessity of focusing on the long-term transformations of administrative organization. Developmental analysis which seeks to understand organizational change can take the form of a concern with the restructuring in the pattern and character of authority. Developmental analysis is not descriptive history, but it is analysis with a strong concern for the historical context.[2]

As organizational forms have grown more complex, bureaucratic authority has tended to be transformed. In order to maintain their organizational effectiveness authority systems have had to become less arbitrary, less direct, and even less authoritarian. The significance of persuasion has grown with the growing complexity of society. From this point of view there has been under industrialism a relative shift in the basis of authority from status toward morale in all types of bureaucratic organizations. An authority system based on status is an expression of a simple division of labor where co-ordination involves no more than

This chapter is from *Administrative Science Quarterly*, III (March, 1959), pp. 474-493.

compliance or adherence to rules; the morale system implies that co-ordination is too complex to be mechanical and requires positive involvement and incentives.

In this analysis the relative shift in forms of authority is described in terms of the shift from discipline based on *domination* to that involving *manipulation,* concepts which will be elaborated later. While the analysis is applied to the military establishment, since it can be considered the bureaucratic prototype, the transformation is also found in other authority structures. One major proposition is that the military, despite its rigid hierarchical structure, has nevertheless been forced to modify its authority system from domination and rigid discipline to more indirect forms of control, as have other types of bureaucracies. In its own terms, the recent transformation of military authority may be even more extensive than that found in nonmilitary organizations. Of course, a shift in authority from domination to manipulation is hardly an all-or-none change; we are only speaking of trends and countertrends.

A second basic proposition, therefore, emerges—that the shift in organizational control to an emphasis on manipulation and persuasion is highly unstable and transitional. Already one can see the outlines of emerging patterns of authority which will be required if the military establishment is to achieve its organizational goals. For lack of a better term, such a change from present forms might be called a "fraternal type" of authority system. Moreover, these transformations of authority relations in the military establishment in some respects anticipate and foreshadow developments in civilian bureaucracies. Thus the similarities and differences between the military establishment and other types of large-scale organizations require continual comparison.

The contemporary military establishment has for some time tended more and more to display characteristics typical of any large-scale nonmilitary bureaucracy. This is the result of technological change, which vastly increases the size of the military establishment, elaborates its interdependence with civilian society, and alters its internal social relations. Nevertheless the typical sociological analysis of military organization does not take into account the consequences of these trends and continues instead to emphasize its authoritarian, stratified-hierarchical, and traditional dimensions as a basis for distinguishing the military from the nonmilitary bureaucracy.[3]

Thus Campbell and McCormack in their study "Military Experience and Attitudes toward Authority,"[4] supported by a United States Air Force research contract, began with the hypothesis that air cadet training would increase authoritarian predispositions among the officer candidates. Since they assumed that the dominant characteristics of military organization were its authoritarian procedures, the consequences of participation in its training program would of necessity heighten authoritarian personality tendencies among those who successfully passed through such training. (Authoritarian personality tendencies imply both the predisposition arbitrarily to dominate others of lower status and simultaneously to submit to arbitrary higher authority.)

When the results of the research, as measured by the well-known authoritarian "F" scale, showed a decrease in authoritarian traits among cadets after one year of training, the authors were tempted to conclude that perhaps their research tools were inadequate.[5] Now even a superficial examination of the organizational processes of combat flight training would have indicated an emphasis on group interdependence and on a team concept of co-ordination to ensure survival which should have cautioned these researchers against their initial hypothesis.[6]

The view with which these social scientists approached the military establishment is partly based on civilian ideology. Partly, as Hans Speier points out in his critique of the *The American Soldier* research series, such a view exaggerates the differences between military and civilian organizations by overlooking what is common to large-scale organizations in general.[7] Many of the bureaucratic features of military life are in fact to be found in civilian organizations in varying degrees.

Military Structure and Combat Goals

One can hardly deny the significant differences that exist between military and nonmilitary bureaucracies. The goals and purposes of an organization supply a meaningful basis for understanding differences in organizational behavior, and the military establishment as a social system has its special and unique characteristics because the possibility of hostilities is an ever-present reality.

A realistic appraisal of the implications of combat and combat preparation on military organization obviously starts with the social consequences of the changing technology of warfare. Although the narrowing distinction between the military establishment and nonmilitary bureaucracies does not eliminate fundamental differences, three trends need to be emphasized.

First, military technology both extraordinarily increases the destructiveness of warfare and widens the scope of automation in the use of new weapons. It is a commonplace that both of these developments tend to weaken the distinction between military roles and civilian roles. Nevertheless, conventional units employing the airplane, the submarine, and airborne assault troops need to be maintained for limited warfare. Despite the growth of missile systems manned auxiliary methods for the delivery of new weapons require organization similar to conventional combat units. Even more important, no military system can rely on expectation of victory based on the initial exchange of firepower, whatever the form of the initial exchange. Subsequent exchanges will involve units and formations—again regardless of their armament—which are prepared to carry out the struggle as soldiers, that is, subject themselves to military authority according to plan and continue to fight. The automation of war civilianizes wide sectors of the military establishment, yet the need to maintain combat readiness and to develop centers of resistance after initial hostilities ensures the continued importance of military organization and patterns of authority.

Second, it can be argued that the revolution in military technology shifts the military mission from that of preparation for the use of violence to that of deterrence of violence. There can be no doubt that this shift in mission is having important effects on military thought and authority. Military elites are more and more forced to concern themselves with broad ranges of political, social, and economic policies. Again, there are limits to the consequences of this trend. The role of deterrence is not a new one for the military. Historically the contribution of the military to the balance of power was not the result of its civilian character. On the contrary, the balance-of-power formula operates, when it does, because the military establishment is prepared to fight effectively and immediately.

With the increase in the importance of deterrence, military elites have become more and more involved in diplomatic and political warfare, regardless of their preparation for such tasks. Yet the specific and unique contribution of the military to deterrence is the threat of violence which has currency—that is, the threat can be taken seriously because the possibility of actual violence is real. The types of weapons available do not alter this basic formula. In short, deterrence still requires an organization prepared for combat.

Third, the assumption that military institutions, as compared with civilian institutions, are resistant to change has been eliminated as the process of innovation in the military establishment itself has become routinized. Analysis of the relative impact on technological development of the requirements of war versus the requirements of civilian economic entrepreneurship has produced volumes of historical writing. Schumpeter in his brilliant analysis of modern imperialism argues that capitalist economic organization succeeded only as it opposed the military establishment.[8] For him the technological development of the capitalist economic system stood in opposition to the interests of the feudal aristocratic elements, which, unable to find their place in the changing social order, supplied the ideology and personnel for the military and imperialistic expansions from Western Europe up through the nineteenth century. In this view capitalism produced social change through technological innovation in order to accumulate capital and to make profits. By contrast, the military, concerned with honor and a way of life, stood in opposition to social change and technological innovation and accepted new developments in military organization with great reluctance. In all probability military organizations of the middle of the nineteenth century were strongly resistant to technological innovation and derived their goals and tasks from other sectors of society—from the religious, from the political, or merely from a negative effort to escape the powerful dogmas of capitalist profit and business pacifism.

However, it is impossible to find support for Schumpeter's view of the antagonisms between business enterprise and the military order as a basis for understanding social change during the twentieth century. Military institutions, because of the nationalism on which they rest and the vast resources they command, can no longer be thought of as merely reacting to external pressures. The articulation of the military establishment with the business enterprise system is indeed too complex to be considered as simple antagonism. Moreover, the military creates requirements of its own for technological innovation which modify industrial organization. The classical view of the military standing in opposition to technological innovation is inapplicable as the present cycle of the arms race converts the armed forces into centers of support and concern for the development of new weapons systems.

Leadership based on military customs must share power with experts not only in technical matters but also in matters of organization and human relations. Specific organizational adaptations of the military even foreshadow developments in civilian society, since the military must press hard for innovation and respond rapidly to the strains created. For example, the continual need for retraining personnel from operational to managerial positions and from older to newer techniques has led to a more rational spreading of higher education throughout the career of the military officer rather than the concentrated dosage typical of the civilian in graduate or professional school.

There are of course powerful pressures against innovation. As long as imponderables weigh heavily in estimating military outcomes, and as long as the "fighter" spirit is required for combat, the military establishment cannot become completely technological in its orientation. The heroes of former engagements can with some validity press their personal experiences as a basis for decision making. The need to protect privilege as well as all the classic devices of bureaucratic behavior—military or civilian— imply that outmoded militarism persists even though technological necessity becomes dominant. Nor does acceptance of technological change necessarily imply acceptance of changes in approach toward political and diplomatic conflict. The residues of conservative military authority become manifest at times in an overemphasis on the use of force to regulate competing national interests.

Thus neither the increased automation of military technology, nor the military shift in mission from war making to deterrence, nor the decline in traditional military opposition to innovation can give a completely civilian form to military institutions. The function of military authority—the key to military organization—is undergoing systemic change; yet the character of military authority remains an expression of organizational requirements for combat and combat preparation—goals unique to military and military-type organizations.

Changing Military Authority: From Domination to Manipulation

Although a preponderance of military personnel is engaged in administrative and logistical operations, military authority, if it is to be effective, must strive to make combat units its organizational prototype.[9] For combat the maintenance of initiative has become a crucial requirement of greater importance than the rigid enforcement of discipline. In the concise formulation of S.L.A. Marshall:

The philosophy of discipline has adjusted to changing conditions. As more and more impact has gone into the hitting power of weapons, necessitating ever widening deployments in the forces of battle, the quality of the initiative in the individual has become the most praised of the military virtues.[10]

Close-order formations based on relatively low firepower could be dominated and controlled by direct and rigid discipline. But continuously since the development of the rifle bullet more than a century ago, the social organization of combat units has been altering so as to throw the solitary soldier on his own and his primary group's social and psychological resources. In World War II and again in the Korean conflict, the United States organizational crisis centered on developing the ability of the infantry soldier to make the fullest use of his weapons. The decision to fire or not to fire rested mainly with dispersed infantrymen, individually and in small primary groups. Thus the military with its hierarchical structure, with its exacting requirements for co-ordination, and with its apparently high centralization of organizational power must strive contrariwise to develop the broadest decentralization of initiative at the point of contact with the enemy. Any new nuclear weapons systems short of total destruction creates the same organizational requirements.

The combat soldier—regardless of military arm—when committed to battle is hardly the model of Max Weber's ideal bureaucrat following rigid rules and regulations. In certain respects he is the antithesis of this. He is not detached, routinized, and self-contained; rather his role is one of constant improvisation. Improvisation is the keynote of the individual fighter or combat group, from seeking alternative routes to a specific outpost to the retraining of whole divisions immediately before battle. The impact of battle destroys men, equipment, and organization, which need constantly and continually to be brought back into some form of unity through on-the-spot improvisation. In battle the planned division of labor breaks down.

The military organization of today is forced to alter its techniques of training and indoctrination. Rather than attempting to develop automatic reaction to combat dangers, it requires a training program designed to teach men not only to count on instruction from superiors but also to exercise their own judgment about the best response to make when confronted by given types of danger. The designation "combat team" exemplifies the goals of such indoctrination since it emphasizes the positive contributions of each person regardless of rank.

Obviously technology conditions these changing internal social relations in the military. Modern weapons involve a complex division of labor and high levels of technical skill. The morale and co-ordination of the individual members of a group cannot be guaranteed by authoritarian discipline. The complexity of the machinery and the resultant social interdependence produce an important residue of organizational power for each participating member. All the members of a military group recognize their mutual dependence on the technical proficiency and level of performance of others as well as on the formal authority structure.

Moreover, the increased firepower of modern weapons causes military forces to be more and more dispersed so that each unit becomes more and more dependent on its own organizational impetus.

Thus the impact of technology has forced a shift in the functions of military authority. Military authority must shift from reliance on practices based on *domination* to a widening utilization of *manipulation*. By domination we mean influencing an individual's behavior by giving explicit instruction as to desired behavior without reference to the goals sought. Domination involves threats and negative sanctions rather than positive incentives. It tends to produce mechanical compliance. By manipulation we mean influencing an individual's behavior by indirect techniques of group persuasion and by an emphasis on group goals. Manipulation involves positive incentives rather than physical threats; though it does retain the threat of exclusion from the group as a form of control. The indirect techniques of manipulation tend to take into account the individual soldier's predispositions.

Despite its hierarchical structure and despite its legal code the military establishment presents a striking case of this shift from domination to increased reliance on manipulation. The transformation can be seen in every phase of organization behavior—for example, the narrowing of the differences in privileges, status, and even uniforms of the enlisted man and the officer, the development of conference techniques of command from the smallest unit to the Joint Chiefs of Staff themselves, or the rewriting of military law into the new Uniform Code. The report of the Doolittle inquiry following World War II on officer-enlisted man relations represented a high point in this development. Emphasis on manipulative control varies as between the various services, depending mainly on the rate and nature of technological change. The Air Force in some respects has gone the farthest in modification of its organizational behavior.

The Instabilities of Manipulative Authority

The long-term outcome of the current transformation of the military from an organization having an underlying emphasis on domination to one showing increased reliance on manipulation is problematic. It is abundantly clear that present forms are highly transitional. Since the shift in military authority is a function of organizational requirements, it is not surprising that armies in totalitarian political systems display these same features. The organizational effectiveness of the Wehrmacht was based on highly developed practices of manipulation and group cohesion, within the context of radical repression of political and ideological deviation.[11]

Likewise the contradictory interplay of practices designed to stimulate group initiative and those required for organizational co-ordination are again general contemporary bureaucratic processes which are certain to create built-in strain and dilemmas in any large-scale bureaucracy. It can be argued that they are more extreme in military than in civilian organizations. In the military the requirements for initiative in the face of combat are very great, and simultaneously the professed need for more rigid organizational co-ordination is powerfully sanctioned. Organizations can and do function effectively despite internal strains and dilemmas, but the military has special characteristics which complicate and disrupt the successful incorporation of authority based on indirect control, group decision, and other manipulative techniques.

Devices for maintaining organization balance are slow to develop under these conflicting requirements. Thus, for example, it requires extensive training and great expertise to develop an officer cadre that is skilled in applying indirect techniques of control and whose use of indirect techniques of leadership will be accepted by subordinates as valid rather than mere sham. Likewise, the gap between formal regulations and the informal realities of command is especially great. This gap becomes a source of tension and confusion.

Equally disruptive to indirect discipline is the ideological orientation of portions of the military elite. In the United States and elsewhere the military elite holds a conservative ideological and political orientation which often is alarmed by and misinterprets the new requirements of military authority.[12] Segments of the military elite see the new requirements as potentially undermining the fundamental basis of authority and as threatening decision making on the strategic level. Their interest in technological change is not necessarily accompanied by an interest in organizational change. They fail to see how manipulative techniques supply the basis for developing the necessary strong subleadership required to operate effectively within a closely supervised larger military unit. In fact, they fail to see that indirect and manipulative control of rank-and-file leadership based on positive group cohesion is essential to maintain both decentralized initiative and operational control over widely dispersed military formations.

Furthermore, it does not necessarily follow that indirect organizational control interferes with strategic or tactical decisions. On the contrary, staff work in support of the strategical commander has traditionally been extensive before the commander arrives at a decision. The requirements of command have pushed this form of decision making down to the lowest operational units, and it is understandable that such a trend is resisted by military traditionalists. Typically, military elites are concerned that indirect control should not undermine the authority structure, and therefore they repeatedly attempt to limit the scope of manipulative and group consensus procedures on the part of lower commanders. As a result, as the older techniques of military domination break down under technological requirements, newer forms based on manipulation emerge highly unstable and laden with dilemmas.

The outlines of dysfunctional responses by military authority to the strains of organizational change are all too obvious. A number, illustrative of United States experiences but more generally applicable, are worthy of note—organizational rigidity, ceremonialism, and exaggerated professionalism.

ORGANIZATIONAL RIGIDITY

Organizational rigidity means the handling of new problems through the mechanical application of traditional practices rather than by innovation. Some degree of organizational rigidity develops in any military establishment as soon as combat ends and the organization tends to return to simple forms of routine. But disruption follows the efforts to re-establish traditional discipline. The lessons of the necessity of initiative remain alive in those units whose routine training most closely approximates actual combat or is most hazardous, whereas concern with traditional discipline is a particular expression of ritualism among members of the military elite, who see their particular weapons systems becoming obsolete with no opportunity of regaining their organizational dominance.

Some quarters in the United States military have pointed to the events in Korea as justification for traditional discipline. There is no doubt that during the first phases of the Korean conflict ground troops lacked sufficient exposure to realistic training. However, improvised and realistic adaptations having little or nothing to do with formal discipline produced in Korea one of the most effective military forces in recent American military history. The performance of military units in Korea is a striking example of the conditions under which civilian apathy was prevented from influencing battle behavior by the performance of a professional officer corps, especially its junior elements, who were convinced that their organizational integrity was at stake.

The Womble committee of the Department of Defense, which sought to investigate the professional status of officers as an aftermath of the Korean conflict, issued a report in 1953 that contained strong overtones of concern for traditional forms of discipline and officer prerogatives.[13] The report, written as a reaction to the results of the Doolittle Board, dealt not only with basic matters of pay and promotion in the military establishment but gave emphasis to a formalism which seemed to be more oriented toward past ideology than the realities of military life.

A return to an organizational structure based on domination can only be achieved at a high cost. The repressive mechanisms of a totalitarian state are needed to enforce consistently such a high level of conformity; indeed we are now witnessing the partial renunciation of such levels of repression by totalitarian elites themselves. Given American cultural traits, the officer corps runs the risk of losing its most creative intellects, while the noncommissioned ranks, as discipline becomes harsher, attract those who are unsuccessful in civilian life. Besides, any widespread and conscious effort to reimpose stricter discipline is tempered by the political pressures that draftees can exert.

CEREMONIALISM

Since any serious return to the discipline of domination is blocked by the realities of military life and by civilian political pressures, nostalgia for the past expresses itself in increased ceremonialism. Ceremonialism refers to those organizational processes that are conventional gestures and formal observances. The opportunities and evidence for increased ceremonialism are ample, from the reintroduction of the dress sword for naval officers to more close-order military parades.[14]

Ceremonialism is functional when it contributes to a sense of self-esteem and to the maintenance of organizational efficiency. Psychologically it is a device for dealing with the fear of death. But at what point does it interfere with the realistic requirements of the military establishment? Military ceremony seems at times to be a device for avoiding concern with unsolved problems of military management. Much of the increased ceremony appears to focus on patterns of social intercourse outside the military role. Ceremony thereby becomes a substitute for career satisfactions and a device for regulating the off-duty life of the military officer. As such it is a profound source of tension between the professional soldier and the citizen soldier. Both the latter and the public at large often fail to see its purpose or significance.

EXAGGERATED PROFESSIONALISM

Because of the drive for efficiency in the military establishment, ritualist tendencies toward ceremonialism are diverted and are more easily expressed in the form of exaggerated professionalism. Professionalization can be defined as the process by which the members of an occupation develop a training procedure, a body of expert knowledge, and a set of operating standards. To speak of overprofessionalization implies that concern with the forms of professional status outweigh concern with functional performance.

Overprofessionalization is an expression of professions with low social status—and officership, despite public acclaim of individual military heroes—is a low-status profession. The results of a national sampling of opinion placed the prestige of the officer in the armed services below not only that of physician, lawyer, scientist, college professor, and minister but also that of public school teacher.[15] In this respect there is much similarity between the army officer and the social worker, especially since they are both professional groups dedicated to doing other peoples' "dirty work."

Overprofessionalization leads to an exaggerated concern with the specification of missions and roles and to organizational morale based on parochialism rather than on a sense of competence. The result is an emphasis on mechanical principles of military science at the expense of creative problem solving. Exaggerated professionalism increases interest in status differentials and, given the low ceiling on income and prestige in the military, results in an intensification of the struggle for minor advantages.

The professional status of the troop leader versus the technical and logistical expert becomes particularly acute and contributes to the dilemmas of developing consistency in authority patterns. In order to enhance the authority of those responsible for operational formations, strenuous efforts must continually be made to differentiate the "fighter" from logistical personnel on the basis of pay, dress, and status. Yet the maintenance men press heavily for rewards and for control over the conditions of their employment, and technical specialists demand both special consideration for their professional qualifications and at the same time the status and authority of combat personnel.

Moreover, the authority systems of technical and logistical formations are at variance with those of combat units. Here professional perspectives increase organizational strains. The leaders of technical units operate without recourse to authoritarian domination and often decry the disciplinary character of operating and line units. Yet they fail to recognize that combat units must develop much higher levels of positive group identification than technical units in order to be able to seek and to face danger. On the other hand, troop and operational commanders see in the standard operating procedures of technical and logistical units bureaucratic resistance to military effectiveness. Exaggerated professionalism deepens these differences.

The Prospects for Organizational Balance: Fraternal Type Authority

Each of these illustrative responses—organizational rigidity, ceremonialism, and exaggerated professionalism—has an adaptive counterpart simultaneously at work. The functional adaptations if successful would seem to be transforming the authority system of the military into a "fraternal type" order—the recognized equality of unequals—which theoretically would permit initiative and creativity within a hierarchical organization. The organizational behavior of the emerging fraternal-type authority system would have two elements. On the one hand, the formal structure of authority is recognized and accepted by those in both superordinate and subordinate roles. There is less attempt to hide the facts of power and authority, as can be the case when manipulative practices become extreme. On the other hand, from the highest levels of the organization down to the very bottom, technical and interpersonal skill plus group loyalty qualify subordinate personnel for effective but circumscribed participation in the decision-making process. Since strategic decisions are centralized, the authority system accepts the decentralization of implementation as a desirable goal rather than as a threat to its existence. The gap between formal organization and the actualities of informal procedures is thereby reduced. Fraternal-type authority is only one possible outcome of present tensions.

At the risk of a dangerous analogy the outcome of the shift in authority from *domination* to *manipulation* can be highlighted. Organizational behavior based on domination is the authority system analogous to the classical authority of the father over his son, comprehensive and absolute. Under fraternal-type authority the system reflects the authority of the older brother over the younger, circumscribed and functional. Although the older brother's superior authority cannot be denied because of the biological facts of age and the forms of family structure, the younger brother has his forms of equality because of the very same considerations.

More revealing than this analogy undoubtedly are the procedures and processes for modifying authority in the military which have the potential to render the fraternal type of discipline effective and functional.

1) *Organizational rigidity* does not develop if fraternal-type authority

becomes established. Not only is traditional discipline seen as ineffective, but those in authority consider undue reliance on powerful negative sanctions as personally degrading. Instead there is a growing concern with those managerial techniques involved in the successful exercise of authority. The military career becomes defined as a career of managerial skill; true it is a career that is unique since it involves leading men into battle, but it is still an honorable managerial career, which ultimately requires public respect.

Thus the adaptive segments of the military elite seem to be interested in overcoming the types of criticism that the citizen soldier is prone to level at the military mind. In order to negate the criticism that many of those exercising authority are unqualified for their jobs, the commander must demonstrate his ability to exercise authority. If he performs the same task as his men, it is not simply a manipulative device—"Look we are all in it together"—but rather to show that he has passed the initiation rite and is fully qualified. In order to avoid the charge of senseless and arbitrary exercise of authority, he is careful to explain his "reasons why" whenever possible.

But most crucial under an ideal type system of fraternal authority is the fact that the officer must avoid exercising his authority as if he assumed a low level of intelligence among his subordinates. The fraternal-type organization is based on the assumption of open equality: any individual who can demonstrate his competence can rise. Since in the United States military establishment some enlisted personnel can and do become officers, this assumption is grounded in reality. Most social deficiencies in a man's background that might hinder his exercise of authority can be erased by military education. Thus officers exercising fraternal-type authority must assume that each soldier is a potential officer. This is like civilian society's dogma about the possibilities of social mobility.

Concern with technical competence, explanations of the purposes of commands, and assuming high performance potentials among subordinates are all incompatible with a continued demonstration by military leaders that the sanctions they hold in reserve are severe and ultimate. There is something of the older aristocratic outlook to be found in the successful and competent leader who is aware that to threaten is to demonstrate actual or potential weakness. He rather attempts to base his authority on his very presence and on his expertise. The older military dictum that authority inheres in the office rather than in the occupant is being modified to a considerable extent. "You salute the bars, not the man," is no longer tenable. The attempt is made to justify authority on the basis of personal qualities as well as role criteria.

2) A military elite concerned with adaptation avoids *ceremonialism* and concentrates instead on developing organizational cohesion and group solidarity. Cohesion and solidarity on the job are a function of technical competence and of the quality of interpersonal relations among the members and leaders of a military unit. Social research has emphasized the importance of practices which promote cohesive primary group relations if complex organizations are to operate effectively. The standardized procedures for replacing the human components of military organization operate to weaken social solidarity. A wide variety of techniques are available and are being employed to assist in the maintenance of primary group solidarity. These range, for example, from the modification of the replacement system from one based on individuals to one based on groups and units to special training academies for noncommissioned officers who figure so prominently in maintaining group cohesion. Fundamentally under a fraternal-type authority system, especially in a democratic society, organizational *esprit de corps* rather than ideological indoctrination supplies the basis for positive morale. This is strikingly the case for the Israeli Army which can be considered a military formation closely approximating the fraternal type of authority.

In addition, the military must have institutional devices for linking military life to family life and for controlling the tensions between these two spheres. In the past garrison life resulted in an intermingling of place of residence and place of work, especially during peacetime. Although these practices may have served to isolate military from civilian society, the military community was a source of social cohesion for its members both to the soldiers and to their families. The changing technology of warfare and changing patterns of military life are eliminating the geographically isolated military community. Now the military must assume on an organized basis many of the services rendered informally to military families on the basis of self-help. It is indeed striking to realize the extent to which the military has built into it many of the features of the welfare state. Private commercial interests are continually criticizing the military for its organizational socialism, but these features are important sources of its organizational solidarity.

3) The military establishment incorporating adaptive change would be constantly altering the content and scope of professional roles in order to avoid the dangers of a rigid division of labor and *exaggerated professionalism*. One measure of adaptation is the extent to which the classic struggle between the troop commander, the manager of men and machines, and the staff officer, the manager of plans and organizational co-ordination, can be overcome.

Professional training must be concerned with exposing the individual to a wide variety of experiences so that he can broaden his perspective and be prepared to deal with new and emerging tasks. If it is true that combat requires authority oriented toward maintaining initiative among a group and possessing the skills of indirect control, then the skills of the combat commander and the staff officer are in effect converging. Skill in interpersonal relations even more than technical competence is necessary. (One is struck by the number of United States higher staff officers who have combined achievement in both spheres as a result of their World War II experiences.) Thus the job requirements of the successful professional soldier in an adaptive army are not those of a disciplinarian, although he must be prepared to use the powerful sanctions at his disposal. This is not to deny that an important element of tension still exists between the emotional and technical requirements of many of the initial assignments of a combat officer, such as the fighter pilot or paratrooper, and the emotional and technical requirements of a commander. Yet for all those who survive the rigors of indoctrination, training, and initial assignment, the professional career of the officer holds the prospect of permitting the development of general managerial skills applicable in a wide range of assignments.

The changing content of professionalism in the military establishment alters the relationship between the civilian and military elites. It is not only the greater size of the military establishment and the increased importance of policies of national security which pose the problem of the interjection of the military elites into roles traditionally reserved for civilian leaders. More fundamentally it is the fact that the type of training and experience of military leadership are more relevant for and have greater transferability to civilian bureaucracies—both economic and governmental.

Conclusion

Throughout this analysis it has been assumed that the military establishment as a social system is no longer a major point of resistance to technological change—at least no more resistant than might be expected by an elite involved in a highly dangerous task. However, organization innovation encounters powerful resistances. Organizational adaptations to these technological changes have been analyzed mainly in terms of the requirements of the military system of authority. The result has been a transformation of military authority from one based on domination to one employing more and more techniques of manipulation. Organizational processes of manipulative discipline are unstable and transitional. Adaptive and maladaptive responses in organizational behavior can be observed whose final outcome remains problematic. The strains associated with transition produce powerful demands in the military to return to earlier and "traditional" patterns of authority and organization. One possible functional outcome would be a "fraternal type" of authority which would maintain organization co-ordination and yet ensure the high levels of initiative required for combat. Whether such an organizational transformation develops depends not only on factors within the military organization but also on political and ideological considerations in civilian society which are not discussed here. The conditions under which selective service and conscription are modified or abandoned as air formations and nuclear weapons become more dominant will be extremely important. But even with professional armies, so to speak, there can be no possibility of a successful return to earlier forms of military authority, although one common response to the strains of change is an effort to reconstitute past arrangements.

Finally, these processes by which organizational authority is being transformed in the military are present in all types of large-scale bureaucracies. The movement from domination to manipulation seems to be a general pattern of social change. The fact that it is present even in the military is of particular theoretical importance.

Notes

1. See David Easton, "Limits of the Equilibrium Model in Social Research," in Heinz Eulau, Samuel Eldersveld and Morris Janowitz, eds., *Reader in Political Behavior* (Glencoe, Ill., 1955), pp. 397-404.

2. See Heinz Eulau, "H. D. Lasswell's Developmental Analysis," *Western Political Science Quarterly,* XL (June 1958), pp. 229-242.

3. Samuel A. Stouffer et al., *The American Soldier* (Princeton, 1949), I, p. 55; Arthur K. Davis, "Bureaucratic Patterns in the Navy Officer Corps," *Social Forces* (December 1948), pp. 143-153; Arnold M. Rose, "The Social Structure of Army," *American Journal of Sociology,* LI (March 1946), pp. 361-364; Felton D. Freeman, "The Army as a Social Structure," *Social Forces,* XXVIII (October 1948), pp. 78-83; Harold Brotz and Everett K. Wilson, "Characteristics of Military Society," *American Journal of Sociology,* LI (March 1946), pp. 371-375; C. D. Spindler, "The Military—A Systematic Analysis," *Social Forces,* XXVII (October 1948), pp. 83-88; Charles H. Page, "Bureaucracy's Other Face," *Social Forces,* XXVIII (October 1949), pp. 88-94.

4. Donald T. Campbell and Thelma H. McCormack, "Military Experience and Attitudes toward Authority," *American Journal of Sociology,* LXII (March 1957), pp. 482-490.

5. T. W. Adorno et al., *The Authoritarian Personality* (New York, 1950), pp. 222-280.

6. In fact, there is some empirical evidence that selection boards in the Air Force tend to select for promotion the less authoritarian officers, presumably in part through selecting well-liked men (E. P. Hollander, "Authoritarianism and Leadership Choice in a Military Setting," *Journal of Abnormal and Social Psychology*, XLIX (1954), pp. 365-370.

7. Hans Speier, "The American Soldier and the Sociology of Military Organization," in Robert K. Merton and Paul F. Lazarsfeld, eds., *Studies in the Scope and Method of "The American Soldier"* (Glencoe, Ill., 1950), pp. 106-132.

8. Joseph Schumpeter, *The Sociology of Imperialism* (New York, 1955).

9. The distinction between logistics and combat is a functional distinction and not a formal organizational distinction. It, too, is more and more difficult to make as the military establishment becomes more complex.

10. S.L.A. Marshall, *Men Against Fire* (New York, 1947), p. 22.

11. Edward A. Shils and Morris Janowitz, "Cohesion and Disintegration in the Wehrmacht in World War II," *Public Opinion Quarterly*, XII (1948), pp. 280-315.

12. C. S. Brown, "The Social Attitudes of American Generals, 1898-1940," unpublished doctoral dissertation, University of Wisconsin.

13. Department of Defense, Press Release, December 3, 1953, "Final Report—Ad Hoc Committee on the Future of Military Service as a Career that Will Attract and Retain Capable Career Personnel."

14. The close-order drill parade which was introduced with the advent of musketry was not only ceremonial but also a training exercise for the field of battle. Today a fire demonstration would be the appropriate equivalent of a combined combat training exercise and public spectacle.

15. Public Opinions Survey, Inc., Princeton, "Attitudes of Adult Civilians toward the Military Service as a Career," prepared for the Office of Armed Forces Information and Education, Department of Defense, Washington, 1955.

U.S. FORCES AND THE ZERO DRAFT

After a quarter of a century, the United States has taken the essential steps to phase out conscription and to maintain an all-volunteer force.[1] In the 1970s, American foreign and military policy will not only be constrained by the technology of weapons and arms control, but also by the numbers and quality of the manpower that an all-volunteer system will produce. This policy is not a short-term or stop-gap measure, but a fundamental transformation of military organization which has its counterparts in most Western industrialized nations.

The purpose of this paper is first to examine the underlying factors which have brought about the decline of the mass armed force based on conscription and a mobilization format. The weapons systems and the politico-military necessities of international relations require that NATO, including the United States, rely more on an effective 'force in being' to achieve the goal of deterrence. Second, it seeks to explore the consequences of an all-volunteer military in the United States on her international political and strategic position. Third, it seeks to identify the problems and dilemmas of recruiting and retaining manpower since the issue of personnel emerges as crucial under an all-volunteer system. In this connection, various strategies and policies for dealing with manpower and with the larger issues of 'armed forces and society' are reviewed and assessed.

The conclusion of this analysis is that an all-volunteer force could meet the strategic requirements of effective deterrence in the decade of the 1970s provided that there are fundamental professional and organizational reforms in the American military forces. The key manpower shortage will

This chapter is adapted from a paper of the same title, Adelphi Paper Number 94, London, International Institute for Strategic Studies, 1973.

of course be in the ground forces; these are required primarily to maintain a stable commitment to NATO requirements. It is doubtful that the projected 2.3 or 2.4 million force level can be achieved after 1975 within a cost level of 7 percent of the gross national product. However, there is reason to believe that a lower force level ranging from 1.7 to 2.0 million could be maintained during the second half of the decade of the 1970s and that such a force, if properly deployed and with appropriate political leadership, would be sufficient.

It is possible to take the position that the manpower and professional problems of a modern all-volunteer military force can be solved by economic measures. The number and quality of military personnel in this view is a function of the economic wages that a nation is willing to pay. One can speculate about a scheme of economic reward under which the commanding general would receive compensation equal to that of the 'captain' of industry.

This paper is based on a different set of assumptions. The officer corps is a specialized profession and the career-enlisted ranks a type of craft or skill group. A volunteer force in a democratic society will require and will obtain pay competitive with civilian occupations, but the military is facing a professional dilemma which cannot be solved by economic incentives alone. Such incentives do not guarantee the required mixture of numbers and quality of personnel, especially of the most dedicated and innovative types. Military men do not want to think of themselves as mercenaries and a democratic society cannot treat its military as if they were mercenaries.

The military profession requires a sense of purpose, an operational logic and a basis for social cohesion. The heroic model of the traditional military officer no longer suffices as a basis for career commitment, but military professionals cannot and do not operate as a group of technicians or administrators.

Although the questions of war and peace are paramount because of the utter destructiveness of nuclear weapons, the prestige and moral worth accorded to the military profession in Western democracies and in the United States is not conspicuous. On the contrary, there are widespread attitudes of indifference or disdain where there is not hostility. In turn, military men are uncertain about their career commitments and the legitimacy of the enterprises they seek to command. The great magnitude of their operating budgets do not reassure them.

It is not unwarranted to speak of a crisis in the military profession in the industrialized nations of the West, as distinct from the Soviet Union, which articulate with a nuclear strategy, although circumstances vary from nation to nation. For Germany and France, the idea of the military officer as civil servant has an element of validity, while in Britain, the military style of life, social standing and tradition still hold operational relevance. The dilemmas are deepest for American officers. With their strong sense of commitment to organizational innovation, they are hard pressed to draw on past tradition for a future history.

An examination of the manpower and professional issues of the military has emerged as being of equal importance with the strategic balance of hardware. It requires an examination of the decline of the mass armed force which in turn is an outgrowth of changes in military technology, new socio-political contexts of international relations and internal societal developments of advanced industrialized nations.

Trend Towards An All-Volunteer Force

DECLINE OF MASS ARMIES

We are witnessing the end, or at least the transformation, of the mass armed force in the West. The decline of the mass armed force is truly the end of an historical epoch since the new format of the military profession will profoundly influence military and political relations between major powers. Nuclear weapons technology, the altered international environment and the basic international socio-political changes in the 'affluent' nations are all at work. Practitioners and students of international relations are being forced to broaden their horizons beyond conventional analysis of war-making and traditional concepts of the international balance of power. Basic questions of legitimacy and organization of the military and the sources of military manpower ('Who shall serve?') have to be answered. The sociological analysis of emerging military institutions and of the transformed links between armed forces and civilian society has moved more into the center of the stage.

Historical epochs do not start or conclude on specific textbook dates. The mass armed force had its origins not only in technological innovations which concern military historians, but also in socio-political factors. The technology of the mass armed force was rooted in an organizational system created by increased firepower of the infantry and artillery, plus improved means of transportation of military personnel and supplies. There are those who argue that the technological basis of the mass army was in operation during the American Civil War and in the Franco-Prussian conflict, but prototype elements, especially organizational elements, could already be found in the Napoleonic Wars.

However, for the purposes at hand, the mass armed force also had its origins in the socio-political struggles of the American and French Revolutions. These rebellions defeated the post-feudal armies as the revolutionary leaders armed the rank and file. These revolutionary movements initiated the idea that citizenship involved the right and the duty to bear arms—truly a revolutionary notion. To be a citizen of the nation-state was to have the right to bear arms in defense of the nation-state. The fusing together of the concept of 'popular' military service and its political legitimacy with the ever-increasing destructive power of military weapons provided the basis of the mass armed force until the end of World War II. (See Table 1 for manpower trends.)

TABLE 1

Historical Trends in U.S. Military Manpower

Total Uniformed Personnel—Officer and Enlisted
(including Academy Cadets and Officer Candidates, excluding Coast Guard)

World War II Period

1939	334,473
1940	458,365
1941	1,801,101
1942	3,858,791
1943	9,044,745
1944	11,451,719
1945	12,123,455
1946	3,030,088
1947	1,626,130

Korean War Period

1950	1,460,261
1951	3,249,455
1952	3,635,912
1953	3,512,949

Vietnam War Period

1965	2,655,389
1966	3,094,058
1967	3,376,880
1968	3,547,902
1969	3,460,162
1970	3,066,294
1971	2,714,727
1972	2,330,000
	(preliminary figures)

Mass armed forces culminated in the strategy of total war, which is a prenuclear notion. It refers to the development of mobilization plans during peacetime, to comprehensive conversion of the civilian population into mass armies and their supporting base in production during war, and to the military use of air power. The distinction between the military forces and the civilian population is weakened. Both become the subjects of military organization and the objects of attack, propaganda and political warfare. Likewise, the boundary between military forces and the larger society weakened as total mobilization required that an ever larger segment of the population became part of the war apparatus. Within the professional military, recruitment shifted as officers were drawn from more and more socially representative backgrounds. The concentration of personnel with civilian skills increased, and the patterns of military authority shifted from authoritarian command to organizational decision-making. The civilianization of the mass military was not only an outgrowth of technology and organizational control. The vast resources needed for military operations and the justification for prolonged hostilities and massive destruction require an egalitarian ideology in both democratic and totalitarian societies. But men in political democracies are progressively less prepared to fight for nationalist sentiments alone; they must see the cause as morally justified.

As in the case of its emergence, both technological and socio-political factors which became manifest during World War II started the decline of the mass armed force in the 'affluent' nation-states of the West. The deployment of nuclear weapons marked the technological transformation of the armed forces of NATO nations. A vast literature has been written on the impact of nuclear weapons on military strategy and organization, most of which is superficial or irrelevant. Nuclear weapons weaken, but do not eliminate, the strategic concept of the inevitability of war—the essential logic of traditional military forces. The concept of strategic deterrence has to substitute for traditional notions of 'victory.' The lack of clarity in military purpose forces a continuous and uneasy search for a new and acceptable rationale. The manning of nuclear weapons, while still defined as a crucial societal task, is not a military function which can be readily endowed with mystical and highly honorific subjective purpose for the individual soldier. For the military, or at least for segments of it, mere maintenance of the technology of deterrence is a highly passive task. Either by doctrine or by training and spirit, the military requires a more active and positive outlook. Modern society, as Max Weber has stressed, experiences a process of demystification. The military has resisted this trend longer than other sectors of society, but nuclear weapons have taken their supreme toll on the military image and its mystique.

Moreover, from 1960 to 1970, the American military establishment was given vast resources to impose on South-East Asia, by force, the policy of containment. This military effort and its failure during a period of domestic social and political tension produced the most violent anti-militarism in modern American history. The impact of Vietnam, projected into United States consciousness by the dramatic content of the mass media, especially television, not only called into question the effectiveness of American military institutions, but also produced a profound moral unease. The United States moves to an all-volunteer force in the context of the most extensive anti-military sentiment in its recent history.

The movement towards a greater reliance on volunteer armed forces is a trend among advanced industrial nations in Western Europe and in the United States and Canada. The tremendous destructiveness of conventional weapons and the havoc they wrought in World War I and World War II might well have called into question the mass armed force and the military strategy of offensive warfare in the interest of national security. But clearly the advent of nuclear weapons is crucial since it altered the strategic role of the military and called into question the validity of the mass armed force.

However, technological determinism is no adequate basis for explaining military developments; technological innovations must be placed in the broader context of socio-political change. The decline of the mass armed force and the rise of the modern all-volunteer force are an expression of underlying processes of societal change under advanced industrialism in the non-Communist nations. First, externally, neither small professional forces nor large conscript armies are able to maintain Western-type colonial hegemony over developing nations. The strength of nationalism in these nations is too powerful; the assistance available to them from the Soviet bloc and China is too extensive; and domestic rejection of old-style imperialism is too powerful. Likewise, civilian political leadership and mass public opinion in those nations with parliamentary institutions react with horror or withdrawal at the prospect of a 'broken back' nuclear war and force the redefinition of military strategy into the format of defensive deterrence. Second, internally, in the advanced industrial societies without totalitarian social control systems, higher levels of education and a more ample standard of mass consumption have led wide segments of the population to a diffuse but persistent reluctance to serve in the military. Important segments of the population come to believe that service to the nation and the solution of pressing economic and social issues require skills and outlooks other than those associated with military life and military organization. In the absence of hostilities, conscription is seen as unnecessary and undesirable because it involves compulsion and interference with personal decision-making.

IMPACT OF NATIONALISM AND INDUSTRIALISM

Nationalism, the very basis of the military establishment in the nineteenth century and a rationale for universal military service, has suffered an important erosion. The military accomplishments of World War II—that which was avoided by the Allied victory—have receded and the reality and image of tremendous destruction instead persist in the public consciousness. The affluence of the post-World War II period has had a double effect on nationalist sentiments. It has created or permitted a series of social and moral problems to persist which are defined as not solvable by military preparations, but rather by international cooperation. Likewise, there has been a partial exhaustion of the organizing myths associated with nationalism. It is as if nationalism and the defense of the Western political and ideological values had been oversold. The growth of literacy and the increase in the number of persons in Western Europe and the United States who have been exposed to ideas circulating at colleges and universities have served to dampen nationalism—an old-fashioned utopia—and popularized international or at least transnational values and utopias.

In advanced industrialized societies, with some notable exceptions, the goals and style of military institutions have been subjected to massive criticism and the belief is that the moral worth of conscript service has been shaken. In part, hedonism and the importance of self-expression supply a new basis for resistance to military authority among young people. It is difficult to draw the line between highly personalistic opposition to military institutions and broader, more moralistic and political viewpoints which generate a powerful sense of neutralism and new forms of pacifism. The sheer destructive power of weapons systems and the apparent feeling that political leaders are unable to control the nuclear arms race are essential ingredients. These sentiments are concentrated among an important minority of young people, but they can be found in varying degrees in all parts of the social structure. Thus, even in Germany, with no political involvement in Vietnam, reluctance to serve in the armed forces has dramatically increased. One measure of this is the steady and sharp increase in conscientious objectors in Germany. Of the

men subject to the draft born in 1944, 1.33 percent were conscientious
objectors, while for those born in 1952, the figure had risen to 5.05
percent. In terms of those eligible to be drafted, the percentages were
slightly higher.[2]

The basic features of an advanced industrial society create complex
problems in the recruitment and management of military manpower.
Although political leaders seek to limit military budgets, in the contemporary scene the military must compete for military manpower against
civilian occupations by paying higher wages because of the decline in the
inherent attractiveness of the officer profession. For enlisted personnel
(other ranks), the traditional pools of manpower from culturally isolated
areas have declined. The rise of the welfare state with unemployment
compensation and social security payments, plus mass education, also
undermine the traditional system of recruitment. Those who can be
impressed into military service because of sheer poverty are fewer in
number and marginal persons have the alternative benefits of the welfare
state. To the extent that the military faces declining opportunities to be
stationed abroad, both the tasks of recruitment and the maintenance of
military morale become more and more complex.

The all-volunteer force can be thought of as one response to the
economic and social pressures operating in the United States, which are
not unique but more or less common to advanced industrialized societies
of the NATO nations. These pressures reflect the effort to limit military
budgets—that is, to keep them under a fixed percentage of the gross
national budget and hopefully to allow them to decline in order to release
resources for domestic programs. Moreover, elements of the new style of
civilian life—leisure and relative affluence—find their way into the military
establishment. Although it continues to retain some of its traditions,
protocol and heroic features, the military becomes one profession among
many and one which, because of its function and internal organization,
faces particularly special problems of manpower recruitment and retention.

It has taken 25 years for these trends to become fully evident in the
United States. With the emergence of the all-volunteer force in being, the
pattern of civil-military relations alters. The trend towards civilianization
of the military is temporarily arrested as the military seeks to assert and
maintain its organizational identity. The issue arises whether the military
profession may become unduly separated and socially isolated from the
larger society. Thus, the introduction of an all-volunteer force does not
solve the problems of military manpower, but rather under an all-volunteer

force the number, quality and professionalism of the military emerge as critical and persistent issues of national security.

COMPARATIVE NATIONAL TRENDS

The speed with which a specific country accelerates or retards this transformation of its armed force from conscription depends on historical traditions and the details of its strategic position. On the one hand, Britain was the first European nation in NATO to implement the all-volunteer concept, in part because of economic pressures. Her historical reluctance and resistance to conscription were also at work. On the other hand, Germany, despite the newly emerging opposition of her young people to military service, appears heavily committed to some form of conscription because of her strategic and political requirements. But the Germans are exploring alternative systems including an all-volunteer core augmented by short-term conscripts, organized as a modern territorial militia.

In France, because of her large Communist minority, the conscript army is believed by the political leadership to have crucial internal security functions, and the French do not have the same extensive historical tradition of opposition to conscription found in Britain. Nevertheless, the trend in France is toward shorter periods of conscript service with a smaller proportion of each age group serving in the military. In parliamentary debate, the prospect of the end of conscription has already been raised, while in the Netherlands planning for an all-volunteer force is underway. Norway may well be an interesting exception. Since the end of World War II, conscription appears to be compatible with youth culture and accepted as an aspect of national independence following the model of Sweden. In short, there is no reason to expect that the trend towards an all-volunteer force will be arrested during the next five to ten years in Western Europe. If anything, an agreement on mutual troop reduction with the Soviet Union will hasten the trend. This observation does not imply that contingencies—unanticipated eventualities—could not arise which would create pressure to return to some form of conscription, but the probabilities are low.

It is unlikely that the impact of these technological and socio-political trends on the armed forces of the Soviet Union will be the same. Fragmentary evidence does indicate that the Soviet armed forces face fundamental problems of manpower and professional redefinition. There is a strong emphasis on volunteer service in the key strategic weapons systems, especially in the rocket forces. Soviet youth displays many of the elements of personal hedonism and skepticism found in the industrialized nations of the West. But the system of totalitarian controls renders personal attitudes less relevant to the decision-making of the Soviet elite. Moreover, the military forces of the Soviet Union perform crucial security functions in the occupied nations of Eastern Europe and internally at home. Military service in the conscript forces of the Soviet Union—despite its relative unpopularity—can draw upon a considerable sense of diffuse nationalism and a limited degree of personal attraction based on material comforts, uniforms, opportunity to travel away from home, etc. For the Soviet Union, the years of the decade of the 1970s are likely to see the continuation of conscription and of mass armed forces. The profound disparity in mobilized manpower between the power blocs will remain as an overriding component in the increasingly deconcentrated world balance of power. No doubt, this imbalance is of real importance, particularly in calculations about the defense of Western Europe. But it remains a profound error to conceptualize military affairs in conventional terms without regard to the changed role of force both in the industrialized and the developing nations.

Despite the prospect of continued conscription in the Soviet Union, by 1970, military leadership in the United States was aware of the political pressures which brought important segments of both the Republican and Democratic parties to support the all-volunteer force. Richard Nixon, as a presidential candidate in 1968, understood the popular appeal of the all-volunteer force. Selective Service was a rigid bureaucratic agency with highly unfair rules, which favored middle class, college-educated young-sters and which had an arrogant, over-aged General, Lewis B. Hershey, as the director. Nixon used his call for a volunteer force as a device to indicate his desire to end the war in Vietnam. He had also been influenced by economists such as Milton Friedman, who claimed that an all-volunteer force would be more efficient and that it was more compatible with his notion of personal freedom and the proper 'conservative' role of the state.

Initially, the Democratic Congressional leadership was more oriented towards reforming the draft; the Southern wing because of its sense of patriotism and support for the military, and the liberal Northern wing because of its fear of the political dangers of an expanded all-volunteer force. However, the opposition to Vietnam by liberal Democratic Congressional leaders moved them rapidly to support the all-volunteer system since it represented an effective means to protest the war in Vietnam. The resulting coalition on this issue grew rapidly in strength and only the grim realities of supplying ground force personnel to Vietnam prevented an earlier termination of Selective Service, which was finally set for 30 June 1973.

The United States Congress has not debated the emerging functions of the military, or the basic problems of creating an all-volunteer force. It has mainly been concerned with passing appropriation bills to raise military pay. A Special Subcommittee on Recruiting and Retention of Military Personnel of the United States House of Representatives conducted a series of hearings during 1971 and 1972 which consisted of presentations by high ranking military and civilian officials of information on recruitment and retention, which had already been released to the press.[3] The recommendations of this Subcommittee were limited, highly conventional and commanded very little attention.[4]

International Consequences of an All-Volunteer Force

PRESIDENT NIXON'S PROPOSALS

For its post-Vietnam foreign policy, the Nixon Administration projected that an all-volunteer armed force could supply the manpower required for the more limited overseas deployment. An essential element was the declaration of 'no more Vietnams,' although this necessity had to remain relatively undefined. The estimate of the required force and the ability of the volunteer system to produce such a level has been steadily scaled down. In 1970, the President's Commission on an All-Volunteer Armed Force estimated a manpower level of approximately 2.4 million or slightly less than that of the pre-Vietnam build-up. This was the work of the economist Milton Friedman and his associated specialists.[5] In the spring of 1972, Secretary Melvin Laird already reduced the target and stated that a volunteer force of 2.3 million was required.[6] In President Nixon's budget message of January 1973, delivered after the departure of Laird, the figure was further reduced to 2.23 million as a target manpower ceiling after June 1973. This figure was close to the estimates that civilian officials in the Department of Defense had been stating privately since 1970 as the post Selective Service force and they did not rule out that a lower figure of 2.0 million was a possibility after 1975.

In the spring of 1972, in *Foreign Affairs*, the outlines of a military posture based on 1.75 million men was described for the period after 1975.[7] While there would be an element of risk, it was argued that a military force of 1.75 million could support a meaningful military policy of effective deterrence rather than merely a balance of terror. With or without mutual balanced force reduction agreements, the original estimate of the Gates Commission appears much too high if the military budget is to be kept near 7 percent, let alone reduced. Increasing unit personnel costs, the tremendous projected increase in the cost of military retirement for personnel no longer on active duty, and the rising cost of new weapons result in unending pressure to limit active duty manpower. The major reduction will, of course, be in the ground force, since further contractions in the size of the naval and air forces are very difficult to accomplish. (See Table 2 for trends in service allocations of manpower.)

Senator George McGovern introduced this lower figure of 1.75 million in his election campaign. As described below, such a military force could also undertake a variety of national emergency tasks which cannot be performed by civilian organizations and which would enhance the force's military effectiveness. But it would have to re-deploy effectively and reorganize professionally as described below.

It is indeed a paradox that, at the end of the Vietnam phase, one of the central strategic issues—if not the central issue—of the nuclear deterrent force was the size and deployment of the ground element. In part, the structure of the strategic nuclear force was being fashioned both by economic restraint and by negotiations with the Soviet Union. The general purpose forces had to face much heavier budget pressure and the manpower limitations resulting from an all-volunteer force.

Yet, by 1972, within the American military there had emerged a broad outline of strategic consensus concerning ground force deployment, but not without crucial and unresolved differences in emphasis. Faced with a changed politico-military world environment, the assumption was accepted

TABLE 2
Trends in Active Duty Military Personnel, 1950-1970

Year	Total June 30		Army	Air Force	Navy (excluding Coast Guard)	Marine Corps
1950	1,460,261	(N)	593,167	411,277	381,538	74,279
		(%)	40·6	28·2	26·1	5·1
1955	2,935,107	(N)	1,109,296	959,946	660,695	205,170
		(%)	37·8	32·7	22·5	7·0
1960	2,465,065	(N)	868,116	814,153	611,500	171,296
		(%)	35·3	33·0	24·8	6·9
1965	2,655,389	(N)	969,066	824,662	671,448	190,213
		(%)	36·5	31·1	25·3	7·1
1970	3,066,294	(N)	1,322,548	791,349	692,660	259,737
		(%)	43·1	25·8	22·6	8·5

Source: Selected Manpower Statistics, Department of Defense, 15 April, 1972, p. 21

that only in Western Europe did there remain a positive reason for the stationing of a significant number of American ground troops. (In South Korea, the prospect of an American military presence limited to air and naval units is no longer being ruled out.) A contracting system of naval and air bases, plus military assistance missions, and an overseas scattering of specialized personnel for communications and logistical purposes would be the augmenting elements.

To implement the evolving concepts of deterrence, the services had had to plan and initiate changes in military organization and professionalism, in anticipation of the target date of 1 July 1973, for the all-volunteer force. The patterns and degree of response from service to service have varied markedly. At the one extreme, the Marine Corps, with a strong sense of self-assurance, has made practically no adjustment as far as mid-1972 and could well succeed, especially given the projected decrease in its manpower. On the other hand, the Army, faced with the gravest problems, has revealed a deep lack of self-confidence and has only been able to proceed on a piecemeal and limited basis. Interestingly, the Navy has responded energetically, in anticipation of more severe problems than one would have believed to be the case. The Air Force seems less concerned than the Navy and has modified itself to a lesser degree.

The Marine Corps, fully aware that in the years 1946-1947, there was a determined effort to eliminate its existence, has developed a strong skill in organizational survival. It insisted and succeeded in being the first to withdraw from Vietnam in order to regroup and maintain its operational capabilities. Marine leaders see the Corps as a specific purpose assault force. Drawing on its tradition of a volunteer force and on the image and reality of its tough training, its officers believe that there are enough young men in the United States who will be sufficiently attracted to its style and meet its manpower needs. During the period of transition from 1970-1972, it has instituted practically no changes in its procedures, except to be alert that its training procedures did not get out of hand and create any public scandal.

By contrast, the Navy, although a volunteer service, has been deeply concerned with its manpower requirements. The 'gentleman' style of life in the Navy, together with a sense of public service and the pleasures of going to sea, were at the basis of its traditional system of recruitment. However, the pressures of the modern Navy, as for example the stark conditions of service in the missile-carrying submarine fleet with long separations from family, had already in the early 1960s started to weaken the attractions of a naval career. To meet the end of the supply of draft-motivated recruits and officer candidates, the Navy displayed a strong interest in maintaining and enriching its style of life and its internal social cohesion. It has extended its tradition of allowing personnel a sense of personal autonomy which would be compatible with its military requirements. Under Admiral Elmo Zumwalt it has taken steps to permit areas of personal freedom and individuality and to reduce needless harassment, but it has experienced deep tension in adjusting to new race-relations realities. It has shown a concern to reduce excessive personnel transfers. At the same time, the Air Force believes that it is already a modern technological organization and it has not revealed a concern about its professional and manpower needs and has, therefore, made only very limited adjustments.

The ground force is faced with the deepest crisis since its personnel have been heavily recruited by the draft. Why does the ground force face the most difficult problem in recruitment? The social status of the ground force is perceived as lower in part because the style of life—both in its operations and in its communal existence—is seen as the least desirable. As compared with the Navy, its base of social recruitment in the past was somewhat from a lower social stratum; more important, the Navy considered itself a more elite service both socially and operationally. In the current scene, the Army has the highest concentration of black personnel. The image of the ground force, more than other services, has suffered from Vietnam and from the scandal of corruption. Finally, the prospect of sharp reductions in personnel deeply limits the ground force's ability to offer stable career prospects and opportunities for promotion.

The ground force established a special staff section to deal with the problem of transition to an all-volunteer force, 'Project Volar,' and launched a series of reforms and demonstration units. Emphasis was placed on improving physical and material conditions of base life, especially more privacy in the barracks and in eliminating the requirements of non-military duties, such as kitchen police and maintenance of grounds. In contrast to the Navy, the Army defensively responded to the demand for greater personal autonomy. It sought to improve basic training by making it more meaningful and to introduce more adventure and range training to deal with the problems of boredom and underemployment after basic and advanced training.

RECRUITMENT

Can the military in an affluent society, where there is a profound reluctance to serve, recruit on a volunteer basis a sufficient number of personnel and, at the same time, personnel of adequate quality (including a cadre of potential leaders)? Moreover, the manpower must be relatively socially representative. Social representativeness implies a wide dispersion in geographical origin, a mixture of social class background, and a limitation—difficult to specify—on self-recruitment from within the military. American military leaders are sensitive to the specter of an enlisted cadre drawn from the lowest strata of society and increasingly black, officered by men recruited from the hinterlands of the south-south-west, where military virtues are presumed to be still respected.

The transition to the all-volunteer force during the period 1968 to 1972 has meant a marked decline in draft calls as indicated in Table 3.

To meet the manpower requirements of the all-volunteer force, a total of 514,000 enlistments per year must be forthcoming for a force of 2.35 million which the Department of Defense announced was required for the year 1973-1974. Congress re-enacted markedly improved pay bills to achieve that level of voluntary recruitment. Manpower costs as a percentage of the total annual defense budget had already risen from 34 percent in the fiscal year 1964 to 40 percent in the fiscal year 1973, according to one set of Department of Defense estimates, and the percentage may be higher depending on the system of calculations. With the new pay scale and the commitment to vastly increasing costs for military retirement pay, personnel costs will consume a much greater proportion of the military budget in the decade ahead. (Retirement pay was 1.2 billion in 1964, 4.4 in 1973, and will rise to more than 20 billion in the 1980s.)

TABLE 3

U.S. Force Levels and Draft Calls

Year	Active Duty Military (in millions) June 30	Annual Draft Calls
1965	2·65	102,600
1966	3·09	334,530
1967	3·38	288,900
1968	3·58	343,300
1969	3·46	299,000
1970	3·07	289,900
1971	2·71	98,000
1972	2·33	50,000
1973	2·35	(Department of Defense projection)

In 1972, Congress authorized a pay scale which established a base pay of $288 per month for privates with an automatic increase after four months to $320, while other ranks were given corresponding increases. Because it was apparent that even this high pay level per se would not attract the necessary new recruits into the combat arms of the ground forces, a special combat enlistment bonus of $1,500 was authorized for an experimental three month period. At the officer level, the pay rates, except for such specialists as physicians, was by the summer of 1972 'very competitive' with civilian pay. At the lower ranks it was in fact superior. For example, a married captain with more than three years of service earned a salary equivalent to about $14,000 (based on regular military compensation and including a tax advantage) while the comparable civilian salary for a college graduate with three years' experience was about $12,000. The annual costs of these pay increases have already been estimated at 2.7 billion and requests for 400 million additional funds have already been prepared.

Although considerable progress towards an all-volunteer force has been made, the impact of the pay rises and internal changes in the various services have not produced the necessary level of enlistments. Additional measures would be required if the appropriate mixture of numbers and quality and rates of re-enlistment were to be achieved. The main locus of the shortfalls was in the ground forces and in the combat arms, although the Navy still faced difficult problems. In part the Air Force appeared to be benefiting from the high rates of civilian unemployment, especially in technical skills, since unemployment influences re-enlistment more than initial enlistment.

By the spring of 1972, defense authorities were explicit in asserting that required goals were not being achieved. During the fiscal year 1971, the total enlistments both draft motivated and 'true' volunteers was not the required 440,000 but 367,000 and in the fiscal year 1972, the number rose only to 371,000. In May 1972, the ground forces announced 'excellent results in true volunteers for combat arms and delayed enlistments. At the same time, 'we still have a long way to go.'[8] At that time it was estimated that on the basis of a required 200,000 annual enlistments for the Army, recruiting without a draft would produce an annual shortfall of 80,000-90,000. In the summer of 1972, a similar estimate was produced by the staff of the Department of Defense in response to a memorandum of 15 January 1972 from the Special Assistant to the President for National Security Affairs. This study concluded that there was 'the probability of a sizeable and growing shortfall of Army enlisted personnel.' For the fiscal year 1974, the Army shortfall was estimated at between '15,000 and 85,000,' or could involve up to two divisions and support personnel. In particular, combat arms enlistments in the Army increased from a monthly average of 250 in the last half of 1970 to approximately 3,000 in the last half of 1971 and remained at this level until May 1972. This figure was below the required 6,000 per month and indicated at least a 36,000 annual shortfall. In the fall of 1972, the Department of Defense and National Security Council were more optimistic about the impact of pay rises and intensified recruiting efforts. In part, this represents the result of a relatively large number of high school graduates entering the labor market during the summer and thereby supplying an enlarged pool for military recruiters. The further reduction in the projected manpower goal, announced in January 1973, as mentioned above, helped to close shortfalls in manpower over the short term. In fact, as of June 1975, the ground forces were able over the short run to meet their requirements because of the impact of high unemployment rates and intensified recruitment.

One measure of the relative problems each service faces can be seen in recent changes in first term re-enlistments. Re-enlistments—the percentage of men who complete initial enlistment and opt to continue in service—is indicative of the power of attraction of a military career in each service. A re-enlistment rate of 25 percent is thought to be optimum. For the Army, in 1970, first term re-enlistments had dropped to 9.4 percent from 17.6 percent in 1964, according to the testimony of Assistant Secretary of Defense Kelley. Short-term fluctuations in 1971, the wind-down of the war in Vietnam and efforts to improve recruitment resulted in improvement with the re-enlistment rate returning to approximately 17 percent. However, for the period July 1971 to March 1972, the rate for first term re-enlistment dropped to 13.3 percent. Interestingly enough, the Navy performance was not much better. In 1964, the rate was 18.7 percent and by 1970, it had dropped to 11.7 percent. In 1972, it had risen to nearly 20 percent. The Air Force performance was much higher and served as the basis of their greater self-assurance; by 1972 first term re-enlistment had temporarily reached the high level of nearly 30 percent.

The experiences of 1972 and 1973 remain only transitional, since the effect of the draft was still at work. The overall size of the force was being reduced and therefore increasing the relative size of the re-enlistment pool, and the unemployment rate was very high. Moreover, the temporary advantages of the pay rise in comparison with civilian employment had not yet begun to erode. An indication of the magnitude of the recruitment task facing the armed forces is the requirement for 630,000 new enlistments for all the services during the fiscal year 1973, including both requirements for active duty and reserve forces. This figure represents about one-half of the males qualified for military service who will reach 19 during the year and, therefore, constitutes a most ambitious goal. Although recruitment will not be confined to this age group, it will be heavily concentrated there. Moreover, the annual size of the youth population will not increase markedly during the decade of the 1970s. Already by 1972, there was a 44,000 short-fall of reserve personnel and the prospect of increasing difficulty in recruitment.

Recruitment of numbers, not necessarily of quality officers, has been temporarily less of a problem because of the backlog of candidates in the subsidized Reserve Officers Training Corps (ROTC) program. However, ROTC enrolment dropped from 218,466 in 1968-1969 to 87,807 in 1971-1972 and to prevent further drops below minimum requirements, added financial incentives would be required.

In the transition to an all-volunteer force, increased emphasis has been placed on the use of women both as officers and enlisted personnel. Since 1965, the total number of women on active duty has gradually increased from 31,540 in 1960 to 44,305 in 1972. It is anticipated that the number will continue to rise from the current 2 percent until it reaches approximately 4 percent by 1975, which would be comparable to the percentage of the British forces. Likewise, an increased use of civilians can be expected; again for the United States, the ratio is lower than that of Britain after a decade of an all-volunteer service.

What about the level of quality? The military, in searching for universal standards and equality of treatment, relies heavily on educational level and educational performance standards. The four year college degree has come to be used as a measure of quality at the officer level. In the past, military services followed a more flexible system of recruiting young men with some college and, in a few programs, high school graduates, extending to them the opportunity for college education while in the services. But recent trends have emphasized the recruitment of college graduates, especially through ROTC programs. The services do maintain programs of officer recruitment from the enlisted ranks which carry with them the opportunity to complete college while on active duty. But, clearly, increased emphasis on such programs is required to prevent arbitrary exclusion of talented and energetic officer candidates and to obtain the appropriate numbers of such candidates.

The ability of the military to retain outstanding officers in the post-Vietnam armed force is also a pointed aspect of the level of quality.

Military academies recruit young men of very high academic performance. However, in recent years the resignation rate upon completion of the minimum tour of obligated service has fluctuated up to levels of nearly 25 percent. With the winding down of the war in Vietnam, numerous outstanding junior officers in the ground forces have either opted out or were seriously considering doing so. For the eighteen-month period preceding June 1972, 33 officers who were teachers at the United States Academy at West Point resigned. In part, the contraction of opportunities for advancement influenced some; others were concerned with what they believed to be a failure of the military to confront the military and moral issues of Vietnam. In addition, they felt the military had failed to take sufficient steps to adapt to its changing role in international affairs.

At the level of enlisted personnel, the key indicator of quality in recruitment is the so-called concentration of Category IV personnel—men with limited performance on educational achievement tests; high school graduation is an alternative and more stringent measure. The services have been energetic in containing the number of Category IV recruits, but the Army must rely on a significant segment of such personnel. For the period January to April 1971, new enlistments contained 23.9 percent in this category. This number temporarily dropped, but was still 17.0 percent for the period January to April 1972. Personnel in this group are heavily weighted with blacks.

Thus, on balance, it appears that the services, especially the ground forces, will continue over the short run to face real problems in the recruitment of adequate numbers and particularly, quality of personnel. Over the long run, budgetary considerations will only serve to compound these difficulties. However, improved personnel and organizational procedures and realistic deployment constitute the only effective remedies.

STRATEGIC DEPLOYMENT

As far as the United States is concerned, it is difficult to anticipate changes during the next decade in the international environment which would produce a shift in domestic public attitudes favorable to the reinstatement of conscription. The American military, because of the criticism of Vietnam both morally and technically, is hardly likely to be seen as a vital instrument for the massive solution of internal domestic issues. There is even a profound reluctance to make use of it marginally in this regard or to draw on its standby forces. No doubt because of the inability of existing institutions and market-place economics to solve many basic issues in the United States, the idea of national service has been

growing and will continue to grow. But such service will be on a voluntary
basis and outside military jurisdiction.

Of course, one cannot rule out the limited eventuality that international relations could cause or create socio-political conditions leading
to the reintroduction of some form of conscription in the United States.
The emerging definitions of national security under nuclear deterrence
limit such contingencies; but more important, military manpower as
generated by a volunteer system will set the limits and outlines of
American military policy.

Within the military profession, there are endless debates about the
meaning and content of strategic deterrence. One school of military
professionals is deeply concerned that, in the decade ahead, the United
States will not realize the full impact of its military forces unless it
maintains a 'forward' military posture. A force structure and a deployment
of aggressive patrol—air, sea and forward positioning of ground forces—and
a potential for significant intervention and assault outside Western Europe
are required. These are the military professionals concerned with maintaining the personal qualities required for combat. On the other hand,
there are those who, while committed to the force in being for
contingencies, see the military as operating under powerful political and
moral constraints. They see the possibility of a successful American
foreign and military policy without an overt or conspicuous assault or
intervention ideology. For them, the function of the military is in the
political intentions it conveys as much as the sheer destructive power it
can wield. At the professional level, they prepare for and hope for careers
without combat.

These differing conceptions of strategic intent translate themselves in
day to day struggle over the allocation of the manpower pool and the type
of weapons systems that will be acquired. Two different and hypothetical
staff plans for a force of 1,750,000 indicate the meaning of these
alternative conceptions. The 'forward' or 'assault' model leads to advo-
cating a large Marine Corps of 200,000 with capabilities for tactical
nuclear weapons, an Air Force of 525,000 and a Navy of 525,000 men
which would emphasize attack aircraft carriers to support amphibious or
airborne warfare. The ground forces would be limited to 500,000 men and
most would be stationed in the United States, with 50,000 ground troops
in Western Europe. The character of these troops is crucial. The American
ground troops in NATO would be part of a highly automated battlefield of
electronic surveillance with 'modernized' weapons, and would operate
with tactical nuclear weapons as a trip-wire. In addition, there would be a
strong emphasis on 15,000 men in Special Forces and related units for

armed reconnaissance, operations behind enemy lines and counter-insurgency.

Alternatively, the 'constabulary' model would limit the Marines to 100,000 men and have a Navy and an Air Force of approximately 500,000 each. The naval emphasis would center on submarine missile deterrence and would include anti-submarine warfare. Six hundred and fifty thousand men would be allocated to the ground forces and the Special Forces would be limited to a few thousand specialists. On the crucial issue of ground force deployment, 150,000 men would be stationed in Western Europe (representing half of the current 1972 force level) and they would be closely articulated with the emerging military manpower systems of the various NATO nations.

Clearly, the central issue resulting from the transformation of the American military into an all-volunteer system is the impact on the size of American ground forces in Western Europe, locus of the major strategic role for American military manpower. In both political parties in the United States, there is a powerful desire to scale down the size of these ground troops; the major difference hinges on linking these changes to negotiations with the Soviet Union concerning mutual balanced force reductions. Although analysis generally proceeds in terms of the required troop levels to maintain a credible deterrence, the core point is the stability of American politico-military commitments in Western Europe. A 5 percent reduction, if seen by NATO partners as the first step in a continuous withdrawal, could undermine the military alliance system, while larger reductions if linked either to renewed long-term commitments or negotiations with the Soviet Union, would not be de-stabilizing.

Let us assume that the negotiations over mutual balanced force reductions take three, five or seven years, or even alternatively that they fail. The introduction of an all-volunteer force complicates the strategic problems for the United States, but hardly renders them unmanageable. The pressures will be greater on the United States to reach an agreement because of budgetary and manpower factors than on the Soviet Union. However, if two conditions are met, a new strategic balance could emerge. First, the United States after 1975 does not station any significant number of ground troops outside her continental limits except in Western Europe and parts of South Korea. Second, American military leaders explicitly seek to confront the difficult professional and organizational issues of an all-volunteer force as described below. If the military budget is to be kept roughly at 7 percent, the total manpower level will be less than the projected 2.3 million, but large enough to supply a basis for effective negotiation with NATO partners and with the Soviet Union concerning mutual balanced force reductions. The essential requirement for the United States is to convince NATO members of her long-term commitments in Western Europe, a most difficult task in the light of internal American political arrangements. There can be no doubt that the prolongation of the Vietnam conflict has also complicated the political and organizational problems of maintaining an effective military presence in Western Europe.

Nevertheless, despite the complexity of contingent elements, an appropriately managed American all-volunteer force could produce the ground manpower requirements for effective deterrence and avoid the possibility of a destabilizing independent European deterrent. The range of possible alternatives remains wide. There is good reason to believe that a 5 to 10 percent American unilateral troop reduction could be brought about without significantly altering deterrence. Administrative reorganization based on current strategy and alternative approaches would reduce the ratio of overhead to combat forces. For example, the RAF over the last decade has demonstrated that important reductions in personnel did not decrease their operational efforts and state of readiness. If accompanied by long-term reaffirmation and ratification of NATO, such reduction would be politically reassuring to the West and would serve as an incentive to the Soviet Union to negotiate realistically. On the other hand, successful negotiations with the Soviet Union could lead to reductions of up to one-third of American troops stationed in Western Europe. There can be no doubt that the continuation of a draft—administered equitably and with civilian service options—would have given the United States a more effective base for negotiation with the Soviet Union over mutual balanced force reduction, but the impact of Vietnam has ruled out that alternative strategy.

The introduction of an all-volunteer force, plus the gradual disengagement from Vietnam, do have an important impact in that they increase the ability of the President to mobilize political support for nuclear weapons expenditures. The situation is analogous with the introduction by General de Gaulle of the *force de frappe* at the end of the Algerian war. Hostility towards personal military service, a desire to end the Vietnam war on some reasonable terms, and even concern with military budgets, is not incompatible with popular support for increased investments in nuclear weapons. American military expenditures will in essence continue to be influenced by the political support that can be mobilized for particular weapons systems. A scaling-down of conventional forces in Europe and expansion of American expenditures on nuclear weapons could lead to the emergence of an independent European nuclear deterrent, with highly destabilizing effects.

The all-volunteer force of the United States is also being designed to meet unanticipated contingencies outside Western Europe. However, under current American foreign policy, the tension areas of the developing nations are not likely to be the scene of military intervention which would require a commitment the size of even a small Vietnam—150,000 ground troops—and which would require extensive mobilization of the reserve or the reintroduction of a modified form of conscription. Ground-force intervention in particular appears remote in the Middle East, the focal point of great tension. American intervention in South Asia has already been limited to volunteer forces. The expropriation of American overseas assets no longer produces 'US-Marine type' intervention. Such intervention is too costly and unproductive and alternative means are the more attractive, as witnessed by recent developments in South America. For the period of the next five to ten years, even a major civil war in a presumed 'strategic' nation such as Brazil would not be likely to result in significant ground-force commitments. The shadow of Vietnam remains much too powerful.

There is the problem of territories immediately adjacent to the United States. Military planners trained to think in global terms resist realistic analysis of such limited and localized issues. To the north, the prospect of a Canadian withdrawal from NATO cannot be ruled out. However, it does not appear that any neutralization of Canada in the next decade would move to the point where the United States would anticipate or be concerned with hostile penetrations. In the case of Mexico, current policies and the Mexican government give reason to anticipate the limited possibility of a governmental breakdown and a radical leftist government. It is difficult to anticipate the American government's response to a hostile Mexican government. Would even a relatively passive response strain the resources of an all-volunteer force?

There is much speculation in the United States that an all-volunteer force will give the President additional initiatives in committing troops to combat in case of international emergencies. No doubt the absence of draftees in the active duty force removes a restraint on the President. But any extensive engagement will require either the call up of segments of the reserves or the reactivation of the draft, so that these restraints still operate directly. No doubt there are strong restraints when draftees are utilized or when reservists must be mobilized. Moreover, as a result of the Indo-China War, there is a strong movement in Congress to limit the President's 'war-making' powers. The structure of American government and the Constitutional basis of the President's powers to conduct foreign affairs are likely to limit these Congressional efforts, but they will have strong symbolic value.

The introduction of the all-volunteer force in the United States will produce little immediate and dramatic impact; its consequences on domestic society and on foreign policy will be felt gradually. The violent opposition to military institutions and military service has already been defused by the de-escalation of ground operations in Vietnam and by the reduction in draft call-ups. The radical youth movement in the United States has been closely tied to opposition to the war in Vietnam and does not have its own base of existence or linkages with large-scale leftist political parties, as is the case on the continent of Europe. While criticism of the military budget will continue to be a major and intense political issue in the United States, criticism and opposition to the armed forces will be pressed mainly through the parliamentary system.

Professional and Organizational Issues

ALTERNATIVE MILITARY CONCEPTS

In the past, men have been willing to make a career in the military because of its style of life and without holding a clear conception of their tasks or purposes beyond that of national need and honor. But in the contemporary world, in the context of 'rational' analysis of institutional life, this is no longer the case. Professional soldiers want to know the purpose and presumed logic of military preparations.

Likewise, the advent of nuclear weapons and the all-volunteer force have led specialists to formulate new, alternative models of the military —models which have as yet attracted little popular attention. For example, there is the outlook of specialists such as Albert Biderman who calls for a reconceptualization of the military into a national emergency force.[9] He asks the question, what is the military? and believes that, in the post-Vietnam period, the risks of personal danger in the military are no greater than those in civilian life. In the military, the tasks which are purely military continually recede as the institution becomes more and more technological and logistical. However, the military retains a capacity—its instinctive quality—to mobilize itself for emergencies, while most institutions in society are committed to routine functions. Purely military emergencies are not a viable basis for organizing the military. An advanced society is faced with continual emergencies—resource, natural and man-made—oil spills, atomic energy disasters, etc. The contraction of the war-making function can only be balanced by its entrance into a wider set of emergencies and, therefore, the notion of the national emergency force.

Alternatively, there is the school of thought which proposes civilian defense or civilian resistance as a means of national defense. Each nation interested in its defense would commit all of its citizens by means of formal and informal instruction in passive or non-violent resistance and in various forms of massive and popular opposition to an invader—potential or actual. This strategic concept has its spokesman in Adam Roberts, the British political scientist.[10] The resistance of the population in Czechoslovakia to the Russian occupation after the 1968 invasion is cited by Roberts as the modern prototype, although the political effectiveness of this resistance can well be disputed.

There are various active operational equivalents in the contemporary scene. In Yugoslavia, politico-military strategists emphasize the notion of mass partisan resistance as an adjunct to conventional forces in order to repel invaders and as a modern equivalent of the *levée en masse.*[11] The idea of the armed citizenry in Yugoslavia clearly has its political role for the Communist Party as a balance to the professional military cadres.

As another approach, one proposal to maintain the legitimacy and vitality of the military, the notion of linking or broadening military service to forms of volunteer national service, has been discussed. For the United States, I have sketched out the details of a manpower system of volunteer national service in which volunteer civilian national service would parallel volunteer military service.[12] A national youth agency, representing the interests of young people, would assist an estimated two-thirds of each new age cohort to complete different forms of national service for periods of varying lengths of time. In this view, the option of either military or civilian service would both increase the number and quality of recruits for the military and enhance their validity. For Britain, a professional officer, J.C.M. Baynes, in his analysis of *The Soldier in Modern Society,* rejects conscription and concludes with a similar volunteer civilian national-service system in which military personnel could serve for one year.[13]

Despite this intellectual debate, the notion of deterrence as implemented by a professional military force 'in being' has persisted since the end of World War II as the essential 'mainstream' strategic concept to supply a rationale for the legitimacy of the military as the mass armed force declines. The operational content of deterrence and the role of reserve forces are subject to a variety of meanings and differing specifics. The military has been under overriding internal and external pressure to spell out the details of effective and realistic deterrence, both because of the awesome responsibilities and because of growing budget restrictions. The result is a vast amount of detailed planning which may not be linked to emerging realities and an under-emphasis on reconceptualizing professional ideology and the standards of professional behavior.

The details of the deterrent force—nuclear and conventional—require a mammoth set of technical, logistical and organizational decisions. Yet, at the same time, deterrent forces, especially the ground element in Western Europe, represent a pool of resources, with a variety of contingent potentials, which project the political intent of peace-keeping through a military presence. Over a decade ago, I offered a definition of a constabulary force as one point of departure for rethinking the military function. The constabulary concept provides a 'continuity with past military experiences and tradition, but offers a basis for radical adaptation of the profession. The military establishment becomes a constabulary force when it is continuously prepared to act, committed to the minimum use of force, and seeks viable international relations rather than victory, because it has incorporated a protective military posture.'[14]

In this regard, there may be important differences between the military in Britain and in the United States. In Britain, it is reported that senior officers accept the new military role of deterrence, even though it appears to have strong 'passive' overtones. Prolonged hostilities in Vietnam have retarded the American military from effective debate and internalization of such professional norms. Some military officers implicitly hold the view that a military—especially a ground force—which does not engage in even limited combat from time to time loses its vitality; others are realistically aware of the difficulties of recruitment and morale of a force which performs mainly passive functions. Nevertheless, the overall drift in strategic outlook has been in the direction of acceptance of deterrence concepts even though hard cores of 'traditionalism' persist and even flourish. Thus the all-volunteer force which is being developed to implement strategic deterrence faces new and unprecedented professional and organizational problems.

In examining these professional and manpower issues of the all-volunteer force in the United States, the experience of the military during the period between World War I and World War II when they operated on such a basis, supplies little guidance for the emerging period of the 1970s. First, the total size of the military was tiny, little more than 300,000. The military force of 1.7 to 2.3 million which is under consideration is a large-scale establishment and very different from the scattered collection of military posts and naval stations that then existed. Second, that former all-volunteer military establishment had a very different and very limited function from the current forces which are deeply involved in deterrence. Third, the all-volunteer force of that period was a mobilization cadre while the contemporary one is essentially more of a force-in-being, although it is designed to have significant reserve components.

CAREER AND RETIREMENT

In the first instance, the all-volunteer service in the United States requires a redefinition of the content and duration of the military career which would strengthen its civil service basis. In essence, a redefinition of the military career in the American scene requires an increased flexibility in the number of years that personnel will serve, greater diversity in career lines, different patterns of promotion and clearer articulation with civilian employment.

A significant number of both officers and enlisted personnel will continue to serve in the armed forces for six years or less. For them, military experience is an interlude in an essentially civilian existence. This type of military service does not involve a career commitment and the transition back to civilian life is relatively manageable, although there are specific attendant problems. However, for another group, military service will cover extended periods, often up to twenty years. This is a smaller group, but it represents the essential cadres and the question of what constitutes their career is unclear. For them, military service could be redefined as one step in a two-step career which is essentially a life-time career in public service, with the military part being the first step and the second step being in the civil service establishment.

For enlisted personnel, successful completion of a specified period of service, such as three periods of enlistment, could constitute effective entrance into civil service employment. The United States Civil Service and/or Department of Labor would be responsible for their placement in the federal service or, by negotiation, in state or local government. Such a career-system would broaden the basis of recruitment, attract personnel of appropriate quality and eliminate the costly system of re-enlistment bonuses and high-cost pension plans. When an enlisted man transferred to the civil service establishment, he would take with him pension benefits equivalent to civil employment that would be paid to him on retirement.

An equivalent system would operate for officers, but would go into effect only after the size of the officer corps was reduced. In addition, the length of the officer's term of service would be made more flexible. Retirement with appropriate pension benefits after 10, 12 or 15 years is essential to ensure a flow of personnel into the Civil Service which would meet the forces' requirements with regard to rank structure and military tasks to be performed. These arrangements are also designed to bring the costs of the current military retirement system under control. Retirement pay in the United States is based on an outmoded system which is a carry-over from the pre-World War II system.

Under a modernized system, more comparable to civilian retirement, an enlisted man or officer transferred to the civilian establishment would take with him pension benefits equivalent to civil employment. His pension benefits would be incorporated with those of his new job and paid upon retirement from civil employment at 65. He could, if he wished, opt for private employment and get a lump sum payment.

The number of years that short-term personnel will serve is also subject to re-evaluation. The military in the United States has taken a firm stand that a two-year enlistment is the minimum. In fact, only the Marines make extensive use of two-year enlistments. However, a shorter term enlistment could be thought of as a trial enlistment designed, in part, to recruit men for longer terms. The trend towards higher skill requirements in the armed forces should not obscure the extent to which the military and especially the ground forces still have an important segment of their personnel engaged in tasks which do not require extensive skill. Recent studies document in detail that there persists a core of jobs which can best be performed without extensive training or after limited on-the-job training.[15] Already the military forces of Western Europe make effective use of personnel who serve less than two years. Such a trial enlistment would appeal to young men from a variety of social and educational backgrounds who are not initially prepared to make a longer commitment. As a result, fifteen months or shorter enlistments would increase the social representativeness of the military recruits and would, for young people who have completed high school, serve as a moratorium before post-high school vocational training or during college or before regular employment.

Likewise, the length of traditional short-term enlistments which tends to be three years could be lengthened on a flexible basis. In the United States, there is excessive emphasis on 'promotion up' or selection out. While there is considerable concern about reducing personnel turn-over and thereby containing training and logistical costs in the all-volunteer army in the United States, the projected typical length of service remains too low. For the ground forces, the average period of duty of enlisted personnel including re-enlistments is projected as being between four and five years. In Britain, basic infantry enlistment includes a seven-year option and there is no feeling that such enlistment creates personnel stagnation. Likewise for officers, it should be possible to retain technical and staff specialists at the rank of major or colonel and make use of their skills without requiring them to be subject to promotion reviews. They could remain in grade and receive pay increments based on length of service. The approach has been used with success in the all-volunteer service of Britain.

A system of lateral entry would articulate with such a trend. The military uses lateral entry in order to recruit doctors and lawyers at the officer level and for some specialists at the enlisted level. By lateral entry, it is possible to draw on a larger and already trained manpower pool. It has been more extensively adopted by the volunteer systems in Britain and in Canada, where recruits with appropriate skills are given higher ranks.

Finally, the all-volunteer force in the United States must confront a rank structure which evolved as a result of the expansion of the war in Vietnam. The services are already experiencing a slowing up in promotion opportunities which is made worse by a hump—a bunching up of the selected ranks. This hump is to be found at the rank of major and also at the colonel level, thereby decreasing the opportunities for promotion to colonel. The previously mentioned flexible retirement system after 10, 12 or 15 years of service would be an important step in handling the 'hump' in the officer ranks. In addition, in the three services, an excessive number of general officers have been accumulated. This concentration thwarts the assignment to important posts of young men prepared to adapt to the changing environment.

The Army, in particular, has a deep division between junior and mid-career officers who actually fought in South Vietnam and the ranking personnel who flew over the battlefield or were in top command positions. Men in their forties who are more prepared for change could be rapidly incorporated into the general officer group to heal the breach and to offer an incentive for able mid-career officers to remain in service. Beyond the normal retirement, as many as 50 to 60 percent of the general rank officers might well be excess personnel and some steps have been taken to produce early retirement. One rank deflation for all assignments at the general level is also needed.

EDUCATION

The military educational system, particularly for officers, also requires consolidation under an all-volunteer force. The essential format for career officers in the United States is a three-step system—military academy or the college level equivalent, command and staff level, and, subsequently, war college or inter-service war college. If one adds to these steps a variety of specialized courses, plus advanced degrees in civilian universities for an important minority, the result is that the professional officer spends a considerable portion—more than 20 percent—of his active duty time in education. This three step system requires consolidation. It is wasteful, often mechanical and repetitious as well as excessively time-consuming in diverting officers from operational assignments. Military officers require extensive education, but many competent officers consider the present system an excessive diversion from professional service. The system should be reduced to a two-tier one, with the inter-service component distributed to the service war colleges. A stronger emphasis on brief courses for handling new developments in organization and doctrine would be desirable, as well as permission to substitute civilian schooling for advanced military professional school attendance. In addition, the military academy programs should permit one year of attendance at a civilian university, in the junior year, for example. Alternatively, the academy could have a five-year program with one year free for civilian work experience or service in the enlisted ranks.

There must also be a greater use of Officer Candidate Schools for recruitment and training of new officers. The end of conscription will reduce the pool from which qualified officers can be selected. Since there is a danger that officer candidates will become less socially representative, ROTC units must be reorganized so that any college student in the United States, either on entering college or when a junior, will have access to a collegiate ROTC program. In each of the ten major metropolitan areas, there should be a composite program, administered by an existing ROTC group, enrolling students from any accredited college in the area. Such an approach would increase the supply of applicants for ROTC and would tend towards greater social representativeness.

ROTATION AND DEPLOYMENT

The existing world-wide personnel system, which leads to continuous, excessive, expensive and disruptive rotation can no longer be justified. The rationale for this system is that it prevents stagnation and trains personnel for high command. Between World War I and World War II, the necessity of training a small cadre which would be prepared to expand rapidly during the war gave validity to a continuous service-wide replacement system. But, for a post-Vietnam force in being of less than two million men, these procedures are outmoded because they weaken military cohesion. They are the cause of important family discontent which leads to resignation and failure to re-enlist.

In contrast with other comparable military establishments, the American forces have high degrees of personnel rotation, although exact data are not available. There is growing resistance to these procedures and, at a minimum, stabilized tours of duty of three or four years would make a marked difference.

More comprehensively, ground forces must develop a modified version of the British regimental system or, in the present context, a modified brigade system. Each man would have a basic unit and would spend a significant portion of his military career within that brigade. For the Navy, a home port concept, and for the Air Force, a home base, would serve as equivalents.

A modified brigade system becomes an essential device in the recruitment of personnel. The ground forces have started a program by which volunteers can select their operational unit and have the opportunity to remain with the unit even as it changes its home station or place of deployment. Three units have been so designed: 197th Infantry Brigade at Fort Benning, Third Armored Cavalry Regiment and 212th Artillery Group at Fort Lewis and 192nd Infantry Brigade at Fort Knox. Research indicates that the opportunity to make such a selection has increased voluntary enlistment.

Unit solidarity and stability is a vital issue for dealing with the sense of under-employment which is a powerful source of negative attitudes towards a military career, especially among young officers. In the past, military personnel were less sensitive to the stimulus and responsibility of initial assignments since they could always assume that war would break out and they would be fully engaged. To develop a sense of active engagement in a military involved in deterrence is more complex and the avoidance of boredom and futility are very important.

When the U.S. Army undertook opinion surveys to facilitate planning for the volunteer force, results underlined the obvious conclusion that meaningful work was a very important element of satisfaction for enlisted personnel. The services have sought to eliminate kitchen police and maintenance of grounds. The ground forces, in particular, have introduced more adventure training in order to maintain the sense of engagement generated in basic training. Young men who enter the ground forces expect a rigorous life and are disappointed if there is little to engage them. Likewise, traditional forms of personal harassment, once thought to be a means for teaching discipline, are deeply resented. (The Marine Corps system of basic training is apparently not resented by the limited cadres which they require and are probably attracted by it; however, the ground forces require larger numbers and these recruits seem less willing to accept Marine Corps procedures.) Reduction of the size of the forces will help military morale since fewer men will be called on to perform more operational assignments and missions. One of the most promising potentials is that many training functions can be transferred from specialized units to operational units both in order to improve training and to reduce the actual amount of under-employment in the latter.

Deployment and utilization require a fundamental restructuring of the reserve component. The reserves have been heavily staffed by men seeking an alternative to full-time service in the draft. With the reduced pressure from the draft, reserve enlistment has declined and already, by 1972, there are shortages of more than 45,000 men in the reserves, with the rate of enlistment indicating increasing deficits. At the officer level, reserve quotas are being met, to some extent, by the short-term procedure of assigning ROTC graduates to the reserve rather than to active duty.

Current official planning sets a required 1,000,000 level for the reserves. For an all-volunteer force committed to a deterrence concept, a smaller reserve might be feasible if it is adequately organized and maintained. One can postualte three different types of reserve personnel. First would be the fully alert units which can be assembled and deployed within 48 to 72 hours. Such personnel should have a reserve status, pay system and active duty training periods which realistically reflect their commitment. Second are the personnel who, in the normal course of events, would rotate, as individuals or small groups, through active duty assignments for various periods of two weeks to two months to even longer periods of duty. Third would be a general manpower pool of persons who would receive limited training and be available for various contingencies and requirements. Moreover, persons should be able to move from reserve units to active duty units, depending upon national and personal need. In general, the function of the reserves would be less mobilized personnel and more manpower resources to be actively utilized by the forces in being. Such reserve forces would serve as an additional and important link with civilian society. It is possible to estimate the total size of a reserve force with these three components as totalling between 700,000 to 800,000.

More effective deployment involves a restructuring of the internal organization, equipment, and division of labor of military units. In this regard, the military organization of the U.S. forces is being subjected to continuous critiques.[16] The basic logic of such critiques is that military forces, especially ground forces, have an excessive investment in overhead (the teeth to tail ratio) and that there is a wasteful commitment to excessive technological devices. Moreover, they are designed on outmoded strategic assumptions which lead to a concern with prolonged hostilities rather than the most effective fire-power for deterrence. It is important to note that under the pressures of a volunteer system, the British Royal Air Force has made noteworthy progress in maintaining the number of operational miles flown with reduced military personnel. It is to be anticipated that the all-volunteer force in the case of the United States will produce a reduction in the size of overhead manpower and resources.

SOCIAL REPRESENTATIVENESS

How representative will the volunteer force be? A volunteer military can be expected to have selective social characteristics, but if it becomes highly unrepresentative, it creates internal socio-political problems.

Before 1940, the American officer corps had a strong element of selected social characteristics, although there were mechanisms at work limiting this social selectivity. First, there was a component of self-selection from service families. Self-selection in this regard included not only military father-military sons, but also officer recruits who had families in which other relatives—uncles, grandfathers, cousins—had served as career officers. Moreover, there was also a southern, old family, upper-middle class, hinterland and Protestant cast to the other cadres, especially at the upper levels. Yet the growth in the size of the officer corps and the process of social change in the larger society had already weakened this selectivity before 1940. The massive expansion of the officer cadres during World War II made a further contribution to the 'democratization' of the officer corps.

Since 1945, the issue of social representativeness has centered, to a considerable extent, on the question of self-recruitment. As compared with the pre-World War II period, there has been a clear increase in self-recruitment if only because of the size of the career manpower pool and, in consequence, great expansion in the number of military sons. One important measure of self-recruitment is that the composition of cadets at the three military academies has increased. In the 1960s, more than one-quarter of entering cadets at the service academies came from career military families. They had fathers who either were on full-time career duty or had completed twenty years of service. If one were to include uncles and close relatives who were career military, the percentage would, of course, be larger. A major component in self-recruitment is sons of non-commissioned officers. For these young men, who have strong military commitments, entrance into the officer corps, especially as academy graduates, is a sign of real social mobility and personal achievement. Among military offspring, linkages with civilian society tend to be attenuated and a sense of social isolation is an often present potential.

Demographic analysis indicates that, given the size of the military establishment during the 1950s and 1960s and the high birth-rate among military families, an effective supply of military sons will continue into the 1970s. Their interest in the military is a problematic issue for all the reasons which make a military career less attractive, but the number of opportunities to serve will be diminished so that comparable concentrations of self-recruitment could well continue. Father-son succession is, of course, an element in any profession and probably essential in the case of the military. Occupational inheritance serves to transmit basic values and loyalties. The medical profession has a pattern of recruiting about one-quarter of its members from the sons of doctors. Military service families in particular have, in the past, been prepared to accept the ups and downs of service life. However, the issue at hand is the potential danger of excessive self-recruitment which would, under conditions of an all-volunteer force, contribute to social isolation. This is especially the case when these are the sons of non-commissioned personnel, whose family horizons are indeed restricted.

Another noteworthy trend has been the enlargement of the percentage of working-class sons in the officer corps, as measured by the fact that more than 20 percent of the cadets at the military academies have come from working-class backgrounds. The military academies are less socially exclusive than the elite and high prestige major state universities. In part, this represents a decline in the attraction of the military career, especially for the upper-middle class and, in part, it is a reflection of the search for talent whereby intelligent young men with strong academic backgrounds and athletic skills could compete in the examination regardless of their social origins. One might assume that men from a modest background would be particularly loyal to the military establishment because of the educational benefits they accumulate and the social position they achieve, but there are no real data to establish this point. However, in broader terms, there is no reason to believe that recruitment on a more democratic base—that is from a wider base—has the consequence of selecting men who have stronger loyalties to democratic institutions and to the process of civilian control or are more professional in their commitments.

The massive expansion of the officer corps during World War II and its persistent enlargement for 25 years thereafter reduced regional selectivity. However, the projected reduction once more raises this issue. The nation itself has drastically changed during this period. To some degree regional differences have declined and, in particular, the hinterland culture which has been conducive to the military tradition, has been penetrated more and more by urban values. Congressional leaders have displayed some concern that ROTC units, which have been eliminated as a result of anti-Vietnam agitation, were located in liberal arts and prestige colleges in the northeast and mid-west, while new units and requests for new units have been located in the south and southwest.

Geographical selectivity involves more than an ecological area in which military values persist. The American military has had a regional base because its military installations are heavily concentrated in the south and again, currently in the southwest. As a result, the military develop many of their social contacts in these regions; they marry the residents from these areas and they retire there as well.

In addition, in the post-World War II period, a new stream of officer recruits has come from the urban day-time universities, located in the center of the northern metropolitan areas. These universities, often Catholic institutions, serve the ethnic lower-middle class and working class population and their ROTC graduates diversify if not make representative the emerging officer cadres.

RACIAL COMPOSITION AND RACE RELATIONS

But more visible than self-recruitment and regional balances, at the officer level, is the under-supply of black officers in all services including the ground forces. In the past, discrimination excluded or limited their participation. Likewise, the requirements of a college degree worked a powerful hardship against blacks who wished to serve as career personnel. Desegregation and the operational requirements in Korea brought about an increase in opportunities for black officers. Those without sufficient education were offered resources to complete their education while on active duty. In 1949 the percentage of black officers in the total armed forces was 0.9 and by 1970, it had risen to 2.2 percent. The highest concentration of black officers was in the ground forces (3.4 percent) and the lowest (0.7 percent) in the Navy.

Paradoxically, in the 1960s, as opportunities for black officers in the services increased, it became more difficult to recruit them. Opposition to the war in Vietnam was strong among many blacks who would have been eligible to become officers. Moreover, as opportunities for college-trained black personnel expanded in civilian society, the services experienced greater difficulty in attracting and retaining them. By the end of the 1960s, there was a higher concentration of blacks among captains, majors and lieutenant-colonels than among first and second lieutenants, an indication of the persistent deficit of black officer personnel and of the increasing difficulty in recruiting them.

Since 1968, the service academies have engaged in intensive recruitment drives for black cadets and the number has risen sharply. In 1968, 9 blacks out of 1,243 entered the U.S. Military Academy and the number increased to 45 out of 1,439. The Navy reached 50 out of 1,250 in 1971 and the Air Force had approximately 30 out of 1,400 that year. Likewise, efforts were made, especially by the Navy, to establish ROTC units in southern black colleges. Even with these steps, the deficit is most pronounced and there is little guarantee that new recruitment will produce personnel who will remain in the military beyond the obligated tours of duty.

Social representativeness for enlisted personnel focuses mainly on social class and racial composition, elements which are highly interrelated. In the past, the military recruited enlisted personnel heavily from the south and from rural areas. This is only in part an economic issue since periods of depression have demonstrated that the economic push into the military has only limited power. (Re-enlistments are more likely to be influenced by economic conditions.) Enlistment involves both a psychological and a cultural dimension. Enlisted personnel, to some extent, have been drawn from those areas where 'going into the service' is still viewed with favor. Over-recruitment from rural and southern areas persists but at a much lower level. This is described by the remarks of General Conrad S. Allman, Commander of the U.S. Air Force Recruiting Service, who stated, 'it is easier to get a person out of the South or South-West than it is out of the North-West.'[17] Although regional goals exist, the relative ease of recruitment influences regional representation in the enlisted ranks.

Within the working class culture of the central city—both black and white—the attraction of the military and the cult of masculinity that it represents still serve as a basis of recruitment. For the enlisted ranks, during the mid- and late-1960s, the Selective Service System with its medical and mental screening, under-selected the very poorest, while educational deferments exempted many middle-class youths, with the result that the cadres in Vietnam were heavily drawn from the solid core of the working class.

If it were not for the impact of Selective Service screening out many blacks with the most limited educational background, the ground forces would have a marked racial over-concentration of blacks. Nevertheless, blacks tended to be more concentrated in the Army and especially in combat units where limited educational background was less of a barrier to a successful career. The Army, through the draft and lower enlistment standards, has made more use of limited education, Category IV men. In 1970, in the ground forces, 30.4 percent of Category IV personnel were black. To the extent that an all-volunteer forces must utilize this group, the concentration of blacks will increase.

Trend data on racial composition must be carefully assessed. From an overall point of view, the concentration of blacks in the enlisted ranks in the military has risen from 9.2 percent in 1962 to 11 percent in 1970. This increase represents higher concentrations in the Army, Marines and the Air Force during the period while the figure has remained constant for the

Navy. For the Army, the figure stood at 13.5 percent as of 31 December 1970. While this did not represent a marked over-concentration, the trend has been one of steady increase. By June 1972, the percentage of enlisted blacks in the ground forces was 15.1 and it reached 18 percent in September 1972.

Observers look at the re-enlistment rate of blacks as a sensitive indicator of emerging trends. Blacks have re-enlisted at a very much higher rate than whites in the ground forces and thereby contribute to the higher percentage of blacks in the Army (13.5 percent of total enlisted manpower and almost 20 percent of career personnel). The re-enlistment rate for blacks at the end of their first term in 1964 was 33 percent of the eligibles as compared with 15.6 percent for whites, or twice as many. By 1970, re-enlistments in the Army fell sharply because of the impact of Vietnam. Likewise, temporarily the differences between re-enlistment rates of blacks and whites decreased, but this convergence in re-enlistment rates was temporary. In part, it represents black hostility to the war in Vietnam and the ending of hostilities will reduce the importance of this factor.

Moreover, the pool of blacks with high school education will be growing as public schools make special efforts to assist blacks in achieving higher levels of education. Thus, the pattern of higher rates of re-enlistment can be expected to return, even if not as high as in the past. The Gates Commission estimated that the percentage of black enlisted personnel would level off at 16 percent, but their argument is hardly impressive and has been exceeded by the 18 percent in September 1972. There is no reason to believe that this will occur without conscious policies to enhance the social representativeness of the military.

For the future the dilemma is clear-cut. A democratic society does not want the military to be a 'school of the Nation' or to over-recruit from the lowest social and deprived minority groups. However, the military has the capacity to make use of men with limited educational background and to offer them a second chance.

Race relations in the armed forces is not only a matter of numbers, but also a reflection of the larger civilian society. Yet the military is expected to operate at higher standards of social justice and due process than civilian society because it is a federal institution and one charged with such grave responsibilities. The military cannot be expected to solve the problems of civilian society, yet it is expected to solve its own problems without reference to the defects of civilian life.

Race in the American armed forces reaches back to the very origins of the American Revolutionary War, and was given its powerful and persistent salience during the Civil War. In the Post-Reconstruction Period, as civilian society reintroduced racial segregation, the military in its own logic resisted to a considerable extent and sought to offer blacks a form of legitimate existence within its ranks. This meant to accord blacks a position as a fighting man—the essential sign of the military profession. After the Reconstruction period came to an end, blacks fought in the west in segregated units and were armed, while in civilian society the black community was suffering increasing repression and discrimination.

During World War I, black soldiers were not only segregated within the military, but their combat-role under white officers was most limited. Black civilian leadership demanded that they be armed and given the right to enter all branches. In a fundamental sense, to be armed was thought to be fully accepted, to become an equal member of society, since military service was taken to be an essential sign of complete citizenship. During World War II, the black community continued to press for the same goals, and slowly the role of black military personnel was broadened. Under white officers, larger formations were organized which produced mixed results in combat and much mutual recrimination. The operating philosophy of the professional military—reflecting the mores of the larger society and especially the patterns of its southern component—was indeed reluctant to make use of the military as an agent of social change, although in effect military experience stimulates black veterans to more militant demands.

During the Korean war, the military officially accepted the goals of racial integration, and higher headquarters pressed harder than did comparable civilian institutions. Integration was assisted by authoritative sanctions and by the performance of blacks in combat. Most officers believed that the armed forces performed an important public service when they demonstrated that racial segregation could be eliminated.

Although progress at the officer level was painfully slow, the success of blacks as enlisted personnel and non-commissioned officers was striking compared with their progress in civilian industry. In the Army and in the Marine Corps, as Charles Moskos has demonstrated, intelligence measured by test scores, rather than racial characteristics, accounted for assignment and advancement in the decade of the 1960s.[18]

The rapid rise of black self-consciousness in the late 1960s created in the military resentment precisely because the white officer had come to believe that integration was the correct solution. Military morale was such that signs of racial identity, in contrast to religious identity, were viewed as disruptive. The first indications of racial self-consciousness were shown by black draftees during the Vietnam build-up and had overtones of opposition to the war. Black non-commissioned and commissioned officers, with many years of service, resisted these new sentiments fiercely, but their opposition served only to strengthen militant feelings which intruded into duty assignments and on occasion erupted into resistance and hostility. In the fall of 1970, field reports from West Germany indicated extremely high levels of racial tension and discontent which seriously strained the command structure. Dissatisfaction with promotion opportunities among blacks developed and there was a widespread feeling that they were given harsher disciplinary treatment than white personnel for the same offense.

Military officials have struggled to come to grips with these issues. They came to acknowledge the existence of an Afro-American subculture by permitting Afro-haircuts and by encouraging open and frank discussion of race relations and by energetically investigating complaints of discrimination and sources of tension. It was even necessary to remove one of the top-ranking officers in Western Europe in order to insure that positive steps of accommodation were expected from field commanders. New patterns of adjustment began to emerge in 1972 with the re-deployment of troops from Vietnam and as more black officers in the ground forces were selected into the general rank. It was opportune that blacks who had entered service at the end of World War II and during Korea were eligible for promotion into high rank by the early 1970s. In June 1972, six were placed in the promotion list of the ground forces for brigadier-general.

While racial tension in the armed forces must be dealt with in terms of procedural justice and new forms of mutual self-respect, for the military the issue of sheer numbers is still a dominant question. Efforts to recruit adequate numbers of black officers can be expected to be pursued with vigor since this represents a concrete goal which the military can objectify. On the other hand, the over-representation of enlisted personnel cannot be handled by a direct or simple solution, especially since a quota system would be unacceptable and unworkable. Nor can the military accept the point of view that when civilian society accords full equality to blacks, they will not be over-represented in the military. Instead, the military can be expected to adopt policies which will facilitate transfer and training so that no single unit or service will become over-concentrated. Second, adjusting entrance requirements—particularly educational ones—will have an influence. Both of these steps are negative measures with built-in limitations. On the other hand, positive efforts can be made to distribute black personnel through the various branches and services of the military. The extension of training programs in technical skills and preparation for transition to civilian society offers the opportunity to facilitate the outward movements of blacks. Black groups are already involved in cooperating with the military in such a program, including sending their representatives to military bases in order to offer employment counselling and recruiting.

Changing Civil-Military Relations

The transition from a mass armed force to an all-volunteer force means a continuation of long-standing issues of civilian control as well as new ones. During the period of the dominance of an expanded military force from 1940 to 1970 in the United States, there was paradoxically a civilianization of the military establishment. The dependence of the military on civilian industry and science, plus the immense political and public relations efforts required to justify military operations, weakened the boundaries between the military and the civilian. The trend towards civilianization of the military had its counterpart in increased penetration of the military in civilian society. The task of civilian socio-political control during this period was to prevent excessive politization of the military and to contain its influence which derived from its size and importance. Notions such as C. Wright Mills' 'power elite' or Harold Lasswell's 'garrison state' were concepts designed to highlight these persistent dangers. A body of scholarship, more pointed in its conclusions, has come to focus on details of the impact of the military as a powerful pressure group both on civilian society and on foreign policy, but a pressure group under civilian political leadership.[19]

Under the all-volunteer system, the need to contain the pressure group influence of the military remains an overriding goal. There is no reason to suppose that civilian control will become a simpler and more manageable task. In fact, political control assumes new dimensions. The trend towards civilianization has probably reached its limit even before the end of the draft. But with the advent of an all-volunteer system, the military will develop more clear-cut boundaries and dangers of social isolation and political particularism. Once more the task of public policy is to strengthen the integration of the military into the larger society. Already, by the end of the 1960s, top American military leadership was displaying a strong preoccupation with maintaining its boundaries and corporate identity and exercising initiative in this direction. For example, it is pressing for, and succeeded in getting, an enlargement of the military academies in order to increase the concentration of academy-trained officers on active duty. Estimates as high as 30 to 35 percent academy-trained officers have been offered as desirable. The concentration of academy officers in the highest ranks was again increasing. Insistence on the prescribed career for entrance into the elite remained all-powerful.

The prospect of an all-volunteer force only increases the potential for internal rigidity and a sharper boundary between the military and the civilian sector. As mentioned above, there already can be noted an element of self and internal recruitment of officers—recruitment from the sons of the military—which, together with excessive in-service education, could result in a narrow and uniform outlook for its top officers. It would be dangerous and an invasion of personal privacy to probe excessively the public attitudes of active duty officers. As civil servants they are expected to perform their duties regardless of personal outlook. But it would be in error to overlook the fact that self-selection into the volunteer force is already recruiting men with an inclination towards conservative thinking. An in-bred force, which could hold resentments towards civilian society and could, accordingly, develop a strong and uniform conservative political ideology, would in turn influence professional judgments.

Conservatism in the officer corps will require continuing exploration in the American setting. Despite its 'revolutionary' origins, the mass armed force in the West has been traditionally officered by men who have strong conservative inclinations. These inclinations have been grounded in their family and social attachments and have been developed by their schooling and career experiences. In Britain and in the United States conservative-oriented officers have adjusted to the emergence of a parliamentary system while they managed citizen soldiers in time of war. However, for the United States, right-wing extremism can supplant conservatism. The attitudes of retired officers indicate that such outlooks already exist, as exemplified conspicuously by men such as Curtis Le May, former Commander of the Strategic Air Command and later associate of George Wallace.

Military officers are civil servants and therefore have the right to hold private political views if they do not lead to public pronouncements or partisan affiliations. It is not the responsibility of military personnel to defend and publicize military policies; this is the task of elected officials. But the military are not hired 'mercenaries.' They cannot be arbitrarily deprived of participation in community and public affairs. Thus, the vitality of the military profession depends on a delicate balance between a special sense of inner group loyalty and participation in the larger society. The military may well retreat more and more into the military base or garrison, but residence on or off base is not the crucial factor. Rather than residence per se, the quality of integration into civilian society depends on personal initiative and membership in voluntary religious and community associations. Military regulations and practices encourage participation within the format of non-partisanship, i.e., without direct affiliation to political party groups. But rotation from one assignment to another limits the ability of a military man and his family to make contact with their community. Some research studies indicate that the level of community participation of military personnel is similar to that of persons in other occupations which have a high degree of job rotation. One would hope, therefore, that the introduction of a modified brigade system with less job rotation would increase the possibilities for more meaningful community integration.

However, new perspectives on civic participation are required if the United States military under an all-volunteer force is not to become socially isolated, and if it is to maintain and enhance its self-respect. In West Germany the idea that an army man is a civilian in uniform has been pressed to the point to which regular personnel—both officer and enlisted—are permitted to stand for political elections while on active duty. In the American context, the need to avoid a political party affiliation probably is essential. However, military personnel should be permitted to serve on local school boards, run in nonpartisan local elections and be members of government advisory boards and public panels wherever they have the essential qualifications, competence and interest.

Moreover, the military cannot maintain its vitality unless it uses facilities for a wide range of other national emergency functions. The basic issue is not, as traditionalists hold, that the military should not be diverted from its fundamental mission. The military has traditionally been engaged in national emergency functions but the nature and content of these functions change. In fact, in the reconstruction of the military, it is essential that it use its manpower and vast resources to keep it an active and responsible institution. Such a professional outlook is required to attract and retain bright and highly-motivated men who wish to avoid under-employment and get on with social change.

Clearly, the military cannot engage in activities or programs which are better performed by civilian agencies. The essential issue is to make use of the military's stand-by resources; that is, its ability to respond to emergencies broadly defined, and to improvise in a crisis. The military is already deeply involved in the control of natural disasters. Floods, hurricanes and the like pose emergency situations which require its flexible resources. By 1970, the United States could not operate in a variety of such tasks without the support of the armed services. To natural disasters can be added the increasing scope of man-made disasters. Oil spills, power failures and chemical and atomic accidents are likely to increase rather than decrease. The armed forces are indispensable in a great deal of air and sea-rescue work, to which is being added, experimentally, medical evacuation, especially of victims of road accidents where alternative facilities are not available.

But the major frontier is in environmental control and the handling of particular aspects of pollution and destruction of natural resources. The Army Corps of Engineers has moved in this direction, but only the first steps have been taken. Many units in the armed forces have a contribution to make. The concept of a military career as part of a civil service career means new patterns of assignment between military and civilian agencies. An armed force of more than 1,500,000 men is a significant manpower pool—one that is urgently needed, given the economic pressures of contemporary American society, not only for national defense but for alternative forms of national emergencies. To speak of contemporary society as an 'affluent' society is a mistake in rhetoric, especially in dealing with the all-volunteer force, since societal needs continue to outrun society's resources.

Thus, the overriding conclusion is that the format of the all-volunteer military is not predetermined. Options still remain open for civilian political leadership and military professionals to make adaptations which would enhance the viability of the armed forces and restore its legitimacy in the post-Vietnam period, as well as increase its responsibility to political authority. But each day and each month that the all-volunteer force develops its own logic, the potentials for adaptation decrease. It would be a profound error to assume as some military leaders do that the United States is only experiencing a traditional 'post-war' reaction and that the return to conscription is only a matter of time. Of course, it would be equally in error to extrapolate the emerging forms of the all-volunteer military into the future without recognizing the possibilities for change and modification.

The essential reality is that the all-volunteer force will increasingly come to have its profound effect both on domestic society and on international relations. The domestic issues of 'armed forces and society' may be relatively manageable if civilian universities and colleges improve their instruction and research on these matters and offer, via ROTC and other programs, advanced officer education as a mechanism for integrating them into the larger society.

The central international issue rests on the construction of a new sense of military professionalism which realistically accepts the meaning of deterrence and is prepared to make efficient use of its limited manpower. Many of the arguments of military conscription—which were compatible with and even at times reinforced political democracy in the West—no longer hold in the current situation. The United States, as an advanced industrial society, does not seem prepared to accept imaginative and bold programs of voluntary national service, military and civilian, in order to demonstrate civic responsibility and to make a contribution to the national welfare. The tensions created by Vietnam in the United States are alone too great for that to be a realistic alternative.

On balance, the all-volunteer force does seem about to supply minimum manpower requirements although, no doubt, at a very high cost. But there is no basis for arguing the moral superiority of this manpower system. Nor is there need to argue the case on grounds of a strategic superiority, namely that manpower reductions will force a more humane and realistic foreign policy. The best that can be said is that the all-volunteer force can be made to work in a period of very difficult negotiations and a renewed search for a new international order.

Notes

1. U.S. President's Commission on an All-Volunteer Armed Force, *The Report of the President's Commission on an All-Volunteer Force* (Washington, D.C., 1970).

2. *The Force Structure in the Federal Republic of Germany*, p. 215; see *Survival* (January/February 1973), p. 35.

3. U.S. House of Representatives, W. C. Daniel, Chairman, *Hearings of the Special Subcommittee on Recruiting and Retention of Military Personnel* (Washington, D.C., 1972).

4. U.S. House of Representatives, W. C. Daniel, Chairman, *Report of the Special Subcommittee on Recruiting and Retention of Military Personnel* (Washington, D.C., 1972).

5. *The Report of the President's Commission on an All-Volunteer Force.*

6. "National Security Strategy of Realistic Deterrence," Secretary of Defense, Melvin R. Laird, *Annual Defense Department Report* (FY 1973), (Washington, D.C., 1972).

7. Morris Janowitz, "Volunteer Armed Forces and Military Purpose," *Foreign Affairs* (April 1972), pp. 427-443.

8. Laird, "National Security Strategy of Realistic Deterrence."

9. Albert Biderman, "What is Military?" in Sol Tax, ed., *The Draft: A Handbook of Facts and Alternatives* (Chicago, 1967), pp. 122-138.

10. Adam Roberts, ed., *Civilian Resistance as a National Defence: Non-Violent Action Against Aggression* (Harmondsworth and Baltimore, 1969).

11. Olga Mladenovic, ed., *The Yugoslav Concept of General People's Defence* (Belgrade, 1970).

12. Morris Janowitz, "National Service: A Third Alternative?" *Teachers College Record*, LXXIII, No. I (September 1971), pp. 13-15.

13. J.C.M. Baynes, *The Soldier in Modern Society* (London, 1972).

14. Morris Janowitz, *The Professional Soldier: A Social and Political Portrait* (Glencoe, Ill., 1960), p. 418.

15. Harold Wool, *The Military Specialist: Skilled Manpower for the Armed Forces* (Baltimore, 1968).

16. For example, Steven L. Canby, "The Wasteful Ways of NATO," *Survival* (January/February 1973), pp. 21-26.

17. *Hearings of the Special Subcommittee on Recruiting and Retention of Military Personnel.*

18. Charles Moskos, Jr., *The American Enlisted Man* (New York, 1970), pp. 108-134.

19. Stanley Lieberson, "An Empirical Study of Military-Industrial Linkages," *American Journal of Sociology,* LXXVI, No. 4 (January 1971).

RACIAL COMPOSITION IN THE ALL-VOLUNTEER FORCE: POLICY ALTERNATIVES

With the all-volunteer force entering its second year, it becomes more and more appropriate to raise and discuss the implications of the overrepresentation of blacks in the U.S. armed forces. This paper seeks to explore alternative strategies for dealing with the long term trend toward increasing concentration of the black minority in the military system. Although, of course, the minorities composition of the armed forces includes Mexican-Americans, Puerto Ricans, American Indians, Asian-Americans, and others, it is the high visibility and significant number of blacks entering the military services which bring them to the central concern of attention. For, in the ethnically pluralist society of the United States, race constitutes our country's most fundamental cleavage. If our American society is ever to realize its democratic goals, the direction its race relations take in the armed forces will be a prime factor.

Overrepresentation of blacks in the armed forces, while not yet an issue of national debate, can be defined as a problem from several perspectives. Thus, professional military officers and civilian commentators view a large concentration of blacks as exacerbating racial tensions and management problems within the services. A few of these are apprehensive about the internal reliability of such a force. Conversely, others, not only blacks, are distressed over the potential disproportion of black casualties in time of war. This paper, while fully cognizant of these issues, attempts to reformulate the discussion of the racial composition of the military in terms of representativeness of core institutions and political legitimacy. Can a political democracy expect to have a legitimate form of government if its military is not broadly representative of the larger society? Can a

From *Armed Forces and Society: An Interdisciplinary Journal,* November 1974, written with Charles C. Moskos, Jr.

military force whose combat units are overweighted with a racial minority have credibility in the world arena? What can be done to deal with the possibility of a concentration of casualties in one segment of society?

Trend Data

To examine the question of racial composition in the all-volunteer force is to focus on the enlisted personnel of the ground combat units. The trend toward increasing concentration of black personnel is underway in all services and branches, but the crux of the problem rests on the overproportionate number of blacks in the combat arms of the Army and Marine Corps. The experiences of the all-volunteer force to date have not indicated a serious shortfall in qualified entrants in the Air Force, Navy, and non-combatant elements of the ground forces. Indeed, quite the opposite, there remains an underproportionate representation of blacks in most technical military occupations.

Moreover, the expectation that the all-volunteer force would essentially be led by an all-white officer corps does not appear to be a likely eventuality; although, of course, projections of the racial composition of the officer corps have their marked limitations. It was the case that with the initial advent of the all-volunteer force, the number of blacks entering the officer corps began to decline. In good part this reflected the broadening of opportunities for college-level blacks in the larger society. But the armed forces have engaged in aggressive recruiting of potential black officers including an increase in the number of black cadets in the service academies. The most pronounced trends in minority officer recruitment, however, are in the very marked increase in ROTC programs at predominantly black colleges. In fact, by the academic year 1973-1974, 18 percent of the cadets in the Army ROTC were black. All in all, there are sufficient grounds to believe that the armed services have instituted programs such as will produce the requisite number of black officers. It seems reasonable to expect the economic and social advantages of ROTC and a short term military career will persist to a greater extent for blacks than for whites; and that blacks will constitute five to ten percent of the newly commissioned officers in all services for the second half of the decade of the 1970s. This is to say that while blacks are still likely to be underrepresented in the officer corps of the foreseeable future—as they were similarly underrepresented during the era of conscription—this deficit will not be to the extent that it will produce a profound racial distortion in the officer representativeness of the all-volunteer force.

We come back then to the root problem—the overproportionate

number of blacks in the enlisted levels, especially in the ground combat forces. The "Gates Commission," termed after the chairman of the President's Commission on an All-Volunteer Force, estimated in 1970 that an equilibrium over the short run would be for the total force approximately 15.0 percent black, and it even projected a decline to 14.1 percent for the 1980s. "Our research indicated that the (racial) composition of the armed forces will not fundamentally change by ending conscription."[1] As was apparent to many students of the U.S. military establishment during the preparation of the Gates Commission Report, there was no sound basis for this projection. Equally unsubstantiated was the Gates Commission estimate that only 2.1 billion dollars in additional pay was required to maintain an all-volunteer force of 2.5 million active-duty personnel. (By 1974 the military force was only 2.1 million and the increase in salary expenditures far exceeded the original cost estimates even without adjustment for the declining manpower quality.) More recent private estimates by Department of Defense officials in the spring of 1974 anticipate the number of blacks will reach about 20 percent for the total military manpower strength with a higher figure for the ground forces.

Despite the confident prognostications of the Gates Commission, it ought to have been apparent that there was no effective basis for making definitive manpower estimates on the quantity and composition of the all-volunteer force. At best one can report current trends and offer informed speculations as to the future.

During the period of conscription in the two decades following the Korean War, there was a slow and gradual increase in the proportion of black military personnel, both at the officer and enlisted ranks. As given in Table 1a, the proportion of blacks for all services was 8.0 percent in 1955, 8.3 percent in 1962, and 9.8 percent in 1970. The black concentration was highest—13.5 percent in 1970—in the enlisted ranks of the Army. The transition to an all-volunteer force, as reported in Table 1b, immediately

TABLE 1a

Blacks in the Armed Forces as a Percentage of Total Officer and
Enlisted Personnel, Selected Years 1954-1970

	All Services	Officer	Enlisted
1955	8.0	1.4	9.0
1962	8.3	1.7	9.2
1965	9.5	1.9	10.5
1968	9.3	2.1	10.2
1970	9.8	2.2	11.0

TABLE 1b

Black Enlisted Personnel as Percentage of Total Enlisted Strength
By Service, Fiscal Years 1971-1974

Fiscal Year	All Services	Army	Navy	Marine Corps	Air Force
1971	11.4	14.3	5.4	11.4	12.3
1972	12.6	17.0	6.4	13.7	12.6
1973	14.1	18.6	7.7	16.9	13.4
1974 (first half)	14.9	19.9	8.1	17.7	13.8

SOURCE: Department of Defense statistics.

reflected itself in a sharp increase in the concentration of blacks, again especially at the enlisted levels. The overall percentage has risen year by year, from 11.4 percent in 1971 to 14.9 percent by the end of the first half of fiscal year 1974 (December 1973). The overproportionately black distribution was most noticeable in the ground forces where from 1971 to 1974 the number of blacks increased from 14.3 percent to 19.9 percent in the Army, and from 11.4 percent to 17.7 percent in the Marine Corps. Moreover, by September 1973, 23.6 percent of all Army infantrymen were black.

A sharper picture of the changing racial composition of the enlisted ranks can be obtained from Table 2 which presents the figures on the number of blacks among the new volunteers in the military establishment. This table requires comment in two respects. First, it highlights the differing numbers of black personnel acquired by each of the services. Thus, in April, 1974, the Army recruited 3,390 new black enlistees contrasted with 840 for the Air Force and 560 for the Navy. Second, the percentage of blacks among those entering the military for the first time in April, 1974, reached 27 percent for the Army, 20 percent for the Marine Corps, 16 percent for the Air Force, and only 11 percent for the Navy.

TABLE 2

Black Proportions of New Enlisted Volunteers
(non-prior service)

	April 1974		July 1973-April 1974
	n	%	%
Army	3,390	27	27
Navy	560	11	10
Marine Corps	300	20	21
Air Force	840	16	16
All Services	5,090	21	20

SOURCE: Department of Defense statistics.

That the April, 1974, figures are atypical is seen by the comparable black percentages for the cumulative period July, 1973, to April, 1974. Moreover, the indication of growing black concentration at the enlisted levels is compounded by the fact that the reenlistment rates among blacks remain distinctly higher than among whites. Thus in fiscal year 1973, the reenlistment rate among first-term Army enlisted men was 52.0 percent for blacks compared with 35.1 percent for whites. The evidence is quite persuasive that the paramount trend in the racial composition of the ground forces since the end of conscription is toward a heavily disproportionate concentration of blacks.

In purely statistical terms, one could project a point at which a racial equilibrium would be reached; say, for example, 30 percent black throughout the ground forces. But such an approach encounters two problems. A 30 percent black distribution throughout the ground forces would probably not be random; some units would be markedly more black than the overall percentage. Already by the summer of 1974 there were combat units in the ground forces which were upwards of 35 percent black. Such an equilibrium model also avoids the qualitative issue of "tipping." By tipping we refer to the point at which the proportion of blacks becomes so high that large numbers of whites are no longer prepared to enter the particular service or branch involved. Such an occurrence could be engendered by factors including the perceived status decline of units overproportionately black, or the very real fear of black "hooliganism" on the part of many lower-ranking white enlisted men. It can be expected that the tipping point will operate in a gradual fashion in the military rather than in the dramatic threshold fashion of residential communities. But the end result nevertheless could well be a significant diminution of white recruits for the ground force units involved.

The Socio-Political Context of the All-Volunteer Force

We can only surmise as to the lack of public debate on the racial composition of the all-volunteer force. Undoubtedly, the underlying crisis in political leadership associated with the Watergate scandals and related matters has overshadowed the issue. The academic community, typically opponents of conscription if not of the military system, may perhaps not want to address the question in anticipation of egalitarian arguments to restore the draft. That a generalized racial tolerance accounts for the low concern about the composition of the armed forces seems naive. Indifference is probably the most adequate explanation. In any event, elected officials have almost completely avoided public statements of the problem.

Excepting a few news stories and columns, the mass media have also eschewed coverage of the growing concentration of black service personnel. One would have expected that the media with their increased identification with the adversary role could be expected to oppose conscription when it was operative and in turn to be critical of the all-volunteer force when it came into being.

Within the black community public leaders and elected officials have also generally been indifferent to the issue. In the main, views among black leaders seem to represent a widespread outlook among black adults that the armed forces represent an important source of job opportunities for blacks. Within the black community, moreover, there is a strong feeling that military service is particularly relevant since it appeals to young blacks who have the highest rate of unemployment, and by implication, the military is seen as a desirable alternative to life on the streets. Only on rare occasions has a black leader raised the issue of the legitimacy of the manpower system which has disproportionately recruited from minority races.

The absence of public discussion on the racial makeup of the military is not to say there is a lack of concern within the confines of the defense establishment. But even there the concern is felt more strongly by uniformed personnel rather than civilian officials. And even among military officers discussion on the black concentration in the services is sporadic and muted. A few military officers believe that the point of no return has already been reached in the combat arms of the ground forces; others view the emerging situation with a deep sense of personal frustration. More typical is the attitude: "Yes, we have a problem, but somehow, someway, a solution will be found." Concurrently there is some resentment in military circles that Congressmen and Senators will frequently issue pronouncements supporting the all-volunteer concept without making mention of the difficulties the services are encountering. There is a vague sentiment among many military officers that our national legislators voted to end conscription for political reasons, but these same legislators are reluctant to confront the unpopular problems associated with the all-volunteer force.

Nevertheless, the principle of civilian control over the military is so powerful that the general response of the professional military officer has been an unquestioning—almost "can do"—effort to make the all-volunteer system work. Indeed, the response of the military professional could be described as overprofessionalism; the uncritical acceptance of a mission without sufficient professional dissent. There has not been a single major statement about the racial composition of the armed forces by a military officer which has raised the fundamental issues involved, nor has there been a single token resignation from active duty on this issue. Instead the military officially has sought to minimize the issue. There has been repeated emphasis on the fact that the armed forces are an equal opportunity employer. There have been repeated statements that racial quotas would probably be unconstitutional and, in any event, would not be considered a policy alternative. Strenuous effort has been focused on the immediate concern to meet enlistment goals, rather than questioning the demographic premises of the all-volunteer force.

By the spring of 1974, however, there were indications that civilian political leaders were beginning to be alert to the dimensions of the racial and ethnic composition of the armed forces. Howard H. Callaway, shortly after becoming Secretary of the Army, boldly and clearly stated the Army goal to recruit from a relatively representative cross-section of the civilian population. In 1973, in the name of quality control, Congress passed legislation requiring 55 percent of new enlistments to be high school graduates. The Marine Corps was subsequently denied permission by Congress to reduce its educational standards for new enlisted personnel. Also, in 1973, the Army implemented for six months a recruiting policy requiring 70 percent of its new accessions to be high school graduates; but this standard proved to be unrealistic and was dropped in the wake of declining enlistments. It is very important to note, however, that unofficial Army recruitment data show that racial composition has consistently been most balanced among those choosing the shortest possible enlistment tour—two years.

Policy Strategies

In exploring alternative strategies for dealing with racial imbalance in the armed forces, this paper assumes that national and black leaders will increasingly be forced to confront the implications of the trend toward greater concentration of blacks in the combat arms of the ground forces. It is also assumed that a return to conscription, whatever its merits, will be politically unfeasible in the near future. This is not to assert that racial imbalance in the armed forces will suddenly constitute a dramatic "crisis," but that it will come more and more into the center of public attention. Furthermore, it is posited that the steps required to make the U.S. armed services—and especially the ground forces—effective in their emerging politico-military role of deterrence and constabulary professionalism are precisely the same steps which will contribute to a resolution of the problems of racial and ethnic imbalance. Put in another way, the disruptive potential of the race issue supplies pressure for internal reform. The character of this needed reform is not embodied in the report of the Gates Commission which programmed the all-volunteer force by emphasizing visible and competitive monetary compensation. Rather, our approach seeks to specify a series of steps and strategies which deal with the organizational climate and professional integrity of the military as a social institution.

These strategies are also based on the presumption of the constitutional authorities we have consulted who have asserted without reservation that a formal quota limiting the number of blacks would be illegal and unconstitutional. (Though Congressional statutes raising or lowering educational standards will have indirect but important consequences on the proportions of entering black personnel.) But even more pointed, such a quota system ought to be morally objectionable to the citizenry at large as well as an affront to minority groups. It is therefore doubly essential to propose and examine critically a variety of positive steps which aim toward recruitment and maintenance of an all-volunteer force which is broadly representative of the larger society.

Reduction and stationing of U.S. forces. The most direct approach to handling racial imbalance would be to reduce the size of the military establishment, and especially to reduce the size of the ground forces. Already the overall size of the all-volunteer force has been reduced to well below that estimated by the Gates Commission. The basic issue is the extent and timing of such reductions and the restraints that operate for an effective foreign policy. A smaller military establishment would have higher educational standards and thereby have less of a concentration of minority group members. It is important to remember that, in part, the short term success of the recruitment drives of the Navy and Air Force since the introduction of the all-volunteer force is to some degree related to the reduction in the overall size of these two services. During the same period, the manpower requirements of the ground forces were not reduced; in fact, they were slightly expanded for the next fiscal year, 1975.

The United States is already clearly in a position in which manpower requirements restrain its politico-military posture in Western Europe. It is therefore understandable that a great variety of approaches are being explored to reduce the number of personnel stationed in Western Europe without reducing their presumed military effectiveness. It is striking, however, to note how the numbers of American military personnel abroad have been translated by NATO allies as indicators of the stability and credibility of U.S. intentions. It may well be the case that even small reductions overseas will be seen as the initial step toward longer term withdrawal. It is also conceivable, however, that with proper restructuring and diplomatic groundwork, force reductions could be accomplished to satisfy the political requirements of Western Europe, e.g., reratification of NATO, new budgetary arrangements, innovative force structures, and the establishment of a NATO rear headquarters in the continental United States. Moreover, it is becoming evident that race and strategy are fusing inasmuch as our Western European allies are hardly predisposed to accept an increasingly black ground force as the appropriate instrument of U.S. foreign policy.

In the event of further reductions of total U.S. forces, the almost certain consequences would be that a higher percentage of the American military will be stationed within the United States. This would entail deployment from the Far East and elsewhere as well as from Western Europe. Until recently, it was generally assumed that reduced likelihood of overseas assignments would decrease the attractiveness of a volunteer force with accompanying heavier reliance on minority soliders. But the evidence to date suggests the reverse is the case.[2] That is, overseas duty—partly as a result of the diminished purchasing power of the dollar, partly less willingness to put up with family disruptions, partly to changing evaluations of foreign assignments per se—has lost much of its traditional appeal. In other words, the attractiveness of military service for a wider representation of the American population will probably increase to the degree U.S. forces are stationed at home.

Manpower substitution. Starting as early as the McNamara era, but becoming increasingly pronounced since the advent of the all-volunteer force, more and more uniformed male personnel in military occupational slots are being replaced by female uniformed personnel and civilians. This trend will generally work toward more racial balance in the total defense structure. But inasmuch as virtually all of the civilian replacements for formerly uniformed positions will occur in noncombat occupations, such a trend will not by itself directly affect the racial imbalance in the combat ground forces. Indirectly, to the extent that the demand for uniformed personnel is decreased, there could be some shifting in volunteers from noncombat to combat occupations. Thus, it is especially important that civilianization be monitored for its precise impact on the racial composition of uniformed military personnel.

In the case of female military personnel, the all-volunteer force has witnessed an opening up of many positions previously the exclusive preserve of males. Women recruitment goals have changed from the traditional less than 2 percent to a projected 6 to 8 percent by 1977. But as with the situation of civilianization, the increased reliance on female military personnel is concentrated in the noncombat occupations. Moreover, the proportion of black and other minority women in the Army is slightly higher than the proportion of minority male military personnel —despite the higher education entrance standards required of women as compared to men. In any event, the impact of greater employment of either civilians or female military personnel appears to be limited in terms of alleviating racial imbalance in the ground forces.

Increased social cohesion and organizational identity. Among the internal organizational reforms required for any viable military establishment is the strengthening of the social cohesion of units. This is especially mandatory for the ground forces. The constant rotation and lack of personal integration decreases the attractiveness of military service and leads to deviant behavior. It is not enough—nor even necessarily true—to assert that problems of soldierly dissatisfaction are issues in their own right. Only by a greater sense of group cohesion and less personnel rotation can the manpower management issues be effectively confronted. It is our strong belief that military life can be made compatible for significant portions of contemporary youth without sacrificing required organizational discipline. Such a proposition implies that organizational change is consistent with—indeed a requirement of—military institutional integrity.

The ground forces have taken the first limited steps in this direction by permitting men to volunteer for specific units of their own choice. This procedure has had some measure of success. The next step would be to permit group recruitment and the handling of training and assignment on a group rather than an individual basis. Another aspect of this approach is to allow individual units directly to recruit more of their own personnel. To some extent this is already being done, but the scope for decentralization is much greater than presently envisioned. Likewise, once assignment to a permanent unit is effected, it is essential to reduce personnel turnover. These internal reforms can be thought of as an effort to develop in American ground combat units a modern equivalent of the British regimental system. Not only would steps in these directions increase soldierly satisfaction and thereby military effectiveness, but, and most important, these developments would in turn lead to an increased ability to recruit more broadly for the all-volunteer force.

Military as an educational institution. From the viewpoint of minorities, especially those deprived of effective social advantage in civilian society, the attractiveness of the armed forces is intimately connected with the opportunities which the military offers for education and skill training.

From the viewpoint of the military establishment, training is emphasized to recruit manpower and to serve military occupational needs. From the perspective of civil-military relations and the integration of the armed forces into the larger society, however, trained personnel need be seen as a national resource who, to an appropriate degree, ought to be encouraged to return to civilian life. Although the armed services in effect are a vast training institution, military leaders have resisted recognition of this role, fearing it would divert their attention from their primary mission. But the pressures of the all-volunteer force have compelled the military to accept this role, albeit reluctantly, and to stress education and training in their recruitment appeals. There remains, nevertheless, a great deal of uncertainty and ambiguity about this task among professional officers. In other words, clearer recognition of the secondary functions of the military in education and skill training should lead to policies which would facilitate the return of trained individuals to civilian society and thereby reduce the racial imbalances within the armed forces, i.e., lowering black reenlistment rates.

Again, certain required organizational changes are evident. These demand further study and even experimentation and can only be tentatively proposed here; for example, alternating unit assignments —especially in the ground combat forces—between field training and purposive civilian training; preseparation assignments where education and skill training would be a primary function; job counseling on the most individual and personalized level. What is important to emphasize here is that usable civilian skills are least likely to be acquired in the ground combat forces, the very units which are overproportionately black. The requirement, therefore, is to open up the ground forces to potential civilian employers including black advancement groups such as the Urban League. To facilitate the training and outward flow of black servicemen, moreover, it would be eminently appropriate to receive budgetary allocations from the Departments of Labor, and Health, Welfare, and Education.

More balanced recruitment. The growing racial imbalance in the enlisted ranks of the all-volunteer force is one outcome of the adoption of the monetary incentives advocated by the Gates Commission. Perhaps the ultimate in monetary recruitment has been reached in the "bonus" ($2,500 as of June 1974) used to induce young men to join the ground combat forces. In March 1974, the most recent month for which figures are available, one-third of those who signed up for the combat enlistment bonus were black. That this outcome was not anticipated is surprising in light of conclusive studies which have shown that military earnings for minorities with less than a high school education will exceed their earnings in the civilian labor force.[3] The fact that the all-volunteer force significantly overdraws its membership from America's lower classes simply reflects the tendency of social groups to behave generally in their material self-interest.

It was also true that until recently the military itself followed a recruitment policy not geared to attracting young people oriented toward post-high school education—either technical, vocational, or collegiate. But the military establishment in the spring of 1974 is moving toward a position which recognizes that an important source of personnel are young people who are prepared to serve in the armed forces—relatively short terms, two to four years—as part of their transition into adult life. Social surveys indicate that one of the most powerful incentives for these persons is not immediate pay, but deferred pay in the form of educational benefits.[4] In this regard, a rough rule of equity might be the exchange of one year of military service for one year of post-high school education.

Recruiting single-term enlistments from youth with educational plans beyond high school would obviulsy make for a more racially representative military constituency.[5] It follows also that the counseling system of American high schools—not just military recruiters—must become alert to the possible civilian educational benefits of military service. Even under the present financial situation, existing G.I. Bill benefits combined with an appropriate fraction of savings from military pay (feasible owing to the military's provision of food and housing) would be enough to enable a recruit to afford two years of post-high school education after two years of military service. It would be more desirable, of course, if this arrangement were made explicit by means of a contract enlistment, i.e., in which the terms of compensation were oriented toward educational benefits rather than monthly pay. The military is favorable to arrangements as outlined here but the resistance to such programs is difficult to understand except in terms of organizational inertia. One important element in such arrangements is that the college bound recruit actually be accepted for admission to a college and his entrance postponed for the period of his military service.

Another variant of linking military service with advanced civilian education could be the establishment of a program in which a college education partly underwritten by the military would *precede* entry into the armed forces. Such considerations would be particularly relevant for middle-class families for whom the financial costs of a college education are becoming increasingly heavy burdens. Certainly it can be argued that large expenditures will be required to institute such a scholarship program.

But it must be remembered that already the present combat enlistment bonus alone could pay the tuition for one year at many of our most expensive private colleges. Also the present financial plight of many colleges is such that they would be very amenable to intermesh their curriculum with a military sponsored scholarship program, e.g., two years of military service between sophomore and junior years. Such a program would coincide with the present trend toward abolishing the lock-step educational system. Also on financial matters, it might be well to consider trading off projected E1-E4 pay increases to fund such a scholarship program—whether pre- or post-service. Another alternative could be granting student loans which would be cancelled upon completion of a specified tour of duty.

In return for such educational benefits—whether contract enlistments, scholarship, or loans—youth would be assigned in whatever capacity required by military manpower needs—most especially, the ground combat forces. Whatever the details of such a civilian educational program, a major outcome would be the reintroduction of white middle-class males into the ground combat forces. Moreover, there would be a concentration of single-term enlistments in the very military occupations where such short enlistments are most practical—the lower ranks of the combat arms. Such an infusion of white middle-class males into the combat arms could also serve to improve the chances for black representation in the more technical and support components of the armed forces. In this way, rectification of racial imbalance in the combat arms would meet the criteria of both practical efficiency and democratic representation.

Military and National Purpose

Clearly the impact of the Vietnam War and the difficult clarity of military goals have a negative influence on the climate of recruitment, especially among young men and women from better educated families. Even though minority groups appear prepared to accept the occupational advantages of military service—both short and long term—the broader issue remains the legitimacy of the military for the majority and more advantaged groups. Increased clarity of American foreign and military policy is obviously part of the issue. But the core question inheres in the definitions of the worthwhileness of public—including military—services. A reconstruction of military legitimacy requires normative more than monetary considerations.

We are dealing in point of fact with the modern adaptation of the citizen soldier. It is misleading to regard the all-volunteer military service as a long-term occupation; the vast bulk of military personnel even in the all-volunteer format are and will be single-term servicemen and service-women. In the pursuit of alternative modes of entrance into adult roles, the all-volunteer military will directly affect almost 400,000 young people each year. Currently it is in danger of being defined as suitable only for depressed minorities seeking to enter the larger society. We prefer the alternative definition that views the all-volunteer force as an appropriate process of entering adult society for a much broader segment of the population. Moreover, the wider the range of definitions of military service—educational, athletic, disaster relief, rescue operations, environment control, constabulary professionalism—the more broadly representative and racially balanced will such an all-volunteer force be. The power of persuasive normative goals should not be underemphasized in relating the all-volunteer force to the emerging young generation of this nation.

It goes without saying that in the long run the end of black overconcentration in the ground combat forces requires the attainment of effective racial equality and dignity in the larger society. To some extent the armed forces have contributed and will contribute to this goal. But in the immediate future, the basic issue is to prevent the military from becoming a racially distinct enclave.

Notes

1. President's Commission on an All-Volunteer Force, *The Report of the President's Commission on an All-Volunteer Force* (New York, 1970), p. 15.

2. Charles C. Moskos, Jr., "Coping in Europe," *Army* (November 1973), pp. 12-15.

3. Morris Janowitz, "The U.S. Forces and the Zero Draft," *Adelphi Paper* No. 94 (London, 1973); and Charles C. Moskos, Jr., "The Emergent Military," *Pacific Sociological Review*, XVI (April 1973), pp. 255-280.

4. Gary R. Nelson and Catherine Armington, *Military and Civilian Earnings Alternatives for Enlisted Men in the Army* (Arlington, 1970); Harley L. Browing, Sally C. Lopreato, and Dudley L. Poston, Jr., "Income and Veterans Status: Variations among Mexican Americans, Blacks, and Anglos," *American Sociological Review*, XXVIII (February 1973), pp. 74-85.

5. Jerome Johnston and Jerald G. Bachman, *Young Men and Military Service* (Ann Arbor, 1972).

SOCIOLOGICAL RESEARCH ON
ARMS CONTROL

Have twenty-five years of sociological research made any discernible difference in the progress toward arms control and disarmament? Such a question appears pretentious since the crucial research questions of war and peace have not been of central concern or even emphasized by sociologists. In fact, much of the work in cross-national sociology and the sociology of development has proceeded without reference to the fundamental transformation in international power relations that weapons of mass destruction have brought about.[1]

The question of the impact of sociological research on international relations is relevant if it is appropriately recast. If the sociological writings on international relations during the last twenty-five years are seen as part of a broader social science endeavor, there have been significant efforts that warrant evaluation and assessment. In fact, these efforts, by the middle of 1965, involved over one hundred institutions that were doing research related to arms control. Leaving aside economics of peace and disarmament, much of such research has dealt with the specific subject of public opinion concerning topical issues about international relations and various proposals for arms control.[2]

How shall we assess the consequences of the writings that deal directly with the role of violence in international relations and with the institutions and arrangements for reducing the use of violence in world affairs?[3] Have social science analyses of international relations had a discernible impact on the progress toward arms control and peace-keeping?

From *American Sociologist*, VI (1971) Supplementary Issue, pp. 23-30.

Impact of Social Science Research

A good case can be made that the contribution of the social sciences to arms control and disarmament has been negligible, or at least trivial. Of course, governmental achievements in arms control and disarmament efforts over the last quarter century are also hardly profound. In *World Military Expenditures,* the burden of the arms race is described in comprehensive and global terms.[4] Since 1964, the dividends of economic growth in the world community have been "dissipated in higher military expenditures, rather than contributing to the improvement of living standards."[5] Moreover, recent increases in the burden of maintaining conventional arms have been proportionately greater in the poorer countries.

There have been, however, specific but limited steps in the form of international agreements involving the United States and the Soviet Union and other nations that have served to inhibit the nuclear arms race and reduce the threat of accidental or premeditated nuclear war. These steps include negotiated items such as the creation of a nuclear-free zone in the Antarctic, the limited test ban treaty that prohibits atmospheric nuclear tests, the important Outer Space Treaty that prohibits the placing of nuclear weapons in outer space, and the Seabed Treaty that prohibits the stationing of nuclear weapons on the ocean floor. The most ambitious effort to limit the spread of nuclear arms has been the nonproliferation treaty, which contains provisions for international inspections. Finally the Hot Line communications, designed to prevent war by accident or miscalculation, should be mentioned. All of these items have additional importance because of their symbolic value in mobilizing public attention about the possibilities for more effective arms control and disarmament.

It may be argued that no particular linkages can be identified between systematic social science research and these specific steps. Yet elected officials and policy makers and their administrative staffs have no doubt incorporated specific research findings in efforts to avoid pitfalls in moving toward these objectives. Social science research has been relevant where it has supplied superior documentation to the normal flow of information available to officials, but these incidental advantages have been limited.

Social scientists have used their prestige to press for relevant policies in many fields, and this has been a long-standing practice in the area of nuclear arms and disarmament policies. A number of social scientists, mainly from the University of Chicago, were active immediately after 1945 in the passage of federal legislation that established the Atomic Energy Commission. This legislation ensured that the development of nuclear energy and research in the United States would be under civilian scientists who worked on the Manhattan Project which developed the atomic bomb during World War II. The scientists and the associated social scientists established the *Bulletin of the Atomic Scientists* which has been an active forum for debate on disarmament and a continuing lobby for arms control and disarmament. Initially, these various activities were an expression of personal political interests and not a manifestation of expertise grounded in careful scholarship.

A case, in fact, might be built that the consequences of social science endeavors toward arms control have had negative overtones.[6] Four illustrations are given:

1. Much of the research work done in the name of the "behavioral sciences" has been trivial, naive, or merely a jargonized expression of common-sense knowledge. The efforts of the behavioral sciences have unfortunately contributed to an excessive psychological reductionism in the analyses of international relations, as, for example, the work of Charles Osgood.[7] This is not to overlook the suggestive insights and formulations of psychological perception theory, as, for example, in the work of Ralph K. White.[8] Of course, the psychological dimensions of arms control are crucial, but the thrust of much behavioral science research, because of its amorphous conceptualization, has not stimulated thinking about "institution building," which is required to deal with the psychological dimensions of arms control. In this respect, social science research on arms control is similar to many of its efforts in the area of race relations.

2. Some of the theories of arms control and international relations that have won ascendency in the last quarter of a century are overdeterministic and replete with self-fulfilling prophecies that inhibit creative and positive policies and political action. Originally, war games and subsequently arms-control games were designed to sensitize social scientists and officials to the complexities of international relations by encouraging them to take "the role of the other." However, mathematical game theory, as it developed in the area of international relations, has developed into a self-contained mode of analysis. The application of mathematical game theory to international relations has proceeded on a very high intellectual level and with real logical rigor. However, I would join psychologist Robert H. David in stating that the consequences of such analyses have not encouraged new initiatives, but, rather, have served to explore existing dilemmas and thereby have served to freeze relations in the status quo.[9] The same type of criticism has been made by Martin Oppenheimer regarding the social psychological research that was stimulated by the peace movement and calls itself peace research.[10] Oppenheimer is particularly critical of the absence of concern with political realities and

sees much peace research as a substitute for political action. The work of Kahn and Wiener is another example of work that does not effectively stimulate creative thinking about policy issues.[11] Their book *The Year 2000* is perhaps the most overbearing effort to "predict the future," but it is based on dubious logic and faulty empirical assumptions and results in a pseudo image of reality. Otis Dudley Duncan has vigorously exposed the intellectual defects and hazards of such long-term forecasting.[12] The social consequences of writings of this type are that personal fascination with the future develops and there is a de-emphasis on the voluntaristic elements in social change.

3. Postive contributions of social scientists have been weakened by the inadequacy of professional standards in disseminating findings, assessing policy implications, and monitoring the advice-giving process. Research and advice have not been structured to highlight areas of agreement or clarify the specific bases of disagreement. Each social scientist is in business for himself. Social science has no counterpart to the Council of Economic Advisors that can maintain some semblance of professional standards and continuity. As a result, social scientists have not effectively contributed to the clarification of public debates concerning arms control.

4. The social science research community has not performed its essential function of serving as a relevant "collective" memory. Research on arms control must deal with a wide range of past politico-military events that bear both on contemporary political issues and on the accomplishments and nonaccomplishments of arms control. The basic issue is to analyze past events in order to underline the ever-increasing sociopolitical limitations in the uses of force to achieve political objectives. One does not have to develop a new overdeterminism to highlight the increased likelihood of a negative marginal utility in the use of force and coercion. The technological capacities for mobilizing massive force and the ideological justifications for the use of force have grown rapidly, but the ability of force to achieve specific goals has not. Obviously, there are striking exceptions, but the underlying issues are the broadening restraints on the use of force and the point at which the threat or the reality of force becomes counterproductive.

For example, the war in Vietnam is not only a tragic example of misguided fundamental moral issues, misconceived national interests, and profound political blunders, it is a dramatic example of the counter-productive consequences of excessive force and coercion. From the point of view of social science research, it represents the case of a monumental lapse in the collective memory. Social science analyses failed to negate the overwhelming misconceptions of strategic air warfare and its impact. Social science failed in its function of "enlightening" policy makers before bombing raids were undertaken and it failed in assessing what the political impact of the raids would be. Future historians will be able to point out that research during and after World War II in Europe and Japan, including the massive United States Strategic Bombing Survey and the documentation of the Korean conflict, should have supplied a basis for the intellectuals of the sixties to recognize the limited impact air warfare would have on the political and social structure of North Vietnam.[13] American policy in South Vietnam has never been based on realistically understanding that the social and political impact of strategic air warfare would be negligible and most likely counterproductive.[14]

The main intellectual advocate of strategic bombing of North Vietnam before and after the Gulf of Tonkin resolution was W. W. Rostow, a scholar trained in economic history and a person who had been extensively associated with planning long-range bombing in western Europe during World War II. Clearly, the available research findings on strategic air warfare did not figure prominently in his thinking or in that of Presidents Kennedy or Johnson or their staffs. Likewise, it is well known that research on the impact of air warfare in Vietnam (conducted by the Social Science Division of RAND Corporation and involving such persons as Leon Gurre, Joseph Goldsen, Philip Davidson, and Ithiel de Sola Poole) produced preliminary findings that were at variance with those of World War II and Korea. The findings were made available to selected newspapers and at special briefings. They presented a picture that emphasized the deterioration of Viet Cong and North Vietnamese political and social structures under bombings, a picture that strengthened the personal convictions of United States political leaders, but which was viewed with skepticism and outright rejection by more detached social scientists.

Most competent social scientists were, of course, so politically and morally opposed to the war that they would not have participated in official research if they had been asked; and many were not asked. Moreover, the organization of governmental research was so bureaucratic and the political pressures were so powerful that effective research would have been very difficult, although probably not impossible. It is striking to note, however, that individual American sociologists could have undertaken independent and unsponsored research on these issues in Vietnam. It was only necessary for them, like journalists, to receive accreditation as war correspondents, which would have enabled them to engage in extensive and intensive interviews and field observations. Since they did not, the in-depth studies about the social costs of the Vietnam war have been done by journalists and not by social scientists. Only Charles Moskos showed the necessary professional dedication; his important results are incorporated in his book *The American Enlisted Man.*[15]

The failure of policy makers to expose themselves to and avail themselves of the documentation about World War II and the Korean conflict is clear. But the failure was more than a lack of research continuity. More basic, social science and sociology failed to reconceptualize the role of force in existing theories of social and political behavior.

At the same time that I accept the relevance of each of the four criticisms of the limitations of social science research on arms control, on balance I conclude that the contributions of social science toward arms control have been worthwhile if not dramatic. These contributions have not been primarily of the "engineering" variety, that is, discernible contributions to specific actions. In fact, I am doubtful about whether the sociologist as a sociologist can or does or should make contributions that are of a very specific nature.[16] This is not to underemphasize the importance of the factual information he collects for policy and social action, but to say that, instead, as is generally the case, his contributions have been toward an understanding of the social context in which planned intervention must operate. The results of social science research have contributed to the general enlightenment of those engaged in political action or arms-control negotiations. The more direct effects of such researches have been to help transform arms control from a technical to an organizational problem. They have served to sensitize various publics. Indirectly, they have helped to sustain a more balanced, long-term, and continuous commitment to arms control. I would argue that without these research efforts, national commitments to arms control would be more unstable and would take on more of the character of the current fadlike interests in environmental problems in the United States.

Moreover, various American social scientists in cooperation with European and especially Scandinavian social scientists have sought to maintain contacts and stimulate communications with Soviet scholars. There can be no doubt that research inside the Soviet Union concerning the technological aspects of arms control has matured in the last five years and has produced an increased realism in Soviet negotiations. It is more difficult to assess the vitality and consequences of Soviet social science research on arms control. However, the growth of a self-critical research effort is the modern equivalent of the intellectual preconditions for progress toward peace as set forth by Immanuel Kant in *Eternal Peace*.

Basic Intellectual Issues

Because the years from 1945 to 1970 were a delimited period in American foreign policy, it is appropriate to explore possible new directions for sociological efforts in arms control and disarmament. Pieces of research are continuously needed on specific aspects of arms control and disarmament. In looking backward over the last twenty-five years or forward to the next five to ten years, the broad, essential questions seem to concern concepts, reformulations, and research on the fundamental changing character of the world order. What will be the limitations of the uses of force and the conditions and institutions for increasing such limitations?

Members of the American Sociological Association as well as an important segment of the student population no doubt view with considerable skepticism the repeated declaration of President Nixon that it is United States policy that there should be no more Vietnams. The President's political posture is but a manifestation of deep concern in the United States with redefining the nature of the world order. It is commonplace to hear that there are growing limits to the national resources of both the United States and the Soviet Union. These limits to the national resources are in part what is meant by the decline of the bipolar structure of the world community. But the sociological perspective has not produced a basic conceptual transformation that would reflect the changed empirical realities of a world faced with the prospect of a mass-destructive nuclear war. It is futile, alas, to call upon social scientists to adjust their theories to obvious realities—intellectual developments are not the results of command performances. The best that can be accomplished is to stimulate discussion and inquiry.

The task at hand is not only to stimulate research and thinking on topics labeled arms control and disarmament, important as they are; the task is to inject into sociology—from the study of small groups to the analysis of international organizations—a theoretical reconceptualization that sees the world as a social unit and is concerned with the basic transformation in the role of force within and between nation states.

These are intellectual issues that require intellectual solutions, and the organizational capacity of sociologists and the American Sociological Association to confront these issues is of relevance. In my judgment there is much greater interest, concern, and ferment about these issues than is reflected in the formal organization and structure of the sociological enterprise. In the mid-1960s, representations from the membership led the council of the ASA to establish a Committee on International Order, of which I was privileged to be chairman. I was struck by the depth of intellectual interest. It was possible to organize a committee of varying interests whose members defined issues in broad terms. For a period of years we had an active program and stimulating papers for special sessions at the ASA annual meetings. The Committee on International Order found itself responding to the needs and interests of young faculty members and graduate students who wished to develop courses dealing with the issues of war and peace at both undergraduate and graduate levels. In new ways, the courses on wars and revolutions that had been offered in the 1920s and 1930s and dropped after World War II were being reconstituted. Our committee was able to stimulate Louis Kriesberg to prepare an effective volume for course work entitled *Social Processes in International Relations.*[17]

Even though the sharpening interests of sociologists in these matters encountered organizational difficulties, their pedagogical initiatives proceeded rapidly—often more rapidly than the underlying intellectual development. Courses on war, revolution, arms control, and disarmament are now widespread, although their contents are not standardized. The chairman who succeeded me on the Committee on International Order had the committee abolished on the premature assumption that these matters were not effectively diffused throughout the discipline. Kriesberg's book, despite its real intellectual merits, was not reviewed by either the *American Sociological Review* or the *American Journal of Sociology,* more because of bureaucratic problems than because of reasoned or studied neglect.

Meanwhile, theses on war and arms control increase. The number of applications for the limited theses-support funds from the United States Arms Control and Disarmament Agency has also grown. Much of the writing and research is published in specialized interdisciplinary journals. One might say that there has been a premature splitting off of interests instead of an institutionalization of these concerns at the center of sociology.[18] But the central issues remain intellectual.

New Research Directions

As I see it, the basic issues of the sociology of war and peace cannot be defined as a delimited set of topics in "applied sociology" dealing with arms control and disarmament. To the contrary, we are dealing with central topics that are at the heart of sociology and are related to the groping efforts to "internationalize" the sociological endeavor. The essential issue is an examination of a changing world order. The development of instruments of mass destruction by the major powers changes the goals of international relations. The possession of these weapons does not increase the influence of the major powers accordingly, and the balance between persuasion and coercion has to be redefined. Each of the following three illustrative examples relates to a central issue in sociological research and is at the level of world sociology.[19]

1. At the core is the analysis of essential ecological and resource trends from the perspective of a world overview. The renewed interest in basic social indicators in the United States will fail if it remains an American movement. The efforts of economists and demographers via international agencies are producing more adequate descriptions than they have in the past of the stratification of the world community and its inequalities; these descriptions are essential components for understanding persistent patterns of conflict.

The need is for suitable indicators of institutions, especially the institution of political behavior, to be used as a base for comparative purposes. The extensive literature on quantitative cross-national analyses of political behavior—especially of violent patterns—has been produced without much concern for the quality and validity of the basic quantitative data. The search for sophisticated measures of political development and political stability on a worldwide basis has been relatively unsatisfactory.

Concern with disarmament and arms control offers alternatives and more direct approaches. In the last three to five years, data on worldwide arms expenditures have greatly increased and improved although there are still basic problems. The materials produced by the research units of the United States Arms Control and Disarmament Agency and more recently by the Stockholm Institute of Peace Research are impressive. They offer for the first time a comprehensive overview of the ecological distribution of arms expenditure.[20] These data already permit a simple and relatively direct set of measures for comparative and trend analyses, and they may well continue to produce startling findings. Thus, for example, the arms burden in recent years has rested more heavily on developing nations than on industrialized nations; nonnuclear rather than nuclear expenditures have accounted for recent increases in the budget of industrialized nations. As more basic data become available, they will permit exploration of the central proposition that the amount of expenditures on military affairs is unrelated to the role of violence in political change at the world community level.

2. The application of a relevant social psychological perspective to the study of arms control and disarmament is crucial. It offers an opportunity for the reconstruction of social psychology, which currently presents a picture of intellectual defensiveness. Social psychology has become an aspect of sociology that is concerned with the boundaries of sociology—namely, the relationship of sociology to psychology and psychiatry—rather than with the intellectual core of sociology. We are not concerned with a social psychological

explanation of international relations. Such an approach runs the risk of premature closure and low explanatory effectiveness; it also runs the risk of faulty reasoning from analogies drawn between small-group processes and national states.[21] It is not enough to proclaim that we are interested in the definition of the situation as seen by the key actors and agencies; it is not enough to develop research in which the attitudes are seen as component elements of macrogroup processes. The essential thrust must focus on the social psychological processes that operate during periods of tension or crises and act as barriers to planned social change, institution building, or negotiations. The theoretical issues are no different from the analyses of the social psychological aspects of conflict at the community level; they merely deal with a different system of legitimacy and sanctions.

The classic model of the social psychological analysis at the level of world community is Lasswell's *World Politics and Personal Insecurity.*[22] Lasswell's formulation of personal insecurity presents a highly appropriate set of variables—it avoids both cultural relativism and ethnocentrism. It is now more than thirty years since that seminal volume on the collective behavior and attitudinal aspects of international relations appeared. This book has supplied one of the major themes in the contribution of social science to the study of arms control and disarmament. The literature on distortion, perception, and communication in international tensions derives from this effort.[23]

Lasswell's book has supplied a framework for subsequent efforts to evaluate contemporary events. Unfortunately, like the original urban sites of ancient Middle East civilizations that lie buried under the debris of centuries, Lasswell's original ideas have been covered with many layers of added and often imprecise data and speculations. In fact, among the works on international relations done by social psychologists, psychiatrists, and psychologists there has arisen in the last ten years an anti-personality intellectual posture that is most confounding. Part of this is the residual product of political activisim, but part is the product of an intellectual confusion that is the result of an analysis of power that is very unhistorical and unstructured. What is required is a clarification and explication of the assumption that a social psychological analysis is a partial but essential dimension of a sociology of war and peace. A return to Lasswell's original volume to extract a careful proposition of analysis and an evaluation of the intellectual progress, or lack of it, during the last thirty-five years is the first step.

3. At the level of social systems, it is essential to focus on the institutions and the efforts at institution-building that deal with socio-control processes between nations. One can argue that the rapid

development of comparative sociology (that is, cross-national analysis), while it was an indispensable phase in the "internationalization" of social science, had built-in limitations. To consider nations as samples to be analyzed quantitatively, as objects removed from their environments, overlooks essential patterns of interdependence and interaction with other nations. (A similar analogy is the fate of the studies of bureaucratic or formal organizations which for many decades were treated without reference to environment; the emerging focus is on interorganizations and interrelations and on the relations between organizations and their environment.) The focus of comparative sociology is slowly but definitely being reoriented as a result of examining the dominance, stratification relations, and processes of diffusion and institution-transfer between nations.

Analysis of the changing world order requires explicit attention to the planned and purposive efforts at transforming international relations.[24] In this regard, sociological concerns with institutions and institution-building are paramount, but either the topics have been neglected or the results of available sociological studies have been neglected. It is, of course, appropriate as a first step to spell out in hypothetical terms the institutional arrangements required for a world without war. Interestingly enough, this has been attempted by Millis and Real in their volume dealing with a world without war.[25] Millis and Real, who believe themselves to be realistic and radical innovators, propose an organization they label "national police forces," and they see this organization—not world police—as the instrument for the abolition of war. The details of this line of reasoning are worthy of careful study by sociologists concerned with analysis and policy.

On a different level, and much more concretely related to the mechanics of arms control, is the formulation of Schelling on a special surveillance force.[26] This is seen as an instrument for implementing an arms-control arrangement. It is an organizational device for making treaties and formal arrangements enforceable, effective, and expandable. The special surveillance force is an example of institution-building that would function "to help tranquilize crises that threaten to erupt into general war, particularly crises aggravated by the instability of strategic deterrence." Schelling says of its organizational characteristic: "the attributes of the force should be readiness, speed, reliability, self-sufficiency, versatility, and ability to improvise."[27]

Elsewhere I have suggested that if the human community were ever to free itself of disease and illness, the world would not be without doctors.[28] But it is probable that under conditions of a medical utopia, doctors would be called by another name. In fact, the term "public health doctor" is an expression of the powerful contemporary effort to transform the medical profession and increase its capacity for preventive practice. Likewise, a world without war would not be a world without soldiers, or "specialists in violence." But the role of the professional soldier would have to be transformed into some equivalent of a "constabulary force."[29] The structural transformation of the profession to achieve this goal would be immense, but the postulation of the organizational requirement is part of the immediate agenda of sociologists.

Changing World Order

It is evident that the emergence of a new world order and its essential regional and supranational institutions will depend on the formal and informal arrangements that result from negotiations of the nuclear superpowers. In 1945, detached observers anticipated a relatively long period, as much as twenty years, in which the possibility of a major nuclear war was a most unlikely eventuality. They foresaw the United States with superiority in nuclear weapons, but with a declining advantage. The Russians would base their political strategy of international relations on the assumption that the United States would not initiate a nuclear war. This political arrangement, more than or at least as much as the actual balance of weaponry, meant that the probability of a nuclear war was indeed remote. In the late 1960s, as the nuclear weapons of the United States and the Soviet Union presumably became more equal to each other, the calculus was placed under great stress. It has been disappointing that a new accommodation has been so slow to develop. A more explicit and formal set of arrangements, arrived at by negotiation and recognizing the new military environment, is required. A variety of factors thwart the emergence of some form of negotiated limitation on strategy weapons and the explicit stabilization of United States-Soviet relations; they include sheer technical problems, unclear notions of minimum-security requirements, the desire to press for marginal international political advantage, the problem of domestic political management, and the lack of charismatic political leadership. Nevertheless, the possibility of a major nuclear war in the 1970s between the United States and the Soviet Union remains remote. Essentially, there is a set of diffused institutional arrangements between the United States and the Soviet Union that will be able to expedite the self-interest of both sides. These institutional arrangements include elaborate mutual surveillance systems, diplomatic and technical exchanges of information, highly energetic strategic planning and control staffs, and the rudimentary elements of a permanent negotiation system that can, in effect, operate as a control device. Equally important is the persistence of the political assumption that the United States will not take nuclear initiatives. However, the crucial issue is that of incorporating Communist China into this arrangement, a goal toward which little progress has been made.

From the point of view of the sociologist concerned with institution-building for a world community, it is not sufficient to proceed on assumptions that are limited to the key roles of the major nuclear powers. One cannot simply extrapolate existing trends; counter political forces of less magnitude are also crucial. In short, it will be well to assume that the transformation of international relations is linked to the limitations on the power of the nuclear nations to maintain their conception of a world order by their own resources—political, military, economic, and moral. To state the case in other words, the residual powers of nations, the ability of even small countries to oppose the superpowers, is of increasing relevance to the transformation of international relations. The United States in this regard is subject to greater limitations than is the Soviet Union, but the same assumption applies differently to both superpowers and by inference to Communist China.

The conceptual aspects of this assumption are based on an international analogy to Karl Mannheim's formulations concerning domestic problem solving and conflict resolution. Mannheim in the 1930s emphasized that industrialized societies had to face the dilemmas of fundamental demo-cratization, a clumsy phrase and in many respects misleading. But it is a formulation that calls attention to the importance of new institutional arrangements. In essence, Mannheim argued that as the social structure and the division of labor became more and more complicated, effective social control would depend on the broadening of the base of participation in decision making. He was fully aware of the profound limitations that a person's lack of education and low social position place on his ability to participate in political decision making. But he did not believe that in a democratic society the dominant trend was toward an effective central-ization of political power. He saw pervasive limitations of central control because of lack of legitimacy and ineffective instruments of adminis-tration. He saw the development of powerful loci of power scattered through the society; the loci could produce a blind pursuit of self-interest which would disrupt the system of social control. The phrase "funda-mental democratization" is not a political cliché. For Mannheim, it meant a system of viable institutional arrangements (not merely or even essentially a system of voting procedures). But without effective fundamental democratization, instability and social conflict (not overcentralization) would be the proximate outcome.

At the international level, an equivalent set of relations are at work. The increase in the potential for nuclear destruction has not meant a corresponding ability of the superpowers to impose their will on the world community. The transformation of the world order is based on the increased limitations of the superpowers to garner results from their nuclear investments.

The ability of small nations to find their own way and to defy the superpowers and world "public opinions" is striking. The complexity of managing a nation limits the ability of the superpowers to intervene in external affairs and gives the small nation a range of options in response to pressures from without. A variety of apparently self-contradictory, but clearly compatible, policies enhance self-determination in the crude sense. (In 1970, the Union of South Africa, with its racist domestic policies, received arms from France; France was committed to black Africa and also traded extensively with Communist China; Communist China was engaged in training black Africa in guerrilla warfare against the Union of South Africa. None of these nations appeared embarrassed in dealing with the other.) Should the major powers in their search for military alliances assist in the nuclearization of currently nonnuclear nations, the international trends toward the diffusion of power would become even more marked.

There is, of course, no reason to assume that the secondary centers of power will pursue rational and constructive policies, but there is no reason to write them off. Nor in the multipolar world community are the secondary centers essentially minor. It is true that the typical developing nation is small and without resources. But the world ecology of nation states is overly neglected; in addition to the particular phenomenon of Japan's reemergence one needs to be reminded of the developing nations that are looming larger than specific European states, such as Indonesia with over 100 million people.

The tasks facing the sociologist concerned with international relations and arms control are clear, although there is little evidence that the discipline and its centers of graduate training are prepared to undertake them. Sociological thinking needs to be applied to the world community; the world community needs to be seen as an incomplete and highly imperfect social system, in a manner analogous to other incomplete and highly imperfect social systems that concern sociologists. As mentioned above, recent increased interest in comparative (that is, cross-national) analysis has been substituted for research concerned with the issues of how relations between nations are institutionalized.

Sociologists pride themselves on their ability to describe and analyze complex social systems that combine formal structure with diffuse patterns of communications, but such an analysis has not been extensively applied to the international arena and arms control. The task with priority is to focus on the more explicit and more formalized institutional arrangements for managing international conflict. Good examples can be cited and the future agenda is rich. Wilensky has published a book on organizational intelligence and has work in progress on the utilization of intelligence by foreign offices in a period of crisis.[30] Moskos has studied the organizational features of the peace-keeping activities of the United Nations on the island of Cyprus.[31] Another supranational agency involved in arms control is the International Atomic Energy Authority located in Vienna. This is a complex bureaucracy that was originally concerned with international cooperation in atomic research and has been given the responsibility of nuclear inspection in connection with the nonproliferation treaty.

Iklé has undertaken an analysis of the international negotiation process in structural and institutional terms, and he points the way to essential research concerns.[32] If one takes seriously the limitations on the superpowers, the long-term negotiations of the Geneva Conference of the United Nations Committee on Disarmament are seen as a forum of ever-increasing importance.

The range of substantive issues is extensive. Institutional arrangements for arms control include, for example, efforts to prevent nuclear weapons accidents. John Larus, professor of political science at New York University, has prepared a penetrating analysis of nuclear accidents that have taken place in the armed forces of the United States and the military's response to such crises.[33] Laboratory experiments and simulations are undoubtedly part of the research methodology. However, the sociology of arms control is primarily a field problem. Access is not an insurmountable task, and existing bodies of theories—with all their limitations—could be applied with good results. But it does require sociologists of heroic perspectives.

Notes

1. Irving Louis Horowitz, *Three Worlds of Development* (New York, 1966); Charles C. Moskos, Jr. and W. Bell, "Emerging Nations and Ideologies of American Social Scientists," *American Sociologist* II (May 1967), pp. 67-72.

2. A. Etzioni, "Nonconventional Uses of Sociology as Illustrated by Peace Research," in P. Lazarsfeld, W. H. Sewell, and H. L. Wilensky, eds., *The Uses of Sociology* (New York, 1967), pp. 806-835.

3. See Elizabeth T. Crawford and Albert D. Biderman, *Social Scientists and International Affairs* (New York, 1969), for a bibliographic overview of the sociological research and policy on arms control.

4. United States Arms Control and Disarmament Agency (Washington, D.C., 1969).

5. Ibid., p. 4; see also International Institute for Peace and Conflict Research, *SIPRI Yearbook of World Armaments and Disarmaments, 1968/69* (New York, 1969).

6. See A. Wildavsky, "Practical Consequences of the Theoretical Study of Defense Policy," *Public Administration Review* XXV (March 1965), pp. 90-103.

7. Charles E. Osgood, *An Alternative to War or Surrender* (Urbana, 1962).

8. Ralph K. White, *Nobody Wanted War: Misperception in Vietnam and Other Wars* (New York, 1968).

9. R. H. David, "International Influence Process: How Relevant is the Contribution of Psychologists?" *American Psychologist* XXI (March 1966), pp. 236-243. See also P.M.S. Blackett, "Critique of Some Contemporary Defense Thinking," *Encounter* (August 1961), pp. 9-17.

10. Martin Oppenheimer, "The Peace Research Game," *Dissent* XI (August 1964), pp. 444-448.

11. Herman Kahn and Anthony J. Wiener, *The Year 2000: A Framework for Speculation on the Next Thirty-Three Years* (New York, 1967).

12. Otis Dudley Duncan, "Social Forecasting: The State of the Art," *Public Interest* (Fall 1969), pp. 88-118.

13. United States Strategic Bombing Survey, "Effects of Strategic Bombing on Japanese Morale," in *Reports, Pacific War* XIV (Washington, D.C., 1945); "Effects of Strategic Bombing on German Morale," in *Reports, European War* LXIVb (Washington, D.C., 1947).

14. It is striking to note that for a thirty-five-year period the Israelis lived under a garrison type situation and struggled to maintain a realistic understanding of the limitation of force. Their high command and top political leadership succumbed to strategic air warfare for political and social objectives in January and February, 1970, and authorized long-range raids in Egypt. These were counterproductive, and Israeli realism terminated them rapidly after limited self-inflicted damage.

15. Charles C. Moskos, Jr., *The American Enlisted Man: The Rank and File in Today's Military* (New York, 1970), esp. Chap. 6.

16. Morris Janowitz, "Sociological Models and Social Policy," in *Political Conflict* (Chicago, 1970), pp. 243-259.

17. Louis Kriesberg, *Social Processes in International Relations* (New York, 1968).

18. See *Journal of Conflict Resolution* and *Journal of Peace Research*.

19. W. Moore, "World Sociology," *American Journal of Sociology* LXXI (March 1966), pp. 475-482.

20. More efforts in this regard are needed to reconstruct historical data, but this is a difficult endeavor and subject to inherent limitations.

21. Peter Blau, *Exchange and Power in Social Life* (New York, 1964).

22. Harold D. Lasswell, *World Politics and Personal Insecurity* (New York, 1935).

23. Herbert Kelman, *International Behavior: A Social-Psychological Analysis* (New York, 1965).

24. Raymond Aron, *Peace and War* IV (New York, 1966).

25. Walter Millis and James Real, *The Abolition of War* (New York, 1963).

26. T. C. Schelling, "A Special Surveillance Force," in Q. Wright, W. M. Evans, and M. Deutsch, eds., *Preventing World War III* (New York, 1962), pp. 87-105.

27. Ibid., p. 87.

28. Morris Janowitz, *The Professional Soldier* (New York, 1960, 1971), pp. 417-440.

29. Ibid.

30. Harold L. Wilensky, *Organizational Intelligence: Knowledge and Policy in Government and Industry* (New York, 1967).

31. Charles C. Moskos, Jr., "Structured Strain in a United Nations Constabulary Force," in Morris Janowitz and Jacques van Doorn, eds., *On Military Ideology* (Rotterdam, 1971), pp. 248-263.

32. Fred Iklé, *How Nations Negotiate* (New York, 1967). International Institute for Peace and Conflict Research.

33. John Larus, *Nuclear Weapons Safety and the Common Defense* (Columbus, 1967).

ARMS CONTROL, 35-42; 133
ARMED FORCES AND SOCIETY, General 11; Garrison State 59-60; Middle East 146-175; Models; Authoritarian-Personal; Authoritarian-Mass Party; Democratic-Competitive; Civil-Military Coalition; Military Oligarchy 138-139; Western Society 70-88; World Indicators 89-109
AUTHORITY, Fraternal 233-236; Military 122-123; 177-180; 195-199; 221-238; Political 25-28

BUREAUCRATIC ORGANIZATION, 10; 116-121; 144; 221-223

CAREER LINES, See Military Professional
CEREMONIALISM, 231
CIVILIAN CONTROL, See Civil-Military Relations
CIVIL-MILITARY RELATIONS, Aristocratic 58; Democratic 59; Impact of All-Volunteer Force 278-282; Garrison State Model 59; New Nation 136-145; Totalitarian 59
CITIZENSHIP, 70-78; 85-86
CONSCRIPTION, See Military Organization
CONFLICT, 11; 56-68; 82-84
CONSTABULARY FORCE, 19; 129-133

DETERRENCE, 20-21; 48
DOMINATION, 221-223; 226-230

GARRISON STATE, 59-60

HONOR, 191-194

IDEOLOGY, 144; 161-162; 178; 199-206; 279-282
INTELLECTUALS, MILITARY, 11
INTERNATIONAL RELATIONS, 19-55; 249-251

MANIPULATION, 221-223; 226-230
MASS ARMED FORCE, See Military Organizations
MILITARISM, Definition 59-60; 129
MILITARY ELITES, 56-68; 123-124; See also Social Recruitment
MILITARY INTERVENTION, 21-22; 46; 137; 146-150; 163-172
MILITARY MORALE, 112-116; 177-220
MILITARY ORGANIZATION, General 11; Alternative Conceptions 262-265; "Civilianization" 12; 44; Combat Goals 223-226; Conscription 239-249; Industrial Society 110-135; Mass Armed Force 121-129; 241-245; Middle East 146-175; NATO Nations 247; "Stabilizing and Destabilizing" 20-22; U.S. Volunteer 239; 283; U.S.S.R. 247-248; Wehrmacht 206-211; World Wide Indicators 93-105; 140
MILITARY PROFESSIONAL, 42-51; 89-90; 110-112; 144; 265-270; 279-282; Overprofessionalism 231
MILITARY REGIMES, See Military Intervention
MILITARY SOCIOLOGY, 15; 91-93
MILITARY STRATEGY, 19-55; 249-251; 257-262

PARA-MILITARY FORCES, 14
PROPAGANDA, 211-216
PRIMARY GROUPS AND COHESION, 177-217

RACIAL COMPOSITION, 273-278

SKILL PATTERNS, See Military Professional
SOCIAL RECRUITMENT, 79-82; 124-125; 144; 156-161; 271-278
STABILIZATION STRATEGY, 31-35

315

TECHNOLOGY, See Weapons Systems

VOLUNTEER FORCES, See Military Organization

WAR, 56-68

WEAPONS SYSTEMS, 33-35; 35-42; 78-79; 110-112; 143; 223-224

Citation Index

Abrahamsson, Bengt, 8, 55, 87

Abrams, Philip, 88

Adelman, Irma, 107, 109

Adorno, T. W., 238

Almond, Gabriel A., 109

al-Qazzaz, Ayad, 156, 157, 173, 174, 175

Andreski, Stanislaw, 74, 87, 134

Angell, George W., 174

Armington, Catherine, 297

Aron, Raymond, 8, 52, 73, 87, 313

Bachman, Jerald G., 297

Bawly, Dan, 175

Baynes, J.C.M., 263, 282

Bebler, Anton, 8

Be'eri, Eliezer, 146, 156, 157, 158, 172, 173, 174

Bendix, Reinhard, 73, 75, 87

Berger, Morroe, 155, 173

Bernard, Jessie, 52

Bettelheim, Bruno, 8

Biderman, Albert, 8, 115, 134, 262, 22, 313

Blackett, P.M.S., 54, 313

Blau, Peter, 73, 87, 313

Bluher, Hans, 218

Bopegamage, A., 8

Boulding, Kenneth, 56, 69

Bowers, Raymond U., 115, 134

Bradbury, William C., 134

Brim, Orville, 8

Brinton, Crane, 83, 88

Broch, Hermann, 219

Brodie, Bernard, 52, 54

Brotz, Harold, 237

Browing, Harley I., 297

Brown, C. S., 238

Burton, J. W., 53

Busquets, Julian, 8

Campbell, Donald T., 222, 237

Canby, Steven L., 283

Chorley, Katherine, 69, 87

Clifford, Clark, 54

Coleman, James S., 196, 108, 109

Cooley, Charles Horton, 55, 218

Coser, Lewis, 56, 69

Cottrell, Leonard, Jr., 8

Craig, Gordon, 54

Crawford, Elizabeth T., 313

Crocker, G. W., 134

Cutright, Phillips, 109

Dahrendorf, Ralf, 53, 73, 87

David, Robert H., 300, 313

Davidson, Philip, 302

Davis, Arthur K., 237

Demeter, Karl, 79, 87, 112, 134, 173, 219

de Sola Poole, Ithiel, 302

de Tocqueville, Alexis, 82, 83, 88

Dicks, Henry V., 217

Dinerstein, Herbert S., 54

Dore, Ronald, 148, 172

Duncan, Otis Dudley, 53, 301, 313

Durkheim, Emile, 86

Easton, David, 237

Edwards, Lyford P., 83, 88

Emerson, Rupert, 52

Engels, Friedrich, 71, 73, 86

Erickson, John, 45, 55

Etzioni, A., 312

Eulau, Heinz, 237

Fallers, Lloyd A., 17, 54, 172

Fanon, Frantz, 24

Farber, Maurice L., 53

Feld, Maury, 8

Finer, Samuel, 8, 52

Fortes, Meyer, 87
Frankel, Joseph, 52
Freeman, Felton D., 237
Freud, S., 218
Frey, Frederick W., 156, 167, 173, 174
Friedman, Milton, 248

Garthoff, Raymond L., 52, 55
Geertz, Clifford, 52, 54, 145
Gellner, Ernest, 86
George, Alexander L., 134
Gilpin, Robert, 54
Goldhamer, Herbert, 52
Goldsen, Joseph, 302
Grinker, Roy, 16, 17, 218
Grusky, Oscar, 8
Guetzkow, Harold S., 52
Gurfein, M. I., 219, 220
Gurre, Leon, 302
Gutteridge, William, 174

Hackel, Erwin, 55
Halperin, Morton, 55
Halpern, Manfred, 150, 155, 173
Harries-Jenkins, Gwyn, 8, 90
Herz, John, 52
Hill, Reuben, 108
Hilsman, Roger, 54
Hinsley, F. H., 52, 53
Hollander, E. P., 238
Hook, Sidney, 7
Hoopes, Townsend, 54
Horowitz, Irving Louis, 312
Hudson, Michael C., 108
Huntington, Samuel P., 55, 69, 115, 134
Hurewitz, J. C., 147, 150, 172, 174

Iklé, Fred C., 33, 312, 314

Jackson, J. A., 135
Janowitz, Morris, 52, 54, 55, 69, 86, 87,
    88, 90, 106, 108, 109, 114, 116,
    134, 135, 172, 173, 174, 219, 220,
    238, 282, 297, 313, 314
Johnson, Chalmers, 148, 172
Johnston, Jerome, 297

Kahn, Herman, 24, 53, 301, 313
Kant, Immanuel, 303

Kaplan, Morton, 24, 53
Kelman, Herbert, 52, 313
Kennan, George, 54
Khuri, Fuad, 8
Kimcbe, David, 175
Kissinger, Henry A., 31, 54
Kolko, Gabriel, 53
Kolko, Joyce, 53
Kriesberg, Louis, 52, 305, 313
Kris, Ernst, 54

Lane, Robert E., 88
Lang, Kurt, 8, 134
Larus, John, 312, 314
Lasswell, Harold D., 7, 10, 11, 23, 29,
    44, 53, 55, 59, 69, 86, 112, 134,
    145, 159, 278, 307, 313
Lazarsfeld, Paul F., 238
Lebby, David E., 55
Leighton, A., 134
Leites, Nathan, 54
Lerner, Daniel, 145, 168, 174, 175
Levy, Marion, 74, 87
Lewis, Barnard, 148, 153, 172, 173
Lieberson, Stanley, 54, 283
Lifton, Robert, 16, 17
Lindsay, A. D., 218
Lipset, Seymour M., 73, 86, 87, 88, 105,
    106, 108
Little, Roger, 8, 110, 116, 134
Lopreato, SallY C., 297
Lovell, John P., 55
Lyons, Gene M., 54

Maier, Charles S., 53
Mannheim, Karl, 19, 25, 52, 53, 310
March, J. G., 134
Marshall, S.L.A., 16, 17, 69, 134, 226,
    238
Marshall, T. H., 71, 86
Marx, Karl, 73, 86
Mayo, Elton, 218
McCormack, Thelma H., 222, 237
Merton, Robert K., 238
Meyers, Samuel M., 134
Millis, Walter, 132, 135, 308, 314
Mills, C. Wright, 44, 55, 278
Mladenovic, Olga, 282

Moore, Barrington, Jr., 53, 69, 82, 88, 148, 172
Moore, W., 313
Morris, Cynthia, 107, 109
Morton, Louis, 54
Mosca, Gaetano, 73, 87
Moskos, Charles C., Jr., 8, 132, 135, 283, 284, 297, 302, 312, 313, 314

Nelson, Gary R., 297
Nelson, Paul D., 55
Neubauer, Deane E., 109
Neumann, Franz, 147, 172
Nordlinger, Eric, 107, 109

Ogburn, William F., 8
Olsen, Marvin E., 109
Oppenheimer, Martin, 300, 313
Osgood, Charles, 300, 313
Ozbudun, Ergun, 149, 168, 173, 174, 175

Page, Charles H., 237
Park, Robert E., 83, 88
Parsons, Talcott, 74
Pike, Douglas, 53
Plessner, Helmuth, 218
Poston, Dudley L., Jr., 297

Rapoport, Anatol, 52
Radway, Laurence I., 125
Ranney, A., 87
Real, James, 132, 135, 308, 314
Roberts, Adam, 263, 282
Robinson, Richard D., 165, 168, 174, 175
Rokkan, Stein, 75, 87
Ropp, T., 87
Rose, Arnold M., 237
Rostow, W. W., 302
Rummel, R. J., 53
Russett, Bruce M., 53, 108
Rustow, D. A., 173, 174, 175

Sanay, Abdurrahman S., 174
Schelling, Thomas C., 52, 133, 135, 308, 314
Schmalenbach, Herman, 218
Schmitter, Philippe C., 17, 52, 107, 109

Schumpeter, Joseph, 68, 225, 238
Scott, S. F., 80, 87, 173
Sherman, A. V., 173
Shils, Edward A., 8, 52, 53, 86, 114, 134, 137, 145, 173, 175, 177, 238
Silver, Allan, 8
Simmel, George, 69
Simpson, Dick, 109
Smith, Bruce Lannes, 7
Snyder, Richard C., 52
Sohn, Joe Souk, 8
Speier, Hans, 53, 69, 87, 112, 116, 134, 223, 238
Spencer, Herbert, 73, 86, 91
Spiegel, J. P., 16, 17, 218
Spindler, C. D., 237
Stouffer, Samuel A., 113, 134, 237
Strachey, Alex, 53

Tarr, D., 52
Tawney, Richard H., 53
Taylor, Charles L., 108
Thomas, W. I., 88
Torrey, Gordon H., 173

Uyehara, Cecil H., 54

Vagts, Alfred, 69, 87, 129, 135, 173
van Doorn, Jacques, 8, 80, 86, 87, 90, 109, 134, 173
Vatikiotis, P. J., 173, 174
Veblen, Thorstein, 82, 88
von Grunebaum, Gustav E., 147, 172

Walker, Walter, 175
Ward, Robert E., 175
Weber, Max, 10, 19, 52, 73, 86, 112, 134, 148, 151, 243
White, Ralph K., 300, 313
Whitehead, T. N., 218
Wiener, Anthony J., 53, 301, 313
Wildavsky, A., 313
Wilensky, Harold L., 312, 314
Wiley, James A., 109
Williams, R. H., 134
Wilson, A.T.M., 218
Wilson, Everett K., 237
Wohlstetter, Albert, 52

Wolfe, J. N., 55
Wolfe, Thomas W., 54
Wool, Harold, 123, 134, 283
Wright, Quincy, 8, 52, 69

Young, Donald, 8

Zald, Mayer, 8
Znaniecki, Florian, 88